The Dynamics of the
Armed Struggle

THE
DYNAMICS
OF THE
ARMED STRUGGLE

J. BOWYER BELL

FRANK CASS
LONDON · PORTLAND, OR

First published in 1998 in Great Britain by
FRANK CASS PUBLISHERS
Newbury House, 900 Eastern Avenue
London IG2 7HH

and in the United States of America by
FRANK CASS PUBLISHERS
c/o ISBS, 5804 N.E. Hassalo Street
Portland, Oregon 97213-3644

Website http://www.frankcass.com

Copyright © 1998 J. Bowyer Bell

British Library Cataloguing in Publication Data

Bell, J. Bowyer (John Bowyer), 1931–
  The dynamics of the armed struggle
  1. Insurgency   2. Government, Resistance to   3. Insurgency –
  Religious aspects   4. Government, Resistance to – Religious
  aspects
  I. Title
  322.4'2

ISBN 0-7146-4865-5 (cloth)
ISBN 0-7146-4422-6 (paper)

Library of Congress Cataloging in Publication Data

Bell, J. Bowyer, 1931–
  The dynamics of the armed struggle / J. Bowyer Bell.
    p.   cm.
  Includes bibliographical references and index.
  ISBN 0-7146-4865-5 (cloth). – ISBN 0-7146-4422-6 (pbk.)
  1. Political violence.   2. Insurgency.   3. Revolutions.
  4. Guerrillas.   5. Terrorism.   I. title.
  JC328.6.B45   1998
  303.6–dc21   98–10981
                                                    CIP

Typeset by Vitaset, Paddock Wood, Kent
Printed in Great Britain by
Bookcraft (Bath) Ltd, Midsomer Norton, Somerset

Contents

Preface

FOR OVER a generation, for much of my analytical life, in fact for most of my adult life, I have been engaged in a long march as an observer through active and recent undergrounds. Many of the garden spots of internal war, Beirut and Belfast and Aden, the old and new battlefields, Gaza and Ethiopia and the Zambezi valley, always Ireland, Italy and Cyprus and others, have been way-stations, often visited repeatedly – stops on a terrorist tour. With luck or careful planning, I have for years attended wars and coups and the various rituals of structured chaos. In the course of these travels, I have been target and quarry, arrested, expelled, kidnapped, followed by the legitimate, and feted by the dubious, had tea with terror and lectured to policemen.

Spread over a generation such adventures, rare if memorable, are only punctuation to endless interviews and a great deal of waiting. Generally it has been a most unacademic march, often fascinating, especially in retrospect – being shot at without effect may be, indeed is, exhilarating the first time but repetition tends to reduce the charm. And so I have grown if not immune then at least resigned to the occasional complexities involved in research.

Few scholars can have been offered a ride on a carbomb or been kidnapped in order to be lectured on the wisdom of the rebel. I gave up pretending all this was quite normal when, while in Eritrea interviewing without permission those wounded in a war that the Ethiopian government denied existed, I ended assisting at surgery at the Second Imperial Division hospital in Asmara. True I was a doctor, if not a physician, and the patients were delighted to find a foreign specialist when they had anticipated local talent. So it all worked out. Everyone was the better for the intervention: my grasp of the insurrection extended and the recovered patients delighted. It was, however, a method of field research that I had not been taught at graduate school.

At the time there is often little joy in most of the obstacles to investigation.

And in time most of these are taken for granted. Journalists regularly do interviews with someone crouched behind a wall while his friends shoot up a village, so why not a historian? Still, sitting in a ditch in the corner of a far field waiting for the dubious to appear on matters of most parochial concern brings diminishing analytical returns. Is one more bit of evidence needed – is this ditch relevant or another gunman's tale needed? And do I really want the opinion of a frightened young man in a jumble-shop combat jacket with his eyes darting about behind Ray-Bans? Is one more story really necessary? And, after a generation, the answer is, finally, probably 'no', or at least 'no' it is not worth the risks – erratic, rare but real risks.

The march through the killing fields began long ago above the green Irish fields of Kilkenny in a pub next to the Spotted Dog in Inistioge where with enormous innocence I began my time with the Irish Republican Army, a movement that has involved more of my life than I could have imagined. I have spent more time on the IRA than most volunteers have spent on active service. The result has been several books, endless articles, papers and lectures – some to the involved – and some reticence about publishing a final analysis that might alienate the subject.

I have interviewed those out in Easter Week 1916 and those presently active whose fathers and grandfathers I met long ago. Somehow my presence seems to validate each new generation, offers the prospect of a place in the book on the secret army as well as in that army. The new, the old, the retired, the distant have largely kept the faith, but as transient I have tired of those who smell of cordite and possess the absolute truth. Each one is different but much the same and often much the same as African rebels or Italian. In time, now, the heart tires and the fascination with the raw edges of politics fades. It is a good time to sum up, to indicate a special perspective on a world as difficult to describe as it is for a visitor to enter – a dragonworld of violence and romance, killing and sacrifice, and a structure and dynamics still elusive after a generation.

Revolution is a young man's game. And it is true that one ambush is much like the next, one gunman the image of another. Still, the fact remains that even for the observer the smell of cordite and the touch of danger is addictive. Time spent in the regular world, walking across a campus or to a conference, sitting in front of the computer, holds none of the charms of the dragonworld. Those charms, best savored cold, may, however, dominate the day. Field work can become an addiction, requiring regular dosage. The means may become more important than the task, especially to the visitor. The underground that attracts is difficult to define – in a sense the purpose of this work. There is no *thing*, no ground under observation. Nothing is *there*. The underground, a world made real by conviction, is a matter of perception. The visitor enters only on invitation and by necessity as an alien there on sufferance.

In Khartoum, for example, years ago, I sat at a cafe table in front of the hotel overlooking the Blue Nile at an agreed hour. The appointment had been made seven thousand miles away with people notoriously vague on details and matters of time, with people all on the wanted list, with people who had and have no love for Americans and little understanding of academic inquiry. And so I sat, scholar-tourist, as the local patrons began to leave their tables in the rising heat. Then, beside the table appeared a tall man, smart in a long robe, leather sandals on his feet and polish on his nails, a large black man topped with a swirl of turban. There was an odor of musk, a face embossed with scars and no special expression. He was like many of the other patrons if not at all like me. I sat still, volunteering nothing. He said my name and I stood up in the underground.

Twenty minutes before, I had sat down in a chair, in Khartoum, in the real and visible world. To those around me sipping warm Fanta or sweet coffee as I stood up I was the same; a tourist on the terrace. But I was not the same at all. I had become a visitor to an underground, as real to me as to the tall man in his turban and his outlaw colleagues waiting out of sight. In the underground everything, everything is out of sight.

One cannot see love or hate or quantify faith – all real, all causes of real acts. The underground is not a place but a manner of seeing – and so no one sees it clear but only through eyes opened by faith. Those involved rarely even talk about their environment; only the faith that brought them to it. The faith changes everything, enhances life with dangers and possibilities. Walking off the terrace of the Palace Hotel in Khartoum to the waiting car, I came again to see hints and risks, probabilities, potentials and shadows that before did not matter.

In the underground no one talks about this transformation. Few notice. They, rebels for one cause or another, covert, illicit, determined, may, like the lover or the monk, talk about the faith but not the world that the faith shapes. It is a world that has generated enormous interest and has been depicted in all manner of conventional ways – often adequate, sometimes brilliant and useful, occasionally moving and true.

The underground is almost totally closed except to the faithful and, even then, their vapor trails are difficult to see. It is a world of strangeness and new colors and a certain charm. The underground rebel lives in an enhanced reality, lives with a new agenda, with new internal virtues and a new way of seeing. In retirement or success, in jail or power, many remain within the magnet field of the underground, seeing matters differently. Life is rarely as intense again and so the habits of the underground become vestigial. The values of the underground are only crucial underground. These novel and special values are everywhere – Central Africa, Germany, Algeria or Sri Lanka – similar in their effect if not their ideology. Such a rebel perception imposes canons of behavior, patterns on the movement, vapor trails that are of little interest to the involved, if noted at all. The underground is all unstated, unnoticed premises, all assumptions protected by illusions, on-the-job training in tradecraft, luck, and the failures of the center.

The involved are not concerned with the dynamics, scarcely aware of the real anatomy of their movement. Their faith is so compelling they can barely spare the time to wage an armed struggle, learn the rebel craft. They are uninterested in all but the faith and so pursue the armed campaign in the midst of a secret world created by that faith. The only hope of those who would report back – even with visa entry assured – is research by osmosis, long contact with those involved. And driven by invisible gods, these rebels speak little and see strangely.

They are in many matters quite conventional and everyday – to their family and friends or in their allotted occupation. The rebel, like a saint or a new lover, is not really everyday. The saint may have a law degree and the lover can make millions or go to war but both still are shaped by especial faith. They see what others do not. They are as others are not. Yet both may appear normal, orthodox. The rebel, too, is conventional – not as cover but truly. Rebels may appear fanatical in politics but otherwise are normal. They do not always stay underground. Even as rebel they sometimes appear in public. They may talk to journalists and tourists and the passer-by. They may appear only slightly irregular. They can, indeed, be found as assignment sitting in the movement's information offices. There they speak for the rebel, the truth. They see, however, what others cannot: the present promising and the future assured, the will of the people and the fragility of power. They see them all. They know the real truth. And if on aging their vision fades, they lie and keep the faith, faithful bureaucrats of the underground. The other volunteers, some mute, inarticulate, peasants from the outback, some glib urban animals, seldom appear for questions but are in one aspect alike, at one with the spokesman. They are pilgrims engaged in an armed struggle.

The faith permits, demands all. And so the rebels take the most disproportionate risks with their lives and the lives of others. The risks, often ignored, minimized by habituated response, are always with the underground and so add tang to the rounds of the transient. There are those, combat photographers or stringers for provincial newspapers, who become addicted solely to such dangers, attend the war not for the Pulitzer but for the danger game, drive the race for risk not to win. There is a charm in standing in harm's way. The underground, the armed struggle, however, is not simply about the killing, not just about the war or the risks in war, but about the organization of reality by the faithful to permit the killing. Those focused on the spectacular and novel, the violent, the news of the day, miss as irrelevant the dynamics of the underground world. For many the focus has been on to the visible story: the no-warning bomb, the assassin, the suicide fundamentalist driving to murder with a smile. Terror has for years been trendy if abhorrent. Much analytical time is invested in the proper response to such wars, in what to do. The strange world that produces such war is only a secondary concern, if that, to many of the responsible.

Entering that strange world, an invisible force field, the underground as ecosystem, means not only a disappearance unnoticed by the real world, not just risks that attract, the romance of terror, but also time spent in dubious pursuit. No one sensible sits across bar tables from active gunmen or watches gun battles from a terrace, and very few of the sensible want to enter the underground beyond a hurried interview. Academics, even the most curious, find access difficult, finances difficult.

Mostly sensible analytical access is with those rebels who for one reason or another are no longer in the killing game; those in prison, or parliament or retirement; those who no longer smell of cordite. More often the academic and the analyst concentrates on the available and often to great and good purpose. There are profound and useful books on single movements, the Shining Path in Peru, the ETA in Spain, the PLO. There have been those who for years have effectively dealt with terror – David C. Rapoport at UCLA or Martha Crenshaw at Wesleyan, Ted Gurr at Maryland with graphs and charts, the lawyers, the historians, all the others including those who have visited the active. It is the reality of an active underground, an active armed struggle that has been attractive to me. Any source on such matters is grist for the analytical mill, but the real rebel is special. Yet the problems of access, the attraction of the covert, the romance of danger, simply offer the first obstacles.

As time passes, for the observer with a valid visitor's pass to the underground the necessary distinction between subject and object may erode. Bad enough to be drawn by the risk, by the violence, but worse to take part. To accept entry is to be in the underground even if without faith, without conventional mission – and certainly without sponsor or recourse to external aid and comfort. The visitor must be both neutral and sympathetic, disinterested and concerned. And must perforce rely only on existing assets. To be able to use the return ticket, the transient must make do, rely on luck, a feel for the aberrant, experience, and common sense. If there is to be a return to the conventional, if there is to be a written report, an article, a book, the tourist must not only return but return uncontaminated by the faith or by the covert and illicit.

Visitation rights must not lead to commitment through enchantment with the involved. And usually such rights are only granted to those sympathetic, friends of the movement, all but allies. Even then the scholar-advocate Regis Debray as friend of Guevara, or the various Palestinian writers have produced interesting, often valuable if always committed work. The underground naturally prefers their friends. Thus the disinterested is often accepted only as potential convert or a messenger from beyond, hardly ever as a fair observer. And staying clear, staying an observer rather than becoming enemy or advocate is never easy. The rebel, sensibly, remains suspicious. The journalist is briefed, goes home, writes the story – this one sits and stays, promising publication later, much later. There the faith and the faithful may, almost surely will, become commonplace, friends, protectors, reasoned pilgrims. And even the dangers and the exotic grow tame after a time – a second risk of exposure. The irregular becomes regular, the normal, natural.

Usually the faith is easy to deny – except as reasonable for the pilgrims. Wasn't Palestine twice promised? Don't the Basques have a case, but doesn't Madrid as well? Underground, balance tends to be lost by the involved in the light of absolute truth. The visitor may, too, lose objectivity, if not at once, if not altogether. Many causes are not unreasonable, if always flawed. The flaws tend to fade in conversation with the faithful just as the necessary precautions of the underground become habit. What inevitably happens is that the strange and irregular becomes commonplace. The killing game imposes rules and assumptions not found elsewhere. So 'life-threatening research', as sociologists called it, doesn't seem so. Meeting members of the Moslem Brothers in the dark under the foundations of a new Cairo hotel, talking with men wanted by the Greek police who are standing in a clump under a streetlight at the next corner, nodding at the friendly gunman in the street becomes proper, appropriate, usual. It is the way things are done, talking to rebels, and it must be done with care.

So talking to rebels is what I have done, what I do. 'I learn by going where I have to go.' And I do it among those who no longer seem very exotic. Just as one gets used to the street patterns of Cairo or the business habits of Cypriots so too is the case with the killing business, the patriot game. And the habits and assumptions of the underground can be discarded if not as smoothly as the charms of the faith when I come home to the everyday.

The gunmen off Riverside Drive in New York are locals, seldom involved in politics, rarely dispatched from abroad. Once or twice there have been problems. The underground has suddenly materialized unexpectedly. Once two fellow nationals tried to dispatch a dinner guest with iron pipes – a low budget Fourth World assassination attempt unreported, unsuccessful, unwanted. Sometimes those seeking a special kind of detonator or details on electronic equipment have stopped by unannounced. All sorts of spokesmen and transients have my telephone number. Fewer now than once. Mostly off Riverside Drive we have only crack addicts, transient drunks, and not gunmen. Any gunmen are my old friends, retired, tourists in the great city not on assignment at all. There is no dragonworld in New York that concerns me.

Much is now conventional. Much always was, certainly in New York, often abroad. Meetings at the Delegates Lounge of the United Nations are quite conventional. Interviews at the Foreign Office or at the Knesset need not be structured as a meeting on a street corner. And even then gunmen interviews are only somewhat different. There is no more a shift than that from Italian to English, from Rome to New York, from a gunman to a congressman: hardly noticed after a time. These pilgrims move through a new world that enhances, transforms even the most fixed and traditional aspects of life – walking a street, talking to a friend, meeting a plane or stopping by the road. Nothing can be assumed to be simple, clean, benign: nothing is as it seems. Nothing is normal. Any street, every street may have unpleasant surprises – walking is an adventure turned conventional by endless practice.

Actually everything may be normal as normal. The streets are usually safe, unobserved friends are really friends. However, while running with the hares and being funded intermittently by the hounds, I have stayed wary enough to survive, met those I liked, found reentry into the conventional relatively easy, and rarely been tempted by alien causes no matter how valid.

It is better still to become involved with the more savory rebels, those with good causes if horrid means. Every cause is flawed and the means truly dreadful. Yet who is an American to demand perfection from others? After all, Americans at least have a record not innocent of blemishes – Wounded Knee and Dresden, Hiroshima and My Lai. Americans, my own ancestors, were once rebels, licensed piracy, attacked a neighboring republic to get

Texas, slaughtered each other at Antietam and Gettysburg, produced the Ku Klux Klan and the hanging posse. My genealogy may have been politically correct at the time but might not stand up to contemporary moral standards. Thus the investigation of other wars and other terrors can hardly be disallowed because of rebel contamination. Still, the politics of atrocity causes qualms; not all rebels are terrible but certainly many do terrible things.

There is no clean means of access to terror, every rebel is by someone's definition a bandit, a mad dog, and is obviously outside the law and often decency. George Washington was so regarded by King George, Houston by Santa Ana, Robert E. Lee and Jefferson Davis by Lincoln. Separatists enrage the center, decades later the English still hate Menachem Begin just as the Israelis despise Arab gunmen who claim Begin's heritage. The most dreadful may be avoided, but the most awful are often prime examples.

In any case access to terror is not easily granted, is almost never granted to the orthodox by the dreadful. Access by a conventional American has often raised considerable suspicions. Precautions are always in order. And here and there over the years, over cocktails, to prove a point or out of malice, those who announce as an aside their sure and certain knowledge that this chap or that one – or me – is a provocateur or operative or employee out of Langley are into more than gossip. Why the CIA would send out operatives under such visible banners with such obvious intentions is a mystery. Yet everyone likes a conspiracy, especially in the underground. The CIA's hand is found everywhere when once it was the British MI-6 or a fine Italian hand or much earlier simply the devil.

No one wants to be chosen as spy-of-the-week in Aden or Beirut, especially those innocent. At times only the presence of friends in place has prevented me from walking into a room filled with those who have taken rumor as fact, added this to that and found me suspect. Gossip in Washington or Dublin can be deadly to the subject in Beirut or Aden. The chattering classes can kill as well as contaminate. Thus one of the difficulties has always been that without the prospect of pension or the resources of the state I have had false flags tacked to my mast by those idling their minds. It is difficult being an American, citizen of the Great Satan, always responsible for Washington's most recent lunacy and never the beneficiary of American success or decency or even power – not to mention being the tallest person in any crowd when the bricks are thrown – without being a spy as well. It has been difficult but to date, fortunately, never any more, just one more obstacle, the musing of the malicious.

In fact an innocent observer may gain entry simply because he is taken as agent: seeking for meaning, suspecting conspiracy, the fearful and suspicious take the evidence of films, the plots of thrillers as reality. Then I become important, alas. Why else would the man come harm's way to ask questions? Why do the Americans want to talk with us? What are we to say? What is the mission, the meaning, the message? The courier can be taken as the message. The visitor, transmuted into message, is thus damned by the hares for consorting with the hounds. And not all hares are harmless. Yet, sometimes the courier is welcomed as a sign. Men have come with guns to take me away at a time of very considerable tension in Jordan. With a civil war all but scheduled, they came not to eliminate a suspected spy but to lecture an American for hours on the wonders of Syrian Ba'athist ideology, ever a painful experience even when accompanied with much tea and a safe return, much less under a gun. And so it is not how do you meet these people but rather not to worry for they may come to get you. But not often.

Access is easier than most assume. Everyone likes to talk about themselves, none more than the saved. And talking is much easier when your arrival somehow validates the seriousness of the local armed struggle. This alone has become reason enough to retire from active inquiry. Such investigation based on access – achieved after an endless vigil in some largely uninhabited hotel at the back of the beyond – often assures that the orthodox assume sympathy with the rebel. Damned by hound for consorting with the hare. Association with the more conventional undergrounds raises fewer qualms of conscience, but the rebels too have dedicated enemies. Turks abhor Armenians and are detested by Greeks. Who holds a brief for Abu Nidal's terrorist except a transitory patron eager for action at a distance? Who, even now, would give television coverage to an airport killer? Yet who in the West wants to hear of the more unsavory aspects of the Afghan mujahedeen? And are the trendies of the African National Congress terrorists, and were the Contras? Everyone has dubious friends and nasty enemies. There are no clean undergrounds, none is pure in deed and few pure in heart. An armed struggle is always a dirty war – all wars are awful anyway but the rebel fights close, personal, often in plain sight and often with limited restraint. Association must always to some degree contaminate. Some hate a rebel so bitterly that insight bought by contamination is not worth the price.

Many shrewd and responsible people cannot bear too much rebel reality whatever the purpose. Yet rebel contact is all. If the active rebel is sought in the act, there is no other route. The risks really do become conventional. The risk of antagonizing the consumer, the patron, the public is conventional. Most historians must write as if not only their subject were dead but also their readers irrelevant: in theory at least. The risks in the field are almost forgotten once precautions become habit. The dangers do not seem very special. Isn't everyone on some sort of list? Anyway, just wait; in time your name will drop out of the top ten. Doesn't everyone assume the telephone is tapped, the mail read, the police at the airport, the gunman in a ditch? Don't use the phone, rely on the post, fret about police on regular duty or the wraith around the corner. Don't worry about the rules of the trade or the conditions of research. All the risks evaporate through habit. The dynamics of the underground no longer grate.

Much of my work on the rebel is orthodox. Conventional interviews are arranged. The policemen speak at the same conferences, attend the same seminars. The prime minister may be a target or even a retired rebel and can be contacted through his secretary. Much can be learned from old newspapers, others' books, the daily newspaper, even the driver on the way to the airport. Research is research, mostly. Out of the underground, safe and everyday, only occasionally does one worry about luggage left standing by an airport line or strange men loitering outside Zabar's delicatessen. Mostly the underground is left at some foreign airport to emerge in New York only in wisps and faint scents when visitors arrive for whatever purpose – and so for a moment transmute the normal into a contact.

Such contacts, more often out of the past than with the active, are a reminder that the way stations of the long march of others now may include you. One hopes to become a name moving out of the top ten, a fading fancy, an old contact, a far away writer soon forgotten. It is past time to let the underground stay underground.

As I approach my twilight years the delights of interviewing one more generation of gunmen have faded. And so my tangential career within the underground has, I hope, come to an end. There has to be an end to excursions that bring diminishing returns at unnecessary risks. The friends will remain, the contacts fade, the memoirs can be used at a party or conference. The beginning of the end is in part this book. There is no longer a need to skirt harm's way, stand amid alien corn, be thought dubious by both sides, all sides. The time to write in detail on the underground has arrived – not so much betray confidence, endanger contacts and old friends, but to write a text that will surely give displeasure and pain, the inevitable response when an observer does not grasp the truth as given: given by the rebel and given by the center, given by the radical or the conservative. There are lots of truths about any underground, especially the Irish Republican movement with two centuries of history to dispute.

No text will satisfy all and most texts will annoy some. Most rebels do not mind some criticism on the practical, the pragmatic, the details of the trade – after all they, by definition, are not yet successful. To reduce the ideal to techniques, to keep score, to lump their dream with others, may be wrong and abhorrent. Even to pry and poke into everyday dynamics as the crucial aspect of the underground is to miss the point. For the rebel, past or present, the cause determines all: the dream illuminates the underground. And so it does throwing the dynamics into the shadows, hiding even the mechanics, the working parts.

It is a dream the center insists is illicit, warped and illegitimate that should not validate those horrors offered in its name: rebels are monsters, criminals, bandits, not worth notice beyond condemnation, revolting. Few at the center want to talk about such pilgrims. The British are exhausted by the revolting Irish, no more text, no more attention to the IRA is needed, warranted. Dublin has had more than enough of the patriot game. Everyone on the island seems to want no more than peace and quiet. There has been enough dreaming by gunmen to last well beyond the century.

Having followed the devices and desires of my own heart, not the requirements of the profession, the strictures of discipline, I have existed on the margins of academic research and analytical policy concerns, as an eccentric with appropriate connections and doubtful interests. Perhaps more orthodox interests and a greater concern in spending time tilling the proper academic fields would have allowed a more orthodox career – and perhaps not. Most assuredly it would not have taken me on my terrorist tour, exposed me to the alien and the desperate. I would have missed, not so much the wars and romance, but the reality of the different, those who could see what I could not. I would not have known those gunmen, nor the desperate at the dangerous edge of matters. Those who are difficult to explain in Cambridge or Washington but real enough in Rome or Derry have made my life more interesting. Perhaps the old Chinese curse, 'May you have an interesting life', was bestowed upon me.

In my march alongside, if not in, these interesting crusades of our times, I have had not only the toleration and assistance of those actually involved but also the aid of the orthodox, the traditional, colleagues and foundations and individuals. My focus on the armed struggle was encouraged a decade ago by a grant from the Earhard Foundation. This book itself was made possible by the accumulated support of a generation of such aid and in particular by five grants from the Harry Guggenheim Foundation with the oversight of Program Officer Karen Colvard, and two from the Smith-

Richardson Foundation with first as program officer William Bodie and then Devon Gaffney Cross. Both foundations, in fact, funded a general study of the Irish Troubles that permitted a final round of questions before I gave up gunmen in hopes that after writing such a history there might be sufficient material for a detailed analysis of the Provisional IRA – which has proven to be the case to the relief of all except, perhaps, the subject. Rebels do not mind history, being in and part of history, written history, but feel uncomfortable as subjects on a slide. Still, there they are, my image, my perception, not on a slide but on the page.

That perception, acquired over a generation, rests on the aid and comfort of thousands of people – especially the Irish. The hours spent with or about the Provisional IRA have been enormous, usually several months each year; special trips to Britain, to Washington, and through contacts not only within the Irish diaspora but also in Africa and the Middle East – graffiti on Irish matters was to be found in Rome and Jerusalem and Cairo. During all this field work there has been the assistance of conventional colleagues, the kindness of strangers, the enthusiasm of government officials – many with grave distaste for the subject – and access to the special knowledge of many journalists, transient, local, stringers, in-place and retired. There are those whose comments over tea or on the ferry, in the midst of war or after a lecture have been accumulated, weighted, those never thanked, met once, met often or not at all. Some of the most helpful contacts always remain invisible, truly underground. And there are those whose time and talent I have drawn on for years in Ireland, at home, in far places – and most of these like most of the involved are just as pleased not to be listed. It is those not listed, the gunmen and the volunteers, the pilgrims old and new, retired, active, unrepentant and persistent that I have to thank the most – and who will undoubtedly dislike the text the most, for it focuses on the system not the banner on the lance. And the cause for most volunteers is the key – and properly so. Yet, albeit reluctantly, over the years many have discussed the technicalities and so the dynamics of their special armed struggle. These gunmen throw their shadows here.

As for cited sources, the reader will find few. Most of the specific data in the text is general knowledge. What is not, the special cases and the general conclusions, arise from the thousands upon thousands of hours of discussion with all and sundry. Thus there seems little need of academic pretensions for a formal apparatus. Citations are more likely to be asides than sources. What matters in these armed struggles is not so much dates and places and fatalities, all on record, but interpretation and presumption.

And finally, all these notions and presumptions about the underground, discovered at a distance and detailed in the quiet before my Macintosh have often made an easy home life complex. In this I have been fortunate with Nora, my Irish connection, my Kerry wife, who has made my life less of an armed struggle. Beside gunmen and poets, saints, and scholars, the alien has always found on the island warm hearts and blue eyes. Beir bua.

JBB
New York–Dublin–New York

1

The Nature of the Armed Struggle

WE LIVE in an epoch of enormous violence, a time of terror and mass murder. The century has been an age of anxiety at best and at worst generation after generation of slaughter. All but the most primitive and isolated have lived under threat of nuclear destruction. If the great, bipolar cold war with its mutually assured destruction has ended, the legacy is dubious – proliferation of nuclear weapons, proliferation of new states, new ambitions, new rebels, new wars. Nearly everyone is touched by everyday violence even if it comes no closer than the evening news. War is no longer just the sport of kings but endemic.

These conflicts have been generated by reasons of state and because of historical grievances, through blunder and mismanagement, generated by race and class and tribe. There have been national wars and religious wars, civil strife and simple massacre, conflicts that were by-products of the Cold War and a long wave of people's wars, rebel armed struggles, guerrilla insurrections. War has been a growth industry. And, when not so involved, a variety of governments have slaughtered their own in great internal purges, maintained power through terror, pursued security with Gulags of the interned. Once the great monsters disappeared, Stalin, Hitler, Mussolini, there were ample replacements: cannibal kings, warlords, bureaucrats of oppression and lethal idealists imposing in great leaps forward fantasy by terror.

All these horrors continue despite the efforts of the men of good will. And many leaders seemingly have only the will to power and then in power the will to destroy any perceived threat: at worst simply to seek vengeance and at best to correct perceived grievance by recourse to force. The world is filled as well with real grievances – hunger, misery, disease, humiliation. Neither science nor managerial skill have prevented war or even alleviated natural disaster.

Everywhere the meek are wretched, the desperate denied. The post-modern world is the equal of any Dark Age in matters of turmoil, disease and slaughter. And centralized control and technological triumphs of the times have enlarged the capacity to do violence to the many – no longer need armies kill by hand or the news of new taxes arrive on forked stick. Even without an autocrat at the center of the web, the structures of the modern impose conformity – conformity in consumption and conformity in action. The radical sees all about in Moscow and Rio and Tokyo quiet desperation and the denial of hope. The rich live the same everywhere in a transnational society of excess consumption, each great hotel or luxury car a clone of the last, each of the comfortable interchangeable, Hong Kong banker, Swedish manager or Mexican entrepreneur. The workers, paid with promises and consumer goods, are forced into hives, let out for football and tranquilizers. The poor, like the rich, too live the same everywhere – in hopeless misery without prospects or position. The brave and the free, those with prospects and property, are rare. For the cynical or the radical, it seems that much of the world is either a combat zone or structured to deny the many both pride and property. A billion Chinese ruled by jealous old men, the Japanese clerks and programmers stuffed into trains and tiny flats and closed careers, the Celtic margins of Europe depopulated and turned into vacation parks, Africa closed for repairs and Latin America ruled by charlatans and criminal cartels – the world after a century of terror and violence appears comfortable and profitable only for the very few.

If the meek are to inherit the earth, they must do so over the ruins of the nation-state and the efficiencies of the free market and despite the wonders of instant communication – all hum the same tune in the global village. If there is to be revolutionary change for all, it must come not only against armies and despots but also despite the lure of material things, cheap, gaudy and available for all but the most wretched who are restricted to discards and the traditional.

Sometimes, but not often, armed struggles have led, in part at least, to change. A new image is created or old wrongs avenged, if not righted. There may be shifts in power, even real revolutions. The end of an imperial age, chaos in fragile states, and even some changes in the West can be traced underground to rebels with a cause. Revolt may, as promised – but so rarely delivered – lead to institutional change.

There have been all sorts of nasty, small changes in the years after the last great war ended in 1945. Airport security is different, the agenda of prime ministers different, the flags over new nations novel, and the back lists of publishers abound with works on violence and terror. China is Red, Lebanon ruined, Zaire is again the Congo, and Israel exists – as now does the dream of Palestine if confined for a time to Gaza and Jericho. And equally important, the rebel with a cause has grown grand in perception. The media, the sponsoring states, the dictates of fashion, have often combined to exaggerate the guerrilla role. Bosnia and Somalia, Ulster and Lebanon have been focus of the moment, the arena for photogenic violence exaggerated by television news.

Standing on a jungle hill, clad in beret and combat jacket, bearded and bold, armed with an AK-47, the guerrilla in a passing colonial world became hero. The freedom fighter appeared to be able to bring liberty and justice, able to topple imperial, even indigenous, despots, and so proved to many that a just cause can devise a strategy to remove the corrupt.

In time fashions changed and the myth of the guerrilla frayed. Che was dead and despots ruled in the new nations. Only the most innocent and provincial, like the Indian peasant guerrillas in Chiapas province of Mexico in January 1994, would find Che and Castro still heroes and Zapata as ancestor for their National Liberation Army.

Then the Marxist-Leninists found guerrillas in their own empire, first abroad and then closer to home. Guerrillas were not so fashionable and soon replaced by different gunmen. Even the café Left of Europe discovered during the years of lead that their party card did not deter the Euroterrorists. The new Reds shot the old Reds, and not in the outback but in Turin and Berlin. And there were new fascists, new Blacks, as well to add to the din.

The world became more complex, heroes more difficult to discover: a beret and an AK-47, the costume of irregular killing, could be worn by any-one. Serbs slaughtering Croatians or Somali warlords starving competitive clans fit no attractive model. And the killers often came dressed as tourists, slaughtering innocents for obscure causes. These urban guerrillas surfaced in the center of the West and carried killing into the streets of London and Rome. Palestinians, Lebanese, Persians, rebels from the Spice Islands as well as from County Kerry, a new generation of Germans and Italians, all sorts, brought murder to the West.

No one loved a terrorist. In the cities no-warning bombs and shoot-outs in the airport eroded the appeal of the gunman, any gunman, any cause. The covers of popular magazines, the television news, the journals and papers and radio presented so many atrocities: dead judges in the gutters of Rome and Milan or airport lounges strewn with the bodies of murdered children. Even the fashionable African rebels burned their own with flaming necklaces, set no-warning bombs in supermarkets, killed without considera-tion of external standards. And many gunmen were not fashionable at all, only brutal or bizarre, killing tourists in Allah's name or this tribe or that fellow who dared to buy the wrong ticket, fly the wrong airline, stand in the wrong queue: no one was innocent and anyone could be guilty of murder. All that was needed was a gun and the scrap of a cause, a slogan would do. Anyone could play.

There existed suddenly, unexpectedly, new monsters. Cool, urbane, ruthless, young men and women in casual Italian tailoring and RayBan aviator sun glasses, who without compunction slaughtered innocents as symbols. These were the new, polished butchers of the underground, armed with hi-tech machine-pistols and the absolute truth. They appeared only to slaughter the vulnerable. They were the first of the new, awful, feral gunmen who cast long shadows.

Deeply dedicated or hired with a slogan, these killers became a consumer of Western innocence. And worse, they became a constant, replaced by new killers with different slogans.

Even the old rural guerrilla struggles have grown more awful. Increasingly, the rebel – Irish or Arab, urban or rural – has appeared cruel, a new barbarian. Hidden behind those dark sunglasses, the terrorists have the eyes of a gull: cold, feral, opaque. The romantic rebel is dead and gone.

The rest, the watchers, the vulnerable, the threatened, even the distant and the secure, find rebel ways deeply troubling. Those states who sponsor the rebel do so at risk. Few but the rogue regime pursue guerrilla options any longer, sponsor terror. The Contras brought scandal to Washington. Moscow had its own problems. For even when their surrogates took power, the Soviets often found escalating commitments, not influence and power. And at the end the Russians had to learn of guerrillas first-hand in Afghanistan. The Libyans as paymaster provoked a United States counter-attack and later isolation, damned as tinkering with terror. Peking squandered moral capital by backing the dreadful Khmer Rouge. In the great game, who wanted to claim as piece or puppet those who murdered an old man in a wheelchair or shot a family friend at his door? Who would write a ballad for those who bombed holiday crowds or shot a soldier dressed as Santa? No one – or nearly no one – and those who would take the risk, Libya, Iran, Syria, grew very cautious. Terror was not trendy but ubiquitous, Egyptians in New York bombing the World Trade Center, the war in central Africa with no one in charge, the Slavic warlords in Bosnia. And for the nostalgic there were in 1994 those innocent Indians in Chiapas, a children's crusade with tarnished automatic weapons, with previously discarded ideas and tactics, with old grievances none the less real. And these guerrillas, like most in Latin America, produced not change, not justice but, as always, bodies sprawled in ditches and the army sweeping through the countryside. Who sensibly would advocate the gun as an effective means forward for the wretched in Chiapas? Who would advocate atrocity as cost-effective?

No one at all wanted to underwrite atrocities if atrocities paid no dividends. Sometimes they did – one carbomb and the United States was out of Lebanon. One more under the World Trade Center and the Great Satan was punished and the grievances of Islam revealed everywhere on the nightly news: the most limited of volunteers working from borrowed manuals and trial and error had charged if not changed history. More often the returns were uncertain. State-sponsored terror revealed unanticipated costs to many, even to many vicious and immoderate despots. Even Gadaffi wavered on the proper posture: now humble, now defiant. For much of the world and the West, the old guerrilla heroes now seemed reborn as monsters.

Hero or monster, the rebel leaders have been visible, become famous. Many became megastars in the media of the times: Mao and Giap, Che and Castro, Carlos, Arafat. Their faces have been on the covers of news magazines and on television, carried emblazoned on banners and painted as icons. Their names are still scrawled on walls. Pop artists paint Mao. They are rebels with names. Names that have purchased fame with a price measured in blood and death. Bobby Sands and Baader and Meinhof and Abu Iyad are all safely dead; but even now, they are names to conjure. Once Menachem Begin was a terrorist wanted by the British. So once was his successor as prime minister of Israel, Yitzhak Shamir. So too were Colonel Grivas and Archbishop Makarios, Anwar Sadat and Jomo Kenyatta. The men in black pajamas now administer the ruins their dream has made of Vietnam and some of those from Oriente broadcast venom against the regime of Castro. Times change.

However, sometimes the armed struggle triumphs and there is no change: another elite in the old palace. Sometimes all change is announced, but the maximum leader speaks of the people and wears designer glasses, urges socialism and allocates the state's assets to his friends and family. Some despots brought to power through rebellion prove enlightened, some kill for pleasure.

These unconventional struggles have been labeled, fitted into analytical typology: urban or rural, nationalist or communist, low-intensity or high, anti-imperial or messianic. A great many have been fascinated by the aura of the gun, by the weak winning, by the myth of the guerrilla or by the transfer of power from the center to the margins. All sorts of analysis has been done by the involved and by the threatened. The advocates of class, the social scientists and the area specialists, the anti-insurgency bloc, the journalists, the historians, and the advocates of revolution have published. An enormous library has been written.

Many analysts have advanced on the armed struggle with a congenial means, a hidden agenda, and often a prepared mind. These analytical advances into rebel territory have had mixed results. Such rebel struggles do not easily fit the usual categories of political and military appraisal. Each methodology had been useful but partial and some generate quite academic results useful in the long struggle for tenure if not much practical help in the outback. Each seemingly can explain nearly all without recourse to the other findings. So some have collated all the parts and yet, somehow, their results still do not make a satisfactory whole.

Most analysts have concentrated on the killing and on appropriate responses, on war. The nature and impact of the rebel ideal has not attracted much concern except as a sort of political agenda. Those observers who factor in the power of the rebel dream do so as ideology rather than as the determinate of the dynamics of the struggle. In Ireland the IRA is considered at best in pursuit of obsolete nationalism spiced with radical slogans, advocated by the simple and self-taught, and at worst a band of killers seeking sectarian vengeance covered in republican banners; a campaign that was waged for years is extended out of spite. The Irish gunman is a wicked, evil man whose dream is nightmare to the responsible and sensible. So too are all gunman dreams. Even a ceasefire does not change matters.

The dream is not only the source of the energy that drives the armed struggle but also largely determines the dynamics of that struggle. Few analysts understand dreams. Much analysis would treat the conversion on the road to Damascus as an event best described by road engineers and tour guides. And so many do not realize how skewed the underground is by perception of the involved, by the power of a dream – any dream. Few have much empathy with the armed struggle, can imagine life on the run or a life unlike their own.

Even the involved, the old rebels, have proven limited witnesses. They tend to remember only the glory and excitement, not the brutality. The blunders, the killing optimism, the corruptions, the lies and the betrayals are edited out of the text. Just like conventional generals writing from their retirement, guerrilla memoirs have been written back to front. Nothing was ever so neat as Mao, nor as ideal as the memoirs of Grivas, nor as righteous as Begin's revolt. Old rebels, too, have their methods and their agendas. They rarely even pretend to the objectivity of the historian. They have myths to fashion, a dream to shape to reality beyond the strictures of the underground – a nation to build, a system to impose.

All this is as expected. The armed struggle is by nature a difficult study. No one sees matters whole. Nearly everyone uses a special methodology and has a private program, special prejudices. There is often a distaste for the topic or a need to rationalize the past for present consumption. Because of the Troubles Irish history has been rewritten, and this is no bad thing. Yet few among the analysts or the responsible find the present IRA legitimate. The Irish analysts define the problem so that the contemporary Irish gunman is aberrant – not to mention abhorrent. This is hardly novel; the threatened seldom love a gunman. This is especially the case with those who assume that the center monopolizes legitimacy – voted into power by the people or ruled by God's divine providence. They do not look into their own hearts to find legitimacy but to election statistics, historical precedent, the rationalizations of those in place.

The rebel, Irish or other, by definition is a usurper, a killer, a figure who causes trouble by intent. Few Western writers now advocate violence except as last resort. In the real underground world perception is vital. Analysis is not just a problem of discipline or commitment, not of prejudice but also a problem of clashing perceptions of reality. The involved see matters in strange ways. They must translate them for the curious as well as the dubious. And those involved within the underground who see reality shaped by the dream are mostly beyond easy access. They can seldom explain and seldom can imagine that their reality is not that of others. And, when they become as the others, underground reality is no longer real to them. And when access can be managed by the observer, the rebel vision is often discounted as warped. The unconverted always find the absolute truth difficult to accept, difficult to accept in others and impossible to imagine as option.

At present most scholars assume rebel analysis if not deluded at best unrealistic – the rebels see what the professor cannot. They, the gunmen, then, move in mysterious ways within a movement beyond easy entry.

Active movements make poor subjects since the disinterested investigator usually must probe at a distance, often across a cultural and class divide. Many rely on analogy, secondary sources, the perspective of the involved, and the evidence of the center. Why not? It works for other subjects. Few are taken by rebel analysis. Few focus on the dream except as program and rationale. Few have experience in a real underground, not at all the flip side of special operations, not at all like the everyday world. It is, then, rare for the disinterested to move through the galaxy of the faithful during an armed struggle.

The rebel is driven by a vision only the faithful can see and this largely determines his world. The rebel underground is molded in a special way not readily amenable to the methods of the social scientists or the analysis of the threatened. They, the pragmatists or the scientific scholars, examine the same phenomena and yet see differently from the involved, from the rebel. They, historians and policy analysts and political scientists, often see not through a glass darkly but with great precision and from a special angle.

This underground is miasma to all, hard to see into and hard to see in. This analysis is a way, one way of seeing from within, the perception of a transient through the underground, many undergrounds. The analysis rests on the assumption that an armed struggle, all armed struggles, are the unconventional means by which the weak seek to transform their dream into reality; change history, capture the future and so erase grievance and injustice. It does not matter what the content of the dream. The dream supplies the impetus that is shaped by the similarity of most opponents and by the rules imposed by incapacities and finally by the need for cover. The end result produces striking similarities in all armed struggles across time and cultures and arenas. All such struggles remain special but all are also alike, examples in a general category.

Certainly some of those involved have felt that this was the case and written manuals for the guerrilla or the rebel even if the texts proved faulty in the field. Mostly the rules by Mao or Grivas are common sense, no more than boy scout rules for the brutal, and the text a manual that more likely will lead to catastrophe if executed by rote. Author of such a primer, Guevara ended his crusade by the side of a Bolivian road, dead, and along with him the hopes of all those who felt to begin was sufficient, one book enough. Still, the rules given imply a singular phenomenon: an armed struggle under whatever banner, however labeled.

Here, then, at the start are the necessary definitions, valid here but perhaps not valid elsewhere, even in the underground. An armed struggle is the means that rebels against the system transforms a dream into power through recourse to violence. The armed struggle is a *means* to acquire power, power over events, power over history, power over reality. The armed struggle is, thus, an act, a procedure – a means of seeing and doing and deploying the dream, a means less than compelling to the dreamer who focuses on the content of the ideal. For the rebel dreamer in the course of human events all other options except the armed struggle have been found wanting, ineffectual or too slow, lacking in psychic rewards or somehow unrewarding, unpromising. All options have been denied in a long train of abuses and usurpations by the power of the center. So the only apparent way into an acceptable future is an armed struggle, a right, a duty, to replace that center.

Once engaged the rebel, if fortunate, is able to persist, hidden within a protective ecosystem, the underground. Cover is assured and so too is opportunity, but at great cost. The underground is a haven that also assures inefficiency, wastes sacrifice, guarantees schism and disillusion, imposes delay and casualties. The underground encourages persistence not victory and so the rebel must be patient, depend on will, the reading of history, seek legitimacy and recognition often while engaged in ruthless brutality. There are to hand only the most limited military assets to pursue the struggle. The ensuing combat may be protracted since escalation by the rebel is usually difficult or impossible – and combat that proves immediately effective can be labelled coup, for there is no long struggle while the rebel searches for effective coercion with limited assets.

Consequently, with the war limited the rebel, if possible, seeks simultaneous other fronts, other means, tests all potential vulnerabilities of the center, seizes all assets and avenues that may repay the effort with power. In effect, the armed struggle bleeds out into other alternatives and options in order to maintain the momentum of the means. These are not alternatives to the armed struggle but additions, aspects and facets. Those rebels too entranced with politics or with non-violence, with the exploitation of injustice or the returns of publicity often run counter to the central command always fixed on the main means. At times, rare times, during an end-game or when protraction has eroded hope that the center will collapse, politics may offer the only means forward. For all concerned this is a delicate moment, the move into the overt: too soon and the rebel dies outside the ecosystem; too late and politics no longer offers any options either.

When the gun is no longer primary, goes on the shelf or is deployed as symbol, perception and so rebel reality shifts. There is always a reluctance to change; the armed struggle no longer fully protected by cover becomes something else. The gunman emerges as an irregular soldier, his organization as a counter-state, his dream defined as program. And sometimes the struggle dribbles away into endemic insurgency, clan war, institutionalized guerrilla opposition, a rebel band without a compelling dream or incandescent hopes.

The rewards of these efforts, of the war itself, of the underground are always shaped by rebel reading, which is different from the everyday. The tactics of the struggle may return not war gains but rather peripheral benefits – all that is available – publicity or improved morale, a witness to persistence or the comfort of action.

These various tactics and alternatives are melded in the protracted combat into an unconventional strategy that will allow the weak to exploit all means forward. This strategy may be implicit or implied, written down in detail or assumed without reflection. It is the big picture, not a primer for tactical application. Little further attention is given to strategy. Those who write polemics and explanations favoring the gunman's goal or course, advocating change, detailing the logic of violence may assume they parse strategy but actually they merely authenticate the dream, offer the theology of the struggle. They number the angels dancing on the pin but do not question the premise. Once underway the struggle must analytically take care of itself.

The capacity to pursue the armed struggle must be husbanded. Far from being opportunists eager to strike everywhere, flexible and fluid, rebels are often conservative, static, rigid, fearful of change. No one can risk the future for one cast of the dice. And to take such a risk, as was nearly the case with the Tet Offensive, an exercise in excess optimism arising from the most orthodox analysis, that to the amazement of the involved proved catastrophic operationally and a strategic and psychological triumph. Usually, most effort is spent repeating yesterday so as to reach tomorrow. And the means most cherished is the one that has proven effective.

At the core of underground purpose is the major priority, the secret army, the crusade for the dream. All else is subsidiary, even when effective. In an armed struggle, the gun, even in the hands of an astute and cunning commander, determines politics; and if not, if the commissar rules without reference to the battle, rebel politics will lose many of the few advantages of the war. When politics subsumes the gun, then the struggle is no longer armed, but fits other rubrics, runs to a different dynamics – and the transmutation is as difficult for the involved as it is for the analysts.

The struggle may not change the balance of power or the course of history but always transform the rebel. Often the struggle proves more important than the result and usually, the struggle, flawed and futile, fails. Still, at the beginning there are those in the grip of a vision. These visionaries often have little more than an ideal and a few weapons, an idea and the arms of the tribe. With limited assets the rebel cannot impose the special vision and so cannot yet determine the end result of history – history as it ought to be. There appears no option but recourse to force against the entrenched and intransigent center, dissolve the political bands which have connected them.

Those who choose the armed struggle for other reasons, romance, fashion, personal gain or the euphoria of the moment, all the secondary factors, treat power lightly. At times the armed struggle has had allure – especially from a distance. Some have been attracted not as last choice but often first. Some want a gun and others to do harm. Some real rebels want to be in fashion as much as power. It is dangerous to lie to oneself and proclaim the armed struggle not the only way but also the best way – optimism is sufficiently a rebel curse without a further withdrawal from reality.

The real goal is power over the past and most of all power over the nature of the future. The past is disaster, unfair; but for all rebels the past should, must, end in future justice. The present is a constant humiliation. A similar future is intolerable.

Those with an alternate, a compelling dream, have run out of patience, out of all practicable options. They have found no easy means into the future and so choose the gun and go underground. They know that it is not the brutal soldier at fault but the system, not the fool that laughs at them or the exam that they cannot pass but the system. The system imposes injustice, drives the dreamer to act. Often the next and future rebels go in trepidation, go reluctantly, go without prospects. The founding fathers, even underground – especially underground – often spend much time in debating the necessity for their presence. They often slip only gradually into killing, cutting off their way back, moving deeper into their own dark world like sleepwalkers.

Few potential rebels want to go to war. Only the second generation rebel can avoid the general reluctance to accept the inevitable. In Ireland, generations of rebels have paved the way so that, assured of the legitimacy to wage war, IRA strategy has often been to seek means to pursue the authorized struggle. All that is needed is an opportunity. Then a beginning can be made, the gun deployed. Once the beginning has been made, the new Irish volunteer arrives because of the nature of the underground not, like many of his predecessors, despite it. And once there is a history of rebellion in Ireland, or elsewhere, each new generation – and underground only a few years may shape a new generation – signs up without qualms to renew an old struggle, pursue the dream.

Most individual rebels go to war because they must. Few go lightly into the underground. Who, after a generation of the Irish Troubles would enlist in the IRA for romantic reasons when all that is assured is corruption, failure, prison and death? In the beginning, only the driven and bold appear always clothed in optimism in trepidation over timing, not outcome. Later, each new levy is as driven and bold but less optimistic. And until much later with power in view or on display few can be conscripted or intimidated into service.

The gunmen volunteer for service. And each does so for various personal purposes and under varying immediate pressures. Each volunteer lives at a special time in a particular culture at the end of a long prologue. Every arena is different in place and time, in nature. Each rebel knows the dream is unique, perhaps universal, like communism; perhaps very specific, like Ibo separatism in Nigeria. Each tends to assume the entire course of the armed struggle is special – it is certainly different from all other experience.

All rebels share the realization that the underground is different. In each, the mix of discernible reality and special perception, the role of history and culture, the evolution of the struggle with the constant impact of objective reality, all vary enormously; but all are different in the same way. And certainly the dream is different, most special of all, different and often contradictory.

There may, as well, be variations and contrasts in the intensity of the struggle, the locale, the stages of war or the details of battle, differences and variations in all matter of particulars; but each complex armed struggle falls into the common genre. All the movements that opt for the armed struggle, are, thus, shaped and circumscribed in large part by the necessity of turning a dream into reality.

Rebels have great dreams, not small. They want too much for the center to cede: the end of empire, an anarchist regime, an Islamic republic, a Basque nation. More. The rebel wants not a passport to the palace but a people transformed. They, the rebels, are not for the easy life, can see no need to compromise the truth or nibble at justice. Keepers of history's legacy, they are possessed with righteousness, the great ideal. Such an ideal ensures the opposition of the center, a center condemned by the rebels and their history to future irrelevance.

Often only through their faith can the rebels maintain a struggle marked by constant defeat, arrests and frustration and the gibbet for the slow. Yet the rebel persists, beyond compromise, for there is seldom a way back out of the underground. And within there is the eternal optimism. What else can there be but optimism with justice on the side of the denied? There is seldom a middle ground in an armed struggle not strewn with bodies left as lesson and reminder by one side or the other that compromise is hopeless. The center at some point, once the struggle is protracted, relies on the imperatives of pain and the returns of attrition: they cannot suffer what we can expend and they cannot do so forever. So the struggle, if the rebel is not squashed in the beginning, is protracted. The rebel calls this winning but the center knows better.

The center can be counted as having ships and planes and men. The center is organized as state, established, legitimate. And all states are apt to respond to threat in similar ways even if somewhat modified by culture, by habit and by local necessity. Often the provincial are transformed by allies,

American tactics or Soviet ideology adding a universal response to the guerrilla challenge. Despite the difference imposed by history and locality, under threat every center reveals a pattern and a dynamics that can readily be described. No matter what strange device flies over the palace or the color of the police uniforms, any center has similar categories of assets: armies and bank accounts, palaces and police. They are assets that observers can inspect. They are deployed to protect power, to repress the rebellion, to impose order and reinforce legitimacy and so deployed in orthodox patterns. Police everywhere are police and know the form of subversives.

Such conflict between unequals is often protracted as the vulnerable avoid the powerful but often do no more than persist. Some rebels skip the underground by trying other unconventional means. The armed struggle is merely an option. The quick way is a coup, an army take-over with rebel flags, orchestrated riots in the street. The slow way is civil war. And there are still other ways. Gandhi chose non-violence for his followers and dismantled the Raj. The Palestinians in Gaza and the West Bank devised the Intifada, riotous attack short of irregular war but, as with the fedayeen's terrorist strategy, the gain was in prominence rather than in power. Many colonies achieved independence by concession – often no one in Paris or London wanted another Algeria or Palestine. The will was not there. The winds of change eventually blew through the Portuguese African empire and then over southern Africa. By the time South Africa became the arena, colonial empires had long been reduced to rocks and tiny islands, scattered residue.

So, too, in Eastern Europe did the will at the center fail. There, freedom came on the installment plan, haltingly but seemingly irreversible. Poland moved out of communism and so the rest of the Warsaw pact followed.

At times during turmoil, as with Kerensky's Russia in 1917, the center cannot resist the dreamers. The dreamers have no moderation, invest everything in the future. They want all now and have no responsibility for the mundane, only the dream. The center must see that the post is delivered, the taxes collected, and a consensus of sorts maintained. Not the rebel. Not Lenin. Seemingly in control of the state, the center in Russia did not really hold power or consensus, only bits of paper and office space – vulnerable to Left or Right, vulnerable to the gun or the mob.

War, conspiracy, coups, violence, orchestrated chaos, even selected non-violence may lead to power, to victory without recourse to a protracted armed struggle. Rebels, revolutionaries, ambitious conspirators often come to power in the turmoil of the times. Sometimes they possess, as did the American colonies, sufficient assets, often including an appropriate terrain, to wage nearly conventional war; sometimes a riot or a coup will do.

In power, the new elite may claim rebel legacy, boast that Ghana evolved through a national liberation struggle or the new rulers attempt to cover the regime in Libya or Grenada with the myth of the guerrilla. Only the most foolish and most romantic actually want a career as a guerrilla-revolutionary. And many who would volunteer are not assets to an armed struggle.

For all rebels only now will do, victory now before too late, before the language is lost, the people co-opted, the past forgotten. And so the crusade cannot wait, cannot wait on time or history, cannot wait for assets, cannot wait for the next generation – the train of abuse and usurpation is too long. Necessity forces action. The wretched will be transmuted into rulers, the peons given power, the nation will emerge and God be honored. Urgency forces optimism, duty to the future demands the risk. And once the shooting has started, even the sensible may find the gun addictive: the way forward closes the way back.

Demands are best met by traditional ways, by concession or oppression, by co-option or corruption. Such demands are best pursued by patience or petition, by democratic means where possible and by recourse to the unconventional when all else fails. The gun is the last unpredictable choice. The armed struggle is attractive only to the driven and desperate. And such rebels are effective only against a center with uneasy legitimacy, limited resources, where there is room to hide, time to persist, an opportunity to protract the struggle. Still, such arenas include much of the world, much more of the world with the faltering of the Moscow center, and at times has included even the post-industrial West.

CONCLUSION

An armed struggle arises when the unreconcilable rebel molds a dream into a means to power. The dream energizes the struggle. Out of weakness the rebel must shape a congenial environment underground and from there wage war even while seeking other vulnerabilities of the center. This very limited war, waged by various means and out of strength of conviction, tends to be protracted so that the will of the dreamers will have the opportunity to erode the determination and assets of the orthodox center.

The rebel usually loses, often quickly. At times for uncertain reasons, the armed struggle may escalate and in fewer cases victory can be achieved in conventional battle as was the case at the end of Mao's Long March and Ho Chi Minh's war of national liberation in Indochina. More likely, victory comes when the center collapses, as was the case with most anti-imperialist wars after 1945, or in Cuba in 1958 and in 1979 Nicaragua in Latin America, or in Ethiopia in Africa. Colonial struggles were successful in part because imperial rebels began to ask a price not worth paying, but national struggles are resisted because the price is too high and those threatened persist: even Angola and Mozambique without talent or assets refused to concede to their guerrilla rebels who could pursue an irregular guerrilla war over much of the arena but not into the capital. The wild zone began with the shantytowns outside the few cities loyal to the center.

The successful rebel wages the armed struggle in the gray area that lies between reactionary and effective coercion by the threatened and assured concession from the center. Most revolts, including classical armed struggles, fail; some are co-opted, a few triumph, and others simply persist, endemic armed struggles.

Every armed struggle is different. Some blend into irregular war on one end of the spectrum and others are endemic, ethnic clashes, the clan war lords in traditional pursuits, at the far end of the spectrum of low-intensity conflict. Each armed struggle is also the same: covert, illicit, largely structured by rebel capacity and intent and by the powers of the center structured as state.

Rebel dreams have been various and often contradictory. Nearly all such visions are flawed, often are denied by the assumed beneficiaries yet can inspire volunteers, often generations of volunteers. For two centuries the dream of an Irish republic has remained an attraction through good times and bad – even when the Irish people as a whole denied that attraction. The dream still lived. And in Ireland those who denied its relevance recognized its legitimacy by endlessly denying the Provisional IRA had any right to act, although year after year volunteers appeared who knew that the movement was the real heir to the past, not the frightened men in suits who were afraid to look into their own hearts. Others, elsewhere have various dreams, each compelling, all engines of the struggle.

Each struggle is parallel in function, one of a type however different the dream. Even those who fight against an international conspiracy or in the name of a universal vision target, not the world but a single regime. If they do not, if they appeal first to the general as have some of the fundamentalist gunmen in Algeria, they offer the state advantage. Even then the universal aspirations are focused on a special battle arena.

Mostly those who would make Allah great therefore lead underground lives not very different from those who seek a Basque republic or a Tamil state. All must cope with the need for cover and the assets of the center.

None are identical but all similar. Some movements are dominated by the middle class and a few not. Some feed on ancient grievance and others on the latest revolutionary text. All are different and yet all are the same.

There have always been rebels and rebellions, often with a dream, many not unlike the contemporary models. The contemporary armed struggle, however, even when dedicated to the imperatives of ancient ancestors, is a child of the nation-state. These states were founded on dreams not limited by rivers or dynasties but ideas and attitudes.

These states stand in the way of the new dreamers, block history, ensure injustice. Revolutionary alliances and alignments exist but the oppressor is always a state. And often the patron of an international movement is, too, a state – Islam in One Country. Iran as first among equals, a posture made difficult by ancient suspicions, Persians are still Persians even when bearing ground-to-air missiles. And the fundamentalists of Iran once in power, once the Islamic republic existed, had to defend it from the secular rebels who once were their allies. In Libya, Gadaffi may scatter odds and ends of arms, checks and favors throughout the revolutionary world but must remain vigilant against his own: in much of the world to be a state is to generate alien aspirations.

The modern state as opposition is a major determinate of the nature of the armed struggle. The strictures of the covert underground and the nature of the opposition define the dynamics of modern rebels, not their dream or agenda – any dream will do, any state, for the same model underground works for all. Iran proved, as is usually the case, too effective for the secular rebels but no less of a target because the dream was in power – rather more so since the dream was exclusive. Most new revolutionary states must eliminate those mesmerized by the purity of the dream, but even then new generations of rebels may emerge – unless the state is truly popular, truly arises from consensus or else brutal and efficient. Even then the danger exists: the demented may shape their mania as armed struggle, the gunmen from other arenas may appear, the very few will opt for the gun no matter the odds or the futility of the cause.

At times rebels cause enormous trouble. They die, their opponents die, vast numbers of those innocent of any such aspirations die. Their struggle gobbles resources and lives and attention, disrupts the normal and usually to no ultimate purpose. No wonder the orthodox and conventional abhor the pretensions of rebel gunmen, messengers of death, dreadful dreamers rank with cordite and truth.

Repressive legislation, extended security, restricted liberty, large security budgets, all comforts to the orthodox and obstacles to the margins, flow easily from a perceived threat from the rebel gunmen and bombers. One of the casualties in an armed struggle is moderation and decency at the center. Even the decent are apt to respond to an armed threat with recourse to coercive force camouflaged as special operations, special courts or forces, special laws and procedures.

When the center is democratic such recourse to order over law, destroying democracy to save it, transforms the legitimacy of the center. Many gunmen find this reassuring: it is easier to attack the center once the mantle of legitimacy is discarded. Many democratic states do not need to opt for coercion and can co-opt demands for radical change. These same states have less room for maneuver with nationalist agitation. Then the gunmen want not intangibles, institutions, psychological benefits, but land. Formulas that adjust nationalist aspirations are harder to devise – not impossible but still mostly the threatened find that the most effective means to adjust to separatism – as was the case with the Ibo insurrection in Nigeria – is recourse to orthodox power. Mostly, then, a protracted campaign, no matter how low intensity, imposes change at the center even when no change is advantageous or desirable or both.

An armed struggle may impose changes no one foresaw and many, even those underground, do not want. In any case, somehow, some way, all these men with guns, win or lose, do matter. In some arenas they have mattered a lot, assuring decades of disorder and turmoil before withdrawing to the margins or disappearing from view. Elsewhere, last year's desperate are replaced with this year's. The rebels may seldom win but they matter. They may seldom plan the changes that occur but the changes that evolve help shape their armed struggle. The gunman is a significant figure in our times, a time of personal terror as well as real war.

So there stands the gunman. His cause uncertain and beyond concession, his means intolerable and lethal, his nature elusive. His movement is not easily approached nor readily described. At times his struggle is simply war in the outback, and at others traditional ethnic strife under a broader banner. At times he or she is crusader or terrorist, faithful to a special god or liberator of an invisible nation. His life is the material of thrillers, inaccurate, romantic, filled with action. His campaign is more dangerous as spur to counter-violence than threat to order. The fact that on occasion the gunman forces change at the center, or that at rare times the rebel does win as the dream promises, is thus fascinating.

Then one special vision may become reality. History may be changed. A mutation survives. In Addis Ababa Eritreans drink in the Hilton Hotel bar while the remnants of the Ethiopian army straggle back to their villages.

And year after year Castro talks on for hours elaborating a dream increasingly without luster. For one bright, socialist moment Nicaragua seemed the center of the world – at least to those on the side of radical angels – the new elite, decent, less greedy, if hardly the people's choice. The rebels in full view slipped into the old ways while using the new rhetoric, failed to be either brutal or efficient and so found the people unforgiving and without gratitude for past favors.

Each underground is special, each dream particular. One can walk the drab, dry streets of Teheran, where once were the huge, tattered posters of the old Ayatollah, black and white, great glaring eyes that traced every heretical step, and there find power in strange hands. The men at the center, fundamentalist clerics in brown and gray, scraggly beards and bloody hands, the past come to rule the present. There is no glow, no trendy admiration of the people's triumph. Between bleak, concrete buildings the streets are dusty, filled with scraps of paper, dry with orthodoxy. And one of those streets, the avenue in front of the British Embassy, is named for the Irish hunger striker Bobby Sands, martyred in the H-Blocks at Long Kesh, Ireland, green, misty and often lethal. He, his IRA, the whole green and deadly island, is truly a world away – except within the underground.

The phenomenon of the armed struggle has, in a sense, remained underground, real but elusive to all concerned, not politics and not war, not subject to consensus. Mostly, it is examined at a distance, sparks in a cloud chamber, bubble lines traced back, assumptions on first causes, analogies, projections, reasoning from supposition and extension. The result has been a vast library, some shrewd, much useful. Witnesses are often involved in special pleading and add to the library, if not always to understanding. No one sees the phenomenon whole. It is not so much perspective as it is that the armed struggle is still a matter of perception, a matter of seeing. And this is as it should be.

2

The Arena

EVERY ARMED struggle takes place within the flow of history at a specific moment in a particular place. Generally the physical arena is amenable to analysis, mountains or an island; but all armed struggles take place in a far more complex setting. Each such arena is a great buzzing confusion ordered by the perception of the observer, historians, participants, the analysts and transients. Each arena may stretch out to include the audience, the distant watchers quite removed from the conflict, and always historical figures and precedents.

Any armed struggle has not only participants engaged in a combat arena often with access to haven or support beyond the battle zone, but also observers. Thus the arena may be global: for example, everyone with access to the international media was in some small degree involved in the Vietnam conflict. Hundreds of millions may watch on television aspects of an armed struggle: the shells land, the bodies in the street, the briefing of the day; often watch live a terrorist spectacular. A movement engaged in terror or composed of mercenaries, a secret army or a tiny band of bombers can have enormous impact on the course of events simply by imposing priorities and agendas on Western opinion. The audience for the struggle may sooner or later and to a greater or lesser extent play a vital role, may even play *the* vital role as was the case during the Vietnam war. The audience's perception of reality is as much an aspect of the arena as the rebel's dream or the number of tanks or the terrain. What matters is not the textbook boundaries and graphs but what is perceived as the arena by the involved.

Even distances and terrain may be adjusted by perception. Because of instant real time access, the very distant event in Khartoum or Jerusalem is no further than the television set. Because the Irish think of their island as grand, the distance from Belfast to Dublin is far greater than a map would indicate. What matters in an arena, what becomes real, is what is assumed to matter, what appears to be real. Often the state may see the jungle as rebel asset, perceive the terrain as obstacle, while the hunted and desperate rebel, fresh from the urban middle class, instead and more accurately realizes all too well that the jungle is amenable to those with conventional assets, helicopters, all-terrain vehicles, good maps.

The terrain is asset or liability because it is so assumed. Some assumptions may be simple and logical – there is little place for a guerrilla to hide in a desert of sand or a city filled with those opposed to the cause. The assumption that decent people will not back a gunman is less easy to validate until too late – either too late for the state or too late for the gunman. The assumptions vary from time and place, for each conflict. And so each armed struggle is always special in time and in place, the arena unique; but each arena, if not alike, can still fit into categories.

The place, the physical arena, can usually be described to the satisfaction of most, jungle or island, desert sand or a post-modern city, North Burma or the South Sudan. Often the physical arena can be expanded, the rebel campaign carried to a new front, or contracted, the rebel driven into a corner. In such a corner after a generation of government pressure in December 1993, the Armed Revolutionary Forces of Colombia, FARC, to protect its remaining financial sources in the drug business crossed into Ecuador and ambushed an anti-narcotics force killing 14 and wounding 14 thus widening a narrowing arena. This is not a novel occurrence since desperation concentrates minds on novel and unsuspecting targets – targets outside the accepted arena. At times a participant may seek if not to move mountains at least to defoliate the forest as did the Americans in Vietnam, spraying 19,000,000 gallons of herbicides between 1962 and 1971, or seal off the Sahara as have the Moroccans with a great sand wall to keep out Polisaro raids. The British have erected a chain of grotesque watch towers filled with electronic monitoring devices along the border of Northern Ireland, perhaps to keep the gunmen in and their comforters out, perhaps to buttress the assumption that outside agitators are the sources of the Irish Troubles, but after some years to no great effect. One part of Ireland blends into the next wherever the border runs or the monitors stand. Everywhere the arena is assumed by most of the combatants, most of the time to be a place, a feature to be found in the atlas, real, intractable, an asset or a liability by estimate. The Irish Troubles, whatever else, are in Ireland.

The Irish republican movement, arising at the end of the eighteenth century with a meld of the ideals of the Age of Reason, the examples of the American and French Revolutions, and the attitudes and assumptions of the island, has for generations defined the battle arena not simply as the island off Britain but in relation to Irish nationalist assets and English vulnerabilities. Ireland, the island, the place is real enough; but the nationalist struggle has been waged far from Kerry or Tyrone, often waged primarily far from the island. The Fenians in the nineteenth century carried the war into Canada from America just as the volunteers of the Provisional IRA have been found in Gibraltar and Germany spending money raised in America to deploy arms acquired in Libya. And what has happened far away, in the American diaspora, in Western capitals, in the Middle East has at times played an important role even in the shaping of operations in Ireland or the selection of future targets.

An arena is not simply a battlefield or lines on a map. An arena contains both immediate enemies and a galaxy of friends but also, around the edges, an audience. The map of an armed struggle, then, is not really the terrain and cannot easily be found in an atlas. That the arena is far more than a printed chart is recognized even by the most orthodox. The population matters, their beliefs matter, their history and present occupation, class and culture and the idols of the tribe are factors. Hearts matter and minds matter. Hearts and minds far away in the United Nations or the audiences watching the evening television news matter, are within the arena. The arena is thus recognized as not simply a place but also a cultural heritage, an intangible but real mix of traditions and attitudes and assumptions.

The first crucial task for the involved has usually been to discover arenas that will foster insurrection for whatever reasons. What for rebel purposes makes an ideal arena? When can the center, the government, feel safe? What arena is easy to police? What cultures legitimize the guerrilla? Where can the rebel best hide? What factors play the most vital role in encouraging rebellion – the terrain, patriot history, class structure, faith denied, social structure? If actual revolts are indicators of rebel analysis, then some arenas have been fertile and some sterile. Certainly, the advocates of rebellion have for generations announced their targets – the old dynasties, the man in the palace or the party in power, the colonies or the capitalist regimes. And once the enemy was defined, the rebel always found the arena promising just as the threatened discovered a world that they had not really noticed until the first shot or the first bomb.

Much of what was to become the Third World was a complex but promising mix of arenas that welcomed the rebel. It was the great era of national liberation if not without surprises. Certain colonies, like the Portuguese, proved unexpectedly difficult. Some arenas produced not swift nationalist success but, like Algeria or Indochina, protracted war. Still, in time the anti-imperial wave swept over all colonial arenas, leaving but a few rocks and islands under imperial aegis. The theorists, mostly of the Left, then predicted a second general assault under the banners of national liberation on national arenas controlled by regimes unpopular for one reason or another: Latin American *caudillos* or African president-puppets.

During this era of national liberation some arenas had been ignored by rebels. The Second World of socialism – the Warsaw Pact countries dominated by Moscow and the Maoists of China – seemed protected by revolutionary rhetoric and the assets of a closed society. Efficient, brutal Marxist-Leninist regimes proved largely immune to even the idea of revolt. Classical urban risings, a rush to the barricades, in the Warsaw Pact states led only to Soviet tanks in the streets. And China was as intractable to change – one billion Chinese and hardly a rebel to be found. Then after 1989 with the collapse of the central will in Moscow, these arenas too could be considered vulnerable – even the Chinese arena, still protected by a ruthless resort to brutality by an elderly and uncompromising elite, appeared promising to some. By 1991 the once solid Second World had been transformed. Some of the survivors sought entry into the West and others appeared to slip into the chaos and uncertainty of the Third World. Few were certain how even to list the arenas, analyze the vulnerabilities.

Elsewhere during the era of national liberation many arena regimes, often those in former colonies, were too fragile to be the site of a protracted war. Mobutu's enemies simply walked across central Africa to run him out of Zaire – massacres but no battles. There was no need for an armed struggle. These arenas were usually the site of coup, a riot and a rush to the palace, or brief tribal war, not the battleground for a long revolt. Many regimes were despotic and dreadful but vulnerable if only brutal and no longer efficient. There was change and violence and chaos; but an armed struggle is more complex, is a means to change history not the name plates on ministerial desks, a means to make the weak strong not to replace one fragile elite with another slightly more effective.

Many assumed that the flexible, efficient democratic states of the West were immune – conciliation playing the part of Marxist-Leninist coercion. Such arenas supplied only a stage for radical posturing and the odd atrocity by the demented. This immunity, however, did not neuter many of the unanticipated internal nationalists. These rebels, representing people that the government thought safely absorbed into the main, began to appear bearing arms: in Ireland, in Quebec, out of Puerto Rico, in time in Corsica. On the Western stage were all sorts of nationalists – from the Spice Islands to a Wales Free Army. Only a few found the arena sufficiently congenial for a long or an effective struggle. Even more dangerous in the West, if as unexpected, were the rebels with ideological dreams. Killing ideologies had been thought obsolete, fascism dead and communism sealed behind the

Iron Curtain or tamed in political parties. The Duce had been a disaster, and so who would emulate him, and march on Rome a second time? The Western arena was assumed to be an arena dominated by consensus. Those nostalgic for Mussolini could vote for the fascist party and let the center rule.

Then, suddenly, unexpectedly, defying the common wisdom, in the 1970s the Euroterrorists appeared waging spectacular campaigns in seemingly congenial cultural arenas. Their campaigns were, as intended, highly visible in Germany, in Italy and to lesser extent elsewhere. The Italians had feared the classical separatism of the tiny German sliver under the Alps and instead found gunmen in the streets killing for the communist millennium or to prevent it. Italy was the most special arena, the most congenial to an armed struggle. There were only tiny sects in Belgium and France, if potentially more serious gunmen in Spain even after Franco had gone. And Spain too escaped the ideologues, if not the Basques. In America the rebels were bizarre or demented and in Britain only a single, brief flash – the Angry Brigade – as sign of rebellion in an English cloud chamber.

Still, the Euroterrorists made up in intensity for their lack of numbers. To add to the turmoil, Europe became a terrorist arena that drew in distant gunmen eager for exposure, eager to exploit the world media, eager to use a congenial operational arena. These were the years of assassinations, terrorist spectaculars, and hijackings. All these gunmen had appeared in a supposedly immune post-industrial Western society. They were at least a dreadful surprise and a distraction – if in Italy a serious matter, potentially so in Spain and thought to be so by conservative Germans. It appeared as if the Western heartlands could be arenas for fanatical gunmen as well as the wastelands at the margins. And these arenas were novel, the tangibles both post-modern and easily found in an atlas, and the grievances often ancient if dressed in contemporary ideology.

Elsewhere, many rebels have assumed congenial arenas that proved fallow. Latin American despotism, chosen as the second arena of anti-imperialist struggles after the overt colonies were captured, proved resistant to such national liberation. African states drawn on a map not in hearts and ruled by brutal and inefficient elites sometimes turned back rebellion or isolated the rebels in the bush. Asian provinces and islands that should have been nations could not generate effective rebellion, only turmoil. At times the rebels found sanctuary but not victory in the cover provided by the arena. These were often in Asia minor rebels, in Latin America isolated guerrillas, in Africa dissident tribes under universal banners. The Philippine Moros and the Burmese Kachins, the separatists in Nagaland or in Papua New Guinea, the *focos* in Central America, the armed tribal opposition in Zaire or the Sudan, all used a promising arena to persist but without the capacity to escalate. Some rebels were highly visible and enormously fashionable, like the Palestinians; and others, like the Irish, seemed almost a historical artifact, the old gunman in a trench coat appearing out of the Celtic mist while the British listened to *Sergeant Pepper* and watched the World Cup. Most of the second-generation struggles failed. Guevara, first in Africa and then in Bolivia, the Ibo in Nigeria, the Fretilin in Timor. The rebels apparently misread the arenas.

Some, the transnational terrorists, made the world their arena, choreographed grand spectaculars for the electronic media, carried the struggle into the living rooms and cafes of all or nearly all. Rebellion was often in fashion, even terror for a time was chic. The guerrilla was hero. All of these rebels were not seized on imaginary grievances or in the grip of trendy fashions: there were real grievances, reasoned strategies, and promising arenas. There were, over a generation, hundreds of rebellions. Yet after this great anti-imperial tide ebbed, vulnerable arenas proved elusive. When Castro won in Cuba, a rare triumph, thousands parsed his example and a great many attempts, all failures, were made in Latin America to emulate his experience. Arenas proved hard to read and rebel mistakes were usually lethal. Even Giap would have to persist for a generation at a cost of millions of lives. Mao's route march was no easier to follow than Castro's experience in Cuba. The rebel tended to sense prospects in an arena invisible to those at the center. Despite the obstacles, many would try anyway, always optimistic; even if such optimism could be a death sentence.

Those in power simply said no to all unnegotiable demands. Even the awful and unpopular held out, held on to power. And at the center supposedly artificial or doomed regimes resisted. Israel would not disappear because of Palestinian hopes, or India allow separatists to dismantle the nation. The very demands of the ideological terrorists were unfathomable, beyond co-option or compromise. The center held, eradicated the infection in the arena that had, thus, been more effectively exploited in the capital than on the barricade.

At times, rare times, the rebel was proved right, found reality in perception, discovered a congenial arena, not on the map but through a dream of an ideal that would rewrite history. The rebel could then persist, relying on the power of the dream, the will of the people, the risen nation, to overcome the odds. Even then history was seldom rewritten, no matter how protracted the struggle and how protective the arena of the rebel.

The real arena, of course, is in the mind of the involved, there shaped by perception, an environment descended from history, molded by present forces, part real, part illusion, partly visible but tangible. There is no map of such arenas, no tangibles to count in a gazette, no rule book for jungles and gross national product to read.

In the texts of anti-insurgency the physical terrain has always played a major role. Tangibles *always* play a major role for the orthodox. Many of the assets of the center can be touched; few held by the rebel can be. From the center the assumption has been that the wilder the terrain, swamps and jungles, the greater the rebel advantage, for the guerrilla is assumed to be intimate with the ground and all agree in need of cover. Cover is thought tangible, the bush or the hovels on the margins of cities.

For the rebel almost *any* terrain will do for an armed struggle and almost every terrain exacts a price. Cover is not supplied solely or often mainly by trees and slums but by the transformation in the conventional that leaves an orthodox shell inhabited by a dreamer, a rebel. If the rebel is to operate full time, move toward irregular war, then physical cover will hide his or her progress.

If there is no cover, then the rebel will operate in other ways, spend the days delivering milk and the nights bombing. The rebel must always adapt to the terrain. During the Anglo-Irish struggle between 1918 and 1921 the premier IRA military leader, Michael Collins, on every British most-wanted list, traveled openly in Dublin, rode a bicycle past the patrols, made a virtue of difficulty, inspired the many by assuming only the most shallow cover but that armored with audacity. Even if the armed struggle is fought on a billiard table, cover of some sort will be found. The rebels in the Sahara found haven in Algeria and a battleground in a classic desert – great dunes, sand fields, a gritty billiard table. Needing cover, the Viet Cong dug endless miles of tunnels directly beneath the orthodox American army, found cover under their opponent's visible power, made their own very real underground.

In an armed struggle any cover will do and any rebel can find cover. For the rebel, however, all such cover comes hard. During an armed struggle everything tends to come hard in the underground.

The Irish armed struggle, two centuries old, has only at times remained in Ireland. There have been the famous risings and campaigns from the first under Wolfe Tone to the last border struggle between 1954–62 that used the island as arena. Yet, the Irish rebel has always been found abroad organizing, operating, widening the arena. The bounds of all, even the most isolated, armed struggles are apt to be as porous as that of the Irish – especially when the state applies pressure to the indigenous rebels.

The state as always had the capital to invest in expansion. The Spanish pursued the ETA gunmen to France, and lesser powers, like Iran and the

Libyans, assassinated the state's enemies abroad. When pressed, some states make use not only of their legitimacy and international security ties but also state-sponsored gunmen – the arena is extended despite conventional legal norms and with only the most implausible denial since power displayed is part purpose of such operations.

The arena at times can be where the powerful say it is – no place for the rebel to hide in the wings. The gunmen are isolated in the bush beyond reach of the media or concern of the citizens, extras in a road show soon to close. Everything is tangible, the dream isolated, perception the reality of the regime. The arena is as tight as a boxing ring. Sometimes the limits of an armed struggle are geographically vague, sometimes the state or the rebel seeks anywhere for a target.

For the rebel, allies may be havens but all havens are not allies. The rebel presence may in some cases engender adamant opposition or severe restrictions, may lead to the creation of a host-enemy in alliance with the original rebel opponent. Denial of haven may be limited only by the local incapacity to expel the underground presence.

All rebel havens are complex, shifting, exist because of rebel needs and host realities. Some host governments must balance the popularity of the rebel with the needs of the state, the costs of monitoring them or even the risks of suppressing them. There are all sorts of risks even to limited toleration. Thus rebels may gain transit rights or residence as long as there is no provocative display, no operations. They are, as political exiles, neutered. Other hosts want no visitors at all, especially armed and dangerous visitors.

Most Western states, mindful of the problem of civil liberties even for aliens, still keep close watch on their guests. This has been especially true in an era of international terror. The spread of the battle arena eroded the number of havens. The Irish guest workers, the Palestinian student, the Armenian or Iranian tourist tend to cause ripples at customs, a pause at the gate, a special check. The Japanese Red Army attack at Lod Airport in Israel meant delays worldwide for Japanese travelers. A Belfast accent closes doors. In effect, the bounds of any rebel arena are not firm and for some with international operations or universal pretensions may barely exist – the Irish gunmen appeared in Gibraltar and Germany, Armenian assassins could appear anywhere, the Japanese gunmen have surfaced in Israel and in Italy and on the New Jersey Turnpike.

Patron governments may not simply aid the distant rebel but involve 'their' gunmen in special operations. Again the patron may be special, one branch of Syrian military intelligence, one ayatollah, even one department of British intelligence; MI-5 sponsoring the unsavory as much to spite MI-6 as to achieve operational results. And special operations may be joint simply because of mutual interest; each uses the other, each assumes their own intention paramount. And for some states even interest can be discounted. Some rebels may simply be hired with a slogan. And from there the state may hire those without a dream but with access and skills, leave the armed struggle behind and deal with the tangibles, rent a terrorist at the going rate.

There are many unconventional variations at the edge of the armed struggle. It is a dark, shadow world of false flags and convoluted conspiracies – killing for one cause in the name of another, killing for a patron using another's name, killing far from the original arena to build up credit, to send a message for a shy patron, to achieve secret vengeance, to keep in practice for another day. Mostly this world, revealed in thrillers and films, is real, lies at the margin of the real world of power and is marginal to major concerns, even to the rebel. The rebel, the real rebel, always seeks power, not permanent haven, seeks to win not to assist a host's government; most of all seeks legitimacy not assignment as a secret asset. Rebels are only drawn into the state's orbit because of needs that insist over the obvious risks and scant rewards. Most, even those with very limited assets, are reluctant to be bought even at high price for a short term. The dream may be corrupted. The truth of the cause can be endangered by operational pragmatism.

The fact remains that many states have resources to exchange with rebels, resources to be had often at decent rates.

THE CULTURAL CONTEXT

All the involved, the distant and the disinterested, the chroniclers of violence and the innocents abroad, are agreed that the *real* arena of an armed struggle is that supplied by history, by the habits and customs of the involved, by institutions and assumptions. The arena is mostly this thick miasma of a special culture largely adjusted by perception not mountains and maps.

Most important for the rebel – and the center – is to exploit the given reality not simply seek to adjust it almost solely through perception; see precedent where there is none, advantage where disaster waits. Yet, the most important aspect of all arenas is largely a matter of perception and such perception is not easily within rebel control although usually is to a real degree to rebel advantage. Insurrection early on cannot stand too much reality, so those who would rush to the barricades need to assume a degree of optimism about their prospects that only a special perspective, special perception can supply.

Arenas are hard to read in advance, much harder than the vulnerabilities of the center. There rebel perception discounts visible assets in contrast to the power of the dream but this cannot easily be done for the stage. There the dream must explain reality, explain it to rebel satisfaction, then explain it effectively to the rebel constituency, and finally explain it so that the center is confounded. Each step is more difficult but taken naturally by rebels who assume their truth is universal, their dream the great tool of analysis, their vision exact.

THE ARENA MIX

The real arena is in the mind of the involved, part physical but mostly shaped by perception, an environment descended from history, molded by present forces, part real, part illusion, partly visible but tangible. The stage for a rebellion requires a special combination of history and culture, a vulnerability, an aura of possibility. The physical terrain as a factor rarely if ever is a determinant. Revolts have occurred in most unpromising physical conditions: on isolated islands like Cyprus, in the desert of the Mideast or the ghettos of post-industrial cities – as isolated as islands. And revolts have taken place out in the wilds with splendid cover, impassable access, and even friendly natives – without effect.

Even when to the amazement of the disinterested and horror of the center, an armed struggle occurs, persists, the rebel, also often amazed and horrified, finds that there are other rebels, other truths, others who would lead or dominate the armed struggle. The arena proves too ripe. Even in the swamps of south Iraq, the rebels, isolated, deserted by the West, scantily supported by Teheran by 1992, were divided into ten major Shi'ite rebel groups. Competition for the rebel habitat is often cruel; only the fit survive. Most rebels believe that there is only room in a specific rebel niche for one species to survive. Their movement is fit to survive no other. Other rebels professing the faith are an especial problem. It should be one arena and one faith and so one armed struggle; but this is rarely the case.

Some new underground may appear simply because the original is too secretive to reach, operates only in one part of the arena, limits membership – the new may seek not to replace or to present an alternative reality but only to participate. Many new rebels, however, have new ideas. And so their competition is challenge to the revealed truth. The ensuing, if not quite inevitable competition for legitimacy and major assets can be, often is, lethal.

The hope for the lesser rebel, short of a successful take-over bid, is to seek survival in a different niche, appeal to another constituency – ideologically, ethnically, whatever is not secured by the stronger rival. While two nets may catch more fish than one, most rebels want only one true direction into the future: one arena, one movement. The truth is indivisible and even slight variations are worrisome underground. Few are interested in the factors within the arena that have encouraged diversity. Few see the other rebels as a sign of center incapacity.

The arena, the stage of action, is different for each rebel, different for those at the center, and often very different for the rebels in a grip of a dream that can determine even the contours of the field. Mostly the arena is as described in the atlas or the classroom. What cannot be described, the lessons of history, the habits of the poor, the assumptions of the angry, is the most important part of the mix to the rebel. It is often not so to the orthodox who depend on tangibles that can be listed and counted. The rebel, however, must scramble elsewhere for assets, the unseen are easier to amass. The real is another matter.

A different and compelling reality emerges: history becomes a struggle of classes or the hand of God writ small. All the arena is just the same but different – like the woman suddenly loved, now, unexpectedly, she is still all the same but all different. Consequently, all rebel analysis, often debased to slogans and graffiti for the simple, seems unfamiliar to conventional history and the first-time observer. The new vision has explanation and inevitably an explanation that can discern the direction of history. Thus for the rebel, reality – the cultural arena – is adjusted to need and then need to the new reality. The analysis may, like that of the Italian radicals, be improbable, demonstrably wrong; but it can still engender an effective armed struggle. Usually, however, the rebel analysis rests on a real heritage and explains, enhances reality, does not simply create it. In the most demanding of dreams, the novice pilgrim is transformed while in less compelling visions all that is needed is the old nation liberated or the old faith followed.

Reality is transmuted into asset. And this alchemy that makes possible the armed struggle is called fraud and farce by the orthodox who cannot imagine the legitimacy of such a transformation. So it is not the hard reality of the arena that the rebel changes but the meaning. And within a cultural context meanings are viable when they last, convince the many, come to power, write the books – and this is what the rebel wants, the dream as reality and so reality as promised. Then the arena will follow rebel configurations, will be found on the map not just in rebel hearts.

3

Analysis and Reality

FOR THE rebel, filled with grievance and denied power by the center, the aspiration shaped as an ideal, the dream, is everything. This goal is turned formally into ideology and internally it is the text that explains the meaning of life and so politics and thus history. Once all is explained, then the necessary action, the armed revolt, becomes obvious, essential, a clearly defined responsibility. And that struggle is fed by the energy of the dream.

Without such a transcendental ideal force, violence, the gun would be – and often in an imperfect world is – deployed solely for narrow benefit, the advantage of the tribe, the enrichment of the involved, the exhilaration of harm done. At the other end of the spectrum of commitment, escalation may permit the gunman to emerge from the underground, become guerrilla or irregular, give up cover, attract recruits more orthodox and less driven. On either flank of the armed struggle there are those similar in tactics but who march to other drummers. Their motives are usually scorned by the idealists dedicated to a vision that shapes for them a new world. Those most dedicated may even maintain the vision after victory and few, win or lose, are not touched by the time of commitment.

So conviction, at times conversion, is the key into the new world. It is a world with explanations, reasons, a role and duties, where renunciation is rewarded with service. The faith, however, always comes first. The believer is offered a secular vocation, usually at a time in life when purity, dedication, and service hold great charm. This vocation is pretense to those in power, who see only ambition and harm flowing from a gun.

Many governments choose to see all challenges from the underground as bandit threats – or the work of the wicked. Certainly those struggles without a central dream, covert conflicts arising from tradition or as custom, are apt to produce not an armed struggle but bandit country. All sorts may, indeed, be attracted to an armed struggle, even employed by the central command for insurgency purpose, but the dedicated dominate. In fact, those at the center of an armed struggle sometimes refuse any talent not shaped by the faith.

The dream is transcendental, commanding, promises salvation and redemption. It offers an end to grievance and a future appropriate to a new reality. Never, ever, for the faithful is the absolute dream impure. Others may find flaws but the rebel none. One of the most persistent dreams, if not one of the most universal or even grandest, has been that of the militant Irish republicans who have transformed nationalism into a complex and powerful faith. Their dream has been adjusted over the generations to historical imperatives but never forgoing the ideal encrusted with the sacrifices of the faithful. It has proved immune to most temporal defeat. In simple ideological terms the Irish united the political ideals of the eighteenth century, the national aspirations that flowered in the nineteenth, and the local grievances and habits of resistance found on the island. Although non-sectarian and so dedicated to uniting the whole of Ireland – the Protestant, Catholic and dissenter – the movement has been shaped by many of the attitudes of the Roman Church, in turn almost always an opponent to militant Irish nationalism.

The Church recognizes the movement as a competitor for the island flock. Yet Protestants, dissenters, even Jews have been converted to the republican faith. The movement is very Irish and the Irish, even those out-side the Church, are often very Catholic, certainly all are mindful of God's role, the power of religious ideals and the ideal of service and denial. The great Trinity is answered in Ireland: the evil is the British, the remedy physical force, and the goal the republic. Repeatedly repressed, often driven to the margins of events, the movement has won a singular victory in the toleration of many Irish nationalists for the movement's recourse to force. The Irish Republican Army may be scorned by many, by most in the 26-county republic, but yet the gunmen operate largely assured that the people will not betray them, will accept their sacrifice.

In every generation there have been volunteers for a vision that offers not so much rewards and promise of victory as service and sacrifice autho-rized by history. The vision was never shaken by the advent of socialist, class-based analysis: the proletariat not the nation as salvation. This was largely because the industrial revolution barely reached Ireland and then only in a few cities: Belfast, Dublin, Cork. Those who sought to wed national-ism and socialism generally after a time found their republican colleagues unsympathetic. The movement was dedicated to those of no property, at times spoke in the language of the Left but never moved far from the nationalist roots. The Provisional Irish Republican Army and Sinn Féin still focus on the basics – Brits Out, Up the IRA, Up the Republic – even if, for the moment, a peace strategy operates. Few others in power or out have so compelling an analysis of the complexities of contemporary Ireland.

Each Irish generation has contributed adjustment and often an experience misread by their heirs; but what has been passed along, generation after generation, was the right, assumed and often conceded, to wage war, wage an armed struggle, in the name of the Irish people to achieve an Irish republic. That republic, so long delayed, became an almost mystical grail, luminous, appealing, demanding, requiring personal sacrifice but beyond easy definition. Each generation responded within the times, within the special Irish context, but always within the long republican tradition, thus fashioning a rich history. This long saga detailed the primary forces of Irish history, the patriots and the English, who were engaged in a long unequal battle that must be continued if not won. Ultimate victory would come. 'It is not those who can inflict the most, but those that can can suffer the most who will conquer', insisted Terence MacSwiney, witness to the proposition who died on hunger strike. So for two centuries certain Irish nationalists have become dedicated republicans, sought as their right to establish the republic with physical force. When denied by the conventional and proper, denied by the many, confounded by logic and democratic norms, they persisted – the Irish people had no right to do wrong. The present people and their government could not deny the legacy of past generations, accept the intolerable present rather than the luminous history. In Irish matters the dead vote as well as the unborn and are counted positive by republicans.

These militant republicans, the truly faithful, regardless of talent and capacity, Fenians and Irish Volunteers, the IRA and the advocates in Sinn Féin, served the dream. Many served all their lives, often abruptly ended by such service. And all, the Provo gunman of today and the Fenian of old, dreamed of the ultimate republic. Whatever else, the Irish gunmen have been indomitable, unreconstructed, unrepentant, ever renewed because each generation has been touched by the dream. Some despaired, some found other gods or goals, some withdrew discarded, denied; but most, once touched by the dream, remained enthralled. Even now many doubt that peace offers prospects; they wait on events as always.

Such dreams are lethal. Those possessed feel impelled to act to destroy the old enemy, to convert the many, to change history. Some armed struggles may, however, be driven by most limited dreams, the residue of old hatred, ethnic separatism, habits and customs of the tribe rather than by a universal vision.

In a world filled with demonstrable injustice, for those with a heritage of grievance, there are political dreams and personal dreams. There are dreams of liberation and redemption. There are alien and unpleasant dreams, nightmares as well. In Peru, the Indians follow a 'shining path' bordered by dead peasants, men, women, and children, each guilty of reluctance. The world is full of shallow graves filled with the innocent victims of some dream. Some rebels kill those who can read, wear spectacles or a tie, have soft hands, know foreign tongues – those suspects who are in any way beyond the least. The pure cut off the hands of those who take foreign charity, cut off the noses of those who smoke foreign tobacco. Terror is meant to be terrible. No one is innocent. In Lebanon the volunteer martyrs hurrying to salvation use carbombs, eager to die, eager to kill. Everywhere the rebel target is the others, them, the guilty, the pagan or the heretic, the state, the system, the rulers and their friends. No one is innocent.

Rebels kill first and then explain that all of this group or all that one are guilty. This child was boarding the airliner of an enemy and that barber cut a soldier's hair. No one is innocent. Some gunmen simply kill and their acts are beyond explanation, simply a penny on history's scales. In Algeria, Allah may be the answer but the means is random murder. Killing erodes stability, anybody will do, any body will do. Some rebels are unsavory personally, brutal, coarse, narrow, erratic. The dream assures absolute truth. All the faithful are arrogant in belief, intractable. The dreamer has the capacity to adjust all to the ultimate end, to see what should be as what is.

And some simply use a broken dream as rationale for murder, for personal gain, for power. Other gunmen are covert soldiers, simple and true, not much different from Royal Marines or the lad down the lane except that they kill without a warrant card for a cause without proper diplomatic recognition. Without banners or uniform, self-selected, self-anointed, they kill for a better world others cannot see. All are idealists, some decent, some not, most representative of their own. They, the cruel and the criminal, the hero and the idealist, almost always kill for something. They sacrifice others and themselves for the dream, whether it is a great and powerful dream, a universal faith, or the most parochial cause, the integrity of the clan, the pride of the parish.

All armed struggles in some way, however, reflect the classic and all have similar enemies with similar assets and nearly all reveal a mix of motives – vengeance and avarice often co-exist with the purity of the ideal. So any crusade of reasonable size will contain those untouched by the ideal, the criminal and the adventurous, the vengeful and the fellow traveler. It is the dreamers, however, that matter, not the camp followers. And it is the dreamer who analyzes reality to advantage – a procedure even the irregular emulate.

Some rebels want no more than to be let alone. Others carry arms merely as a tribal right of passage. The world is filled with those organized to secure justice, achieve history's goal: a Kurdish state, a triumph of Islam in Egypt or Algeria, a united Ireland or a communist Peru. The rebel assumes change both desirable and possible and the future malleable.

Instead of understanding the rebel determination to secure justice, the orthodox focus on the means – the gun – rather than the ideal. When the ideal intrudes, indicates that the dream is incompatible with the present, the West is often at a loss: what do they *want?* What future can *Brigate rosse* or Islamic *Jihad* imagine? This cannot be a perfect world with all dreams made real.

The rebel vision insists that their struggle can bring if not perfection at least a tolerable and desirable future, a new world without grievance: a post-communist Italy or an Islamic republic, a greater Serbia. Many dreams seek not perfection, not the future made new, but the return of the lost, the old nation, the pure religion, the golden age.

The provincial dream has a compelling power that often proves more effective than the contemporary universals – the hope for communism or the conversion of all to a global ideal. Some rebels have almost nothing: dated, barely armed, still imagining Castro as example, the Mexican Indians who raised Zapata's standard in January 1994 wanted only a living, another shirt, school for the children, land that produced a crop. Elsewhere, many of the young may not be attracted by class solutions, Castro's example, but they eat fast food, watch the world on television, dress much the same in Rio and Dacca, and so are exposed to the dreams of others. Most have ambitions beyond those of the Indians of Mexico – if as bleak prospects. These grievances of the market can be shaped to more compelling agenda in a world replete with grievance. The old ways are often universal ways. Whatever the banner, the gunman brings a parochial perspective to analysis, to assumption.

Each faith, universal or particular is special, but any will do for the engine of the underground. As in all faiths, the contradictions within the dream are ignored. For the rebel all the obstacles are minimized or ignored. Every rebel dream to each rebel believer is revealed truth. Like all dreams, perfection has a luminous appeal. Life, liberty, and happiness are reasoned goals, salvation possible.

In a sense the rebel is not interested in rebellion, the temporary form of the dream, but in the first truth that will lead to the anticipated result. The dreamer sleepwalks through the process between grievance and triumph. The revolt does not matter as much as the faith. The house scholars of revolution may focus on tactics and techniques; certainly the gunman must be aware of such considerations, but the key is always the intolerable past and the illuminated future. The present is a lesser time of trial and tribulation. The present is the dark hour of the armed struggle, a means, not an end. And as a means, a process, those involved underground are apt to offer analysis by rote, elaborate formulas, rationales that will explain a perception of reality few of the disinterested can accept as valid.

Those opposed to radical change under rebel auspices, on the other hand, focus on categories of similarities, the tangibles of each struggle: the real and earnest, the guns and tanks and bodies by the road. They, more than the rebel, are concerned with an analysis of the rebellion. They find the revolt, the present, is the key, not the special grievances of the past or the uncertain promise of the future. Those with responsibility focus on the moment and so seek categories and explanations. How does the war work, not why. So the threatened seek patterns, models, directions, tangibles. They find such patterns in categories and alignments but rarely in any general rebel dynamics.

The armed struggle is almost always and perhaps by necessity approached by those with orthodox minds and policy needs. The center focuses on what can be parsed, counted, countered. The military seminars have outlines and order. The political analyses have recourse to data and rigorous methodologies. Pick up any rebel tract and discover the value of right thinking in contrast to the techniques found in the anti-insurgency texts. The rebel is concerned with grace and the government with good works. The rebel seeks justice and the center pursues order. Justice may come in many flavors and so too may order. And one is not the obverse of the other. The underground is not the dark side of state politics nor the armed struggle just a special kind of war. The confrontation is asymmetrical – the will against deployed power. That is what is unconventional, not gunman tactics nor the skills and technologies of counter-intelligence. One can wear black pajamas, slip through the wilds, absorb tradecraft and never understand that what makes the rebel is faith not techniques, not irregular opportunities, not matters that can be taught or learned but only felt through conversion.

The dream, then, is shaped by the faithful to control history through a successful armed struggle that rewards truth with power. One need only believe and so act. States pursue the real and the rebel the potential. States rarely lose. Most alternative futures are fantasy. If the rebel copes somehow, if the underground can survive the reality of power deployed, the resulting armed struggle is inevitably asymmetrical. The center is determined to hold by denying rebel reality and deploying legitimate power.

THE PERCEPTION

The rebel dreams are various, often contradictory, but always the primary factor in the dynamics of all armed struggles. The dream is a nexus of perceptions about man and history, about reality. What this dream guarantees is an explanation of the course of history and the nature of the future. The first step may simply be to begin – kill the Tsar. Some beginnings are recognized as an end as well – the Jews rising in the Warsaw Ghetto in 1943 as witness to evil, as historic example of defiance. Such blood sacrifices are rare. The Irish in 1916 had hoped to win. And most rebels are optimistic. For the conventional, most rebels are, in fact, criminally optimistic.

The Provisional IRA's campaign began with seven men meeting around a deal table in a cold kitchen to take on a kingdom: seven men who could read history. They had a few old dumped arms, friends and colleagues, kith and kin, and most of all an absolute assurance that their time had come. Sometimes, as with Guevara's dream for the *foco*, the faithful assumed that everything could be changed simply by example of an armed struggle taking place. Revolution would be a chain reaction. The *foco* would be a detonation, small, deadly, easy to assemble and capable of engendering a vast explosion. Guevara's own last adventure detonated nothing, became, perhaps as intended, a blood sacrifice to inspire the next struggle for the dream. Che became a legend but not an example. There is a limit even to rebel optimism: few rise assured of failure, few test the efficient and brutal, the democratic and accommodating. Mostly rebels want to win, not die in a *foco*, not die unnecessarily at all.

The Irish rebels in April 1916 chose to revolt with scant prospect of success. They had hoped for better but were willing to persist. Yeats in his 'Easter 1916' wrote that after the failure of the rising the Irish rebel leaders had been transformed, and all else as well, 'All changed, changed utterly, A terrible beauty is born.' And all was changed. Irish nationalism emerged on the island as the dominant dream and the Irish republic as the proffered ideal. What had really changed was not the reputation of the rebels nor the correlation of forces but the validity of the Irish national dream. For the Irish all was different.

Where Che had represented a universal ideology and a specific strategy, the Irish after 1916 gave form to the national dream previously thought in Ireland a matter for cranks and romantics, most dead and gone. Romantic Ireland appeared in the grave. After 1916 the source of all evil was the British, the armed struggle legitimate, and the republic a reasoned aspiration. The logic behind a renewed armed struggle seemed obvious, the proper means to realize the dream. And the Irish people – all but the Protestant loyalists – would tolerate, even support, such a course. The Irish conflict between 1918 and 1922 became the archetype of most subsequent national liberation struggles that deployed physical force.

To the Irish gunmen all had changed because the dream had touched them. Actually nothing tangible had changed in that the British soldier and the police constable were the same; same uniform, same oath, same role. To the gunman they *seemed* different and so they *were* different, legitimate targets. Everything, the people, the purpose of life, the world, seemed different and so everything was different – and for many stayed so. The dream through the sacrifice of the Easter Rising and the blunders of the British had become contagious: the task was to institutionalize that dream.

All those about to enter the underground where the possibility, for many the surety, of the armed struggle awaits, are agreed on the basics. They do not agree with each other: Begin the Zionist could see no parallel with Arafat the Palestinian nationalist, nor could Colonel George Grivas, a conservative Greek rebel on Cyprus in 1955–60, see a parallel with the communist rebels in Greece in 1946–49. Others, less committed to one dream, see the similarities, not just in the techniques of the underground, the deployment of the center, but in the analysis of the involved.

REBEL REALITY

What confounds the conventional, those without the urgency of the dream, those long mature, orthodox in politics or cynical by nature, is the change wrought on the rebel perception of the real then incorporated into ideology. The rebel simply sees what the conventional do not, elaborates meaning where those at the center find none. That the rebel vision makes a difference in the correlation of forces, in the meaning of the tangible, is hard for the orthodox to accept. That orthodox perception is not the same as reality is even more difficult for the conventional to perceive.

The British, never especially perceptive about the values and perceptions of others, found that the Cypriots of EOKA had been somehow transformed from cunning Greek traders who put a price on every gift to ruthless gunmen. That gunmen were needed could not be countenanced. In Kenya the British could only imagine that the African nationalists were in the grip of primitive witchcraft since colonial policy was so obviously to their best interests. After 200 years of the revolting Irish, the British establishment still denies that recourse to violence is necessary, since from London their presence is only for the general good and to prevent greater chaos. What the British did recognize everywhere an armed struggle arose was that something had changed in the nature of the rebel. The Greeks, the Kikuyu, the Irish, like the Jews and the Arabs and the Hindi, had changed, become intractable, acted against what the British assumed was reasoned interest for some flawed and foreign cause, for criminal purpose, out of malice. There was a clash of assumption and perception. And never even as the last soldier marched away – never driven away but always withdrawn for the greater good – did the British grasp the power of the rebel dream or the contrasting legitimacy that generated rebel assets not easily weighted. The world had changed, again, for the worse. Somehow, in some way, the empire had been tricked, the British denied their proper due: Nasser or Ben-Gurion had conjured up unexpected assets. Even the Irish hunger striker Bobby Sands, a simple criminal, had somehow turned legitimate authority into oppression, reason into ruin. Reality for Britain, for most of those threatened by rebels, is not as tangible as imagined, not an asset held by the powerful.

What had changed for the rebel was this perceived reality. What makes an armed struggle so difficult for the orthodox is that the rebel reality cannot be touched and weighted and measured. Bobby Sands' days can be numbered out, but not the impact of his sacrifice. All that can be certain is that during an armed struggle belief in such reality can kill as well as convince. When the Germans fought in Stalingrad or the Americans on Iwo Jima everyone knew who had won and lost, how much the battle cost, what might happen next. The side that killed the other won, won on the ground, won in the end. Not so in an armed struggle, where it is difficult even to tell if there is a war or if the rebel is winning. Certainly the rebel intent on persisting, sheltering the faith, waiting for change in the will at the center sees through the glass of the faith. He sees differently and so acts – unconventionally. Those under threat at the center find persisting in a hopeless struggle unconventional, unwarranted, evil and wicked, a denial of reality. An armed struggle is about forcing the pace of history, shaping a dream to action, persisting until events justify the sacrifice – not about winning or losing. The rebel may err, follow the devices and desires of his heart and snatch a dangerous operational opportunity, exploit a vulnerability, open a new front or go for the jugular, but not often.

Few rebels can imagine persistence will not pay. The Malayan communists persisted for 41 years before signing a formal truce, accepting the reality of failure. The Irish republicans, so long denied, have shaped responses to operational disaster that transforms the secondary benefits of service into the primary reward of salvation. To persist is to win and the ultimate republic will surely come in time – like the messiah, ever sought, never found.

Most rebels hope beyond reason, beyond the end. All, even the Irish, sense victory as possible, if not immediately then later as history unrolls as ordained by the vision.

Mostly the rebel is wrong, the real is real, the big battalions win; but sometimes the reality imagined by the rebel is valid, but not often. The Irish rebels of 1916 were rounded up, the leaders executed, the Irish people outraged and British confident that the asp was smashed in the egg. And the British and the Irish people were wrong – all had utterly changed. All those underground are incurable optimists, see not only through a glass darkly but also with an intensity others lack. That special vision makes possible the underground, the armed struggle, the persistence of the rebel and those few victories won over conventional reality. And this vision has always been shaped, made articulate, extrapolated and polished, not as intellectual exercise but as an act of faith: exegesis as good works.

THE DREAM AS IDEOLOGY

The incandescent dream is accessible to all, to the poor and innocent, the limited, the uneducated, to those who are most likely to be called upon to shoot, to sacrifice, to suffer at the cutting edge of the struggle.

Most of all the dream can be transformed into a multi-faceted ideology that as the struggle is protracted generates more answers, new texts, and valid positions on all sorts of relevant issues: boundaries and legends, civil rights or the language, the single tax or the rights of women and the duties of men. The dream generates not only an armed struggle but an elaborate text, histories, tracts, proposals, the clotted nexus of elaboration.

The rebel's dream may be expanded, elaborated, made manifest by the printed word; but revelation comes first before all. In the individual case it is, perhaps, triggered by a book, perhaps not often, but arises from experience, personal grievance, and the exaltation of friends. Revolutionary political ideas without revelation, without a dream, often appear the product of cranks, the grist of academics. Ideology without a dream is politics without power, love by other means, sterile. It is simply dry words in a dry season. The real truth is luminous, transcendental. A revolution without a transcendental ideal is merely tribal ritual or local dissonance, bandit politics.

Once there is a rebel dream, a revelation, both the cranks and the academics may well come into their own as explainers, elaborators, even at times leaders of the crusade. Some armed struggles move ahead on the lubricant of the proper words ground fine in fine minds as well as the sound of revolvers. And those words may co-opt the bandit, convert the war lord, involve the pliant and the peasant as well as satisfy the learned.

At some times and place, the dream as ideology is a hasty mix of imported fashions, popular analysis, local prejudice and slogans that may ill-cover most parochial ambition. A few, often those who write the tracts and mail off the position papers, may believe in the imported ideas or the patina put on prejudice; but the many are usually content that the old ways now have a new validity, a contemporary relevance. A renascence, a rush to the basic, has the same luminescence as first revelation. The tattered men in pious drab, blacks and browns, a touch of green, shouting through the dusty streets of Cairo or Khartoum under banners blazoned 'Islam is Our Religion' and 'Allah is Our Ideology' march, as do the others, for the dream, perhaps into an underground, but they are at the moment no less illuminated by the truth. Others have no grand heritage but real grievance and a glimpse of the future. This is for the desperate often sufficient: in time even the Mexican Indian can be recruited. Some ideologies like some revolutions are shoddy, quick-made, and tatter on examination, bandit rationales or excuse for avarice and malice. In Somalia the habits of the clan and the humiliation of foreign charity permitted an armed resistance and a return to internal war but offered no convincing banner, no national dream, no rationale that went beyond ambition and resentment. There was no wonder in the killing, only familiarity. In Zaire, Mobutu lost not to a dream, a risen people, but armed interests.

Most ideologies arising from a valid dream become for the believer wondrous. Grand and complex philosophies for the grand or complex and the simple truth for the truth. Many rebels neither need nor want complexity. The truth will do. Anyone can be awed by the truth. The ill-prepared may move their lips as they pore over badly printed mass-produced pamphlets in mean rooms at the margins of events, but they worship nevertheless. These are the consumers at full-circle, at one with the tribal converts to Lenin. They are at many removes from Mazzini and Bakunin, but the power of the dream need not be confined to the reading room of the British Museum or the tracts of Italian sociologists. Its power is often released by the simple, simply attracted.

All share the convictions that arise from acceptance of the revelation of truth. The revelation, unlike love, is seldom at first sight. It may come on the road to Damascus but only if there is time along the way for contemplation. Only a few are there at the creation. The others come later. Even when revolution is in the air, when recent history's movement can be tangible, felt in the streets, sensed in events, conversion to the dream is not immediate. Often that conversion may arrive only after the volunteer is actually within the movement and finds his mind surprisingly set, his vision the same as the others, all without recollection of conversion. Volunteering for war, the recruit finds instead he has volunteered for the future, finds all utterly changed. In a traditional underground, the rebel finds that the old varieties learned at the mosque or in primary school suddenly have been transformed, are novel and compelling. The orthodox texts are revealed as corrupted by the powerful. The old is new and true. Even then the dream is grasped, sooner rather than later. It comes with all necessary conviction rather than in a blazing light, comes not unlike romantic love rapidly but rather after some familiarity. Most people fall slowly into love, day by day, deeper and deeper. Conversion at first sight is known but not common. Delay is equally rare – a rebel becomes convinced for the truth is all about.

A novice moves out of the dark and suddenly realizes that the dream is at work. A book may do it, a friend, a moment in the mosque and all is clear. A final insult on the street may do or a special insight or a single speech – all, however, act on a prepared mind. Interest, attraction, involvement, and the revelation that there is no way back, indicate that commitment has come. Then, all is changed. Life, action, everything is enhanced by the new perspective, by the new grasp of reality. Ideology will never be merely sacred texts and recruits classes, never dry, until the power at the center has extinguished the dream and requires regular attendance and graded exams in faith. The truly faithful need no instruction but seek it.

Some ideologues may seek to translate this new reality into appropriate form, compose arcane dissertations beyond reach of all. In Italy there was Tony Negri, the sociologist of the autonomists, who wrote dense texts beyond reach of nearly all, even his colleagues, acts of devotion rather than explanation. In public, he spoke not in tongues but with parables that sent radicals out with guns citing his analysis if not his text. Some of the more philosophical advocates of Arab nationalism produced arguments divorced from history or experience seeking to make the translucent mirage real.

To read the stilted academic prose of a provincial academic – the Fourth Sword of World Communism Revolution – will give little clue as to why many have followed in harm's way the Shining Path in Peru. The dream has arisen despite the jargon of the creed. Even the poetic academicians of the armed struggle cannot desiccate the faith nor greatly enhance it. Each offers the available gift, radical sociology or a room for the hunted. And some take up the gun or at least stand near the front lines of the war. Trotsky rode in his armored train, Che wandered the Congo and Bolivia, Pearse and Connolly died in Dublin for Easter Week: all wrote at length but each was first moved as were those who came later by the ideal, new, compelling, and infectious.

Thus the new complex of explanations and ideas that surround the faith are cherished and detailed, enriched by example, elaborated by the skillful and the involved. Volunteers spend more time on the articles of the faith, the implications of history, the meanings embedded in proper analysis than on military training or tactical planning. The limited repeat the basics over and over and the more complex extend the faith to newly perceived reality.

There is explanation, agenda, and promised salvation. Each culture adjusts the process. Each armed struggle is different. Some oppose others but all arise from a dream. The nationalists usually have the simpler task, for only the complex want to define the future, discuss government form or the class structure of the ideal. The simple want a nation once again, a flag, pride, a culmination to history's denial. Those Irish republicans who went out to fight the British on 24 April 1916, first posted a proclamation of aims, short, obscure, and, with something for everyone, appealing as a poster might best be. The Italians of *Brigate rosse* had first to convince their own that the faith demanded a gun, could only deploy the dialect skills and academic training of the university to shape reality to their aspiration. And for some time the thicket of analysis kept the core small until the violence of the vision transformed those less inclined to seminars and communes. Each ideological compound arising from the dream is different but the faithful act everywhere alike.

Ideology is merely the orthodox form of the revelation, the means to move the dream through the galaxy to reinforce the faithful. It is directed at the converted and those beyond the galaxy of belief who insist on conventions and arguments. Ideology is merely one factor, one force, that structures the galaxy and in so doing gives evidence to the alien eye that the faith is valid. The faithful really need no evidence, no fine-spun arguments. They have found their way not through the clash of thesis and anti-thesis, not from logic or rigorous disputation, but by revelation. And all find themselves utterly changed.

4

The Faith's Galaxy

THE ANALYSIS of reality that often seems so at odds with the truth of the conventional arises not from investigation but from conversion to the dream. An armed struggle runs on the energy of this compelling dream and so the institutionalizing as ideology is a major priority of each armed struggle. The dream is the great asset in a real world filled only with enemies and obstacles. The dream must be enhanced, shaped, applied. The analysis rises from the dream and is shaped from it.

In the very beginning the movement, the self-chosen, the desperate and dedicated, can be satisfied with a rapid exchange of revelations. Each has found a tool of analysis, the meaning of meaning, a community of the like, often if not always alike in nearly all ways: the same faith, same class and culture, same age and experience and now with the same agenda. Some armed struggles represent the nation, resist an alien occupier or shape a counter-state, are grand and include all estates and categories; but most are a cadre of specifically discontent, the few, the very few. So many, most if by no means all, armed struggles start small with the first disciplines of the faith.

Even the great mass movements often began with one or two – Hitler making a speech to the German Workers' Party or Lenin sitting at his cafe table in exile in Switzerland. The French Resistance in 1940 was merely a scattering of patriots, a universe of discrete, largely independent parts – and not too many parts. Some revolutions may begin as mob or a committee of correspondence.

An armed struggle may arise among the many who had waited only for an opportunity to act, waited for a perceived vulnerability; suddenly national resistance is possible by all those who are nationalists, not just the few dedicated to an obscure vision. Obscure visions tend to wither and die, raisins in the sun, dreams denied. Not all dreams are denied or even arrive with a long history or special credentials. Other struggles arise from general turmoil or the denial of traditional habits and ways. At the core of nearly all is not only grievance but an ideal, even if the ideal is primitive.

Without an ideal violence is always possible, irregular war, pogroms, havoc and slaughter for profit; but such adventures are structured by opportunity, ambitions, prospects or malice – all transitory indicators unless the turmoil can be made endemic. An armed struggle may be protracted but those involved are engaged in process, not a permanent struggle nor one engendered by greed or gain or simple malevolence. An armed struggle is rather a means to change history as to what it promises to be to what it ought to be – a means, not an end.

There are for whatever reason those who are first to say 'no' to the existing course of history. In the classical armed struggle those who enter or are driven underground go dedicated to the ideal as history's goal. This ideal can be made from the simple currency of nationalism, the driving idea of the last century, compounded by strategies of class or church. This has been the case in Ireland. The ideal can be a secular heresy, an elaborate rationalization for ethnic greed, a complicated and dense cloak for charisma. Whatever the shape or purpose of the nexus of ideas, it inspires conviction.

The very use of words like dream and ideal to label the convictions of the galaxy of believers resonates with decency and legitimate aspirations, but the central icon of belief almost inevitably is flawed – or power would be more readily available. The dream must often be achieved at the expense of others – a cost the dreamer wants paid in full. The dream may attract only the few, may evoke the worst instead of the best in the avowed constituency. For many, even at times for many in the constituency of the struggle, the dream is nightmare: consider the good German caught in Weimar between the dreams of Stalin and those of Hitler defended by those without talent or conviction. Many nationalisms deny those of others and are often so shaped to deny old enemies perceived or real. Palestine was twice promised, and who is now Lebanese?

THE PERCEPTUAL ECOSYSTEM

In a sense the community of the faithful, however formally structured, is rather like a galaxy, a great whirling light source that pulses with energy, magnetic, monolithic at a distance, mostly black and empty when viewed from within. The galaxy, too, contains black holes that gobble up whole stars, novas that burst into light, glow with great intensity, and sputter out spent and dark. Some galaxies may merge or overlap. Nearly all are unique at point zero in a universe soon to be absorbed by the absolute truth.

The rebel galactic structure exists amid the everyday universe, the real world of getting and spending and day jobs, a world visible if often inexplicable. To the orthodox, the real world is real, the only world, what you see you see. Those with a vision are not themselves especially visible unless costumed. Those who live in a special galaxy seldom attract attention, for most are under cover. A visitor may wander through Egypt and miss the fundamentalists or travel in Ireland and never see signs of the republican galaxy. Sometimes the signs are scant, a name scratched on the wall, a grimace, a sullen look, signs useful only to the astute. The innocent, the tourist, the foreign journalist, often sees nothing. The police and the army may find evidence of treason difficult to collect but suspect much that is seemingly normal is not. To the involved, the community of the faithful, their world and all their works is patent, easily grasped: this village is ours, that house is safe. Most of all, the faithful see the meaning of the ordinary, the real is enhanced for they too see what they see and so analyze reality.

All of this, the hidden and the vital, inevitably has somewhat similar form anyplace that supports a classical armed struggle. Each such galaxy is like each rebel special and each the same. Within the galaxy the major factor is the movement that given shape and purpose through the organizations of the faith. Once the shooting begins, all of these organizations are focused on the armed struggle of the secret army. Many within the movement are not joiners, carry no party card, no gun, belong to no secret army, but yet count themselves as one with the chosen. These chosen at times appear to be identified at least by their own, appear as mob, stand as a funeral passes, fail to vote, wear an arm band or give a penny – make some sign, but even this may not be required. To keep the faith is the first and often the last requirement.

ORGANIZATION

What the dream requires of the faithful is duty, sacrifice, good works. Some of these good works are words, books, the faith explained. Codified, the explained faith becomes traditionally ideology, a matter of tracts and texts, many volumes or analytical journals: Mao's Red Book at one end and the works of Lenin at the other with the middle ground heaped with libraries of class-based work. Such work may appear to be the movement's ideology, but this is only partly the case. The Soviet empire or Mao's China erected all sorts of monuments, rituals, habits and signs that gave form to the ideal, indicated the nature of the dream – a dream in power.

It is the faith made manifest that matters. If the movement cannot cope with organizing the ideal as movement, the center, the state, any state, need have no great fear of the rebel armed struggle. The dream will wither no matter how compelling the ideology or elegant the books. This is a consideration that those attracted to ideas, to theory, to politics and to concepts often miss. Ideas about the faith matter enormously but can be effective only if organized – and still kept pure: so that the form the movement takes must be congenial to the ideal and to the arena challenge, must indicate that ideal and also shape it to battle.

For the gunman or the guerrilla, ideology is a process structured to pursue the armed struggle. The secret army, the column in the hills, the armed conspiracy is part, the vital part, of the whole. And that whole, the galaxy, is elaborated and embellished, molded to need, displayed and carried in secret hearts. Ideology is not merely, not only, often not particularly analysis, ideas in print, in books, in dispute and discussion – the seminars of the *Brigate rosse* or the didactic instructions of the Fourth Sword of Marx – but in words scrawled on a wall, in the ritual of the IRA funeral when a volunteer ends active service in a grave but begins a contribution as one of the patriot dead; in the weekly riot or the banned banner displayed. An Arab boy eating a watermelon – the color of the Palestinian flag, red, white, green, and black – is no less involved in giving form to the national liberation struggle than is the editor of a party newspaper. The march of the many under red flags and the uneasy eyes of the police, the intensity of conviction found in a mosque as well as in the works of Marx, the conclusions of a lecturer and the rock thrown at a police car, are all outward and visible signs of the faith.

Many of these signs arise from the organizations devised to shape the faith to deeds: newspapers, front groups, commemoration committees, even choreographed riots and well-financed dissent. Some forms of institutionalization are less conventional: the great rituals of the rebel trade. Funerals as a beginning and end, orations at the grave, defiant procession with the martyr's coffin as prize, flags and the roll of drums, real or imagined. The people risen in riot or simple in mass. The people withdrawn are often even more awesome – a town closed, dusty in a Central American sun, not even the dogs left on the street, silent, sullen, threatening, the strike general and the police driven to beating on closed doors and dragging owners to their shop counters. Appropriately ideology is the dream enhanced in action – the dream as energy drives the armed struggle but must be seen to do so, seen to act on all, act on history, on reality, on life as lived, be visible not only on the page but on walls and in rites.

None have been more effective in shaping ritual to need than the Irish, and none have had more practice: two centuries of experience, the example of the Church of Rome and the glitter of the British empire. The greatest, most powerful ritual at present on the island is in Irish republican practice, not in possession of any state, not even held by the Protestant unionists with their great Orange Masonic marches with all arrayed in sashes and derbies led by huge Lambeg Drums under towering banners proclaiming faith and domination. The funeral of an IRA volunteer transmutes burial into rebirth, brings into existence for a transcendental moment the mystical Irish republic when the final volley is fired over the patriot dead.

The ritual was best transformed into words by Pádraic Pearse, who was to be president of the Irish republic proclaimed on 24 April 1916, before the General Post Office in Dublin and die before a British firing squad, thus becoming, too, one of the patriot dead:

> Life springs from death: and from the graves of patriot men and women spring living nations. The defenders of this realm have worked in secret and in the open. They think that they have pacified Ireland. They think they have purchased half of us and intimidated the other half. They think they have foreseen everything, think that they have provided against everything; but the fools, the fools! – they have left us our Fenian dead, and while Ireland holds these graves, Ireland unfree shall never be at peace.

At the graveside the Irish mix was complete, ideas in action, the dream institutionalized. The ideology made manifest, explanation, reward, promise, analysis all charged with emotion and display. In this matter none could have organized more effectively or to greater effect. Soon all in Ireland would be utterly changed, many instead of few would perceive reality as did Pearse, many – not all, not nearly all but sufficient – instead of only the few would be converted to the dream. Few would be attracted alone or even partially by the purity of ideas, by the works of Pearse or the others, by the printed word, by conventional ideology, but rather by the meld of symbols and rites, the reality of grievance, the prospect of change, the hope to alter history, to sacrifice, to serve.

All of this in Ireland and elsewhere, all these facets of the faith, must have form, must be organized, must make meaningful, relevant and effective the ideal – not just the ideas. An armed struggle is merely a process that turns dream into reality, achieves with force the ideal. It is the ideal so organized that moves history and the faithful, moves the true to stand in harm's way and feel the winds of history, sense the republic, become part of the dream.

COMPETITION: HERESY, BETRAYAL, AND SCHISM

The faithful cannot imagine the decay of the ideal, the great asset, the revelation. They always fear its destruction through violence, through corruption, and worse through division – an error of perception. There may, then, be optional revelations – and always such visions can, often do, inspire recourse to other directions, different strategies, seek other constituencies; but always may threaten the orthodox faith. Faith, in fact, invites apostasy.

At any stage, such alternative ideals and interpretations are potentially lethal because the option may be enormously attractive to those who want to act differently, who want to escalate or to shift directions; enormously attractive to those who want to serve who cannot be found place in the secret army or who have tired of the costs of persistence. All sorts of reasons may actually inspire variant reading of the basic faith and initiate theological quarrels more readily pursued than mere tactical disagreement. The faith is not called into question as much as enlisted in special arguments, arguments often made more intense because of the covert nature of the eco-system that encourages isolation and separatism. The underground encourages schism and revealed convictions are always open to further insights. The faithful, so sure of the vision, are also equally sure that some will diverge, some falter, some betray the singular revelation.

It is not the center, the declared enemy, that often concerns the faithful most. History has already doomed the unjust and promises victory to the faithful. What is needed is to persist, to husband the faith. To suffer, if not gladly, is the nature of the armed struggle, to win its culmination. It is rather those who would either twist or betray the dream who are the real threat.

These heretics read reality through similar but different lenses. They would steal the faith or corrupt it or most deadly of all deny it. The Irish writer and rebel Brendan Behan used to insist that the first order of any republican meeting was the split. The Irish tended to split over the introduction of politics into an organization dedicated to military means; split over compromises necessary to escalate or open new fronts; split over tactics argued out as principles. It always comes down to principles, first causes. There can be only one faith, pure, indivisible – and that is possessed at the core of the galaxy, at the center of the movement, by the organization inviolate.

According to Hardin's Competitive Exclusion Principle, no two species can share the same ecological niche without the better adapted replacing the less well fitted. A rebel inevitably assumes that what makes the movement effective is a monopoly on the truth. This permits the reading of history and so control of the future. Not military assets, not numbers, not the conditions of battle but the ideal legitimizes and assures the ultimate triumph of the struggle. Thus in matters of faith, the rebel is adamant and uncompromising with those who would steal the truth or would profess from within an alternative reading. There *should* be but one niche, one faith.

The truth allows the rebel to exist in that one niche. No other crusade should be allowed to draw away potential and legitimacy and so access to the future. No other reading is possible. And there are always other readings and sometimes the same reading produces other rebels. Once institutionalized, once there is an ideology for all that imposes structure, the faith forms the medium of disputes. Who should be shot by whom becomes a theological question. And outside the core of the galaxy are those who don't even bother with the revealed text.

Some newly coined militants, encouraged by the visible armed struggle, may begin their own independent operations against the center at times motivated by the orthodox faith and at others by a variant reading. Some may have tried to join the first levy but been unable to find the underground – often the case with the Euroterrorist who had to weave very heavy cover. Other rebels may be tolerated only if useful for tactical reasons or at the moment too dangerous to be eliminated. It is a truism that there is room in the rebel's ecological niche for only one movement, but this is a rebel wish not reality.

In any case there may be more than one niche that will shelter rebels. Most rebels doubt this, want to possess sole claim to both the faith and to the armed struggle. At best the faithful see the others as yet unincorporated independents and more often as competitors. Much worse are those who leave the movement, split the faithful, claim a novel insight or insist on an alternate direction. Even when the schism is peaceful the dispute over the distribution of assets is likely to lead to violence.

Those in place want to keep their assets, keep their guns and will shoot those with uncongenial convictions more readily than conventional enemies – the latter threatened only lives, the others endanger the faith and want to take their guns with them as well.

Some of these alternate readers can be co-opted, some must be tolerated because of battle conditions, and at times the arena is so large that true belief arises variously and so engenders compatible armed struggles. Rivalries often can be prevented as well as encouraged by distance. Many in Afghanistan who fought the regime at the center would, geography permitting, have fought each other – and now do so. Opportunities to act may so abound that rivalry over survival is not apparent. In 1991 the Punjab in India was filled with all manner of Islamic armed volunteers but no single, rebel command center. One truth, many niches. The nature of the arena may provide many niches as it did in Italy. On the other hand, dissidents from the faith mostly are seen not as simple defectors but as armed rivals pursuing a corrupt ideology – a real and present danger to the faith.

If the goal and the means are alike, rebel toleration may be possible, for then the difference is perceived as momentary. This difference is a matter of ease and degree and connection. One enlists with friends and family, serves in this town not that. Such a difference is not the same as heresy, not at all the same, not an attempted theft of insight. The real danger remains those who use the glass of the faith to see an alternative reality.

With all revealed religions and most rebel dreams, such alternative interpretations are almost inevitable – the nature of belief, the limited communications of the underground that encourages dissent, the inevitable divisions that arise over tactics read as ideology, mean variant readings. There is always confusion over ends and means, tactics and principles, personalities and true prophets. And so the galaxy can contain other secret armies, may grow larger because of their special constituency or smaller because of the confusion. The only good bet is that there will be schism unless the rebel commanders maintain a ruthless monopoly.

No matter the particular point at dispute once principle is involved, once heresy is announced, the prospect for violence increases. It is quite possible to have many secret armies pursuing various armed struggles against a single enemy – there were in 1991 actually over 200 anti-government commands in the Punjab arena. It is quite possible to subsume, in theory at least, several disputatious organizations under one umbrella as is the case with the Palestine Liberation Organization, a triumph of attenuated consensus over competing charismas, an Arab solution to an Arab problem.

Always, however, the risk that disputes over the nature of the faith and so the action to be taken will lead to violent schism within the movement. Always different kinds of rebels operating within the same arena, even if to similar purpose, are as likely to clash as to co-operate.

Thus still another problem of the underground is that while the faith emboldens and strengthens it also induces divisions within the galaxy. The more complex the ideology and the most orthodox its form the more likely disputes will arise on details of the dream. There are none so bitter as those who fail to win an ideological struggle and none so determined as those who seek to maintain the faith. Generations later in Ireland, winners and losers in matters of no interest but to a few at the time and no one since still nurse grievance, pass without speaking, turn from those whose grandfather strayed from the true way.

And such divisions on matters of principle as much as priority are apt to lead to schismatic violence, often more avidly pursued than the armed struggle. The lost sheep is often hunted down and killed as a goat while the flock strays. The monopoly that matters is not so much over rebelling as reading, the interpretation of the basics of the faith. This may not produce independent congregations but a rival church. Such variants may arise because of the nature of the revealed truth or the lack of underground communication, because of the imposition of a new reality that can be adjusted variously, because of personality or predilection.

What is certain is that the underground shaped to protect the faith will also encourage the very dissent that threatens to destroy the faith. All sorts of factors, internal and external, inevitable and contingent encourage heresy and only a few movements escape unscathed – those too short, those too vague, or those not really about a dream at all.

In very small movements that never grow grand, Zionist LEHI, the early Italian and German Euroterrorists, the People's Will in Russia, the Japanese Red Army, the ideological quarrels may be fierce and personal, lead swiftly to schism and convulsion, even murder in the case of the Japanese. Some movements escape because the danger hides division, because repression leaves the faithful nothing but tactics as strategy, because of skill or luck – and sometimes nothing works and the quarrels begin. Then the faith often leads not just to the gun but also to canker and venom: small movements, great hatred.

Larger groups simply have more faithful to quarrel over details, over strategy or tactics, over the means and the risks of escalation, over anything. Rivalries between the edge and the center, between the operational and the others cause trouble. Personalities and operational disasters all feed disputes. Some cultures tend to organizational schism. Some movements copying their society or right theory stress consensus as remedy. Some groups clot around a personality. Some institutionalize the quarrel. The Arabs, a most difficult culture to organize in Western ways, have tried all means as well as relying on the old ways whether found in the mosque or the habits of the clan.

The more secular, urban Arabs often fashion organizations using either consensus or charisma. Thus the Palestinian movement is riven by deep divisions based on personalities operating under special ideological banners – Marxism or the Arab National Movement, the secular, socialists or the Ba'athists and finally the devout Islamic fundamentalist. The fedayeen descendants of the Arab National Movement – the first split – shattered and divided repeatedly: the Popular Front for the Liberation of Palestine

(PFLP), and then the Democratic Popular Front and then the Popular Front: General Command, each time revealing a single, strong individual, George Habash or Naref Hawatmeh, Ahmed Jibril. Even inside these organizations a strong commander simply chose his own path without explanation and at times without being disciplined. For all the Palestinians to create even the forms and impression of unity and a consensus that included not only the small rivals but also those within the greater Fatah and the scattering of dissent groups was the great triumph of Arafat and the PLO.

Not only were the special problems of any underground present but also Arab society was wont to schism and division. That the PLO not only exists in theory but also in fact, has both a reality and a role, has been a triumph of consensus over the intensity of charisma. The great failure is that the consensus is so fragile that almost any policy has to be avoided for fear of schism. The Palestinians have an umbrella that only works when folded. The rest of the time the whole movement achieves stability through the constant and often contradictory movement of the parts: each more apt to punish their own than the Zionists but all integrated into the greater galaxy of belief. It is a galaxy rife with internal explosions, intersecting orbits, great violence that has cost more to the faithful than loss to the Zionists.

Consensus in any rebel movement is no easy affair in an underground environment. When a general cultural arena encourages schism as well, the individual will face all manner of options that were not apparent at the moment of conversion. To the observer the rebels agree on so much, on so many lethal matters – ideology and the text, the strategy, reality – that the disputes often appear strained: gunmen dancing on the point of an ideological needle. Often these theological gunmen seem more determined to kill their own than pursue the avowed enemy. And no wonder, for their own can betray the dream while the enemy can only destroy the dreamer.

The fact that faith is at the core of the galaxy of believers assures division. It is the nature of the faithful to divide and the faithful in a rebel movement underground are driven to such a position by the additional imperatives of an armed struggle: their very ecosystem that allows the movement to persist also encourages division. So schism for the movement and confusion for the individual are guaranteed as they often are for more conventional faiths. If heresy is the danger, then the ultimate villain is one who not only denies the validity of the faith but also betrays the cause to the enemy.

Every movement fears the informer, the once faithful now corrupt. This is the great revolutionary crime: plagiarism for the scholar, cowardice for the soldier, heresy for the saint and informing for the gunman and the guerrilla. To betray one's own faith, one's own fellows, implies a weakness not only in the villain but also in the faith, a breach into the castle keep manned by the band of the chosen.

Ideologically it is disastrous and operationally deadly. The informer may be intimidated by the enemy or the information extorted, but the crime is still inexcusable. To inform is to betray everything. To inform is witness that everything can be betrayed. Faith is not enough, eternal vigilance is required, suspicion is an aspect of devotion. Every movement abhors the informer, suspects anyone, everyone; for no matter how sound the faithful, how solid the dream, someone, anyone may stray. The secret army, the organizations of revolt, the movement, the very galaxy depends on the energies of the dream. And such a dream is most vulnerable not to force and to state power but to apostasy.

Every underground is a band of apostles always at risk to the one unsuspected Judas: absolute certainty comes at the cost of constant anxiety. The very threat may paralyze an armed struggle, disrupt a movement caught in a tangle of possibilities and no hard evidence, the rebels lost in the maze of mirrors, seeing in themselves the enemy.

Many movements are prone to the divisions of tribe or clan, the divisions of region or class, disputes of generation or culture. In January 1991, armed irregulars in Somalia, one of the few countries in Africa inhabited solely by one people, not divided by tribe but only by clans, began to turn on each other as much for redress of perceived historical grievance as to secure control of the country. In the capital disorganized irregulars replete with modern arms began killing. Teenage gunmen sped through the city in jeeps shooting at movement, shooting just to shoot, shooting because there was ammunition and no restraint. Gunmen killed patients in their beds or those in line for water. Artillery fired without aim into this quarter or that. This clan was arrayed against that.

Technically General Mohammed Farah Aideed was trying to depose Ali Mahdi Mohammed. Members of the same clan, the Hawiyes, they came from rival sub-clans. Neither they nor their irregulars were motivated by principles, political agenda or seemingly even self-interest as the capital was reduced to ruins and the population to despair. There was no functioning government. By November 1991, the capital and much of the country was a free-fire zone. The irregulars killed each other because the means existed, the arena was there, the opportunity seized, the thrill of murder and power assured. The city burned, the streets were littered with uncollected dead. There was no food, no compassion, no order. The people began to starve. Somalia was a photogenic nightmare.

In the North, the Isaak set up their own Somalia while in the country there was no order, not much hope and the starvation relayed by satellite to Western viewers. Simple delight in murder overcame all rationalizations and Mogadishu became a clan killing ground, a random slaughter by boys with machine-guns and their elders without restraint. In Somalia ideology was irrelevant. The means had become an end and so shaped the arena.

Even tightly organized rebels have problems, face internal pressures to kill or not to kill, to open a new front or to remain quiescent. There are inevitably the troublesome questions over the proper tactics to persist and the inevitable quarrels over escalation. And every armed struggle exists within the general ecosystem where the dynamics assure that in return for protecting the rebel the cost will be paid by imposed inefficiency and assured schism. An ecosystem both protects and punishes.

The great asset remains the faith that makes the ecosystem and so the armed struggle possible. That truth is assumed not only inviolate but eternal. Mostly the truth is shattered, usually forever, when the state triumphs, as is usually the case. Sometimes a dream may persist despite the defeat, despite the imposition of reality. The Tatars of the Crimea, some 350,000, were removed to Central Asia, mainly Uzbekistan, by Stalin in 1944, accused of collaborating with the Germans. They dreamed of redemption for a generation and began to trickle back over the years so that by 1990 some 166,000 had arrived on the peninsula. They wanted not simply to return but to control their avowed homeland populated by 2,500,000 Slavs, 70 per cent Russian and 22 per cent Ukrainian. Realistic or not, their dream as the century draws to a close looks more practical than it has for decades. After all, a decade ago Croatia and Azerbaijan were known only to stamp collectors and Soviet bureaucrats. Who would have believed a Free Macedonia, surely less viable than a united Ireland and no less unlikely than a free Puerto Rico. Who in 1944 but the most militant Zionists could imagine an Israel in four years capable of repelling conventional Arab armies.

Pragmatism is never very useful to the rebel, certainly not at the beginning of an armed struggle when criminal optimism is required. Later the dream must be somewhat flexible and not without relation to the real. Even then all sorts of dangers exist beyond the security forces or internal betrayal. The universal may collapse, as has been the case with the Soviet empire. This came too late to delay victory for the Marxist-Leninists of Eritrea and Tigre in the Horn of Africa, but coupled with other considerations led the Farabundo Martí National Liberation Front in El Salvador to abandon certain orthodox aspirations and assumptions in order to share some power rather than acquire absolute victory. The negotiated accommodation was made practical because the dream had shifted over time. It is easier for dreams to be inviolate when power is distant – as the Provisional movement in Ireland have discovered – again, nothing is for the first time in Ireland – reality creates internal problems where frustrated insurgency did not.

Thus, dreams are neither eternal nor isolated from events. They may persist despite all – like the Tatar aspirations or even the residue nationalism in Wales or Brittany – or they may simply die out with failure like the strategy of national liberation pursued by Latin American rebels by various means after Castro's triumph. What is always remarkable about dreams that inspire armed struggles is not simply that they dominate the underground but that they and so the rebels fashion a reality that persists despite almost all, not quite all, not absolute military defeat, not corruption or internal schism, not the long abrasive effect of unappealing reality. The dream may outlive the armed struggle, outlive the rebel, even outlive history. When deployed to achieve power through an armed struggle such a dream can be a formidable and not easily assaulted opponent to order, to the center. It is difficult to deploy tangible assets to war with a dream, to thwart an armed struggle that is rarely visible and never concrete, a process, an alternate reality.

IN SUM

Most movements entering an armed struggle shape their faithful about a military mission, irregular, unorthodox, covert but still a form for a killing mission. The structures may have political priorities but in a war of perception all action has mingled purpose: killing is propaganda and politics, murder and a military mission, all one, all the same. The faith requires the war and so the war is waged by shaping the faith – sometimes with real organizations but always with an agenda of need.

This revolutionary reality, a galaxy structured and protected by an invisible ecosystem, makes it difficult for the orthodox to respond. The conventional seek conventional categories of explanation, party or army, communist or nationalist, cells or militia – and they are hardly aided by rebels who use the same titles.

Rebel reality is simply the form given during an armed struggle to the dream, to the necessary and various sacrifices required. Ideology is simply an outer form for the internal faith. Those who order the deeds may be commissars or commandants, the deed may be labeled operation or mission, action or ambush, the purpose may be to persist or to escalate the struggle but all are manifestations of the faith. Faith thus ensures power at the core, makes the galaxy glow. And the light of the faith, the responsibility of the dedicated, in part result of the structure imposed, will in time change history as written, bring the dream to power. And so the dream, invisible and often unreasonable to the orthodox, ensures persistence beyond reason. The faithful may be implacable but not without some flexibility, not without pragmatism and cunning, tactical flexibility as well as depth of conviction. Their dream shaped to use permits an armed struggle, may procure victory. All that is needed is an appropriate form, continued conviction, some skill and indomitable will. Then history can be transformed, redeemed, as ideology promises, by means ideology makes possible. Time does not matter, nor the correlation of forces, nor the doubts of others, nor the voice of moderation. All that matters is the dream.

5

Recruitment

THERE ARE always those who were present at the creation of the movement, who recruited themselves, who first found the dream and first grasped its power. Then come the others, recruited by an ideal whole and compelling or by the needs of the times, recruited to a crusade, a movement, a cause, simply to a war, and recruited always for various, often contradictory, reasons. In fact, many arrive seeking not an ideal but action; to defend, to possess power, a gun, a uniform or a name. Some appear because the faith calls or the tribe or the opportunity is too good to miss, because tradition demands it or friends so suggested. Some of these recruits in time, sooner rather than later, may find themselves within an armed struggle, while others become irregulars in various low-intensity conflicts, volunteers in a tribal levy or a faction. Armed struggles are the classic, contemporary form of resistance to tangible power; but the margins, the poor, the wretched and denied have often resorted to means little different, shaping for protection an ecosystem not unlike that of the liberation movements or urban conspiracies of this century. And all who must seek cover and are united by an ideal denied are apt to volunteer for similar reasons, fit a similar profile.

Most recruits to an armed struggle are young – even most leaders are young, but not all. Grivas was from a different generation as were the members of the first IRA Provisional Army Council – for revolution is a young man's game. Those who are older, self-recruited in certain ways, remain young, tunnel blind to options, see with the stark vision not focused by the practical or blurred by experience. And the motives and drives of the young, the young recruits, are often everywhere similar. The potential recruit is shaped always by the times: a great war, the collapse of order, the intolerable present, a sense that history moves, a feeling that others are acting or that if no one acts now there will be no later. The young seek action, testing, always an opportunity to risk, especially for the pure and the worthy, to display competence. Some are narrowly ambitious and others want a vocation of denial, but all want a disciplined independence, a new direction but clearly signposted. They seek heroes and example, explanation and insight. They may seek the respect of their elders, the comfort of the faith or the admiration of their own rather than to transform history. Still, they are open to causes. And the rebel cause seemingly offers opportunity and challenge, risk and reward, offers a special role that is historically valid and, given the times, legitimate.

Those with ambition and capacity and without credentials see an armed struggle as opportunity; those sheltered by skills and resources see it as a different opportunity. All seek the difficult, the daring, and the absolute certainty that the dream offers. There are as well other factors present in a rebel role – the taint of violence and power, the lure of the gun, the identification of violence with capacity, operations as rites of passage. Some women, like some men from comfortable backgrounds, too, find the movement an opportunity to compete, to risk and to sacrifice in a manner denied by their society, their own. Recruitment to revolution is a rite of passage, rare in advanced society until the process is institutionalized, but often sanctioned where the old ways can be adjusted to new purpose.

When resort to force is not sanctioned by practice or experience, as was the case with the Jews in the Irgun – determined 'never again' to be passive, the result is often an even greater commitment to the means. The means is the key to the volunteer even if the grievance and the ambition are the core of the ideology and the analysis of those who control the movement.

Any rebel movement, the secret army at the core of the galaxy in particular, by nature has an appeal to the young. What the movement needs and offers is what most young people want and seek. Unlike some more complex institutions the movement's offer can be made to anyone young enough in heart and aspiration, the clever and the dim, the trained and the crude; for all dreams have general appeal and all undergrounds require first the desire to believe. To grasp the dream is within the capacity of all. Thus the sophisticated idealism of the university, the truculent and superstitious resistance of the peasant, the habits of the exiled poor, or the learning assets held by the bookish by conversion to the ideal can be transformed into underground colleagues; not friends, not equals, but comrades in arms.

Mostly the recruits, however, are alike, many even if younger are often like their leaders; but whatever the class or category, however special, most are young. And mostly the young have special needs easily supplied by an underground – not supplied alone by the underground, not even necessarily supplied most effectively by the underground. Some aspects of the underground attractive to the recruit are misread. What the secret army wants is commitment to the ideal, not talent, not uniformity, not necessarily the bold or the best but rather the dedicated. Real armies want professional soldiers, want tangible assets, bombers and guns and artillery men, commandos and main battle tanks. Secret armies run on faith, on the will.

Those who seek tangibles are poor recruits to secret armies. Those who seek power or an opportunity for profit, the special high of power or a life enhanced by the gun, those whose assumptions and intentions are fashioned alone by anger or resentment, by a desire for vengeance or on the opposite pole by romance and through a reading of patriot history often find few of the expected rewards underground. They tend to find the movement has no use for their services, holds no promise of advance or opportunity to exploit murder for personal use. And there is no romance amid the killing. The drifters and those caught in momentary enthusiasm, those driven by base emotions or simple hatred, those who seek a career, to advance, not to serve, those with major and minor vices do not find a congenial home. They may find refuge and they may, if persistent, escape the purges and the dream, pursue their own ends, but not often and rarely for too long. They are unsuitable and often find that the underground is generally unsuitable to their ends as well. Even irregular armies, the factions and the clans, need a commitment, a band of brothers rather than a collection of scavengers – not that factions driven by individual aspirations, greed or blood lust, a desire for adventure or to inflict pain – do not appear to ravish and wander on the edges of order; but those involved are beyond the dynamics that determine the armed struggle – those recruited by opportunity or lust follow other, older rules.

Even those who are moved by the dream, committed to the ideal hardly become paragons of virtue. Rather participation in a dirty war, access to guns and power, the charm of the covert all work to produce volunteers less than splendid. Many were and remain crude, violent, ignorant, apt to anger easily, confuse personal gain with political advantage, opportunity with duty. Secret armies no more than regular armies attract only the pure in heart. And the fact that secret armies always have problems with internal discipline compounds the matter. There is rarely the opportunity for graduated punishment or overt correction. Volunteers can seldom be forced into proper conduct but must be guided, trained, urged – and when this fails, as it often does, early error may be overlooked. And early and late there are such errors: personal vendettas, misplaced funds, guns used for gain, for pleasure, for power and so used often by those who profess the faith.

The volunteer can punish and find rationale, allocate resources to personal advantage but for good reason or simply display arrogance and still excuse all by recourse to doctrine. The result is often brutal and bloody: a frightened boy maimed in a lane, knees shot away for joy riding in stolen cars by men who will drive bombs into the center of the city in stolen cars. Decent people are intimidated, innocents shamed or killed on whim. A hooded man with a gun in the door is more than a momentary fright no matter the outcome. Terror for private motives, terror for any purpose is a horror. And much of any campaign is horrid, arson, theft, torture, extortion, a life-time business ruined in a moment, a son blinded with acid, old people burned and children damaged. And some of the damage is done wantonly, not by error or necessity but by volunteers for special, private purpose.

There is a time when the individual distorts the ideal, betrays the organization – embezzlement, wanton violence, public displays will engender punishment – but often because of the needs of the moment, the corrupt or merely unsuitable volunteer may persist long enough to damage the supposed purity of the ideal. And no matter how disappointing the individual, how many fail to last the course, fail to accept the precepts and examples, the dream still dominates the struggle.

Those who come to the underground with proper credentials find a different world. The ideal is compelling – makes the desire to defend or to use the gun coherent, compelling not just attractive. Still the opportunities are much as anticipated, but the underground is not at all as expected because more is on offer than imagined. And always the appeal of the dream that gives the underground coherence and energy touches the young, the eager, those avid to act – often for the first time, always to act for good purpose. Even those older and more complex retain this enthusiasm. And it is crucial that the dream attract such recruits; those who can be converts, can be inspired, serve. An armed struggle can rarely persist and never escalate unless the founders find such volunteers – or the volunteers can find the founders.

The core of the Irish Republican Brotherhood, the IRB, in 1916 was a strange mix of experience, idealism, innocence and the age. Tom Clarke was an old Fenian, an icon from a Ireland supposedly dead and gone. Pádraic Pearse, poet, Christian idealist, was a not very successful Irish schoolmaster. James Connolly, half English, was a radical, international socialist who had preached the gospel of the workers as far away as upstate New York. Constance Georgina Gore-Booth, child of the Protestant Ascendancy, as Countess Markievicz was a feminist and a radical; and John McBride, William Butler Yeats' rival, was a bluff officer who had fought for the Boers against the British. George Plunkett was a poet and so too was Thomas

MacDonagh; even Connolly wrote poems. The mathematics teacher Eamon de Valera, only half-Irish, had been born in America and raised in County Clare. They were representative of all the strains and stresses of Irish nationalism: mostly Catholic in ethos and personnel but often led by Protestants – certainly the first great Irish republican had been the Protestant Wolfe Tone. They were all romantic about an Irish history created by need, often advocates of the Irish language lost in practice. They were founders and followers of Irish separatist organizations with the great movement: the Fianna boy scouts, the Gaelic League to propagate the language, the Gaelic Athletic Association to encourage Celtic games – Irishmen should play hurley and Irish football rather than the English games. They were all sorts, pious, determined, often thought cranky by the conventional and yet representative of time and place.

When the Rising came in April 1916 and then, surprisingly to most, the armed struggle after 1918, all the forces that were unleashed and harnessed to the new nationalism were represented by such cranks, for everything had changed. What had changed was that the melding of the separate streams of Irish-Irish nationalism by 1918 had created an ideal, a dream structured as an armed struggle, that appealed to many on the island and received the toleration of all but the loyalist Protestants. The Protestants saw Irish nationalism as Irish Catholic betrayal of an empire at war – and many recognized the risk of their island privileges. The others, the rest, the nationalists, the Irish-Irish, mostly Catholic but not exclusively, became a pool of recruits, the daring, the curious, the dreamers and the determined could volunteer. From this dream arose the first modern national liberation movement that appealed to a substantial proportion of the Irish, appealed to all sorts, to every estate but recruited and deployed mostly the young within the Irish Volunteers – the Irish Republican Army.

Fatah was in the beginning a tiny band of Palestinian nationalists – no organizational chart was needed, not even roll call at the meetings. Almost all went off on the first operation. These Palestinians and their early converts who accepted the proffered way of the revolutionary-guerrilla were much the same: exiles, alienated, middle-class or lower-middle class, men in their 20s, impatient with their elders and old allies. They were attracted to guerrilla revolution as a means to act when the Israeli 1967 victory seemingly had closed all other doors. Within a year the recruits had clogged the system, turned the fedayeen into a mass movement. With all other doors closed, with frustration and despair everywhere, the way of the guerrilla guaranteed ultimate victory to those without assets. The appeal was general across the spectrum of Palestinian Arab society even if the guarantee was written in the fashionable script of the class struggle and the leadership composed of unknown exiles.

The new guerrilla was hero and all sorts wanted a place. Only the young and faithful found a military role but many were given a place, often not an opportunity to serve but rather to be added to lists and rolls and counted as formal assets. The real asset deployed were fedayeen sent across the Jordan to die and those being readied for a guerrilla revolution. The new crusaders were without adequate training or operational prospects but possessed great faith. The Zionist entity was brittle, the armed struggle potent, victory and so Palestine assured.

The first few fedayeen were little different than most nationalists of the time, spoke in the language of the Left, admired the guerrilla heroes, faced the challenge of not only defeating the alien occupier but also of fashioning a latent people into a nation. Their dream was of a nation. The armed struggle would establish this dream-Palestine in the hearts of all, those aliens in their own land, those in exile, all those unredeemed who were barely aware of their name or nation. The Palestinians' galaxy would light up, form a constituency for the movement, be mobilized, organized, transformed into a nation, a real nation. When Palestine was real to the people, the risen nation could drive out the alien occupiers, the seemingly strong but actually brittle and artificial Zionists. The Algerians had given example, created a people out of the struggle, and everywhere there was the glory and triumph of national liberation over the old empires, even in Cuba over the United States. It was the strategy that would lead into the future. And so they, the self-recruited, began with a few, themselves, those who believed in the power of the gun, the myth of the guerrilla.

A movement, any movement and all movements, once the founders have begun, offers a different menu at different times. Most recruits come later, enter when the great choice over beginning has been made, when the armed struggle dominates life, when the lines have been drawn, names taken, and shots fired. The many are attracted in periods of escalation when there is room for all and the few when times are hard and so places for volunteers are few. The mass movements often arise in turmoil, during invasion, require instant armies, militias organized on the week-end, the many, anyone; but such structures tend to evolve into the conventional, real armies and militias, find the times changed and no armies or militias needed, or pare down and go underground. There is only so much room underground. Every arena has a guerrilla overload and so any armed struggle must deploy the many without cover in visible and legal tasks while keeping the guerrilla and gunman underground.

Each recruit comes to the underground aware of the immediate past, the prospects and obstacles of the moment, comes for various reasons but hardly ever as an innocent except in great mass movements that suck in all and sundry. Then, suddenly, order is lost. The streets are filled with defenders. Anyone can be an irregular. Chaos drives recruitment. Soon everyone, the foolish and the innocent, the talented and the marginal, can find a place, often is recruited to a place in a people's army, in a column or on the barricades. The struggle is irregular, may become orthodox. Then places are available on application. Everyone is recruited, can be recruited. Everyone, anyone can be used and no one need really go underground. When cover is needed, when order is deployed from the center, the nature of the conflict shifts. Then the dynamics of the armed struggle determine the underground. Most such covert rebel movements are smaller and more discriminating. The volunteers seek the underground rather than find themselves in it.

And for an armed struggle it is always the recruit who volunteers. There is no draft, no co-option into a faith, only conversion of the recruit. There is, however, picking and choosing. There is, in fact, picking and choosing on both sides. The recruit may seek more than the rebel has on offer. The rebels, too, have criteria, standards, ideals – may seek workers or their own, always seek their own; but the entrance exams to the underground are always adjusted for faith, real or potential. This is what the movement really has to offer beyond the expectations of the recruit, not a gun, not an adventure, not challenge but an ideal. The prospective rebel always finds that both more and less is given than had been expected. And surprisingly always more is asked than imagined. The recruit assumes enthusiasm and dedication, avidity to serve would be sufficient and so rarely at first grasps the significance of the dream that makes all else possible. The dream requires everything and returns not only salvation but risk, sacrifice, ruin and privation. The latter to the young is as attractive as the former.

THE PRIORITIES OF THE MOVEMENT: THE RECRUIT SOUGHT

Most rebel movements, once the founding fathers open the recruiting offices, seek not numbers – or not often – and not even capacity but their own as acolytes. The volunteer must want to serve the faith. Sometimes, of course, the need to defend, the requirements of the armed struggle, the difficulty of filtering the eager, forces the rebels to accept into the crusade those who are far from perfect, those untouched by the ideal. The Provisional IRA found those who sought to serve in 1970–71 wanted to defend Catholics not join a secret army to provoke the security forces. The recruits had to be educated. Ideological movements spend much of their time educating the faithful, forced chapel to ensure correct responses honed to doctrine. Mao was as interested in instilling communism as defeating capitalism.

Sometimes the operational needs of the times encourage the rebel commanders to deploy violence against those in their declared constituency who oppose or ignore the crusade – those who consort with the enemy, indulge in foreign vices, refuse aid and comfort to the guerrilla. Such campaigns of violence to catch the conscience of the constituency are directed against the reluctant, those who support the system at one or two removes, those unobservant to rebel ritual. The people have no right to do wrong. In an irregular war the mass movement, the not-so-secret army may even resort to drafts and coercion for recruits. Yet the rebel wants not the cowed but the converted. The IRA wants the Protestants to be Irish even as they kill the local Protestant police as enemies of Ireland. Holy *Jihad* in Egypt targets those of the faith not sufficiently faithful just as the Mau Mau killed Africans and the Viet Cong their own villagers who took Saigon aid. In Algeria the killers kill any they find vulnerable. All the faithful are apt to find heresy, apostasy, and willful ignorance within their constituency – or simply victims.

The costs of the underground are seldom denied by the movement, are usually detailed. The risks stressed are often the lure. Those attracted are not for the easy life but as volunteers often find not drama but routine: books to keep, meetings to attend, errands to run and long waits. Only those driven by the dream can find fulfillment in an armed struggle; all risk, mostly boredom and rote, the rare moment of terror best savored in retrospect, and the long hours of preparations. The long march of Mao was mostly marching and lessons, and so too everywhere.

Most movements offer a lay vocation, often a long novitiate before a gun can be used, offer always service not rewards, risks not returns. And this is what the majority of volunteers want most of all: an ideal to serve, a dangerous service, an immediate future. They want a gun first as symbol not as tool and then to use it as means not end. They want to make a difference, to be, at once, a factor in the real world. And this the underground can give if at a price none who are so attracted can easily foresee. The orthodox may contend the rebels recruit only the depraved or criminal, may insist that there is no honor in such a cause; but the underground has no place for fools or knaves, the innocent, the romantic. Some always find a niche underground, serve time not the cause, kill for pleasure, shape a career, exploit opportunities – most especially if the underground is extensive. They are largely the exception. The classical struggles are more discriminating, more apt to seek to discard any but the true.

THE RECRUIT CONVERTED: THE MOVEMENT'S RETURNS

Once the recruit has become engaged at whatever task in the armed struggle, membership is perceived not so much differently as more deeply. The truth becomes a filter. Those who sought solely personal gain soon find other paths. Those who were romantic become realistic or leave. Those who wanted personal power find little, even with a gun, in a movement dedicated to the general good, where power is disguised as responsibility. The young who escape the cynicism arising from the necessary distance between the grand ideal and the bloody, bloated body at the side of the road become hard in hard matters but only more deeply engrossed in the dream. Individual and special grievances are subsumed in general understanding: this soldier is not to blame, this Zionist or that politician is agent of evil, not necessarily evil. This is in theory: in practice, there are always those who hate; hate the Russians or the Jews, hate the soldier not the system, despite the strictures of ideology. Hate is momentary, the faith forever. And the faithful may, indeed, be brutal, cruel, coarse and too enthusiastic, too care-less of life, any life, the enemy, the innocent, his own, but acts for that truth. Crusades kill no matter how wondrous the grail.

Neither a movement nor a recruit focuses on the psychological benefits of membership. The dream is idealistic, disinterested, disembodied, a vision turned into ideology. The movement and the recruit focus on the meaning, the details, the causes and effects, the grievances explained and the future predicted, not the transcendental nature of the medium. The recruit rarely arrives as believer: a Moslem but not pure, a nationalist but not truly militant, a rebel but not a revolutionary. Conversion seldom comes in a single blinding moment and seldom does the rebel recognize exactly what has been received from the underground. Understanding is assumed to come from reality, from the power of the text and experience not from revelation. Usually only in reflection does the process that transforms the recruit into a volunteer, a new and different person, become clear.

> It's like a process of conversion, conversion in a political way. And it goes very fast. You arrive at a vision that you can alter history, that history doesn't

follow its own fixed course. And I made my commitment, I gave up my career, my family, my social life, and began doing what I had to do. You also develop the clear sense of belonging to a group, a new group, different from the one you were given by your parents. Though my family were tolerant and very supportive.

The idea of commitment contained the idea of physical risk. It's simple. If you are doing what is correct, you think that you are being correct, and you have a regard for what you do. At a certain level of action you are trying to cope with your own anguish and solitude. But in my case what was most important was not the action itself, but the self-esteem that came to me from the action. The self-esteem came to me from doing the correct thing.[1]

The ideal does for everyone, all sorts. It is accepted as politics but most surely has enormous psychological effects on the individual and so the movement. This transformation is seen as the reward of service and is shaped to the practical needs of the underground.

The individual may, indeed inevitably does, gain an enhanced sense of personal worth from conversion, a new sense of personal being and acceptance, an identity in a confused world. Everything is new and so too the volunteer. In the midst of an armed struggle, there is little time for reflection; so the volunteer may hardly be conscious that the faith has deepened, that maturity has come, that the movement has shaped reality, made a deeper, more effective person from the innocent recruit. This new identity is made manifest by good works and is strengthened by the nature of the movement: closed, intimate, dedicated and dangerous. There are shared ideals, shared risks, shared lives. The isolation and lack of direction on the outside are gone. Service enhances grace and so the circle moves on, closing the volunteer off from those without the faith.

Some movements are closed, often small, isolated, societies filtering all reality through a dark, ideological lens. These movements absorb the complete life of the volunteer. No movement recruits those who offer only an eight-hour day or a single talent. The movement wants everything. And the movement gets a lot, often all that is needed. Sometimes not all is needed and the volunteer can in many matters appear conventional, carry the faith as an invisible badge, come home to television and a family, work not even an eight hour day but only a few minutes at the right time, and for the rest appear everyday. Some armed struggles need rather conventional service, can deploy only so many guerrillas, can use only a few hours. Others consume everything, the volunteer has enlisted in another world, an underground without exit.

Much of this is unknown to the volunteer. He, or sometimes she, joins for many general reasons. Often as far as the movement is concerned the volunteer arrives with the wrong reasons and must be transformed. The prospective gunman often finds the day dedicated to revolutionary texts, to seminars, to classes and instruction on doctrinal matters. The gun is merely incidental to the creed. More time is spent on the litany of the faith than on weapons or tactics. In his red book Mao urged proper conduct, wanted a communist to be politically correct and so a friend of the people, an asset, and thus a proper revolutionary soldier. Grivas, a soldier, was more pragmatic, wrote a guerrilla guide while Che, who had discovered the faith in the jungle, wrote a jungle handbook that he ignored – placing his faith as did Grivas in will over power. In the end the faith in the will produces good works – and perhaps victory, not for Che, partially for Grivas, and in time for Mao.

Many volunteers for the underground have some grasp of the nature of the armed struggle even if not the power of the dream. Through contacts and exposure, the volunteer may be aware of the intensity of the experience as is an orthodox recruit aware that the United States Marines need a few good men or that only the best can be a Ranger or a Commando. Once amid the faithful the psychic benefits come into play but rarely become apparent directly. And again these benefits are in part parallel to those of elite units and societies above ground. These benefits are, however, intensified by the nature of the covert underground, by the need to be easy and free only with one's own, by the impact of conversion and by pride of good deeds – and by the risks and dangers. Increasingly the recruit finds a full and satisfying life among his own. Increasingly the underground becomes more real than the everyday life outside. Out there in the everyday world, in school or at work, with the family or at prayer, a vital aspect of self must be hidden that within the underground can readily be displayed. In time the faithful are never fully at ease except with their own, their extended, underground family, never fully at ease outside the galaxy.

The recruit may be attracted by all sorts of factors, anticipate all sorts of returns. Those analysts who focus on the psychological nature of recruitment often touch squarely on the appropriate point – the rewards of conversion, but these rewards in rebel movements accrue after membership not before. And the intensity of the rewards is guaranteed and intensified by the environment of struggle. Thus the attitudes of Shi'ite sacrifice or the vocation of the Roman Catholic may be retained, intensified, and transmuted into revolutionary virtues. The Argentine sociologist Juan José Sebreli pointed out that members of the *Montoneros* carried their Catholicism with them 'which endured well into their Marxist phase: irrationality, sectarianism, asceticism, the cult of individual sacrifice for the greater good, a preference for absolutes, a near-longing for death and martyrdom'. All without exception revolutionary virtues. The parallels with religious faiths are more striking because the rebel can and does fashion transcendental institutions – The Republic or The Masses, the Nation or People. The rebel faith is, however, not *like* religion or *like* romantic love, it is a faith unto itself, *sui generis*.

There are, of course, all the other reasons beyond the psychological and the political, the two poles of the spectrum. There always are. Volunteers hounded by society enlist in the French Foreign Legion for a variety of other purposes than to fight France's battles. So, too, is the case with those who join the Marines or the Legion of Mary, a *Jihad* or a children's crusade. In troubled times, given a choice, some chose the Waffen SS and others the partisans. Some saw either route as equally attractive. There are all sorts of mixes built on the aspirations of the young. And there are always ignoble noble proximate causes, personal ambition, psychological urges, opportunities for criminal gain, even delusions of grandeur. These may be more varied than the drives that bring volunteer to a conventional recruiting office but are hardly unexpected. The deathless dream may attract the common, the everyday, the limited, the distasteful and despicable – and some of these may last the course.

The commanders in the underground inevitably believe in the purity of their motives even amid a dirty war and so want only the pure in heart to sign on the crusade. The recruit rarely is quite so pure. Even those with proper motives cannot deny the pleasure available from the gun, the joy of driving a stolen car without need to consider maintenance, the display made by Semtex or the returns of a secret shared. An armed struggle has romantic by-products, especially for the young and innocent. Since the movement seeks rebels with a cause, those who will do battle for or against Allah or in the name of the people, they will tolerate, if not in theory, those who also seek to punish, those who enjoy operations, those who find satisfaction in killing well done. They try not to tolerate those interested in nothing but revenge or murder or self-interest but at times necessity works underground as well. A secret army must make do with the limited, the greedy, the crude and the cruel just like regular armies.

And unlike the Foreign Legion or the Grenadier Guards an underground movement generally prefers to discard rather than mold those without appropriate ideals. Conventional armies can impose necessary loyalties, force compliance, assure standard through discipline while underground movements can only elaborate ideals and, if there is time, craft capacities.

Redemption and revelation can not be imposed. Underground coercion, even at times discipline, is counter-productive. No one retains a gunman by keeping a gun on him – except in thrillers. Discipline is not maintained – or not maintained for long – by kangaroo courts, summary executions, or a bullet in the knee. Volunteers stay volunteers. Shrewd commanders never give an order that will not be obeyed. Most volunteers are young, eager to serve, to serve at almost any cost, ready for sacrifice and eager to obey. Few may be not unmindful of their own future, but a remarkable number of potential rebels are more excited by the prospect of service. They perceive enlistment as opportunity. They then do as they are told; but not because they are told, not because they must, but out of enthusiasm.

What the volunteer receives and the movement offers only incidentally is entry on a one-way road. The way in is most assuredly not the way out, the way down into the underground cannot easily or for most be retraced. The faith gained relatively quickly is not easily lost. The way back is not barred but not desired. The time served in the crusade is so special, so addictive, that time elsewhere is dour, everyday. Service in an armed struggle is both hectic and enriched by the few moments of terror and glory. Thus dissent in the underground is shaped as heresy – the dream as well as direction at dispute. Some of those who depart often seek another dream, another way, a similar if conflicting vision and from this new barricade can deny the old with greater ease. Some disappointed in the faith leave and live a life in ruins. Nearly all, since nearly all movements fail, must find the future not in a transformed history but in conventions and accommodation, a family supported, a profession found, taxes paid and a life lived without the promise of adventure. Age erodes the attraction of adventure in any case and accommodation has rewards. Some find a role in conventional politics but none will ever live as intensely as they did within the underground.

Win or lose, persist or escalate, the secret army kills and moves on down the road toward the future. The volunteer is simply not needed underground and so is left to sell party newspapers in the street or vote for the proper candidates. The old rebel can drop pennies in a cup or pray at the mosque for those still active, be asked to do nothing, and so is left with nothing at all but the memory of glory, the time spent on the dangerous edge.

It is all very well for a recruit to know that on enlistment the prospects are death or prison and certainly a broken heart; but youth does not believe in death and prison is merely service – and a heart steeled in the faith cannot easily be broken. None can imagine the twists of the future hidden by a rebel faith in absolute victory. Most regular armies have known defeat, have institutionalized responses to reversals. Those engaged in an armed struggle can imagine only ultimate victory.

Expulsion from service by the faithful is past imagining even when the movement every day reveals the fate of the old gunmen. The whole rebel purpose is to act and denial of opportunity is the greatest cost of service. Worse. A broken heart cannot, as can death or years in a cell, be easily imagined anymore than can the power of the dream. A rebel anticipates a patriot grave or a martyr's cell, never obsolescence. How can the faithful be discarded? And in the end most rebels received this as the last gift of the underground, the least wanted, the price of service, the cost of the dream. And this gift is most likely proffered when the dreamers win, move into the palace to serve conventional purpose and shed the purists still fixed on the absolutes of the faith. In triumph or in failure, persisting or escalating, the one constant in a rebel career is the prospect of that broken heart, the campaign medal for the old gunmen of the underground. Such a fate is far down the road for the recruit who sees not denial but action and even the evidence of the moment will not dissuade the strong hearted, the recruit to an immediate struggle.

MAINTAINED: THE RECRUIT AS VOLUNTEER

The movement is not concerned about old soldiers, retired gunmen, tomorrow's problems but always far more concerned about the needs of the moment. The movement having given the volunteer all, the complete menu including the indigestible risks and inevitable results, has little left to maintain the faith but the service promised. As a result few movements distinguish between operational matters, the dynamics of the struggle, and the spiritual comfort of the rebel. If matters go well, the rebel will be content. If they do not, the rebel will be consumed with tasks and so be equally content. The armed struggle is its own reward. In the underground less is less, the more pain, the more gain.

This is the curious nature of the underground: disaster and service are rewards, not penalties. A movement has more problems when tasking is easy, when everyone stands down for a truce. Then the careerists scent victory and flood the movement. Then a real army may be needed, not the gunmen available.

The later volunteers to the underground who are aware of the experiences of the armed struggle are merely wiser, less romantic, more determined. They volunteer anyway. They tend to be more ruthless and yet less persistent. They have volunteered for the battle but not for futility. They want to win, will risk all but are apt to expect a return. Some who enter a protracted war seeking victory may be content to persist. The others, the first levy, volunteered forever. Those who come later volunteered to struggle, to win if possible but to serve in any case: they are more pragmatic, less visionary, more apt to accommodate to reality but in action are if anything more ruthless.

It is when the galaxy and so the movement expands, has a more universal appeal, that the volunteers become more diverse. The core may never reflect the avowed constituency and rarely the galaxy, but large movements and universal dreams may draw in the diverse, those unlike the founders, as was the case with the Palestinians and the new generation of Islamic fundamentalists. This tends to be the case in escalating nationalist movements, in any movement perceived successful, at any time the avowed, broad constituency really feels threatened and also capable of defense. In other words, at times when the underground becomes more orthodox the recruits will become more diverse, more representative of the avowed constituency: the masses or the nation or the believers.

A classical underground, however, simply persists, accepts rather than seeks replacements and reinforcements from new novices who are much like the old. Most armed struggles are short, failures, often aborted on the first day. There is no opportunity for a new generation. Many revolts last only for a few years, the leaders stay the same and the volunteers are replaced by clones.

Sometimes there are no later recruits. Some rebel organizations are not crushed or triumphant, but just fade away, fade back into the Malayan jungle or into the Kurdish population. There they may wait for a next time or accept failure – they do not accept recruits. Some undergrounds lose heart when the faith proves fallible; but, by then, those outside realize that the rebel vision has faded. A rebel without a cause is seldom a rebel for long. The idealist is dissuaded only when the way into the underground is sealed or the dream dead. Very few armed struggles collapse solely because the recruiting office is idle. Unless the rebel is crushed or the arena made sterile, the lure still remains. It may remain very still – the attraction of the IRA gradually after 1921, each decade fewer of the faithful, fewer volunteers, less action, until the rise of the Provos after 1969–70. So sometimes the underground requires more – the struggle escalates or is protracted, the rate of attrition is high, the arena grows, some crucial factor shifts. Any or all such considerations produces a need for more, more of the same – and the more almost always arrive.

IN SUM

While the underground is engaged in an armed struggle, one of the constants is the process of recruitment; the differences in social profile, in age or skill, in class or caste, will be slight and those concerned with what is offered and what taken slighter. The *Sendero Luminoso* (Shining Path) began with a single marginal academic's special analysis. In 1970 Abimael Guzmán converted a few to his faith, a special dogma beyond Mao. The faith was taken to the Indians of the *altiplano*. Recruits came because somehow Guzmán had found means to mobilize that most intractable people of all the Andean Indians many of whom seemingly waited for centuries, mute and indomitable for the Europeans to return to the old world. Guzmán's dream, a dated, irrelevant, provincial, artificial model, was given luster, appealed to the closed minds and then to those more amenable to a new Marx. Somehow the text worked, worked on the recently educated, teachers, civil servants, social workers. Recruits certainly came because of the intensity of the dream and later the success of the armed struggle. The peasants, the workers too came. They came because hesitation was seldom tolerated, terror was a recruitment tool, revolution in the *altiplano* was not a dinner party. And the others, the more conventional, came because of the intensity of the dream not because of threats; and so the armed struggle spread down to the lowlands and into the cities among the poor and the students outraged at institutionalized misery.

The shining path widened filled with those who accepted the text of Guzmán and the example of the gunmen, tolerated terror, sought not the good opinion of mankind but power – and perhaps vengeance – sought a new world. Escalation was both geographic and ideological, a matter of class and location, a mix that after a decade finally put the state at risk. And as always the state responded with coercion, suppression, and a concentration of resources that put Guzmán in a cage and the armed struggle in reverse. The future was again in doubt except within the galaxy of the faithful.

All undergrounds during the difficult days do not stay the same, even if the size is static and the arena stable, but most do – begin and end filled with the same types. Castro began with a dozen and finished with a legion but the few were still commanders. Most movements, of course, never attract the many but make do with their own. Most movements fail. Those who persist without escalation repeat themselves. Usually only the winners have to worry about novel recruits and the diluting of the faith.

NOTE

1   The quotation is a statement by an unidentified former Argentine *Montoneros* guerrilla, from V.S. Naipaul, *Argentina: Living With Cruelty*, in *New York Review of Books*, Vol. XXXIX, No. 3, 30 January 1992, p. 15.

6

Individuals

A N INDIVIDUAL does not simply become a gunman without rites of passage except in the desperate turmoil of chaos when any defender will do, any refugee with a gun is a rebel. Most individuals volunteer, come to the core of the galaxy and seek entry. Many arrive without prospect of an active service role, too old, too young, too vulnerable, in some way unsuitable. Others appear more promising. Many of these recruits, once they have grasped the truth, may serve the dream. Others otherwise attracted to action may be, and usually are, turned away, if not at first, then in time.

THE CHOSEN

The role of the rebel is the one sought by those who arrive to join the armed struggle, arrive to fight. The recruits come usually innocent of the movement or the needs of the leadership. The underground is commanded by the core of the self-selected, usually the first-generation of rebels, who need a secret army and so seek recruits but of a special kind. They want volunteers for the dream, not the best and the brightest, not the skilled, not the angry or the desperate, but those *sound*, those who believe. The leaders more often than not select these potential activists from their own so that the second generation may be like the first even when others are sought – real workers or all the people. The 'right' recruits may not appear and those who do may not be 'right' in that their motivation is too limited. The result is usually those who stay as volunteers are a type.

The leaders are seldom a type except in the commitment to a dream. They have no single profile, only a singleness of purpose. Doctors and dentists, farmers, professors and workers, ancient holy men and children without remorse can become the core of the crusade. When they open the door to the underground usually they find their own image but younger, less various, just as eager if more innocent. The potential gunman, the first recruited generation, are children of the dream, not at the door yet fully caught by the wonders of the ideal, but capable of the faith.

Sometimes, the movement and the leadership, the secret army and all the galaxy are marginal, Christians in an Islamic world, aliens in their own land, ethnically outcast or students without prospects on the edge of the real world. Sometimes they represent, sometimes they are, the poor, the denied, the peasants, but not often. Sometimes they profile a nation denied but rarely. Sometimes they are merely the angry of one city, one social strata, one tribe denied, one class without justice. Whatever their ethnic profile, their special beliefs, their height or race, the recruits are mostly not yet dreamers only aggrieved; but they are always eager to be a soldier in a secret army and so most fit a soldier's profile. They become soldiers in the crusade only when the faith touches them.

Not all these recruits can be accepted, sometimes there is a rebel overload and no place for the eager to serve, at times the movement is closed for repairs or hidden away from not only the state but also the volunteer. At times the potential rebel may have the wrong qualities, lack the promise of conversion to the truth. All those who seek entry are, if at all possible, held at the door until their credentials of idealism can be checked. The leaders do not consciously seek their own, rich or poor, but what their theory and perception of reality requires. No matter what theory requires in practice they take what they can get, mold those they have, inculcate the truth and deploy the new rebels. It is the faith as always that matters, that assures idealists as gunmen and not simply men with guns.

The commanders lead not only the volunteers of the secret army but also the movement and the entire galaxy of the faithful. They speak as well for the declared constituency, the masses or the true Church. Within the movement there are always various types, various motives, various profiles to complicate analysis but nearly always some general groups and types, some useful generalizations. The greater galaxy of belief is far more diverse. Even then the galaxy is not the same as the avowed constituency but often presents, if a more complex profile, still not exactly what the rebel ideology would indicate. The galaxy is not the nation or the masses or the devout even if it ought to be.

PROBATIONERS

Those who stand at the door of the underground, self-selected, eager, innocent even if shrewd, are judged not as potential assets in a struggle that rests on will, on the revealed truth not on numbers or on talent.

Mostly those who volunteer are much alike – even if the arenas are quite different.

These recruits, except in very special armed struggles and in the larger irregular wars, recruit themselves, for various, often conventional reasons: because of the influence of friends or family, the example of others, the enthusiasm of the moment and to a remarkable degree as a response to grievance, often personalized at some point but still the same grievance that generates the entire armed struggle. Godfrey Nhlanhia Nguenya was a clerk in the Baragwanath Hospital in Soweto in June 1976 when the 16 children killed during a protest march were brought into the casualty ward, and at that moment began his odyssey that led him to 14 years of exile and as Timothy Mokoena, a regional commander of 5,000 of the African National Congress-Spear of the Nation guerrillas in Angola. It does not have to be Bloody Sunday in Derry or Soweto in South Africa but it can be a curse at a roadblock, a slur, a sneer, a sign. And then, those who will go underground feel not just anger but that society is at fault, beyond redemption and the only recourse left for amelioration is the gun.

History must not be allowed to impose injustice. The IRA in the lean years after the triumph of the Free State and the defection of Eamon de Valera and his Fianna Fail to conventional politics, which seemed to offer a means to remedy wrong, still found recruits among their own, recruits who came to the underground from republican families and republican villages; who came from nationalist neighborhoods or often out of the blue from conviction or anger. The result was that the republican residue, the underground survivors after defeat and repeated defections, the remaining dreamers fashioned not simply a secret army but also maintained a secret Irish world unmapped except in rebel hearts. From this republican ecosystem as well as from the outside came the recruits, fewer each year but still faithful.

The Irish volunteer, like all other such recruits, enlisted for good cause and for the usual causes. Those who volunteer for an underground, Irish or Tamil, Arab or German, are much alike. The recruit has often been humiliated. Injustice seems beyond conventional resources.

The recruit, then, comes to the movement for reasons that the ideology anticipates and reasons the faithful chose to ignore plus a personal grievance, often not an immediate one – and for all the usual reasons of youth. The recruit to the movement must appear sound, useful for the secret army or its maintenance, willing even to wait as well as to serve. The movement looks always, if possible, to appropriate motivation – some expression of the faith, good character, the recommendation of friends and family, ties to the energy and will that runs the galaxy. Mostly the movement will write on a blank slate, take a probationer of sound character with an eagerness for service as long as there has been no irreversible contamination by other visions, by other ideals. The leadership wants a pilgrim and so does not discount talent and competence but values them in addition to not instead of faith. Later, if the movement grows, there will be places for the less committed – in fact to assist growth some movements have drafted those less than enthusiastic, even if rarely kidnapped for the cause – just like orthodox navies once did. The ideal, however, is always the paragon, the pilgrim.

There are, as would be expected, differences in detail in each movement's priorities. Each has a theory as to the ideal recruit. Some have experience with categories and types that have not worked for them underground. The IRA from 1946 until 1970 suspected students, university students, as having pretensions of grandeur and potentially not as sound because of other available options – but then the IRA leadership reflected a largely working-class movement. Other leaders in Germany and Italy seemingly trusted no one over 30, directed movements run mainly of graduate students. The guerrilla underground in Uruguay and Italy recruited students while theoretically seeking workers. The student *Napisti* in Italy once recruited their cell mates, not criminals but 'victims' of the imperialist system. The Bretons liked older volunteers and most organizations younger ones. Marriage is often in theory seen as handicap although may be useful as cover and haven in practice. Generally, evidence of the faith overcomes almost all hurdles to membership even that of stability and competence. Who could deny those who want to sacrifice for the truth?

At the moment of enlistment, the recruit assumes acceptance to the armed struggle is assured, but in fact the movement has merely accepted potential. The faith, the crux of the matter, usually must come to flower later as recruit is transformed into volunteer. Even then the faith may be tested although rarely, except in thrillers, by operational criteria – kill to demonstrate loyalty. What each movement wants is inherent loyalty to the ideal not a recruit held hostage by fear or even discipline. A few recruits arrive devout, perhaps converted by family or example; but all who stay are so transformed not simply into followers of the movement but also into the faithful. Conviction cannot be purchased or coerced or long pretended nor easily shaken. The volunteer transformed is an ideological asset, each a validation of the faith, as well as a secret soldier.

Most recruits are considered sound, good and faithful volunteers, willing. Sent into harm's way, they are mostly lost. Some are corrupted by the opportunities underground or discarded by the movement, but most are captured, maimed or killed, falling prey to their own incompetence and the skills of their opponents. A conventional army can weed out illiterates and the dense, the clumsy, all more trouble than return, more dangerous in than out. A real army can exist manned by the skilled and competent and professional and need not depend on élan and audacity alone. A rebel 'army' cannot easily turn away the pilgrim, eager, avid, perhaps a family friend, perhaps a risk on the outside, perhaps not sound at all but well connected. Second, the movement almost always lacks resources, lacks means, often motivation, to train those who are sound – and soon lost – and so must rely on the tools to hand, the volunteers eager to serve.

The leadership often is little more sophisticated than the followers, dentists and lawyers and graduate students, or in the case of the Provisional IRA carpenters and clerks. Many times the ignorant and the innocent are the only volunteers available. And finally there are as well the mix of factors that guarantee general inefficiency: the small personal flaws of character and competence that operations exaggerate, the lack of training that is inherent in secret armies, and the miasma of the underground that assures operational failure. Faith does not move mountains nor guarantee rebel efficiency but only the persistence of the underground.

The recruit is apt to forget orders, to arrive late, leave early, skip appointments, fire too soon or too late, weld the wrong wire and lose the right message. Some take to drink or women or talk to all and sundry. Some lie and cheat and steal and get caught and get others caught. The sound men who *are* efficient often are highly visible, too tall or too short, well known to the authorities, overworked and more lucky than skilled. Those rebels who acquire skill through experience, on-the-job training, combine operation luck, a sense of survival, inherent discipline and rigor, a circle of allies, often relations, a grasp of the local terrain, if very good, can even learn to operate in alien terrain, and if the movement is very lucky reveal decency and honesty. Most volunteers will be less skilled but can still be deadly, can still serve; can for a time, for the moment, be effective. In a protracted campaign, most who last, able or not, possess an indomitable will, a singleness of purpose, a willingness to risk and suffer – and a grasp of the power that comes from a gun. They are the volunteers on active service, the gunmen and the guerrilla.

Crucial to the struggle, they live with diminishing prospects, overused, overexposed, the veteran few that lard the incompetent many, irreplaceable but always replaced as the ferment of conflict always produces another acolyte as substitute for them. There is thus no smooth rise to competence.

Most of the incompetents are lost, often swiftly. The more protracted the campaign the more skilled the irregulars – but always irregular, cunning, persistent, ruthless and still vulnerable.

Each armed struggle is filled with one variant of the closed mind, clones of the arena conditions, the inner circle representative of the inner circle. Much of the avowed constituency may actually be foreign to the faithful. Lawyers seldom have peasant friends or know many workers. Truly foreign volunteers may be accepted but usually only for the special – like the Japanese who carried out one operation at Lod airport for the Palestinians – or for special skills or as signs and symbols. Lafayette was welcome but as much as symbol as soldier. Transnationals tend to be a type – Lafayette, Pulaski, von Steuben could dine with Washington – men of reason. And the radicals attracted to Carlos the Jackal were a type, a type found at the center of violent agitation arising from the generation of 1968, inter-changeable individuals. The Palestinians, a huge movement in various parts, attracted volunteers from the Arab, even Islamic world, but most of these returned to their own national arenas, were a sign of Arab support for the Palestinian cause. Much the same has been the case with the rise of the various Islamic fundamentalist groups backed by Iran and the Sudan, idealistic individuals, old Afghan guerrillas, unemployed mujahedeen, implacable bigots, wanderers with different agendas. Even in such universal crusades each band fits local patterns, is most comfortable in its area of the universal galaxy.

A few movements, like Che's last *foco*, are a meld of nationalities united in a universal dream. That *foco* was divorced from local reality. The guerrillas lived in a dream world not a real world enhanced by a dream. And they represented not the Indian peasant but the traditional Latin American revolutionary leadership, each other, and so were led by a doctor with books to his credit. A dream may, indeed, cross boundaries but most secret armies have an arena-based leadership/follower profile. The small secret armies are very much alike and the large more various outside the core.

Most movements are often remarkably homogeneous; not only do the faithful think alike but the individuals involved are alike and rarely fully representative of their constituency – and this is hardly novel. The congregation at St Thomas Episcopal church on Fifth Avenue in New York is not a sample of Christianity any more than a Tory political conference profiles the population of the United Kingdom. And within the church or the party there appears to be more diversity than is apparent to an alien observer who sees them all alike. Everywhere, even those not so faithful, not so intense as the rebel, prefer their own. And within a galaxy the cohesive power of the faith is enormous, welding together those individuals with differences into a whole – a giant *foco* of the faithful. Thus in things that matter to an armed struggle the movement is homogeneous.

THE REBEL

The core of the movement is the volunteer in the secret army, but others among the faithful often volunteer or at least accept assignment as well. Still, it is the man with a gun who counts most. Seemingly the gunman offers the most dangerous service, runs the greatest risk. This is why most have become involved – to have an effect, however small, on the future. The fact that such a contribution will have risk, even when the risk and so the cost is not properly understood, is a positive not a negative factor. Some few rebels may be misguided, beguiled by romance, harried by peer pressure, brought to the armed struggle under false pretenses; but most, despite the propaganda to the contrary, volunteer with enthusiasm and some real idea of the dangers and risks.[1] Later they and theirs are not dissuaded by reasoned explanations of the horror that is wrought, the misery generated by a nasty, brutal war because the commitment and so the continuing is not amenable to such arguments.

The volunteer has come to the armed struggle anticipating some of the cost and without great interest in tangible benefits or many qualms about the means and the murders. An armed struggle is about killing. The rebel is not duped by the dream nor the leadership nor the cost of the cause, comes not innocent in all. Some come particularly to take risks, to take names and trophies, to survive on the dangerous edge and never imagining the reality of danger only the exhilaration.

What the recruit rarely brings to the underground is competence. Few movements have time or can spare the talent to teach underground competence in the midst of a war. Irregular armies, those which have an exile base, can manage training, but a war pursued from underground must be secret, keep cover. The recruit must evolve into an active service volunteer with limited guidance and does so because of the needs of the armed struggle. A volunteer survives by luck, by natural talent, by compensating errors not because of talents selected in advance nor often even nourished within the underground. The rebel has no marksmanship medals, no diplomas in war or certificates of tradecraft. This seldom matters for the volunteer is seen as pilgrim first. Will arising from faith can win, should win, will win over power at the center. Too often the result may seem a children's crusade, innocents with arms marching off to die.

Yet unconventional war, war shaped small and nasty, does not require enormous skills. Anyone can be taught guerrilla tactics, how to set a timer, to strip an Uzi or make a letter drop – and almost every guerrilla has been so taught, by experience, by friends and comrades, by necessity, even sometimes in class. Most classes, however, are held to strengthen the faith. Guerrilla basics can be taught but no one can be trained to believe. And the power of the rebel is in the impact of revealed truth. Once the recruit has accepted the truth all will be possible. The professionals assume trade-craft is all, cover and cunning, perhaps, and experience, but black pajamas and field exercises do not make a guerrilla any more than a P-38 makes a gunman. The volunteer must rely on his own, on the faith not tangible assets, not promise of pension or promotion, not anticipate medals or hospitalization but only ultimate triumph and the immediate returns of survival.

Belief determines all else, especially the difference between those volunteers underground in the rebel ecosystem and those they oppose at the center possessed of skills and power and machines. Better the incompetent but faithful than skills bought with money or promises. The rebel leaders always look to will, to energy, to dedication, to the sound man. Better the sound man, always safe even if seldom as pure as promised in the propaganda and never as skilled as the professional soldier sometimes assumes. Still there are sound men without training or special talent who survive attrition. Even then, the survivors are often limited in vision, restricted in training, and too dependent on luck and improvisation.

The armed struggle of the Provisional IRA in the present phase has persisted for a generation, giving ample opportunity for the appearance of all sorts of gunmen, most active but briefly, some lost on active service, nearly all now with prison time and retired and, while all of a type, each special. Whatever makes an effective gunman is not apparent on sight, in court, and rarely through conversation – and certainly seldom apparent to the involved. Some, a few, given luck, inherent talent, practice, have become that rarest of rare in an underground professional, not just sound but also effective. One of the Belfast premier gunmen was Bobby Storey, not mad, not feral, certainly deadly and ruthless and, most of all, a survivor in a hard trade.

Storey had come under police notice in Belfast even before his seven-teenth birthday. On that day, 11 April 1973, he had been arrested and interned without trial. He was constantly monitored after that by the security forces. Belfast was a city filled with police and soldiers deploying the most elegant technological devices and all the wiles of a dirty war – everyone tended to know everyone and operating for the IRA was enormously complicated – the city republican districts grew to resemble a low-security prison more than housing estates or back lanes.

The authorities early recognized Storey as a danger, an associate of republicans, a boy and then a man to watch. He was easy to watch. At six feet four inches with a ruined complexion, he was easy to spot, to trace. It did no good. Storey operated despite his name, his height, his assignments – and proved effective. Yet, despite two honest eye-witnesses he managed to be acquitted of a charge of causing a huge explosion that destroyed the Skyways Hotel at Belfast's Aldergrove Airport on 31 January 1976. Similar identification failed to convict him of a kidnapping and murder on 11 March 1976, in Andersontown, Belfast, because of the judge's doubt if he were indeed the gunman. The police were outraged. They had no doubts.

Storey was suspected of various crimes including a series of vicious murders. For their purposes the police had ample indication that Storey was a gunman, good at his trade, without mercy, compunction or moderation. He killed on order, was a valuable IRA asset in Belfast. He was arrested again in December 1977, but the charges were dropped. He was almost immediately rearrested on murder charges, but in May 1979 the judge failed to convict him because of dubious police procedure. The security forces were even more incensed. Storey was a most wanted IRA gunman, violent, ruthless, brutal, cunning and incredibly lucky – and, of course, most visible. Luck in the gunman's trade is a matter of sensitivity to the operational arena, meticulous planning – not always an Irish or revolutionary trait – and an assurance arising from success. Some pay for success with anxiety, live on their nerves, grow not cautious but pessimistic. Some find a natural vocation in a life led on the dangerous edge. Storey had the arrogant assurance that he could not be touched and that made it difficult to touch him – certainly made it difficult to convict him. As a GHQ asset he was deployed again and again: sound, effective, send Storey.

In 1979 for a complex helicopter escape from an English prison to free a key IRA commander, Brian Keenan, IRA GHQ dispatched a team composed of Gerard Tuite, who had taken part in a British bombing campaign the previous year, two senior IRA men, Bobby Campbell and a middle-aged republican Dickie Glenholmes – and Bobby Storey. No matter that he was famous, monitored, most wanted, he was still chosen for the English escape. He was sound, he had proven effective. He was available for an operation that would require a reasonable cover and skills that did not come with a gun. Storey was highly visible, working-class

Belfast, not for the easy life and sent into an area not only alien but also open.

No matter, GHQ depended on a sound volunteer for this crucial operation – not someone intimate with the London arena, not someone unknown to the authorities, not anyone with the proper accent or habits, but someone sound, not perfect by any means but available, eager, dependable. This was Bobby Storey, surely one of the most visible IRA men in Belfast, a man who could hardly be missed by the most inept of constables, even missed by the public. He was sent anyway. He was sound, experienced, a proven commodity. He would, somehow, cope, manage. Who else would be better?

The operation was a failure from the first. There had been a leak in Belfast and British intelligence from dribs and drabs had tracked the operation. The IRA team in London was under police observation. Finally, when the British felt there was no point in more delay, on 14 December 1979, the Anti-Terrorist Squad of Scotland Yard arrested the four in a luxury flat in Holland Park. It was a clean swoop, a security triumph built on information received, sound police practice, and the limitations of the IRA. And the authorities had Storey at last.

Storey pleaded not guilty and although the other three were convicted he was not – the jury did not know his record and accepted his explanation. Lucky again. A gunman's effectiveness continues beyond the moment of the kill. No one plans for failure, ever, but someone like Storey never plans to be caught, if caught to be tried and sentenced, and if sentenced to stay in prison. Audacious and resilient in adversity, he was not just lucky. He was, indeed, gawky, unattractive, provincial, ill educated, crude; but he glowed with assurance, was a survivor. He was tried again and the second jury again accepted his explanation and he was released from the Old Bailey in April 1981. Lucky again.

His gunman's career continued. GHQ was hardly going to retire him, for after all he was sound and experienced and lucky. He was arrested again in August 1981, and this time he ended in the Maze prison there to be a prime leader in a mass escape of 38 IRA prisoners in September 1983 – the largest peacetime prison escape in Europe. He was recaptured almost immediately – within an hour – and returned to the Maze, beyond use of the IRA GHQ. He was sound but no longer available, hard to replace but a patent example of an exemplary gunman. When released he returned to Belfast and the movement, still faithful.

IRA commanders have always relied on the solid, the sound gunman, the proven volunteer of the faith dispatched again and again. Not all have the survival skills of Bobby Storey. In many ways the gunman of the moment is the same gunman selected last time and, if available, next time. When such an asset is lost, all the skills and cunning, the learned trade and the acquired habits go too. The next volunteer must learn on the job. Storey, a simple if deadly man, could not have taught his skills if there had been time – survival had become natural, cover even in the dock natural. His was the gunman's trade, taken up as a boy and practiced for years. How can such practice be taught? Certainly the IRA had no time or inclination to do so.

Storey had none of the sleazy elegance of Carlos the Jackal or the elaborate ideological justifications for each murder of the Euroterrorists. He was working-class Belfast and found in a secret army a trade that returned a variety of benefits. He proved to have the right stuff – rare in Belfast as anyplace, impossible to teach from a text, natural talent and on-the-job training. Assurance, grace in adversity, brutality coupled with a sensitivity to the arena are virtues not found in guerrilla manuals. Those who must will learn on their own if given the opportunity, and those who do not are replaced.

There are the sports and mutations, those who fit no category. For some of these the underground becomes the only possible environment. Che Guevara disappointed in the institutionalization of the dream in Castro's Cuba, disappointed in the impact of the revolution in Africa, disappointed that the exhilaration of the Oriente was transient, formed his only doomed *foco* in Bolivia; better a futile armed struggle than none. Carlos the Jackal lived in an apartment in Damascus, pragmatic and professional, no longer active, no longer a transnational terror; a dead dream that mostly fed on excitement and aid and comfort of governments. An embarrassment, he fled to Khartoum and there fell into French hands – Paris had not forgotten him, the myth of the Jackal redux.

No volunteer who has been touched by the faith will ever be the same. The Irish barman in the Bronx can still taste vengeance denied with his beer and still feel the lost hopes flutter on news of the peace process. The Italian with the dream dead can never be the same, youth lost, wasted, Italy cold and bleak and everyday. The returns are various but real, shift with the time and place, the culture and the cost, but always are tangible to the involved: thus was I once and thus now. Thus we dreamed then and this we have now. Now seldom glitters. It never has.

THE ARCHETYPE

Analysts and the public have always believed that the rebel is a type, that there is a terrorist mind. Few are interested in the real rebel, the name of the gunman or the desires of the bomber. The threatened want monsters.

That the man with the bomb is only a faithful fanatic, a simple soldier for a secret army, not much different from any soldier but for the faith, is hardly satisfactory. And for those who love a rebel this is no less unappealing. Enormous romance swirls around the rebel, a focus of ballads and outrage, thrillers and films and the television news. The shadow of the gunman is long. Advocates see a paragon, a patriot; and opponents see a wicked, evil terrorist. All assume there is a relevant profile, an insight into the mind of the gunman. And the mind of a gunman hardly fits the imagining of the distant although there is a communality imposed by the impact of an ideal and by the trade.

Most rebels are not only quite normal and everyday in most ways but also in most ways are not very professional. A gunman is a sometimes thing. A rebel has a vocation not a profession, is in passage toward the future not in training for a present career. Few last long enough to become skilled. The daring die or are scooped up and are replaced. No matter, the movement concentrates on the faith, on grace not good deeds, for there lies rebel power.

Those who survive usually overestimate their own skills. After all, they have survived. And survival is vindication – something is being done and I am doing it. What they all share is not a mindset or a delight in combat but in some degree a faith that demands sacrifice in the form of underground operations. Even the cynic and the pragmatic, the stupid, the brilliant are in part entrapped by the dream. They may join for excitement and take a salary but the cause touches most. The conventional soldier has patriotism, legitimacy, a profession but the rebel only the ideal. And that is the great difference – or the great difference most of the time.

Most of the time on active service the gunman waits or, if a guerrilla, walks. Operations are intense, dangerous and rare. The gunman must fashion a life under cover – often a 24-hour a day task – and wait for the call. When called there is never enough time or talent or intelligence, always the contingent and unforeseen, the skills of the real professionals and the necessity to cope, to improvise, to scramble. Only a few scramble back to await another assignment, whether their base is in Rome or Beirut or Belfast. Each has been exposed to the reality of an armed struggle and all tend to cope in similar ways – there is little other choice.

Still, a rebel vocation is so various that there is no type. What is valid for the Palestinian fedayeen sent to Europe on a single mission is hardly true for the long-time guerrilla in the mountains of Colombia. Most rebels are young, determined, ill trained and ruthless – hardly novel qualities. Almost all share enthusiasm, dedication, a singular and simple view of the complex world. Most are like their own: middle-class students or radicalized peasants, villagers without prospects, or any member of the tribe. Most have limited martial skills but unlimited optimism and idealism. Some are place servers but most are volunteers in their particular crusade. They are very different from each other in many ways. Yet all have a faith, live covert lives, oppose a legitimate center, deploy a gun for the cause and only incidentally for glory and never for a simple salary. And to survive in a protracted war against a skilled opponent they must have recourse to certain similar techniques and responses relevant to the battle arena. Other than that, they are diverse, more so than regulars and far more so than the thrillers and films would allow.

There is no mind of a terrorist, no universal guerrilla type, no archetype gunman. There are, however, types and sorts because many must operate in equivalent conditions imposed by all undergrounds, and at times in parallel conditions in like arenas. Thus peasant-guerrillas, whether African or Asian, share much as do middle-class gunmen with university educations in Europe or North America. All movements rest on the operational volunteer: the guerrilla from the outback and/or the gunman standing in the supermarket line. Some few are clever, well read in theory, attend seminars and even teach at the university. Most do not. Most are everyday volunteers. Organizations usually depend on the all-purpose rebel, the volunteer who is given a gun and the task to hand. These, urban or rural, become defenders or patriots, enlist as simple soldiers and – but for the seminar gunmen – are in most ways simple not singular. Simple soldiers in the bush or down the lane seldom are great readers, are most content with the basic strictures of the faith, the Red Book, the name of the enemy, the rules of conduct or the legends of grievance. They are in such matters deep and narrow and adequate for the requirements of a secret army.

THE GUERRILLA IN THE COUNTRY

The ranks of the rural rebel are filled, mostly, almost always, with simple soldiers if the movement is engaged in an irregular war or draws in large numbers of the poorly educated. These rebel soldiers are little different except in capacity from any soldiers employed by the center, like class, like aspiration, like habits and expectations. The rebel is, of course, drawn toward the ideals of the movement instead of the symbols of the state. This underground faith is what all classical rebels share – and often almost all that they share. This faith may be hardly noticeable to the observer who sees only the young enamored with war and guns and romance or it may be flaunted by gunmen eager to explain each atrocity in tedious detail.

Many who fight in the country have only a swift time as guerrilla, appear like the IRA in 1920 for the ambush in broken brogans and cloth cap and go home again for tea. Others cannot go home so easily but can find cover where the IRA volunteer could not. They can be transmuted into real guerrillas. The simple soldier may want to costume rebellion in the fashionable habit of the faith – wants to look like a guerrilla as well as be one. So the guerrilla appears in camouflage gear with black beret and AK-47, appears so at least during photo-opportunities. The Iranian zealot wears grays and brown, no red shirts, no black berets, no paramilitary garb but the dress of the mullahs with a touch of white in a headband. The real peasant-guerrilla back in the hills has posed over and over in the rebel photograph. There in memoirs and far-away newspapers, in a photojournalist's book or an intelligence officer's file can be found a carefully posed group of the poorly dressed, rags and patches and stolen finery, a few bits of martial gear, the guns, always the guns. Half the world seems armed with assault rifles and clad in Fanta T-shirts and flip-flops.

So pervasive is the role that Grivas had his EOKA pose as guerrillas even though the arena could hold only from time to time a symbolic leavening. It was a front, another front for public consumption like IRA roadblocks in Armagh and the tour through the African outback with this or that liberation movement. Guerrillas became fashionable, a sign of the times, a role for the rebel.

And all these wild guerrillas wear a serious look for serious business. All appear in the requisite photograph as 'guerrilla' – the village elders with their shot guns, the tribal marauder in Liberia with a top hat, the war lord in Beirut surrounded with stern young men draped in heavy weapons. As time passes and the armed struggle unfolds, the garb becomes more uniform, no more high hats and fur coats, no more old shotguns or fedoras – instead the uniforms of the irregular. The first levy have mutated into soldiers of the underground.

One can trace the escalation of some rebellions by the gradual emergence of the uniform – first villagers and farmers with local guns and finally hard-eyed, fit men with automatic weapons, burnished insignia, revolutionary soldiers who are in sight of the palace. A few come down from the hills as mullahs or peasants in black pajamas; but they bring with them concentrated rations, German field glasses, oiled machine-pistols, elegant, Japanese miniature radios, and are tied to command central with a portable telephone, tied to those who know the cost of a fax and the time in New

York and ambassadors by their first name. They are moving out of the dark with polished weapons.

These are the fundamentalists of revolt. The transmutation from peasant to commandant has been a wonder. The old uniform is no longer make-do, no longer cover but at last the outward sign of the faith vindicated. There may be many detours along the way, a way lined with unmarked graves; but those who trod the shining path to power do so as soldiers, become more like soldiers and less like guerrillas and gunmen or even rebels as they go. They act like soldiers, talk like them. If they fight out in the bush, they focus on the food and the distance traveled, on women and home and the events of the day, and the food. They wait and then walk and wait and keep their weapons clean and wait.

For the bright and analytical these rebels are not very interesting at all. Most soldiers as individuals are not very interesting at all as source of a seminar. All that makes the rebel different is what illuminates them – the expression of the faith. It may be, often is, simple nationalism or the faith or tribal exclusion – Allah or Sikh separatism as grail but without need of elaborate explanation. The classical guerrilla is mostly, then, an inchoate soldier without adequate training, a soldier with a field commission whose profile is not much different from that of the opponent's soldiers.

THE GUNMAN IN THE CITY

The urban rebel tends to be more revolutionary than military, more apt to be middle class, if marginally so, perhaps a son of the village who has found a position in the city but no place, more likely a student of some sort. These gunmen are at ease in the cities, lead more complicated lives, have more education and more detailed aspirations. They may play at simple soldiers but are not. They rarely wear uniform, rarely go on public parade. They may have ranks but no insignia. And, unless the movement is very small and thus a sect illuminated by the dream, these gunmen are rarely much more interesting than their rural parallels. If tempered by prison where instruction is inevitably given in the cell-classes, they may be more intimate with the dogma. And few in many movements miss prison for long. From their years in class, they may be more articulate in discussion, more conscious of the variety of the world, more glib but are still of a kind.

Many active gunmen lead everyday lives, still go to class or the office or appear on the factory floor. Some may have wives and children and nearly all have families, a home as sanctuary. The very few who remain on active service, like the IRA's Bobby Storey, are often on the run, chased by the authorities, in a position of leadership, or on a mission. They must spend all their time just to survive and yet operate as well. The others who appear for one operation or another, shoot and go home, bomb on the weekends, operate out of a normal cover, are in nearly every way normal. They, too, cram two lives into one. A gunman's values and rationales, motives and aspirations, may be quite different from those of his conventional classmate but their lives run in parallel courses. They pass the same exams, go to the same films, walk the same streets most of the time. One does the killing and the other reads of the result in the morning newspaper. And the killing is cold and cruel, close up, personal, not the single shot from the ditch.

Since most armed struggles are short and violent and fail, there are simply not many survivors who evolve into effective underground rebels. There is one small group of those inherently capable of survival – the naturals. These bring special and often unsuspected talents to the cause. Their commanders discover the astute, the novice who can operate in an alien and dangerous atmosphere. They are chosen by chance, selected on the nod, discovered with enormous delight by commanders with perpetually wasting assets. These volunteers are the naturals, endowed with an effective personality, special unexpected capacities. And then there are too the others, just as rare, who survive and learn and emerge as classical gunmen, not naturally but with effort. They have learned on the job and so benefited from the often premature demands of the moment.

Despite the inherent inefficiency of the underground, they become skilled in a vocation otherwise dominated by amateurs filled with goodwill and courage. The two, the natural and the competent, are rare in reality but everywhere assumed to be a credible type: the gunman – a stereotype profile accepted as real by the threatened as well as by many observers. If there were, in fact, such gunmen on the ground then the center might not hold as often.

The natural is the predator of the thriller: the jackal on the loose, the assassin and hijacker of films and novels – crafty, cunning, astute in all matters, eternally vigilant, ruthless and lethal, confident in demeanor with feral eyes. Here in legend is a murderer for all seasons, articulate, often elegant, and inevitably sophisticated. And such special people do exist. They must be natural for there are no underground classes in tradecraft, no book of rules to learn, no texts, no teachers. There is no way to make a natural, although a few have attended classes in Eastern Europe that taught the conventions of the unconventional, not the responses required underground.

The natural simply appears, talented from the first, a complete gunman soon perfected by experience. The rebel faith permits murder, cold and calculating. A photograph of Michael Collins' squad of IRA gunmen in 1921 Dublin shows a class of young men, well clad, fresh of face, pleasant and normal, perhaps recent graduates or a group of solicitors' clerks, not the hard men they were behind the neat cravats and fashionable pose. Few looked less like mad dogs or monsters; and few truly good gunmen ever do.

Some contemporary naturals even look as type-cast, slender, cool terrorists in fine tailoring and expensive aviator glasses, Rolex and Guccis, men, and at times women, with a hard presence, a surface glitter, an aura of violence leashed. Some of the naturals, however, are various, less elegant, may look like everyone else or no one, pudgy students, men with bitten nails and polyester suits, intense, fragile students with large eyes and halting speech, all sorts. Some have never operated much out of sight of their neighborhood and others can find their way through Heathrow or Schipol, know the chic hotels in New York. There are not many of these sophisticates. Most stay within the parochial arena, survive at home rather than move in splendor in great capitals. And those in such capitals are often guest workers, students in bed-sitters, lodgers in shoddy hotels. They are ordinary in most visible things and so covered, invisible. Sent abroad for the cause they are lifted at customs, arrested for loitering, stay in a watched house, telephone the family and find the police at the door. They find survival in alien fields difficult.

A very few terrorists must do for the authors and film directors. There are fewer terrorists than terrorism experts, almost no classical assassins and only a few complete gunmen. Most effective rebels are not much different from their colleagues except in their inherent capacity to survive a brutal and dangerous life, to operate despite the odds and without training. The naturals have a remarkable sense of the aberrant, a capacity to filter out signals to find the potential danger. They sense the dog that did not bark, the tension in a bus, the time to turn back. They have a feel for the door slammed in anger, the movement where there should be none, the shift in the hotel clerk's posture. The cost of eternal vigilance is an enormous expenditure of energy – except for the stolid who survive on rote and good briefing. The natural survives on the narrow edge. Ever alert, ever suspicious, rarely reflective, they act without need for thought. And often, they act as if all will always be well, confident, for they are confident, assured because they cannot imagine disaster. The others often hardly survive at all.

Some who seemingly take easily to the trade have found not a skill but an opportunity to live out lethal fancies, to savor killing authorized by others' dream. These gunmen often hide calculation and exaltation behind a mask of geniality. Theirs is a warm hand, a ready smile, and a cold heart. They kill for pleasure and frighten even and often especially their own. They are not soldiers of the armed struggle but killers authorized by a secret army and have found a vocation, not in the faith but in the deed. The stolid kill on the way home with the groceries, murder without reflection or emotion, the loss of awe is their gift to the movement, unimaginative killers, not the stuff of thrillers. They are not interesting, dull, everyday without spark. The stolid can be deployed for brutal tasks and the daring for desperate ones, but most movements prefer the sound man to those not shaped by the ideal.

For the observer all gunmen, even to a degree the stolid, have an enormous bottled energy and bring with them the sense of danger. The most effective such gunmen often have to be run on a short leash, watched to see if it is the killing they like, not the mission well done or the risk evaded. The risk is the thing – and the power. This is the lure for the gunman living on the dangerous edge. The enormous feeling of capacity and control drives the natural. Everything is more exciting when a volunteer moves into the strange world of personal killing, killing at risk. Life is there lived to the full, every second enhanced with threat. For the natural this life on the dark side is the ultimate high. For others, often less talented, it is the ultimate trap, warps vulnerable personalities, transforms potential into psychosis. The stolid avoid this, turn killing into task, but without a focus on challenge they are a limited asset – useful but limited. They are too simple to be tempted but also too simple to be operationally effective: shredders, not computers; executioners, not even simple soldiers.

Armed struggles guarantee horror close up, nasty, horrid. Those involved are often thought horrible, monstrous, responsible for the victims destroyed, the bodies in the rubble. All wars are nasty and dirty wars are worse, often close by, visible and so doubly awful. The guerrilla may perform horror in the outback but the gunman must do so in plain view, often under the eye of a minicam, regularly on the evening news. Millions watch the death of a child, the murder of an old man, the atrocity of the week – and blame the gunman not the system.

Increasingly, even in the wilds, there is no place to hide, no buffer of time and distance, no censorship: horror arrives not on forked stick but in living color. And so what sort of people become so involved? No one asks why a lad wants to be a soldier, march with the Grenadier Guards or jump from airplanes. Everyone tends to understand the admiral and the general but few the gunman, a killer without authority, a demon of the shadows, an enigma and a horror.

Only the most stolid can kill without being touched by the enormous power, the danger, the risk, the deed. The gunman, like the professional soldier, may enjoy the psychic returns of legitimized – or at least rationalized – killing. There is the risk, the danger, the moment: the single shot and the jerk and sprawl of the arrogant, the frantic chaos after the echo of the bomb, the bold dismayed. Those underground responsible, those who give the order, those who drive the carbomb or pull the trigger are rarely personal monsters, mad dogs or psychopaths, but much like real soldiers if more desperate and less disciplined. They too are in a killing trade. In war a job well done, done precisely, is still killing, inflicting harm under whatever the banner, for whatever god.

THE LEADERS

Those in command of an underground, chosen, often self-chosen, at the creation ordinarily last the course. Their circle may widen if the campaign escalates but they remain at the center: Castro in the short run and Mao or Ho and Giap in the long. The commanders at the beginning are usually there at the end, whatever that end may be. Few recruits enlist in a struggle that persists long enough for promotion to change the central command. These commanders are most various indeed, old men or young, well educated or crude, some with great experience and skill and others who simply have tongues of fire or ruthless purpose. Each arena, each special history produces or encourages a special figure, often typical of the movement, the galaxy, even the constituency. Some may share cross-culture traits in that nationalism makes an appeal to certain classes and categories, or students everywhere often have time and inclination to devote to radical politics. An Arab Christian dentist, however, shares little of a sociological profile but profession with an Irish colleague. And those rebels who share age or education, career or a marginal place in an ethnic pure community still do not make up a satisfactory category.

The leaders all share a faith, live mostly underground, operate with the necessary assumptions of the illicit and covert militant, and they are all in these matters alike – less alike than their volunteers. The followers, like recruits in a regular army, generally have similar attributes, some more middle class and others more conservative, but all eager to act, to serve, to risk, to fill a role. Leaders, however, are different, not very different from their movement, not alien to others in the rebel game but still different.

All leaders are volunteers, some at the beginning must volunteer to lead.

A few are for one reason or another in place or chosen from beyond the core of those underground, but always to the involved the selection of specific leaders is obvious: the talented faithful, perhaps visible, perhaps charismatic, but most of all *sound*. The natural gunman needs no followers and the professional is a tool. A leader must be general example, source of energy and the most faithful of all. The one in the center must have the attributes of command, a sense of power, an understanding of the gun, may be charismatic or simply effective. All to some degree command by the intensity of their vision, the commitment to the unseen, and all invest all of their resources. At times the volunteer who learns on the job becomes a leader through service, rises to command, as did Collins in Dublin. A clerk who kept a clerk's books on the armed struggle, he also proved an organizational genius, a ruthless and if need be brutal operational commander, and displayed all the genial charm inherent in the Irish and so often missing in the gunman. Mostly, however, as in 1916 in Ireland, the leaders chose themselves, co-opted each other – and mostly, unlike Ireland in 1916, they co-opt clones.

Since all movements must have a beginning, however ancient, there is always a first generation, those who moved from the everyday world to the underground. Later they may have to be replaced if the erosion of a protracted struggle takes a toll; but at the beginning they arise from the needs of the moment. The galaxy of the faithful coalesce around their decision to act. The movement's organizations do not spontaneously appear. Some existing structure may be co-opted but always someone must be at the center – and often there is only a center, no organizations, no movement, only a potential galaxy and a dream constituency.

Some movements do begin grand, a swirling mob of thousands, hundreds eager to defend, the people outraged by invasion or the peasant risen for arson. The people are not mobilized, merely desperate. The rebels must shape the mass to the struggle. And most are conspiracies without masses. There are all sorts of beginnings but almost none without the presence of the leadership.

At times the shift to the underground simply involves taking an existing structure and its leaders into the armed struggle where the dangers and risks and novelty will shape both. The legitimate structure is most likely to be a political party, often a legitimate political party, but at times other organizations – militias or unions or communes – have served. The very small, whatever the titles, resemble cults more than movements, closed, intense, sects of the gunmen. Here the leaders are also the followers. The very large are often underground states, liberation movements that mimic the legitimate. Then the leader need be administrator as well as charismatic.

Parties, however, most readily and most often fit the needs of the faithful before an armed struggle.

Thus the Malayan Communist Party was transmuted into the Malayan Races' Liberation Army, a mix of marginal communist theory and practice within a largely overseas Chinese milieu, that remained as much party as secret army and fought the armed struggle largely with party leadership and party responses to novelty. The party supplied the leadership and these were chosen as much for party reasons – to maintain control – as skills evidenced in the armed struggle.

In the Palestine Mandate, the existing militant Zionist Irgun leadership in 1944 chose Begin, the former leader of the Polish Betar – the crucial youth movement – who had escaped Hitler and Stalin to arrive in the Middle East, as the dominant figure who could end the uncertainty about attacking Hitler's enemy Britain. The new commander had a reputation, a strength of character and singleness of purpose that the organization needed – he had no military skills but a strategy based on assumptions that could only be tested by events, luck. He did have a wicked tongue in public and a driving sense of destiny. It was his aura of assurance and authority that made him obvious to the involved.

In Malaya communist functionaries moved the party underground; but in Palestine Begin came to a very simple organization, a High Command and a scattering of volunteers, a limited political program unlike the orthodox Zionists and even more limited operational assets but great faith. Any competent Malayan communist might have run the armed struggle using the proper text, but Begin was special and so molded his volunteers to purpose with little concern for structure or program. Begin's selection as leader by his own for the battle was more typical than the descent of the MCP leadership into the jungle. Orthodox communists have been prone to opt for subversion rather than insurrection. All the movements, blocs, circles, seminars, *focos*, all the structures that go underground tend to be in the beginning small – and even when grand only the secret army – the African National Congress's Spear of the Nation or the Irgun or the tiny EOKA in Cyprus. No matter the form in theory, often the leaders choose the moment to begin and then shape the faithful to the underground. Many Latin American *focos* were merely extensions of one or two eager rebels. This was true in Cyprus with EOKA where Colonel Grivas with the help of a few early conspirators came from Greece to the island and set up his underground army. He allowed by default the political activity to coalesce under the natural leader of the Greek community, Archbishop Makarios. Grivas, twice as old as his volunteers, a regular officer, a Greek colonel, monopolized the armed struggle, ruled as patriarch, allowed as little freedom at the margins of EOKA as did the communists in Malaya. Begin ruled as elder brother, Che as myth, and many of the Euroterrorists as idealistic ideologues rushing from one atrocity to the next.

Whatever the form the leader was special, very much of a time and place, intimate with the arena, difficult to categorize even when shaped as all are underground by the armed struggle. The effective leader capitalizes on the special but by necessity deploys similar followers in similar ways.

Many undergrounds are simply a band of idealists who, having with reluctance accepted the necessity of the armed struggle, must, like arms and money, find leadership. At first they are all leaders, followers of the dream. They are *Brigate rosse* or Fatah. Grivas was EOKA. The Stern Group, LEHI, in the Palestine Mandate in 1943 was literally two or three gathered together in defiance. One of them, Yitzhak Yzertinsky – 'Shamir', who used the underground name 'Michael' in honor of Collins – in the fullness of time became premier of Israel as had Begin before him.

The individuals with the greatest moral authority, the capacity to articulate the faith through deeds, perhaps through words, emerged at the center. What is vital is the sense of commanding power. For the Arabs this power often has visible charismatic form – the movement as an extension of the leader. Yet the attraction at the center is hardly universal: it was possible for some, not all, in the West to sense Nasser's power as conspirator and later overt leader, but few in London understood his charisma. Few in the West even knew that Anwar Sadat had lived underground, been involved in operations, not always sat in French tailoring initialing Nasser's drafts. And over a generation even fewer understand Arafat's appeal, his hold over a turbulent and volatile Palestinian people.

What hold can Arafat have: a pudgy unappealing man without the voice of the lion or a taste for drama? He sits in meetings, waits on an agenda, talks and repeats and seemingly inspires no one. Yet Fatah is still the main component of the galaxy, the one great movement, and the PLO is an international factor and Palestine a nation in many hearts and some resolutions. And Arafat's rule runs, more or less, in Gaza and Jericho. There is no doubt why Khomeini dominated the fundamentalists of Iran: his great black-and-white poster-portraits over mean streets, even when flayed by time and frayed by the wind, are stark images of faith and power, a man and an icon. Collins was the stereotype of the Irish rebel, mostly absent underground where charm has played a small role. Grivas was a small man with a vast sense of history, an enormous presence, a figure to respect, to fear – even later in exile or during his futile attempt to replay history with

EOKA-B. Begin was the reverse of the sabra, spiny outside and soft inside, for he had all the social charm of a kindly Polish lawyer, solicitous, formal, kindly, mild in discourse. But his mind was seized on justice, a hard and complex man without compromise or seemingly a sense of the possible: soft outside, steel within. All different but special and effective among their own.

Sometimes the nature of underground leadership defies logic. Few of the conventional would have bet on Hitler in his Bavarian jail cell scribbling nonsense or Lenin reading at his Swiss cafe – that little man thinks he can change the world – or the Ayatollah too far out on the Paris metro for most journalists to invest time in an interview. Guzmán before his transformation into the four swords of communism was an obscure and marginal professor in a provincial university of a small Latin American country, was not even of interest to the police in Lima. Dentists and pastors with politics, stringers for great newspapers, students, especially of advanced age, somehow become the core of a galaxy. Few would advocate all power to Grivas in a hillside dugout or putting a Polish lawyer in charge of a Middle Eastern liberation movement, or could have imagined that the fate of South Africa depends on an aging agitator long resident in a mean, prison cell on Robben Island, cut off from events and prospect of power.

All underground leaders are interesting, none more so than the charismatic and various conspirators of the Middle East – and not all Arabs. The most fascinating of all Middle Eastern undergrounds was that of LEHI, where the martyred founder, Avraham Stern's presence dominated a three-man council made up of a publicist, Nathan Yellin-Mor, an organizer, Yitzhak Shamir, and an ideologue, Eldad. These were the leaders of the men and women without names, gunmen and assassins during the time of despair. It was an underground dominated by a dead martyr and his legacy possessed in three parts. The success of the Stern Group defied logic or any rules. So improbable a leadership, so small a group, and yet LEHI often had a spectacular effect on events. That the leadership worked, could be lost and replaced, persisted despite all, perhaps because of all, was even more remarkable. There are no ideal models for commanders.

What matters to the involved is that the chosen are sound and convinced. Leadership is rarely a gift but rather a duty: one is not in most senses promoted into power and glory but co-opted into further sacrifice, further responsibility. Those at the center of a circle, no matter how small the diameter, arrive because there is no place else for them to go. Mostly the most faithful and most talented clump together in the center of that circle and turn to each other, become the central committee, the council, the politburo, the army council. One may dominate the collective leadership, may at times be the leadership. The very small groups like Italians of *Brigate rosse* or the Germans of RAF (Red Army Faction) were all leaders, similar in background, experience, equally unskilled, marginal, drifters on the edge of society. The Germans never expanded but when the Italians did, often without plan or control, the new commanders were not unlike the founding fathers. In the case of many of the tiny Latin American *focos*, the leader was simply the moving force in the beginning, the magnet of desire that attracted the like-minded. He was the one who sought out a few needed talents and began the walk into the wilds. Guzmán wrote his own text and the first generation university students took it to the illiterates. A generation later he was removed from the scene but the validity of the text was still important, the faith under siege still vital. Grivas fashioned EOKA in his own image. Begin took what he needed and gave direction and moral urgency. Always the followers feel they have merely authorized the obvious, turned to the most faithful.

The skills and talents of the leadership inevitably are greater than the average volunteer in the rebel organization, usually more political than military. The larger the movement the more representative the skills. A national resistance can turn not only to talent – engineers and doctors and chemists – but also to those more skilled in organization, in military operations, in the deployment of underground assets. When the militia at Lexington and Concord went home after defending their rights against the regulars, there were all sorts of talent available to organize, to organize not an armed struggle but a real war.

By and large most armed struggles begin small, depend on themselves. Since those attracted to the armed struggle are largely converts to a dream, young, idealists, seeking, their movement is so led, by the young, idealists. A few, like the young in Cuba or Cyprus, may be attracted by a leader and others, like the recruits to the Irgun, may co-opt an elder; but most must make do with themselves even as they speak for the people or the nation. They speak for the multitude of the faithful who largely are ignorant or negligent of that faith.

So, as in all else, the involved seek faith, good character, a singleness of purpose, personal virtue, dedication and sacrifice, not skill and talent. Somehow they know their own, recognize the spirit at work. When skilled, like Grivas, or charismatic like Che, or talent is found in Begin or political capacity in Arafat, the aura of faith still shimmers over the leader. The marginal and pretentious scholar, a dry provincial academic in Peru's *altiplano* becomes rival to Mao and to Marx. At times the charisma is obvious even to the alien. At times the charm works only on the committed. And at times there is no charm, no charisma, only determination and purpose and a sense of bottled power.

The leader, however chosen, is not a type. Some may be charismatic but one society's charisma is another's flummery. And even within one society, in one struggle various types emerge, may indicate differing appeals – George Habash and Arafat are different and rivals, so too were Makarios and Grivas. Often one generation of the IRA is rival to the next, one republican faction led not by a clone but an opposite. Still, there are analytical pigeon holes – charisma here and operational ability there, persistence and charm and managerial skill – or a mix. Most leaders are middle class, males – Arafat an engineer, Grivas and Sadat officers, Eduardo Mondlane in Mozambique was a professor, the Italians and Germans were often students, Che was a doctor and so too was George Habash, Castro and Begin lawyers, Camilo Torres a priest, Collins a clerk, Eamon de Valera a mathematics teacher.

This is not always so and at times mere talent or simple necessity produces leadership. Most of the Provisional IRA is composed of the working class – a few having worked at nothing but the Irish revolution for a generation. All of these leaders were very different in other ways, each a special person embedded in a special history and at times not even a type admired by the many. De Valera, unlike Collins, was no traditional Irish rebel, wit and talent and a drink with the lads but a cold, austere figure with a foreign name. The first leader of the Provisional IRA, Seán MacStiofáin, was a dour, dark man without the soft word – and born English in North London without any Irish connection; John Stephenson was like neither Collins nor de Valera. Any set of leaders in a single organization, from a single class and category is different.

The IRA has persisted for much of the century and the Chief of Staff has reflected both Irish republicans and the variety of the Irish. The movement has been led by the authoritarian and the quiet, a consensus man and a simple soldier, by various personalities, various accents and ages, various trades and experience. The movement has increasingly become short on elegance and education but the leadership has always been sound on republican ideals. For the generations different but similar Irish republican galaxies have had a different leader for different purposes but all such leaders were first Irish, even if Irish by conversion. And as the republican world narrowed after 1946, the leadership has been the same and different, narrow of belief, limited in skills, a school teacher, a journalist, a painting contractor, usually men of no property, often talent denied, and always men with intense conviction, all different, all different from their ideological ancestors – except in their singleness of purpose.

Leaders tend to be different in most matters that figure in a sociological profile but as one on dedication and conviction. Grivas was not like every other Greek. He, an arrogant and egotistical man, intolerant of dissent, in many ways traditional not revolutionary, orthodox, narrow, was devoted to his own, not a leader for all times or all people but for his Cypriot secret army of young, provincial men. His persona was transformed into a traditional Greek paterfamilias and so his limitations became assets and he a comfort to his EOKA volunteers as well as a painstaking, shrewd, and determined operational commander. His leadership was very much for one time, one place, one small galaxy – and when he tried again a decade later the exercise aborted.

Whatever the personality and predilections of the leader, he must in some role be one of his own, at ease among the faithful, neither an imported gun nor an alien presence. There is among the involved a tendency to stress the faith and the character of the chosen especially, neglecting those other factors that might play a role: class or caste, the nature of the rebel constituency, the need for visibility or reputation. Some rebels, like those who traveled with Guevara, simply chose to ignore the arena, their constituency, entirely, placing their hopes in the intensity of the faith visible in their leader. Others solve problems involved in selecting leaders without reference to the parameters of choice. Some movements have to solve problems that are best not admitted – religion or the family or gender has been finessed in internal discussions but still remains a consideration. The leaders of the African liberation movements had to factor in the tribal composition in every decision, even when applying scientific socialism and so could hardly discuss such primitive matters openly.

More than the conventional, the rebel must tread warily about particulars and visibly appeal only to the general faith. The wise leader will know that Mao's doctrine is not applicable to his peasants or that the Little Red Book has no chapter on tribal loyalties just as Mao knew all about the Mandate of Heaven. The foolish leader insists on the ideal. Wise or foolish, the leadership is most concerned about the purity and application of the faith and thus the strategic analysis. The later, focused on the grand issues, the reading of history, the will of the galaxy, seldom determines the tactical options and operational issues that dominated the life and time of the leadership.

The strategy, somewhat like the faith, is the medium for all action; needs to exist, be energized; is the focus of the leader often at the cost of tactical advantage. Yet rebel strategy is simple, based on a few unchanging assumptions and the text of the dream. The leaders are charged not with strategic decisions but with persisting against all odds, escalating without schism or disaster, pursuing the struggle while radiating confidence and assurance on the course of history – an agenda of the dream and the details.

The leadership may be, often is in a large movement, different from those led, not so much older or wiser as from a different class, the workers and peasants are usually led by lawyers and graduate students. When the movement begins large, the leaders may be those judged competent – past military experience, a profession, the voice of lions or the wisdom of years. The tiny band of faithful, *Action Directe* in France, the Japanese Red Army, or Fatah at first, may be both leaders and followers. Often one man – Grivas or the Mufti of Jerusalem, an ambitious African professional in a colonial backwater or a pious symbol with great ambition like Ayatollah Ruhollah Khomeini – begins and dominates, acts as point zero for the galaxy. In Egypt, when the conspiracy of the Free Officers came to power in 1952, their leader, their own, Gamal Abdel Nasser was thought too young, too unknown for the entire constituency, the Egyptian nation; and so for a time an elder, a leader in title, General Mohammed Naguib, was established. Nasser was leader of the secret army – the Free Officers – and so most of the organizations of governance and almost all of the movement, those dedicated to change through the military but not yet the national constituency. Most rebels have few such qualms about their constituency, their faith, their capacity. And in Egypt in 1954, Lieutenant Colonel Nasser, former conspirator rather than rebel, took charge. Within a year he had become leader of all, the officers, the organizations of governance, the movement, the galaxy that included not simply the Egyptians but many Arabs – the avowed constituency had grown enormously but Nasser was by then involved in the overt world of politics and diplomacy, conventional power. The world of orthodox power is quite different from the underground during an armed struggle.

In the end leaders are those most faithful, most dedicated, the sound and sensible and persistent, those capable of the long haul and largely devoid of the more visible signs of ambition and pretension. In many movements there is a reluctant acceptance by the rebel of leadership, a duty not a joy that cannot be denied and assures only misery, sacrifice, and danger all made irrelevant by the promise of the faith. Others find in themselves the only possible leader. Sometimes the party decided and sometimes all the small congregation lead as one. Vanity may play a part but conventional prospects, even the hope of prominence, even with a faith in history's verdict, are usually faint. Command of the underground is not an attractive career choice although for a very few it brings fame, fortune or even power. Not all leaders are pure; some are arrogant and ambitious, some identify the cause with their rebel career but many accept leadership as duty not reward. And no matter how various the leaders, how similar the gunmen and guerrillas, how diverse the profile of the followers, all are alike in the commitment to the compelling ideal.

IN SUM

Those who pursue the armed struggle are special in that they have been in some way touched by a special dream that requires service, which tends to prove its own reward. Those within the underground vary enormously, not so much within each single ecosystem, where they tend to provide a singular profile even if they may not represent either the galaxy of believers or the avowed constituency, but with other systems, other armed struggles. And just as Italian sociology students are not much like Sicilian peasants so any Italian is not much like any Lebanese or Tamil. There may, then, be a profile for each movement. And each movement usually contains those who would fit similar movements: other armies – gunmen and guerrillas – tend to be young and fit and eager. What makes the individuals engaged in an armed struggle especially similar is their faith and their use of the gun. Much that they do, much that they organize, many operations, most tactical and strategic decisions are forced on the leaders by the environment, by the nature of the underground, and by the institutions of the enemy-state. These molds are forced down upon enormously diverse individuals, mostly middle-class males who lead their own or those less skilled, little different from everyday soldiers.

To share a faith, one that contradicts and often conflicts with that of another rebel, imposes a pattern on each individual. Sometimes it is not a very demanding pattern or long-lived, but no matter how special each individual pilgrim in the underground has many things in common. In a sense at times they have more in common with others underground also possessed of a contradictory dream than they do with their own leading conventional lives. The underground, the nexus of perception and reality, confined by risk and heated by the energy of the faith, the terror of operations, the exhilaration of action imprints each individual, every leader, in a way few other experiences can or will.

Still, almost no individual and hardly any leader is merely a profile, simply a die stamped out by the armed struggle, not just a guerrilla or a gunman but rather this guerrilla or that gunman, tall or short, trained or not, Irish or Japanese, bold or diffident, different from all others and the same. Some are hardly moved by the dream and others driven to desperation by the same ideal. And they are led by their own, equally devout, equally diverse, even more unlike the other commanders underground – and yet too often the same.

NOTE

1   In response to critical letters arising from his article 'Making a Killing: The High Cost of Peace in Northern Ireland', *Harper's*, in February 1994, Scott Anderson, who suggests that the Irish paramilitaries are driven in considerable part by the profit motive, noted that 'Political science professors can argue forever about the root cause of any war, but in my experience this intellectual exercise has little application on the ground. Having spent time with guerrillas and soldiers in a half-dozen war zones around the world, I've come to the rather depressing conclusion that most young men don't pick up assault rifles or throw bombs out of any passionately held belief or political awareness but simply because it is more exciting than working the family rice paddy or sitting at home to watch reruns of *Coronation Street*.'

  And in considerable part this may indeed be the case especially in the midst of irregular wars that attract and deploy the many; but it is also true about many regular soldiers who enlist to see the world or to get out of town – and may not profess patriotism to a passing journalist. Some guerrillas, of course, are eager to explain the ideal and so too are nearly all of the leaders, who are truly driven to an armed struggle by perceived, often by real, grievances not the profit motive. Protracted struggles may be profitable for some and supply variety and adventure for the many, but as most soldiers are patriotic so most gunmen and guerrillas are touched by the aspirations of the ideal – a not always very pleasant ideal but always one that shapes the armed struggle.

7

Organization

To WAGE an armed struggle the individual rebels must adapt or create appropriate structures for the galaxy of the faithful, for the movement and all its operations, and especially for gunmen and guerrillas. What is wanted is a form for the dream. Organized structure matters, should aid the rebel, always exists, inherited, cobbled together, or shaped to theory. Generally those involved give the form little thought, often none. Especially at the beginning the combination of urgency, the power of the dream, and the rationale for action attract all the attention. Few then are aware that often the organization already exists – the few are organized by their desperation and determination. The others assume that the old party will do or the central committee or the leader of the *foco* will run the campaign or do not bother to assume at all but simply begin the shooting and so let events organize the struggle.

THE ORGANIZATIONAL FOCUS

Although not any old form will do, sometimes an old form will, indeed, do. The rebel structure is apt to be the one to hand. This ready-made structure may reflect the reality of the arena or may be selected from the existing menu of fashion. The leaders may be organization men but they are not organizational theorists. They are already bonded by their faith and tend to assume this adequate for the moment for such ties are indicated in the organization before entry into the underground. It is generally apparent that the movement – the visible faith – needs special form during the armed struggle and so those responsible use what they know, what they assume proper, at times what is comfortable or what is fashionable. This is almost always done as an aside to what are assumed more significant matters, escalation, armament, publicity or operations.

Some rebels fine-tune the dream to the arena, to the other actors, to visible experience and tangible factors. Others are content with the model of the moment. For the pragmatic the physical possibilities and the cultural climate become more important by far than any theoretical exegeses. If there is to be a liberated zone or the urban riots are to be exploited, if there is no hope of decent cover, if the dry season matters or the dates of the long rains, then the shape of the rebel structure must be amenable to the task. The limitations of the stage as well as the opportunities for action must be considered. The rebel must find a balance between the incandescence of the dream and the hard edges of the arena – like most else in the underground not a problem with a solution. It is also, like much else in the underground, seldom addressed directly.

The Irish republicans, the archetype, consciously or not, of many contemporary movements, have been since Fenian times in the nineteenth century organized as a conspiracy empowered by history to wage war in the name of the Irish people. The dream, the Republic, was almost established in Irish hearts so that the secret Supreme Council of the Irish Republican Brotherhood was in theory the legitimate government of Ireland. The 1916 Rising required structure for physical force. The central committee of the IRB, engaged in a coup, organized and directed a militia-army – the Irish Volunteers and allies. Failure in 1916 produced, unexpectedly, a rush to insurrection, a vast expansion of the secret army, rapid escalation on many fronts, and a lessening of control by the IRB in the new mix of agencies and activities. Events moved beyond the easy control of any IRB conspiracy but the core of the armed struggle remained the volunteers organized as the IRA. What emerged was a counter-state dominated by the IRA and certain charismatic individuals. The IRA split over the implications of the Anglo-Irish Treaty accepted by the Dáil, the Irish Parliament elected by using the Westminster elections of 1918. There followed an internecine irregular war.

What emerged from the struggle between the IRA and the emerging Irish Free State was a defeat for the 'irregulars'. The survivors dumped arms and went underground as a covert, illicit secret army. This IRA, dedicated to physical force and separate from any other republican organization, was still structured as a democratic conspiracy. A new constitution was drafted and accepted and has with adjustments been the basis for the IRA since the 1920s. The secret army's elected representatives formally met in regular Army Conventions and elected delegates who chose an Executive who selected the seven-man Army Council who appointed the Chief-of-Staff. In practice the core of the secret army made the decisions, dominated the selection process, and guided events until schism. Thus the IRA has been organized as a democratic conspiracy, tempered by schism, whose leadership retains the often rather vestigial legitimacy of the republic as declared on Easter Monday 1916 and since denied by force and betrayed by the pragmatic.

What remained after 1949, when the Dublin government proclaimed a republic, was a small, secret army mimicking the once huge IRA of 1921. This IRA absorbed the few remaining and wasted republican assets like Sinn Féin and the new *United Irishman* newspaper, and sponsored the traditional groups like the youth movement, Fianna Éireann. The movement then moved on toward another campaign. The IRA leaders kept what had been inherited, tinkering with details from time to time, and the new volunteer took what was offered, a form fitted for the past but, therefore, a comfort; but both felt the better for the inherited forms, forms that were maintained by the Provisional IRA after the split in 1969.

THE STRUCTURE ORGANIZED

A movement may be very grand or very small, be small and grow large or the reverse. And the small must be organized differently from the large whatever the ideal may suggest. A great many armed struggles begin small. Even then, at the beginning, there is always the problem of simple cohesion. Although some groups are concentrated, can be ruled by all, others, equally small, must be managed over large areas.

Even a large organization faces difficulties in coping with distance and control no matter what means are used. The IRA GHQ in 1938 and 1939 could exert little control over the actual English bombing campaign other than to send over reinforcements and material and read the results in the newspapers. A generation later the Official IRA in Dublin usually learned what was happening to their volunteers in Northern Ireland on the evening television news. Some Palestinian groups after 1968, limited to reading the newspapers, simply claimed credit for operations that *ought* to have been theirs. Control far from GHQ must be left to the local or to consensus.

What is needed for organizational control is obviously the *means* to control. A form that will allow the armed struggle to function at a distance. The form must supply a medium for contact and so control. Contact is important, vital and must be effectively deployed. What works, works quickly but at risk because contact can be monitored – telephones, cables, even the mails. What does not work, messengers or a return to command central, works slowly. As usual there is no happy solution. Some small groups operate without close control and some take the risk to permit tuning event to intent. There is no solution either in a single arena or over great distances so commanders tend to balance the need for visible operations with the need to maintain intimate control. Mostly, however, organizing assets on a wide arena is a problem of the large and although still without solution is more amenable to the assets of large or escalating movements.

All groups, even the tiny, must be structured in practice to control the operational direction of the secret army. Sometimes the target determines not just the strategy and the tactics but also the form. If there is a perceived vulnerability the rebel with a given set of assets must adjust these in order to act. If Israel is not vulnerable to guerrilla revolution, then the organization must opt for terror and so another form. The task may impose structure on a secret army just as may the arena or the reality of the moment. The Provisional IRA with a role as defender grew from the initial core into an all but visible militia that when times changed was driven back underground into cells.

Small groups have special internal dynamics. Small covert groups tend to intensify these factors – especially when illegal, underground, operating under great stress and with constant risk of betrayal from within or without.

Once the movement begins to grow in size, often without commensurate intensity in the armed campaign, there is a new set of problems. In 1968–69 the Palestinian organizations had a great influx of volunteers at the very time the guerrilla penetration campaign began to falter. In the Spanish Sahara the base for an armed struggle was found only in the exiles scattered in Algeria. In Zimbabwe the guerrillas often swept up recruits, some eager, some not, and took them back to exile bases to be trained. Mostly, however, the problem is simply that whatever the bounds and pressures and peculiarities, the secret army may grow too large to fit the old form.

A protracted campaign often encourages organizational stress to develop – doing nothing or accepting more of the same may not prove possible. In South Africa the evolution of negotiation revealed stresses between the internal and external ANC leadership, between the militant guerrillas and those inclined to negotiation, between tribal loyalties, ideological attractions, between classes, between the city and the country. All to be expected and ameliorated because in reality the ANC was small, distant, and largely ineffectual while central political power was isolated in the person of Nelson Mandela in prison. Thus the organization and heritage of the long and hardly viable armed struggle was subsumed in the internal confrontation with African rivals and Afrikaner interests during the end-game.

In South-West Africa the nationalist leadership was tribal but dominant and conciliatory so that Namibia escaped post-liberation schism. As in Zimbabwe the guerrilla-liberation leadership simply took over new responsibilities and the old secret army was discarded. There was no problem. There are fewer organizational problems in Africa when tribal dynamics, regional interests and personal capacity were – and are – reflected in the function of the liberation movement whatever the wall chart may indicate.

THE ORGANIZATION CONFIRMED

Most movements reach particular accommodations to the general impact of size and arena, growth and decline, that if not always successful at least have been visible. Failed organizations seldom leave much evidence of disaster and any organizational vulnerabilities are rarely of great interest even to the victors.

Each movement is different and some are very different. Grivas ruled his army as a Greek patriarch and Begin was the oldest brother and a moral leader. The African nationalists fashioned counter-states that were often riven by tribal loyalties that had to be ignored for ideological reasons as the leaders deployed the powers and prestige of traditional leadership.

The Provisional IRA's Belfast Brigade on a chart is part of a secret army but it is organized on the ground as a mix of a secular *Opus Dei* with murder around the margins just as the units in the countryside more closely resemble night riders. The Protestant loyalists resplendent with titles – Ulster Volunteer Force or Red Hand Commandos – are neither secret armies nor really even defenders but rather vigilantes waiting for an opportunity to commit sectarian murder – a posse of hard men drinking in the upstairs room of a pub as comfortable in their structure as is the IRA unit on parade.

Arabs seem to work best structured by charisma or through consensus – George Habash of the Popular Front as ideological team leader, part image and part explanation and Yasser Arafat as the agreed center, moderator and gyroscope. There might be one Palestinian movement that shared the main dream and the same enemy; but it was scattered across several intra-galactic systems each composed of organizations that spun about in opposition to the others. Hamas, as is appropriate for traditional Moslems, is structured on the congregation of a mosque – not easy to chart but effective.

What works best for the rebel is what comes naturally. A tribal revolt requires no organizational change, no new dream structure, but only cover to allow escalation. The warriors take to the hills, direction, prospects and operations shaped by the assets of the arena. Some rebels simply take the tribe or the party or the congregation underground. Some rebellions have no problem at all with theory, simply following the practice of the past if, perhaps, under new banners. Some announce a secret army but direct a family or a corporation, a congregation or a community of the saved, a guerrilla column or friends ready to lend a murderous hand.

TYPOLOGIES AND UNDERGROUND REALITY

The analysts of insurrection and revolt have sought to devise categories and types. The problem, as always, is that the armed struggle even as an organizational matter tends to be elusive. Just as all living things can be divided into those with wings and those without, so too can rebels be divided by ideology or size or social class, by the nature of the leadership or the intensity of the campaign; but this reveals very little about the organizational imperative.

There are also a great many general organizational factors that fall outside many typologies – in particular how the movement truly works rather than what the chart indicates. And then how the organization so functioning is shaped by the arena. Many of those involved are apt to believe, certainly in retrospect, that the formal structure was the real structure – the cells worked, commanders moved units and decisions were democratic. Yet the arena is often accepted as a given, the terrain an obstacle, the cultural medium, not as a theoretical asset but a practical hurdle. These are special arena conditions, seldom found in an atlas and often integrated into rebel analysis without great thought.

These unarticulated factors of the arena often in great part determine the structure of the dream, impose a function if not a form, are various but always present. Each rebel must, of course, consciously consider the arena. The terrain, the special needs imposed by cover, the nature of the government's control and capacity, the historical ethos that legitimizes certain structures all matter – matter a great deal.

Often insurrection in the countryside, however organized, works because the state-center does not want to invest in eradicating such distant dissent, even armed dissent. Thus once an acceptable level of violence is imposed the far edges of the arena do not matter.

Insurrection in the city often works because a few of the dedicated how-ever organized can cause enormous turmoil. And urban violence tends to work or be closed down, for chaos near the center is less tolerable whether organized as riot or conspiracy. In all this the arena, both the physical battle zone and the cultural limits and opportunities, plays a role and may well impose form.

More likely the ideology, either universal or local, will come with a strategic model to be applied any place, any time with only a few reasonable adjustments to the arena. Thus general ideas about organization – the vanguard party as the cutting edge of practice or the terrorist cell of equals as the next radical option – may convert the acolyte rebel.

As the campaign escalates or the enemy falters, as the tide finally shifts, the underground may grow, husband not a conspiracy, not a secret army, but all the potential assets of a state. A secret army like the NLF in Aden may go directly from the armed struggle, gunmen smelling of cordite, into power in the palace, first execute their local rivals and then rule. Others build up along the way, even over the short haul like Castro, so that power is achieved by a rebel army – of sorts – or by the irregular army of the counter-state.

What does happen is that the movement shifts from the illicit to the recognized, from the unconventional through the irregular to power and changes. The change to the conventional is difficult, for the movement underground seeks to transform a dream into reality and when reality arrives in the form of power the dream must be institutionalized – not at all the same thing as an armed struggle. So the more conventional the more the organization must adjust as the function shifts – often shifts without the leadership noting the change.

In the underground during an armed struggle *any* change is a problem, a serious obstacle. More can cause trouble and less is certain to do so. How to cope with an influx of donated arms may be a welcome problem but it is a problem none the less. These organizational changes forced on the leaders are most unwelcome. Thus when the movement is forced to give up the military structure for cells or go from cells to a military structure, there are problems, risks, anguish, danger.

And if the underground is filled with imperatives and factors and the aura of individuals, there exist as well the contingent and the unforeseen, the fortuitous: the arrival of unexpected talent that must be deployed by new means, the conversion of the constituency, the death of this one or that. Theory seldom factors in chance but an underground is so vulnerable and so eager for evidence of success that luck matters. And luck that is so important operationally, often matters organizationally – the right man in the right place counts.

The end result of all these factors is not really a typology but rather an insight into the considerations that operate on rebel organization practice – not to mention theory. Any category will yield certain groups – rural communist insurgences or urban ethnic guerrillas – but a single schemata that reveals rather than lists does not seem to be available. Everything matters although some things matter more than others. The ideological ideal, the reality of the arena, the direction and intensity of the armed struggle have long been major analytical concerns. Less attention has been paid to the implications of size, the impact of operational options or the nature of life underground; but these, too, play a part. Generally, there is a balance between the tangible and the perceptions of the involved, between theory and practice.

STRUCTURAL FUNCTION

No matter what organizational variants exist in theory or in practice, no matter the factors that shape such structures, the rebels must cope with the real world. Organizations are always less than ideal, are always faulty and any adjustment painful, often too dangerous to risk and always too uncertain to warrant enthusiasm. Thus most movements put off until tomorrow what might best have been done the day before, tinker rather than resort to surgery.

The command center

Regardless of theory or practice or the actual chart of authority, an armed struggle and so, usually, the movement and the galaxy, must have leadership. Even in a central committee or a high command control rests at the head of the table. The first ring of command and control in most central organi-zations is in regular touch, meet regularly, are in contact on evolving events. When those in the field, those at a distance, those out of touch are powerful, deploying assets, controlling a campaign or a column, must act independently, the organization usually has found a way to control at a distance.

The way to control the margins is almost always less than ideal, either imposing too rigid a control that prevents exploiting local advantage or allowing too great a freedom so that those without instruction often operate without response to new policy directions. For the central commanders to operate with the gunmen or guerrillas means the rest of the organization must cope without them. Real armies have these problems but real armies have more assets and more practice. Sometimes in the underground there is an organizational solution, sometimes the movement simply accepts the stress and dispute as natural, beyond accommodation.

The center always, however, dislikes dissent; for argument over organizational details has a tendency to evolve into arguments over the application and meaning of the dream. All disputation underground tends to be expressed in ideological language – certainly the prerogatives of the center are so defended. Dissent is divisive. Dissent is also inevitable – the necessity for cover means that the organization must struggle to meet, to ease potential dispute, to discuss – and possession of the dream means that even when the movement is tiny, a few gathered together in a borrowed apartment, a *foco* in the bush, there is disputation made intense by personal conviction.

Strict formal control from central command, often control that accurately follows the appropriate organizational chart, is not the only effective means or often the most desirable means to direct an underground organization. Many organizations arise from a general consensus so detailed that any gunmen will always know appropriate targets, proper behavior without orders. Some movements dedicated to the most detailed ideological principles function because of the charisma of a single leader whose articulation of the faith disguises the impact of his person.

At times over past generations, the Irish republican movement has been firmly directed from the center, the formal chart indicating an underground reality, and at others has run on momentum and local initiative. The secret army was generally run either as an underground army or as a centralized conspiracy labeled an underground army. The movement had evolved in such a way that a general consensus on most relevant matters evolved – decades underground in the company of the faithful imposed habits and assumptions that did not require orders to evoke. When the center was weak or isolated, this consensus allows the secret army to deploy, act, and assess without much guidance.

A different response, if not any more of a general organizational prospect, has been that of the Palestinians, a large, diffuse, contentious community, poorly adapted to easy acquiescence and self-discipline. There have been the strains of exile, the complications of the cultural area, the skills of the opponent and the diverse problems of acting as a recognized counter-state, all more visible than effective accommodations by the fedayeen. What was done is to mingle the consensus monitored by Arafat with the charisma of the individual leaders with the variety of forms that have evolved over a generation. Then came the Intifada.

The rise of the Intifada placed severe stress on the center around Arafat isolated from events that the Gaza–Jericho agreement has not eased as Hamas has arisen, closer to his presence but closed to his control. The effort to impose the PLO on top of the Intifada was tolerated by the involved because the Intifada was more process than organization. The creation of a Gaza–Jericho structure produced even more problems: the evolving organizations are overt, formal, recognized. Increasingly both the PLO and Arafat could not maintain the illusion that there was one Palestinian movement identical to the galaxy complicated only by a few loose guerrillas with eccentric orbits. Hamas operations have made this clear.

At times the battle arena for varying reasons has encouraged similar competition that has not produced a single command core at all. The galaxy is large, the movement general, but the organizational structures are isolated in all but ultimate goal. In Italy, Afghanistan, the Punjab, the armed struggle has been a matter of many, often competing, secret armies usually with one general goal. In Italy the neo-fascists and the extra-parliamentary communists were enemies but pursuing different goals by different means that had the same strategic effect. Both created turmoil and tensions seeking the collapse of the center, but both together engendered insufficient turmoil and tension to allow to control the future.

Command requirements

A rebel organization must appear legitimate to the involved, may even have to be shaped to appear legitimate to those opposed to the vision. There is more to an armed struggle than organizing the use of arms. Even the smallest group of rebels has an organizational chart, has a command center and announced lines of control and departments for this and panels for that. If there are more places than pigeons to fill the holes, then the pigeons are assigned more roles. If a uniform assures arrest or death, then it is worn in secret, kept for photo-opportunities. An organization, whatever else, must not only be a comfort, have a leader, be effective, but stand as a symbol of legitimacy.

Thus secret armies often appear afflicted with titles and ranks and pretensions of glory. During the era of the guerrilla, rebels seeking the legitimacy that the myth proffered, wanted to look like guerrillas even at the risk of their lives. In the countryside real guerrillas wear raggedy clothing – ancient trousers, Chicago Bulls T-shirts, never carry guns if possible, and look like everyone else. The romantic rebel wanted a black beret, camouflage suit and an AK-47 so as to look like a guerrilla, look like a guerrilla in the mirror, to his friends and admirers. So, too, do secret armies display the structure of the legitimate and often appear afflicted with delusions of grandeur. There are military titles and ranks, special insignia, red berets or black or blue, pins and pomp, military parades and formal roll calls. In some degree the more elaborate and unlikely the pretensions, the shallower the military legitimacy.

The hooded captains and commanders of the Ulster Volunteer Force, cheap suits embellished with pins of the faith, sometimes appear in home-made uniforms that cover their recourse to sectarian murder as politics. In real life they are hard men, working-class bigots. Their hands worn and stained tobacco-yellow splayed across a deal table, their voices grating with the Belfast accent, they can hardly explain their strategy to the media much less make real a force out of what is a vigilante mob in waiting. Sometimes they can kill Irish republicans but mostly they make do with Irish Catholics and rationalizations legitimized by self-awarded titles and forms.

Each command-center in order to pursue an armed struggle must perform certain functions, whether specifically designated to individuals or groups or in small sects passed about without regard to specialties. The leaders must lead, must be selected by appropriate means with recognized criteria, must offer through example and structure legitimacy, but most of all must use the organization to pursue the armed struggles. The organization must also be a comfort if not an unalloyed delight.

Generally, there is an over-all commander, an adjutant, and individuals assigned to plan operations and often lead them, an intelligence officer, someone charged with responsibility for money, another for arms – acquisition, storage, maintenance, deployment, often someone concerned with publicity and another with recruits and training. Some commanders may do everything, some have no other choice. The Italian *brigati* leaders dabbled in ordinary duties but as acts of grace. Small organizations tend to subsume all facets of the struggle under each operation – those involved cope with the needs of the moment without much aid or comfort from central command – a command that is often one man in hiding.

These commanders are various, culturally diverse, individually often at odds with theory but in practice they work or they are replaced. In some cases they may work so well that their rivals leave and emulate them in cloned organizations. What must work is the armed struggle and that generally means waging war with limited assets in unconventional ways against a powerful and legitimate adversary. There is never a solution to this challenge.

Underground administration is also different from the conventional: the leader must not give orders that will be refused; no records may be kept; all the galaxy may be involved in intelligence, not just a special unit. Communication may not be by message-units but by simultaneous interpretation of operations – internal propaganda of the deed. What is needed underground is clear enough, but how it is organized is not a mirror image of the real, orthodox world. The storage of arms is not simply a matter of a group finding a warehouse but of the faithful performing a service so that the movement benefits doubly. What is clear is that such matters are complicated and often determined not by simple function but by the needs of the faith.

Action and form

It is the capacity to act on events that matters in an armed struggle – or rather the perception that this power exists. To do so the organization may be comfortable, may encourage the faith and hearten the volunteer, may be for the long run and need no adjustment but must ensure that the armed struggle persists. Most divisions within an underground are argued out in terms of the faith not function. The clash of personalities or the size of a cell are matters of truth. Mostly the volunteers are in agreement with the existing form of the struggle – brigades or columns or conspiracy. Most volunteers come in at the bottom and have no interest in such matters, accepting existing reality. Most commanders present at the creation assume that the form once chosen is a minor matter. That form may be subject of dispute later; but everyone concerned knows that the real dispute is over control of the truth, over power, not the size of an executive committee. So organization is simply accepted or at worst tolerated.

Almost no rebel movement can spare too much time contemplating the organizational techniques. What is needed is to persist. What is hoped is to escalate. What is crucial is tomorrow: short views again. How does the organization function now is the real question. And the answer is usually 'not very well' – not well enough but adequately for immediate purpose. And in this at least, the rebel's posture is both logical – what choice is there – and in retrospective analysis astute. No organization formula can solve the problems of the underground. Most forms do not hinder command, do offer control and legitimacy, sometimes are a comfort, and rarely are a burden. This is because the form and the function at the center of the galaxy are not truly the same as the chart suggests – the Italian cells, the Irish Republican Army or the hunted bands of the Mau Mau in Kenya were like all else underground – shaped as much by perception as by reality. They function effectively because the form is congenial, often traditional, cunningly adjusted for a new and violent use. Even the Mau Mau organized by the security presence as hunted big game continued to frighten the hunters.

IN SUM

Those organizations that function most effectively in the underground are comfortable, have devised a form to the armed struggle that erodes ineffi-ciency, eases anguish, and encourages escalation. The leadership legitimately chosen and authorized by the faith must perform certain activities that are needed in an armed struggle, must organize and array the limited assets available, and must deploy the results from underground against the enemy so that the dream can persist. There is no real ideal structure for an armed struggle – often the best is none at all – nor any great interest in finding one by those concerned. What is wanted is legitimacy and capacity. This is more likely if the structure is culturally congenial, not weighted by theory over practice, by idealized form over the reality of the arena. What works works. What is wanted is a means to transform the dream into reality, a means that enhances the dream and assures ultimate victory.

8

Command and Control

IN THE conventional world, commanders control. They plan, deploy, and control. The rebel analyzes, risks limited assets, and exhorts. In the underground before there can be command, there must be control. And control arises not from institutions or even physical force but from a variety of factors, most importantly from the shared dream.

Rebels with a dream often seek control, are eager to be commanded, to be used and deployed. Thus, at times underground control may be easy and every command met with enthusiasm. The leader, however, operates within the bounds of unarticulated but real factors that shape such enthusiasm. The potential commander must adjust to those factors and those factors must or may be altered in reality or through perception to the necessities of command, to the demands of the campaign. The leader must balance what is desired with what can be accomplished – and the latter is not a constant nor easily determined.

Most rebel ecosystems are in considerable part controlled through the inevitable consensus that arises from the faith and is strengthened by the obvious requirements of the armed struggle. Such responses may be automatic but soon may become institutionalized: in Northern Ireland cities and towns the clanging of dust bins to warn that the security forces were intruding into nationalist areas began spontaneously, became the conventional means of alert and ultimately rite and ritual with the old metal bin lids painted in patriotic colors kept for display as well as use. And so security intrusions generated a response without need of command and one that required no control.

Armed struggles are not simply reactive nor self-governing. Control must be exerted by individuals, by those with the charisma to lead by example or by force of character. Despite the domination of these positive factors no armed struggle can endure for long without the promise or the reality of punishment. Recourse to force to impose discipline and obedience runs from exhortation and shame to the execution of the recalcitrant with some movements more prone to the harsh than others – because of the arena, historical experience, the necessity of the moment or personal pre-dilection. Negative sanctions must be used most sparingly in a volunteer army of pilgrims eager to sacrifice and obey. Some commanders are hardly aware that such discipline may be needed. Others seemingly seek reassurance in a troubled world through use of force to maintain order – especially true when the movement is small, sometimes very small, and maintained by charisma.

No commander wants a simple order to engender heresy or schism. Suspected dissents may, usually do, prevent such orders from being issued: the sense of the possible. Commanders do give orders, do command and do control – but often with great care. The charismatic may not imagine dissent – until the schism comes – and the mundane may not reflect on the prospect – until the gunmen resist – but mostly any rebel leader knows the limits. One leads by example. One commands as a result of purpose and energy and faith. The commands may put a volunteer into harm's way but must do so appropriately, the target valid, the operation reasonable, the dream unsullied and the potential real.

In all cases, the crucial difficulty arises when an order is given within the underground. What of dissent? What risk is there of denial? What if there is a refusal? What if the guerrilla won't go, the gunman refuses to shoot? What if the militant insists on shooting, not waiting? In Rome in 1981, Professor Giovanni Senzani, a full-time *Brigate rosse* activist after years as a sleeper, insisted on a major Rome action. He was articulate, dedicated, audacious, was moving underground as a late vocation at the age of 42, a professor immune to argument, a man with assets and aura. Senzani wanted action – an attack on the Christian Democratic party headquarters in Rome. The Executive Committee thought the operation too dangerous. Persuading the reluctant to shoot is difficult but dissuading the determined not to shoot is next to impossible. How deny the militant? Why deny the militant, the determined, the bold? What could be done? Senzani would go ahead if denied, disobey the Executive, split, form his own Roman *Brigate rosse*, open operations and endanger everyone anyway. How could one be punished for audacity, for attacking the very headquarters of the Christian Democratic Party in Rome, at the heart of the state? How could the great virtue of denying oneself, conserving resources, persisting for tomorrow be taught to such a confident militant?

What was done was to incorporate Senzani into the plans for the Winter of Fire operations. If the commanders cannot deny the margins, then co-opt them, give the impression of control that may become reality when a tactical consensus is reached. Punishment was simply not an option; control, like consensus, could not be forced. The leaders simply adjusted to operational reality rather than to objective conditions. Within rebel organizations control is often voluntary, rests on consent and a common faith but not always and especially not when the opportunity to operate without cover exists.

The commanders that are sure to be obeyed must carefully prepare the way by persuasion. Even the charismatic must usually argue change although such argument is exhortation and ritual as much as persuasion. The commanders must, then, always balance the requirements of command, an order, a decision of the Supreme Council or the General Staff, but real persuasion is necessary.

Since commanders are often the most faithful, their own drawn larger, control is often achieved without consideration or confusion. The cunning commander – or the natural one – may know who will do what, who will kill as directed without reflection, and who will not. The killing as ordered also may erode the margins of the galaxy or else extend the ecosystem but simultaneously harden the enemy. There is never a clear road. And those at the center must from time to time choose, command. Those who would argue the point, question the directions from the center may be ordered to be quiet – but at what risk? There is more to orders than sending a volunteer out with a gun. And so the more orders that can be avoided the better – thus the value of the faith that decides all, the consensus that eases all to action, the charisma that leads the doubtful and the uncertain confidently forward. Yet throwing rocks, rioting on demand, resorting to ambush or arson needs structure to be most effective. The Intifada needed control and so commands – certainly Arafat and Fatah needed to appear in control and their commands relevant.

Control cannot be left to military law and practice, cannot be enforced with a gun and resort to coercion, cannot always be assured by individual charm or general agreement on ends. Control must be exerted with care, practice, and subtlety at the expense of other priorities. The rebel commander, far from being free, opportunistic, untrammeled by bureaucracy or government, unrestricted by moral priorities, is narrowly bound by special conditions and consideration that the orthodox can hardly imagine. A secret army invests an enormous amount of time evading direct orders, preferring to repeat yesterday's instructions, hesitating to pay the cost of novelty.

No rebel commander can operate outside the perceptions of the faith nor imagine the faithful refusing the sacrifice and service. Commanders within the galaxy are not disinterested spectators, not strategists operating from a text, not at all conventional military commanders. They, too, are in the grip of a dream. Their orders arise from the vision. Their reality is that of their army.

PERCEPTION AND ANALYSIS OF CORE COMMAND

Nowhere can the differences within rebel movements more easily be found than within the core of the command structure where the dream is most intense, perceptions most adjusted by analysis, and, often, objective reality kept at bay not only by the will of the involved but also because of the structure of the organization. All leaders are both different from others in other movements and from their own – usually even different from their avowed constituency, a constituency that for varying reasons is inclined to deny their efforts in its behalf. Thus the leaders, self-chosen or co-opted by the faithful, are unusual. Their commitment to the faith alone assures that their priorities and agenda differ from the everyday. They do not act to the reasons assumed by analysis, do not act like sensible people, for they are incensed. They cannot be approached easily by analogy or extension or logic. They are different, different in kind not degree.

The rebel commanders are most assuredly different from other underground leaders operating in various cultures and other times. Arabs are different, obviously, from Peruvian Indians, Afghan mujahedeen from Italian neo-fascists or those Italian neo-fascists from the ones in Spain or Germany. The Mufti of Jerusalem, Sheikh Haj Amin Al-Husseini, a Palestinian militant until his death in Lebanon a generation after the Arab Revolt, and guerrilla Father Camilo Torres, killed at age thirty-seven in 1966, while leading his men in the Colombian jungle, were in the same rebel business. Both were clerics of a sort, men of the book. They shared more than is first apparent but were obviously from their titles alone very different. Even when they share Church and language and Latin American arena, one rebel priest is not much like another, much less like a mufti of Jerusalem. And a mufti is not like a mullah.

Each different leader commands differently within a nexus of different assumptions and attitudes not to mention personal predilections. The differences that are most pronounced are not so much the ones easily anticipated – those of culture and language, heritage and arena, but rather the reality of the faith. Each assumes the faith singular and dominant – the content matters not the mere presence. The content makes all different. In matters of command and control, where the very few people at the core matter disproportionately, the differences become exaggerated beyond style and even structure so that the movement and the subsequent deployment and campaign are given a special and particular nature no matter how general the faith or compelling the experience of others.

The leaders, then, share certain not readily apparent logistical and ideological burdens that do give a certain comparative nature to the control of all revolts. Most armed struggles are led from beginning to end by the same individuals. Most leaders stay the course, win or lose. New leaders appear first from schism creating their own structural variant or arise outside the old organizations and pursue different if parallel dreams. Those groups that require new commanders opt for those quite like the old, the next generation rather like the last. The center of most galaxies does not change greatly over short periods – or at times long periods – even if the rest of the faithful drift away.

Most leaders, even those who walk the streets or pretend to be conventional, live circumscribed lives, really live fully only with their own. They rarely if ever meet those without the faith and then not to listen but to instruct. They often seemed divorced from reality.

Thus, leaders' control always reflects the faith. And this faith is voluntary and so is control. The leaders' control arises from the rebel center's moral authority, the power of the faith, and a mix of singleness of purpose, individual charisma and general consensus.

Small movements, almost all movements in the beginning, have few leaders and few followers, and most participate in the building of consensus which is the underground structure of control that will make commands acceptable and ideally largely unnecessary. Commanders rarely can command novelty or with adequate assets and so must risk little, avoid schism, keep the faith first, rely on the unconventional to compensate for operational limitations.

THE LIMITS OF COMMAND

All the rebel movements, ranging from the tiny, a sect in constant caucus, to a counter-state, face similar and insurmountable command problems. The leaders lack resources, the capacity and often the desire to escalate the campaign and so risk the movement. And in the meantime there are the universal problems of operating underground, the struggle to persist, protract the campaign so that the enemy will tire.

There is no solution to command and control within the underground. The leadership almost by definition will be small and unrepresentative, immune to reality, unresponsive, and engaged in directing a campaign without appropriate means of communication and so control. Each command depends on the faith and so the faithful can, often must, judge each not on pragmatic grounds but as witness to the revealed truth. It is easier to do nothing – or nothing very bold. Yet the assets must be deployed, the struggle pursued. The battle edge of the movement, combat, can only be fully controlled with an enormous loss of flexibility and a concomitant rise in resentment: firm control paradoxically often equals loss of control over effective force and so over the faithful. Only when the legitimacy of the commanders is automatically accepted rather than the advantage of operation alternatives is the faith safe in such a situation. Tight control usually prohibits the margins from seizing those operational opportunities. Loose control eviscerates command allowing the margins to act without guidance but often to act in congenial ways. In any case the limited communication in large part imposed by the necessity for cover assures that the center and the margin cannot be in regular, effective, immediate touch. Charisma may work if the leader can personally touch the margins: charisma works well for the small but fades as the needs of secrecy circumscribe the impact of personality.

The leaders of a rebellion cannot lead as they would like – or rarely so. At times the leader's command assures a loss of part of what is to be controlled. Far from being free and easy underground, lethal without restraint or regulation, the leader of an armed struggle feels narrowly confined by the lack of assets and options, the restrictions of secrecy, the fragility of the consensus arising from the dream, the power of the tangible. It is often sufficient merely to protract the struggle – and that by a desperate search for a means sufficiently unconventional that the state will be unprepared. Mostly command appears all limits and few opportunities no matter what the arena or what the structure of control.

THE STRUCTURE

The structure of command and control is everywhere much the same – a core of commanders, sometimes fully underground and sometimes wandering about in plain view in a safe haven or in exile. Most operational commanders who direct secret armies without an exile-base or the advantages that accrue from irregular war rely on cover, hide and seek to pursue the campaign. They operate on the run, stay in hiding even if in plain view.

Most secret armies deploy a few commanders, some operational, and the others to maintain the campaign and the movement: operators, gunman, agents, protesters, and party organizers. There may be many titles that suggest convention and legitimacy – presidents and generals and ambassadors – but mostly the movement is made up of a few at the top and the many involved in pursuing the struggle. Even then the charms of structure, the lure of titles even without authority or capacity is real. Nearly everyone wants to be part of a visible, legitimate whole, a battalion or a branch office or a publicity department, be a sub-editor or a lieutenant or a delegate.

The local commanders, even in large secret armies, are concerned with techniques and operations rather than tactical selection or policy and planning. They have limited airs and graces and few assets. The gunmen rely on maintenance supplied in various degrees by the faithful, some in the secret army, many in the movement, and a few not even in the galaxy. Simultaneously with the campaign a further circle of support exists – often outside control of the leadership of the secret army but always as parallel and at times dominant means to escalate the struggle, accelerate events. Those who riot seldom have party cards. Those who march at the end of the parade are not members of the secret army but those who read the banners and walk the mile. They are unasked, unstructured volunteers to the ideal.

Almost all movements have two foci, those who are in name responsible for the faith at the center and those further out toward the edge engaged in good works. The existence of a dream does not impose rules of command, but the necessity for an underground ecosystem assures the problems of commanding will be universal. There is no universally appropriate form, only a universal problem. And that problem to control the galaxy is only one organizational challenge. In fact the thousands of movements do not have many options as how to organize. If they need cover, then the covert world permits only so many effective options. The party or the *foco* or the front must adjust to secrecy, the pressure of the state, the limits of the faith – and there are only so many ways to do so.

In most undergrounds the central core of command is small, separate from the many on the margins by distance, by poor communications and differing priorities, and by the necessities of secrecy. The leadership is inevitably unable to balance central control with operational flexibility, often unable to fashion a middle level of command, and always unable to find tangible resources. In fact the leaders are mostly engaged in husbanding the faith as a first, if unarticulated, priority. The structure can be various but the purpose is not simply to wage war, to pursue the armed struggle, but to offer a congenial and tangible form for the dream. As a result the structures of command are diverse but the purpose always one.

DECISIONS

To maintain the faith, the center's authority, the momentum of the campaign, to persist with the armed struggle, the leadership must lead, must give orders. There must always be someone to give orders for operations cannot run on consensus and habit alone. Some large groups are dominated by a single leader for a period, often for a long period. Alternative commanders are hived off, quit or are eliminated. Even leadership by consensus produces dominant figures.

Decisions made by all the involved in caucus or by the one responsible are not easy unless, which is usually the case, no dissent is likely. Those major decisions that require public dispute, actual votes, division – so many for, so many against – are difficult. Most movements try to avoid them – stumbling into heresy is a disaster. No organization likes to make crucial decisions. The nature of the end-game almost inevitably engenders division as the moment of truth emerges when the dream must be institutionalized, operate in the everyday, be defined. Few armed struggles ever get to play an end-game but all must focus on persisting. Then the key is to persist with a minimum of dissent because every decision risks opposition and no campaign can be controlled without at least some decisions, real commands.

Those who captured the world's media by detonating a bomb under the World Trade Center in New York were clumsy, inept, easily caught and enormously successful in elaborating minimal assets into maximum gain – not power, it is true, but prominence, vengeance, and exhilaration on the cheap for the militant fundamentalists of all Islam. No great decision to be made, no orderly agenda, no tidy organization nor long preparation. Those involved, a nimbus not a cell, parceling out assignments, shifting targets, accumulating the explosives and transportation, learning on the job, made the necessary operational decisions as they went along. The big decision, strike at Fortress America, the West, the real Evil Empire, evolved from attitudes and sermons and unarticulated aspirations: the operation, like Topsy, just grew, evolved as process instead of flowing from an agenda and votes and orders.

Complex, novel, high-risk operations are everywhere undesirable and so as much signs of weakness as power. The decisions that divided during the long period of persistence are those operations that might escalate the struggle but at some risk – and the leadership is most likely every time to opt for caution. The problems of persistence are most often solved by repeating yesterday's decisions. Any operational decision that is apt to engender dissent is apt to bring the faith into question. Thus most armed struggles operate within a consensus and if possible without recourse to divisive choices.

In the rare cases when the state begins to appear vulnerable or simply opens negotiations, when the future is more than getting through the day, then the end-game may have begun and decisions will become crucial, not easily postponed. Any decision will produce dissent. An armed struggle is a means to transform the energy of the dream into reality but shaping that reality is an orthodox task requiring different assumptions, attitudes and agenda. Many underground do not want to be different, certainly do not want the dream to be different. Yet if there is to be triumph, the dream must be institutionalized and inevitably less than transcendental.

The decisions related to operational matters, those that produce orders from day-to-day, shift tactics, ensure promotion and reward, all fade before the truly crucial matters but each such formal choice risks assets, may cause dissent, may lead to crucial questions about the faith. And so some movements allow most decisions to be made at the margins by default or by intention.

The leaders of any armed struggle authorize far more often than initiate. The protracted struggle mostly needs encouragement not diversion into new paths – those who discover operational opportunity seldom need orders. The major task of the leadership is not to 'decide', not even to command and control, but rather to protect, husband, shelter and only with great caution deploy the faith.

CONTROL

To defend the faith and to deploy the faithful the commanders must not only be able to devise orders and dispatch them so as to direct the movement but also rest assured that this control is effective. The leaders must be seen to lead, the commands seen to work.

A covert, illicit movement engaged in rebellion, unrecognized, often unrepresentative must deploy gunmen who operate under strange banners who require different kinds of commands. Their orders must possess a different legitimacy, and must reflect the dream however shaped to use.

Nearly all leaders have *some* trace of charisma but some have very little, often only a touch. The great virtue of charisma is that it is quick and cheap and largely effective. The problem is that it cannot be ordered from a store and cannot easily be discarded if a change is needed. Charisma is one risk after another, while consensus is the evasion of risk, over and over. All movements need some consensus, more than they need charisma, and many long-lived galaxies have it to a remarkable degree. Control is internalized, all options are known, all alternatives can be weighted against the strictures of the faith. The volunteers know without asking, are controlled without carrots or sticks or much organization at all.

There are other general means of control. The easiest being the identity of the movement with existing institutions – the church or the tribe. The more fashionable means is to devise or adapt an existing structure, the communist party, the *foco* theory, a commune or military unit. For this structure to allow rebel control all must accept the legitimacy of the form, the imperatives of the rebel faith as prime loyalty. Mostly all organizations are authoritative, controlled in practice by a very few. If there is any democracy, it tends to be democratic centralism – discussion before not after the order arrives. Yet every single order must be obeyed, for the center rarely has very effective means of punishing disobedience – and disobedience is a threat to the faith that legitimizes the order. Thus no rebel commander wants to give an order that will not be obeyed. Hence the iron rules of control are the nature of the consensus and the needs of the armed struggle. What form the movement takes, the more natural in reality whatever the titles or pretensions the better, the key to control is consent. And consent arises from mutual belief.

To control killers one must understand killing. To control gunmen one must rely on both formal order, rank and age, reputation, the power of moral authority but also, at times, simple awe. Gunmen, even the hardest, most brutal, most independent must be curbed to purpose, must fear the center's displeasure more than any armed opponent. When the gunman declines an order, there must be no doubt that there are serious risks involved. When a rebel dissents in matters of moment, there must be a measured and calculated response from the center. And always the margins must accept that the center, the commanders, control, can be evaded only at cost.

In the underground, no order can be given that will not be obeyed. Since there will be orders that are dangerous or unwise that should, must, be obeyed, simple faith in the center's wisdom may be insufficient to assure control. A gunman must accept risk. Thus, as with the formalities of military law, a secret army must have to hand coercion: but except for the great issues this coercion cannot be molded as law. The gunman obeys the center's commands, for the risk of the operation is almost never as great as retribution from the center. Such retribution comes in a mix but the meld is fear.

Any IRA gunman knows that the toll of dead republicans killed by their own – for whatever the reason – is long. The informer's bagged body adds to the power of the Army Council in all things. Every Arab on reflection accepts that the toll of internal murder, punishment shootings, informers suspected and killed, the dubious purged and the bodies dumped in a wadi, is enormous. More fedayeen by a factor of ten have died at fedayeen hands than by Israeli action. The combination of heresy, real or imagined, informers and agents, real and imagined, and the murk and brutality of a dirty, secret war assures an atmosphere of internal danger as well as shining idealism.

The center must be cautious as well as awesome so that the margins will be confident, assured if ever mindful of the power of command. In practice, in real life, this often means the gunman is afraid of the commander; the commander driving hard men in a dirty war can be ruthless, brutal, and demanding, fearsome as an opponent, a rock for the rebel but one with sharp edges. Cold in command, arrogant in troubled times, attuned to the odds and at ease with the killing game, a commander is not easily denied.

He, or very rarely she, rises mostly as personification of the necessary operational singleness of purpose that dissipates dissent. And each, an implacable guardian of the faith, if effective comes with a sense of the possible and the eyes of a gull – cold, predatory and feral.

TARGETS AND TACTICS

The selection of targets is not a technical operational matter but the end process of a long, often inarticulate adjustment of priorities, assumptions and probabilities. Targets are important. When the fedayeen chose airliners, the selection was based only in small part on the vulnerability of civilian aircraft, a vulnerability that after a generation of adjustment, is still very real. What the fedayeen, denied an orthodox guerrilla campaign, wanted was visibility, shock, a spectacular for the media and their masses, for the West – now vulnerable, for all – for all the uncaring world, everyone, for *them*.

What better vulnerability in 1970 than those machines filled with 'innocents' who flew over and beyond, uncaring, who could be brought to earth, brought to book, brought to Dawson Field in Jordan and lined up and destroyed. And if history were not rewritten, justice not done, then history could be written and vengeance achieved. And so such targets were repeatedly chosen by the desperate and the intensity of terror spectaculars increased until the world could, once again, be bothered only briefly.

Each of these spectaculars had primary targets, the victims, and a whole spectrum of real targets, the involved and the constituency, the galaxy and the enemies, real and imagined, history and the times. In some way a murder in an airport lounge, the capture of a liner filled with tourists, a dreadful, awesome deed would target them all but would kill only the few and those few really no more innocent than some of the other targets – and certainly no more innocent than the Arabs killed or the faithful lost to Western acts. Only one body need be dropped from the door of a hijacked airliner, only one crippled old man need be shot and dumped in the ocean – and millions upon millions can watch.

Technically targets tend to be chosen because of vulnerabilities – the volunteer or a friend reports a lapse in security, an unlocked door or unexpected access. Such vulnerability can be assured or at least increased by shifting to soft targets, new and open categories, any journalist or all bureaucrats, by shifting to new arenas, attacking across borders or in the cities, by resorting to new technologies – mortars or ground-to-air missiles or detonators that can be set months in advance. Nearly every protracted conflict sees this expansion.

At times the new target proves counter-productive, the constituency is appalled, the opposition is strengthened. At best the state may respond in kind, atrocity for atrocity, thus eroding formal legitimacy. At worst their own deny the rebels. The rebels may perceive the target as legitimate, any victim in a storm, but be moved to restraint for expediency's sake.

The target choice may run across a spectrum from the general to the special at the same time. The IRA was involved in a lot more than assassinating Lord Mountbatten. Some armed struggles aim at the highly symbolic as well as the guard at the gate. All the rebel targets, from the policeman on the corner to the prime minister, may be, often are, vulnerable to the rebel – what is needed every time is access, means, and egress. When the latter is irrelevant, the driver dispatched along with the carbomb, very few targets cannot be reached. The combination of access and means, however, can be largely if not entirely countered by security and by warning – not even specific warning, only the realization that the president or the premier is vulnerable in an open car, at a public function. An IRA bomb exploded on 12 October 1984 in the Grand Hotel in Brighton and nearly eliminated not only Prime Minister Margaret Thatcher but also much of the British Conservative Party. After that no British politician could ever slam a hotel door with absolute assurance, without thought, even if security cost millions and every venue was swept and cleared and checked. Times had changed: a few IRA volunteers in prison and the British political establishment in armored limousines and guarded premises.

This very vulnerability is rebel triumph for the state must spend resources to counter each new threat, build the fences higher, place X-ray machines in the airport, budget for more police. The deployment of more troops by the state is not a threat but a reward for the rebel. What is wanted is disorder, costs, chaos, especially if military success is denied. Thus even the softest target, department stores or left-luggage rooms or a tourist at a cafe, hit or threatened, requires new defenses that will eat the resources of the state and so will add to the turmoil and anxiety within the arena.

In general most revolutionary organizations seek to cause the most damage to the state, to the pretensions and capacities of the rulers, to the structure of national security. Some go no further. Others to escalate extend the range of targets and so the rationale of action. Most of the specific targets are not chosen *in camera* from a menu but are either obvious or come in from the galaxy where someone has noticed an opportunity. In some rare cases, the spectacular is planned long in advance with the target examined for vulnerabilities. The IRA was always looking for access to Thatcher because she was blamed for the death of ten republicans during the hunger strikes and found it because a timer could be set long in advance of a scheduled appearance. Thatcher was vulnerable because of the combination of technology and prior access – and the novelty of the mix.

At least the IRA had used conventional if unexpected means. But what to do if an author is condemned to death – a call out of Teheran by Khomeini for Salman Rushdie's death? What does one do when the laws of diplomacy are unexpectedly violated in Teheran or hostages taken by unknown rebels in Lebanon who cannot be reached or co-opted or bribed? What to do when rebels incinerate themselves before television or drive carbombs to the door? What to do with the child that throws stones? What is to be done about dead dogs hanging from lamp standards in Quito?

Even on the most technical level the imposition of all sorts of repressive measures may not end terror in a democratic state – efficient brutality will but this can only be effectively deployed by authoritarian governments willing to eliminate the suspect, their friends, and their potential sympathizers. Thus the rebel, if there is room to operate an armed struggle, has considerable freedom of choice in selecting targets, may have access and means, may note old and new vulnerabilities – what often does not exist is the capacity to act with limited assets. Rebels do not live in ivory towers pondering possibilities but in danger and in haste, content to replay yesterday not attack the Super Bowl or construct a nuclear device. Those are for thrillers and seminars not an underground under pressure.

Targets mean what the rebel wants them to mean, are selected by commanders who know the attack target will assure control, over the volunteers, over the secret army, over the galaxy. Just as targets shift over time during an armed struggle so too must the rebels. Nothing stays exactly the same even during the slow unwinding of a protracted rural campaign.

CHANGING CONDITIONS

The fact that today is not quite like yesterday and sometimes very different inevitably causes rebels problems. A changed response from underground is hampered by the conditions required to persist in the armed struggle, in particular secrecy, and by the adjustments necessary to filter new reality through the perceptions of the faithful. Promising events even cause trouble. Even when there is operational opportunity or indication of escalation or a flood of recruits to the movement, the rebel must adjust and adjustment is, if not difficult, then irritating. What the rebel commanders tend to prefer, if victory without question is not on the menu, is consistency, today as yesterday. What most rebels discover is the shifting capacity of the state, constant change in the climate of the arena, the imposition of distant events – global currents or foreign tinkering – and the always pressing underground needs of the moment that can often only be met by novelty. Some commanders will accept any suggestion, thereby evading decisions; others want no change, to make no decisions. No one wants to adjust.

There are no general patterns as to what might happen once an armed struggle has begun, even operationally, the conflict may escalate, may taper away, may move through cycles to no comfortable model. In theory the rebel wants escalation – and this can be achieved, if at all, only by risk, so underground command is a long campaign of wagers by conservative players uncertain of the rules and unhappy with their cards to keep the game going.

One of the few advantages of protracted campaigns is that the rebel can respond today as yesterday and so, perhaps, foresee tomorrow. Underground there is always strong support for yesterday coupled with the assumed returns of doing nothing. Thus the rebel is apt to find not only operational adjustment but also at times strategy a constant because of the change of the agenda and the shift in priorities. Such adjustments, especially over time, can be managed, institutionalized as the struggle shifts in intensity and direction, but they are never welcome, never easy.

There are no rules underground about the future. The only continuing factor is that change underground is more difficult, more difficult to organize and to sell, more difficult to institutionalize, more difficult to imagine. And this is so whether the change is a threat or an opportunity, is merely perceived or is all too real.

INTERNAL

Mostly undergrounds tend to keep the old means to cope even and especially with new situations. Thus in the case of the secret army, the leadership in form and personnel is apt to stay the same even in escalation, no matter what adjustments are needed. Some leaders would be nearly impossible to replace in those sects driven by charisma or controlled by a dominant individual. Someone to run operations might be found but that someone would unlikely be guide and goad, fount of prospects, not *the* leader but rather *a* leader; not the same thing at all.

Most organizations are led by those who cannot foresee defeat any more than the need for their own replacement: no one wants a protracted struggle, no one plans for it; and no one can imagine the need to replace those who have begun a struggle that should lead to triumph. The founding fathers are sufficient until the police take them away or they end as victims of the shooting they began. When victory does not come soon, the surviving commanders tend to seek routine, not means to change, persistence not retirement.

What requires adjustment, great or small, is the response to repression – the intensity of the armed struggle – and this means finding new assets, new approaches, new friends. This operational adjustment, unpleasant but vital, is an operational matter. When change requires change in perception – the need to negotiate, to change the basic program, to interpret the truth, the leadership must persuade the faithful of the new testament, persuade by logic or example, through the charisma of leadership, by resort to compelling arguments and even the display of force against minority dissent. In the first case, as long as the reality of repression is noted by the commanders and not obscured by rebel optimism, the response can be closely held – dissent in escalation is inevitable, but as long as it does not involve the truth still an operational matter.

If the truth is to be adjusted – inevitable victory is accepted as not possible or an alliance with a rival necessary – then adjustment is a matter of perception not tactics; principles come into play. Since so much of the rebel world is a matter of perception, reality shaped by the dream, adjustment is a much greater risk than above ground. When an organization is small, dominated by charisma and the dream messianic, adjustment is often the matter of a single vision.

When the organizations in the galaxy are many, the secret army large, the command a long-standing committee, adjustment may be institutionalized, may be much closer to the conventions of the orthodox than the usual practice of the underground. Since most rebel movements are neither cult nor grand, fall in the middle where there are few easy solutions, adjustment is a painful matter without a satisfactory text.

The big adjustments at the beginning and during the end-game are strategic and recognized by all as vital. The adjustments of protraction – the fine tuning of the campaign – are more various and at times more than minor, equally vital for to fail to continue is to abort the end-game and fail to redeem the beginning. The dream can be lost in the details as well as in the great decisions. It is difficult to shift operational priorities, to change tactics, to authorize new fronts, it is difficult to select new leadership, it is onerous to change political direction, and it is especially difficult to change the perception of reality. Although the entire thrust of an armed struggle is to achieve radical change, great and small, through resort to violence, all internal change, especially a change in the meaning of the dream, is perceived underground as a violent challenge to order, undesirable, dangerous, a risk. And even to continue, to maintain the movement means at the very least the long series of small risks, each little adjustment painful.

IN SUM

Two major factors in command and control that are less dominant in conventional conditions are the perceptions of the involved and the imposed limitations of any covert and illicit campaign. Only because there is an avowed consensus – a faith that shapes general perception – can the command center, whatever the structure, shape decisions, keep control of the struggle. This faith shapes the way commands can be issued and so the way the struggle is controlled, offering both empowerment and reassurance but at a cost of anxiety and illusion. The dream makes the struggle possible and risky, attractive and difficult. It makes the risks and difficulties desirable and so all else possible. Without the dream there would be nothing to command and nothing to control.

Everything underground is difficult and that includes specifically the necessity to respond to changing conditions, internal pressures, all sorts of novelty by imposing control through command. And almost no armed struggle can avoid the surprises of the future that complicates this. Thus what often seems to the conventional a highly effective hidden power-structure is often to the involved a desperate attempt to cope with change, allotment of assets, unpleasant surprises, reactions to events, sometimes with too much discipline and often with too little.

All rebels tend to accept their favorable reading of the direction of history so that obstacles are never seen as terminal. Some will try to get out of the underground. Some will try orthodox responses to indicate their legitimacy, seek irregular war, risk a Tet offensive as in Vietnam or appear in uniforms at the edge of the jungle and so die as soldiers instead of hiding away as guerrillas. Some after years are comfortable in a special world tested by previous generations that at worst will be left to the next generation of rebels. Yet, regardless of theory the practice of control and so the capacity to command is a constant challenge. For those long in the business, it is met with equanimity but often for those fresh underground it is a distressing revelation: to command is not simple and to control even more difficult. Some leaders do it naturally, hardly recognize a problem, some cope in time, and many never manage.

9

Maintenance

T HE ARMED struggle is not a perpetual motion machine, a flood let loose, but an asymmetrical war that can be maintained by the rebel only by constant adjustment and ingenuity. The guerrilla leaders focus not on strategy and grand tactics, the course of the war, command and control, but mostly on details, tinkering, keeping the struggle going day by day. The free, brave guerrilla on the hills is often actually hiding beside some bush counting out the last dozen bullets while waiting for resupply. The urban gunman often waits in vain for guns held up by error and the terrorist is left at the airport without instructions. Couriers are late, safe havens badly stocked, direction misplaced, foreign friends have other priorities, the diaspora has run dry, and always there are personal problems. Gunmen have unexpected attacks of the flu, trouble at home, a nagging girl friend, a fear of flying. There is the contingent, the unforeseen, the flight canceled and the thunderstorm when clean skies are vital. The commanders even in operational matters are distracted by detail – another car needed, the wrong papers forged, the explosives undelivered, money due, always money due. Life is not like a thriller or resupply a matter of routine followed. With the rare exception, those charged with directing an armed struggle soon find that what is needed is 'more' – more money, more arms, more friends, more cover, more time, more of everything.

REQUIREMENTS

After the first shot the armed struggle requires a relatively stable galaxy, a movement that supports, even if not directly, the secret army; sufficient *matériel* to wage war appropriately – and this need not be very much *matériel* no matter what the guerrilla wants or the gunman imagines; and finally replacements for those lost, usually assured if the galaxy is stable. In fact the galaxy of the faithful is the key. The leaders draw assets from the faithful but more importantly must reinvest them to assure a constant supply – a closed circle that often seems to relegate operational details to the periphery of concern.

Inevitably, naturally, the commanders grasp the appropriate order of priorities and while they cannot ignore operational matters winning comes from the will not as a result of skill or assets or body counts or tactical success. Fortunately for most rebels several factors reduce the number of assets necessary to wage an underground campaign. The key is that the galaxy of the faithful is stable, content with little, willing to wait for a better day.

CURVE OF REQUIREMENTS

Some armed struggles remain much the same over the course of time, the intensity seldom increases, the rebels are unable or unwilling to escalate and the center unable or unwilling to crush dissent. The rebels need only replacements and sufficient assets to persist if there is a concomitant rise in repression. If the arena is wild, cover adequate, the center torpid, often the case in many less-developed countries, then a long, lethargic struggle can be waged. Even more intense confrontations may be static. However, for any rebel the goal is to escalate, to increase the numbers, erode the center, acquire real power.

At some stage every rebel seeks foreign friends to funnel aid and supply comfort. At times such aid may be crucial to persist or to escalation: the threat of withdrawal may allow the patron to control the armed struggle; and at times such foreign aid may actually be marginal, more comfort than aid.

Sometimes the aid comes not even from a friendly state but from other ideological sympathetic movements or from a diaspora – the perpetual source for Irish republicans but one also exploited by every national or ethnic group, every religious movement who can tap friends, compatriots, believers outside the battle arena. But most movements rely on a mix.

Operationally the rebel effort is to seek vulnerabilities through new targets or special intelligence. Tactically the rebel may extend the battle arena and hit the enemy in the capital or in foreign capitals or change the battle array and bring in women and children to throw stones. A shrewd rebel may introduce non-violence in the midst of violence, mobilize the prisons or the United Nations. Unable to do today what worked yesterday the commanders must do something different to maintain momentum.

Unless the innate conservatism of the rebel and the incapacity of the center assures a long-running stalemate – the institutionalization of the armed struggle as armed agitation within the system, the war will ebb and flow with rebel capacity to operate.

Whatever the elegant theories of an armed struggle, reality is maintenance, success in the daily details. The erosion of energy is enormous so that only the young or the very devout can manage. Once the armed struggle begins, the underground commanders live under the constant pressure of crises without solution. That is the problem of the underground; there is no solution, only incremental responses to perpetual challenge.

ASSET MANAGEMENT

Commanders of the armed struggle are often ill-trained, ill-equipped, usually quite unprepared. They are driven to act but bring to management only the faith, a deep concern with politics, a limited grasp of military matters and often few technical skills. All are usually consumed by grievance and a need to act and very few have certificates of management or an exposure to organization. Once responsible for the armed struggle, all their decisions are made in haste, on very limited reflection, and without recourse to more than the sacred texts. The more orthodox the armed struggle the more likely that talent can be found to administer the process. Even then, the persistent movements may lack talent, may be unable to escalate even into regular war. What is almost always true is that the administrative skills necessary must be discovered underground among the faithful – there are no classes in maintaining an armed struggle, only manuals on tactics and exhortations to decent behavior and good works.

The needs of the day dominate the deployment of assets and the requirements of the faith, often unacknowledged, weigh as heavily as ultimate victory. The nature of the underground forces certain choices. The commanders underground feel cabined and confined, limited in assets, in options, in skills and directions. From underground the armed struggle is a desperate matter, even to persist often seems beyond reach and to escalate is a faint aspiration. Any move appears bad, contains unacceptable risks. Operationally the commanders must be conservative not radical – and conservation assures ultimate attrition just as radical departures risk all. The rebel has few counters to play. Most choices *are* bad, most comfort cold. It is desperation to maintain the struggle with wasting assets that drives the rebel to the unconventional, to an operation that surprises and dismays the orthodox.

Men

Volunteers, the vessels, of the faith are the movement's and so the secret army's greatest asset – and that not tangible. These volunteers, however, must be spent, not husbanded, for they are often the only tangible asset. Since no order can readily be given that falls outside consensus, the commanders are always trapped between the risks of deployment and the necessity of action. A conventional commander can send off the light brigade reasonably assured that it will charge and if destroyed not ruin the army, the campaign, the war, and the regime as well. Not so the rebel commander, the order must be logical to the volunteer, worth the sacrifice. Commanders seldom think about such logic for they too are shaped by the consensus. The operation, successful or not, must not violate the consensus of the faithful. Volunteers will simply not obey orders that violate the apparent tenets of the faith. Revolutionary discipline is maintained not by threat or reward but by inarticulate agreement and ideological commitment – hardly a sound and orthodox basis to assure that the volunteer will go into harm's way.

Commanders, mostly focused on sending their pilgrims into harm's way, are not unduly troubled by the limited training provided, by the enormous capacity of the center, not concerned with the creep of historical time nor the loss in the field or no more so than conventional generals. Beyond the immediate needs of operations, most commanders continue to focus on those aspects of the armed struggle that will strengthen or weaken the faith. This is an area of control but this is an area that requires decisions that mean dissent. While there are always rites and rituals that enhance belief, the potential for schism, apostasy, and heresy is present always and at the moment of any decision.

Maintaining the armed struggle often means using up the volunteers rather than training them to persist. The dream persists but not so the gunman, with no time for long instruction, sent regularly into harm's way, a wasting asset but one cherished while active and commemorated as dead for the dead to have a crucial role in an army without assets. The armed struggle moves ahead not on imported arms nor crafty structures, not on administrative skills but on the sacrifice of the volunteers. It is a sacrifice willingly afforded for this was always a major attraction of the underground:

risk, danger, service not a uniform or a pension, not promotion nor a career but a vocation.

Training and tradecraft

One cannot be trained to believe. And belief is the key to rebel operations. One is also rarely trained to be a rebel – that is a matter of conscience – so the volunteer is often hastily instructed and quickly deployed. Still, as time passes, as the underground persists, those at the center of the secret army seek means to improve their assets. An underground army inevitably has a training program, at least in theory. Successful movements are inclined to exaggerate this tutelage as is done with all aspects of an armed struggle. True, there is instruction, recruits' classes, bomb-making, guns to be stripped and radios to be repaired. There are classes in the bush and instructors in an attic, but all such exercises are cursory. Most important, they are far more concerned with maintaining the creed than in instilling the techniques of war. Those techniques are learned from experience, at great cost and rarely taught to others – there is no time for tutelage only operations.

Most armed struggles are thus waged by those who have learned the job on the job. It is possible to crouch under fire next to one guerrilla instructing a volunteer how to clear a jam, how to aim, how to be a guerrilla, survive, strike, withdraw. There was not time nor talent to teach the recruit before. There seldom is time. Talent is quickly lost and there is little corporate memory. Those few who go abroad to school often learn orthodox matters of little use at the end of the wadi or in the ghetto – and often learn orthodox politics that complicates their lessons to the indigenous faithful.

The result of a lack of real training is a high attrition rate and a considerable degree of inefficiency. Volunteers detonate their bombs too early, kill themselves, kill the crowd, ruin the operation. And next time volunteers equally innocent just as determined are again sent out – there are often no others.

The actual techniques of irregular war, the use of weapons, the construction of mines, the siting of ambushes, are not enormously complex. Yet some things are inordinately difficult to teach: to kill close up and personal, to move through a city under cover, to react to the unexpected, to be secret about secret matters. Guerrilla schools are often only incidentally about guerrilla skills. The instructors are apt to mimic the conventional, run a school with a standard text and more photo-opportunities than technical classes.

Many armed struggles are not really sufficiently extended in time to allow for professional rebel competence – two or three years, hundreds dead or interned, a few dozen survivors but rarely those who were present at the beginning. Smaller armed struggles, poorer, more isolated, using real guerrillas, succeed operationally because of morale, persistence, physical capacity and lack of alternative rather than because of any military skills.

Armaments

More than any other factor, any other liability, a secret army is apt to feel the inevitable scarcity in arms. Arms matter more than anything else – not more than the truth or the faithful but more than any *thing*. Arms are absolute, the tangible means into the future. As such they play an enormous role, both real and symbolic. The very word gunman is a meld that makes the armed struggle work.

Arms may not make the movement but they are a prime concern. Consequently, there can never be enough nor can the secret army stress sufficiently their importance. Their acquisition, storage, their care and protection are vital priorities. Usually, there is a special department for arms or at least for their acquisition, often special departments for various steps between acquisition and use. Control of weapons is a first priority. Arms are a killing issue.

The enormous importance given to arms within the underground during a campaign is based on logic: they are crucial, hard to acquire, difficult to maintain and dangerous to use. They are a sign of legitimacy and power, symbol of the rebel army and so the dream. The need for arms is real enough. Their importance as obstacle and symbol, however, is apt to cloud the fact that operational needs are always less than imagined and amenable to cunning, ingenuity, and ruthless purpose.

Money

Despite the individual sacrifices of the galaxy, the infusions of charity from friends and allies, the proceeds of expropriation and extortion, and the construction of novel rebel enterprises, money is a real and persistent problem. The movement commanders must pay their way, pay for the prisoners' families, pay for newsprint, pay for advertising time and pay to run the candidates in elections, pay for arms, pay the telephone bill, pay and pay and never be granted credit by the orthodox or advances by the banks. There seldom seems enough money – and when there is sufficient means must be found to spend it before the enemy intervenes.

Revolutions are, given all, cheap; cheaper than feature films or Broadway musicals, cheaper to fund than failed bank scams or ground-nut schemes in West Africa. Insurgency is still dear when the involved rarely have either money or the appropriate skills to manage what they do have. Nearly all the vital galaxy organizations are money-losers: political parties, youth organizations, protest committees, commemoration and exhibitions. Arms cost money. Gunmen are expensive, even those not on salary. Equipment is dear. Even riots cost money. There are often too few banks to rob, too few foreign friends to dole out money, too many not paying their subscription or buying a lottery ticket or remitting the usual to keep the party office open or the arms shipments moving. Too little always too late and when there is enough it is often too much, too soon.

Many undergrounds resort to extortion shaped as revolutionary taxes and all resort to genuine contributions for whatever purpose from outside the galaxy. At times the underground can be analyzed as an effective economic entity focused as much on the bottom line as on the dream. The few movements that persist have fat years and thin, usually thin. Their fiscal prospects are usually but not always related to the prospect of victory. As in the private sector funds are proffered when they are not needed and withheld when wanted. Sometimes but rarely the movement may have halcyon days when there is actually more money than expenses. Obviously, as in the real world, expenses are found to absorb the difference but there are other factors. A million-dollar armed-car robbery or a five-million-dollar kidnapping may flood the small core of the galaxy with liquid assets. Then what? Spending too much is as difficult as not spending enough. There are risks and time must be invested in investment strategies, in cover and in a revised agenda for maintenance. At best most movements stutter along between scarcity and surplus – and some commanders will not be able to recall even one bright fiscal moment in a protracted war always waged without adequate funds.

In the end, money although crucial, is not vital. The rebel does not attack the heart of the state to balance the books. This may come as a bonus. Few kill to induce contributions. Successful operations do matter, of course, but this is not primarily a campaign matter – a secret army does not imagine itself a fiscal institution but a military force. Funds are acquired by military operations for military purpose. That a big boom may induce big bucks is a given but military matters are military matters.

Some operations, defined as military operations, are directed against economic targets – not to destroy but to acquire. The armored-car robbery or even a great computer theft becomes a military matter, organized and directed by operational people. Funds are expropriated directly. And in a tight, well-run movement every cent acquired is accounted for by the involved – percentages and danger money are signs of decay. Any alliance with criminals for mutual profit is a high risk step – even when the criminal is a victim, even when the crime corrupts or damages the target state. The underground feels legitimate, does not want to be underground or taken as illicit – it is the state that is illegitimate, exploitive, criminal. So revolutionary expropriation is difficult to rationalize, complicity in drug smuggling is even more difficult – not impossible but anathema to most movements.

Most movements are often as ill-prepared to manage the funds as they are to violate norms to procure them. After the funds are acquired, underground bookkeeping may muddle the returns or trace every penny, depending on the skills available – an underground without accountants or even bookkeepers is apt to have poorly structured finances. And all movements under cover have problems with records – some destroy everything after a brief period of time, some hide paper away, some try to have no records, stuff cash in the desk drawers, hide banknotes in the attic and trust in faith and providence, while others with a safe haven and professional talent keep books that would be the envy of many nations.

The disposition of money varies with the circumstances. The impression that there is never enough money – unless there is too much – is universal and not without foundation. And money is vital because it buys not only consumer perishables or pays the rent but the time of the volunteer, the security of the prisoner's family, a hospital bed or the key to the armory. Neither faith nor bravery nor sacrifice can pay the rent or bribe a warder, arrange a child's operation or have the party registered. And the galaxy, a whole universe of people, has diverse needs, has an enormous spectrum of expenses, all due, all urgent, and all unforeseen by command central when the struggle was launched.

MANAGEMENT

Someone must decided what is urgent and what is not in matters of money and morale and killing. Who gets a salary and who does not? Which gun is to be bought? What creditor is to be paid? And there are more important matters. Who is to be shot and who expelled? Who sits on the court martial? Who should carry what message to whom? Someone must take charge, for neither consensus nor charisma, habit or delegation will do. The whole galaxy should be micro-managed by professionals, but mostly runs on inertia and the repercussions of action at the core.

At the center the responsibility to find money or to set up safe houses, to store arms or to carry messages, are tasks apportioned, like all else, quickly to those sound volunteers at hand. If possible, each organization within the movement must solve its own problems. Often the secret army is too far underground to help, if help could be managed. And no rebel commander, alike with all defense bureaucrats and orthodox generals, wants to see military money filtered away for non-military purpose. Spending limited funds – except for arms – causes severe strain within the movement, between the organizations that should be allied not competing. And if the funds are unlimited, they must still be allocated, divided, dispatched, recorded. Often there is no court of last resort on the locals holding back money on the periphery and the organizations reluctant to fund the center. There is rarely appeal when the secret army hoards expropriated funds. Disbursement inevitably engenders disputes over priorities and agenda: disputes that soon appeal to the faith, the sacred text, may spawn schism over bookkeeping.

Most undergrounds simply lack conventional managerial talent and what does emerge is crippled by the lack of experience, the need of cover, and the impact of war needs. A revolt attracts aspiring soldiers and guerrillas, activist politicians, intellectual and militant advocates of radical change, not middle managers or investment bankers.

A broad-based movement may be able to draw on existing skills – some volunteers understand a spreadsheet or can cope with off-shore banking – but by the time most undergrounds feel a need for management those with existing skills seldom are attracted by the risks or dangers even if they sympathize with the cause. And the cause cannot tolerate sympathy – only full commitment. So those dedicated to the cause are suspicious of professional charity and doubtful about the loyalty of purchased skills. Consequently, just as is the case with the gunman, the underground manager, even if complete with military title as quartermaster or finance officer, must learn on the job; often when the skills needed are not too complex. Those with simple skills, enriched with a good memory, native intelligence, and hard work, can serve the underground well as administrators of the moment.

In the real world above ground, many everyday people have made millions without a university degree or even a world view. So even those innocent of management skills can often make underground ends meet. When highly technical managerial skills are needed – to manage stolen millions, to use computers to advantage, to discover governmental or industrial vulnerabilities – then only a few hi-tech movements can cope.

MORALE

The question of morale within the movement, morale underground, is a constant worry in those possessed of a revealed truth. Is the truth working? Morale is almost always tied to the perceived success of the armed struggle. If there is action, a feel of momentum, the oil of enthusiasm lubricates all the cogs and gears: money and time are contributed, recruits arrive, the galaxy expands, the media is agog, the nation is risen or the people mobilized. And since many armed struggles are protracted, rarely successful, and mostly hidden from view this happy state is rare. Instead, commanders, even and particularly of the secret army, must buy time from the war to tend to the welfare of the faithful, to the health of the organizations and rituals of the movement.

The most practical demand from the movement is that the minimum practical benefits are assured for the involved: the dependants are protected, the volunteers nourished, the prisoners not neglected. A net must be placed beneath the faithful to catch those at risk, often at risk through no fault of their own. Money for welfare in even the short run is more vital than arms or operations, for the latter depends on a willingness to continue. And persistence arises from a reasonable sacrifice. A volunteer may risk his life but not his mother's. A gunman wants assurances that his family is protected. Some movements absorb whole families, husband-and-wife teams, others make provisions, many seek only the single, unencumbered. Many movements tend to prefer volunteers without responsibilities – responsibilities that might accrue to the rebel welfare office. They seek volunteers with limited expectations – no demand for medical benefits, pension, or an eight-hour day.

Morale is enhanced, maintained, by participation in rituals and ceremonies, in rebel rites: a funeral with shots fired or a parade to protest an alleged atrocity. The size of the crowd and even the life-cycle of the crowd indicates that general capacity is greater than the sum of the parts.

Every act within the underground is illuminated and enhanced by the dream and many of these acts are crafted largely to that end. Morale in the underground is primary because it arises from the only real asset of the rebel, the revealed truth. The truth engenders will and the will energy and so is the ultimate trump in a game where the state holds all the other cards. The care and concern with that truth requires the commanders to tend to the welfare of the underground. And this every rebel leader does. Those who do not, disappear as would the rebellion without the commitment of the pilgrims.

ALLIES AND ALIGNMENTS

Beyond the reach of the immediate truth, lie those who sympathize if not with the dream then with the possible results of rebel victory, who may be touched by the content of propaganda and ritual instead of the faith. These allies, if more pragmatic, often find the rebel difficult, caught up in a special vision that makes for rigidity of response. Rebels are very serious soldiers. A crusade is not a matter of pragmatism. Converts and pilgrims make difficult allies, but still rebels do have allies and often friends abroad that help in maintaining the armed struggle. The great tie is a mutuality of ideological interests. This allows the rebel to trust, trust a fellow communist or Moslem, trust another nationalist or fascist. Such trust is never absolute; but a universal or general ideology often shapes thinking, provides a mutual vocabulary and similar historical vision.

Some supporters are also rebels, also underground, sympathetic often to both the rebel cause and the rebel experience. Few rebels are completely without advocates, friends, often distant, often without resources but friends. Rarely can one underground do much for another, the assets are limited, often the enemy diverse, and the galaxy too special. The examples of revolutionary co-operation are rare and so indicative that there is no international conspiracy of gunmen and guerrillas.

Those who tend to rebel politics and rebel propaganda often meet their colleagues, travel to far places, spread the word, make contacts. When the target arena is to be expanded such emissaries may use old foreign friends, boy friends, girl friends, family friends, vacation or school friends, set up safe houses, co-opt acquaintances. All these duty tours help the movement but the activity is peripheral to the thrust of the campaign. Other rebels can only help so much. After all, all those other rebels have the same problems and the same lack of solutions.

If the armed struggle is to persist, retain a certain level of intensity or even escalate, the rebel may have to have more: more arms or more money or more visibility on the international arena. And all rebels, in any case, want more arms, more money, more visibility. All rebels seek patrons, displaying their banners and creeds, citing their heroes and prospects. None likes to beg, reveal weakness; but there is seldom an option.

What the rebel wants is to maintain the struggle, to acquire assets to that end at little cost, real, imagined or unexpected. The dangers are not really great. Too much is never seen as risk and even humiliation and unwanted interference is a small price to pay for arms or money or skill. The need for international friends at the United Nations, in the media, among the influential is obvious. In fact any underground needs so much, has so little, that filtering donations is hardly a priority. The returns are so great that hardly anyone underground counts the cost at all, can imagine the need for filter.

MOMENTUM

In theory the entire direction of all rebel movements is toward expansion. Persistence, the reward of the protective ecosystem, is rarely considered ample. Maintenance in theory is not simply holding the line, filling holes, making do. Maintenance is either ignored as details of the daily demands or assumed to be part of the grand plan that will lead to victory. No rebel thinks much of the former or feels the need to dwell on the latter. The rebel does believe that persistence in the end will be sufficient, but no one wants to wait until the end, until the will at the center collapses, until justice triumphs. Everyone underground, sensibly, wants to be above ground with power, wants the war over and victory and vengeance achieved. Thus the thrust is always toward more in theory. The problem in deploying underground assets to achieve more in practice is that then all is risked for something less than all. Rarely, rarely does a movement require escalation simply to continue. The choice is almost always between patience and possibility. And possibility charges high cost even if benefits are returned, even if the option is decay.

To escalate militarily the movement must first keep pace with the repression from the center, where escalation has costs but not the same kind of risks. Second, the leadership must then find new means or new directions since they have discovered that the movement has eroding assets. The reason so many armed struggles are protracted is that the leadership cannot find the assets or the will to risk what exists. Rebels are conservators not only of the dream but also of the galaxy, the movement, each faithful organization and especially and always the secret army. At any stage in any armed struggle, change is risk, changed targets, changed political positions, changed rituals or friends or intensity. To clone the *foco* risks old and new, risks two directions, risks the future. And the larger the movement the more complex the prospects.

Thus, if there is to be change, it must come wrapped in appropriate ideological packaging, presented with assurance, and bought at little apparent cost. A movement may thus opt for terror because it is cheap, possible, and an appealing option to pursuing a declining campaign of guerrilla raids – the radical Palestinians. It cost those faithful who found terror abhorrent and withdrew support. It cost the potential of alliances and alignments with those in orthodox power who could not be seen to countenance atrocity. It cost the toleration of many Palestinians. It assured the adamant and uncompromising opposition of not only the Israelis but also much of the West. It did, however, pay immediate returns as promised in vengeance achieved and prominence secured. The visibility of the struggle was escalated, the general impact intensified. Terror was a solution to an inability to maintain the guerrilla revolution in the Israeli-occupied zones. Like all such solutions to escalation on the cheap it proved costly, often in ways not visible underground.

A movement may cause internal turmoil by producing a platform more or less radical or simply different, by changing the time schedule of the war or the shape of the army, by shifting the direction of the political party or even reworking the masthead of the newspaper. Instead of absolute freedom underground unhampered by bureaucracy or moral restraints, the secret army suspects novelty, finds the faith limits most options and change dangerous. Any move, and escalation requires movement, assures difficulties, may engender ideological dissent but certainly will assure costs in all matters, large and small, costs not easily recognized nor readily paid.

IN SUM

Maintenance in small matters, maintenance today, bills paid and bullets found, at least assures a tomorrow, and so persistence pays in that the struggle continues. Maintenance often means more than salaries paid or arms found, often means that in a tumultuous and dangerous struggle yesterday's forms are protected. The movement always clings to the present, raises tactics to principles, suspects alternatives as heresy.

All this is in part because of the enormous importance of the faith. Dissent is apostasy. And so the faith is protected and embellished and maintained at all costs. Another quite real and tangible factor is that change is really an operational risk – new targets, new arenas, new means are uncertain and rebels, like everyone else, like certainties, sure things. Rebels in command positions are especially reluctant to pursue novelty unless necessary – when necessary or when escalation blunts anxiety new means are more acceptable. And the conservatives, if they were to give thought, might point out that the old ways even with the passage of time and the shift in the arena often still work: matches light, Semtex explodes, presidents and premiers are vulnerable to single snipers. The IRA carbomb in the City of London in 1992 that caused a hundred million dollars' damage deployed a means first used a generation before, required six weeks, a few easily replaceable volunteers, audacity, cunning placement – and luck. What had worked, worked, and a year later worked again.

So all views in the underground are short, most are conservative, keep the constituency of the moment, the shape of the dream that exists. Yet the armed struggle even to remain static, to persist, must grow or decay, become more or less, find a new direction or new means if persistence is not to presage decline. And decline is hard to reverse, the light dimming in a galaxy requires action at the core that usually is energized by drawing on the very light of the faithful in the galaxy. Yet escalation, like persistence, assures dissent and never promises success. And always the difficulty with main-tenance is the present, a present filled with demands beyond the capacity of the leadership to respond. Yesterday cannot really be repeated, should not be, and today's needs rarely satisfied, with always tomorrow to consider and no time and no money. All efforts at maintenance can at best be only stop-gap and at worst engender schism.

The diverse priorities of maintaining the struggle and the valid divisions over escalation assure dissent. To a degree this dissent is a sign of vitality – a movement that stays together ossifies together. This is, of course, assuredly not the view from the center of the galaxy where unity, conformity and the orthodox faith are considered cardinal virtues. Heresy that may be the end product of dissent is the constant threat, for it risks the faith, the engine of the armed struggle. And above all the armed struggle must be maintained as the dream in action. Winning or losing is more than who is killed in the Ben-Gurion airport lounge or at a café table in Rome, who is kidnapped and what is bombed, more even than who is faithful and who is not – winning is maintaining the dream in an effective form as the times change. And nearly inevitably the rebel response is to opt for as little change as possible, to delay, to restrict, to conserve because a novel deployment contains most undesirable risks and no promise of triumph.

Deployment of the husbanded assets is not a matter of exhilaration or enthusiasm. There is no joy in command, in responsibility underground, but rather desperation and anguish. The gunman or the guerrilla may go gladly into war, young, arrogant, and sure; but they are sent by those who feel trapped and denied. A few, like Grivas, find a second life. Others, often the charismatic, find command a vocation. All are ground down by the needs of the day, by the paucity of assets and by the demands of the underground. Maintenance is more than housekeeping, for what is maintained is the dream in action, not a matter of paying bills or finding bullets or patrons. The leaders can find no easy way to maintain a dream. They are damned if they maintain the deployment of the moment and cursed if the escalation destroys irreplaceable assets. They can neither run faster nor slower nor stay in place without grave risks. And there is no solution but to persist and face the dilemma once again.

10

Communications

ONE OF the most important aspects of any armed struggle is the nature and efficiency of rebel communications. There can be no command or control without contact, no deployment, no means to rally support, rail at the enemy – or to negotiate with that enemy nor even any means to discover reality, estimate the course of war, sense the direction of history. Most undergrounds, however, tend to see communication as a spin-off difficulty of operations. A leader to command sends a message that arrives – somehow, arrives sooner or later, more or less as sent. This is sufficient even if the trials of transmission are irritating: all undergrounds must learn to cope and to adjust beneath cover and all do without great reflection.

The fact is that the rebel has largely technical trouble communicating within the galaxy, inside and between the various organizations and especially in the secret army engaged in a campaign. When messages must be sent outside, then even the target is difficult to determine. Always, any-time, inside or out, everywhere the routes are vulnerable and the feedback – answers or impressions – face both the same technical obstacles but also the filters of the faith. The rebel may not be conscious of reality bent by the force of the faith but the imposition of enemy filters and dams is obvious, the obstacles to the use of the conventional irritating. In fact communications is most often seen as an irritant rather than an opportunity if always recognized as a necessity.

There is often little internal analysis of the nature of communications within the galaxy, in the movement, between the various organizations and not even concerning operational matters. Adjustments are made to repression by necessity not on reflection and rarely before necessary. The campaign needs are clear: the need for command and the need to keep in touch, not simply maintain the secret army. If at all possible, the movement maintains recourse to the conventional for any internal messages that are not blocked and for nearly all external contact – legal parties and papers, public meetings, formal meetings are all permitted, if often under notice of the enemy. In this world, the galaxy extended, the movement nearly always maintains a second net of covert communications. This capacity is not for emergencies but because the core of the faith in the covert armed struggle is indistinguishable from the structure of the galaxy. The galaxy, then, is at times involved in an internal dialogue and at times under the direction, both through covert communications. The two ends of the spectrum are the curt orders sent from GHQ – 'Yes' or 'No' – and the great rituals of the faithful, overt, visible, dramatic, spectacular – tens of thousands marching in a banned parade or a funeral for the patriot dead.

Outside the galaxy when messages must be sent to the neutrals, the disinterested, distant friends, others not adamantly opposed to the faith, those responsible within the rebel ecosystem tend to opt for the raw truth as message. The most convenient means as link to these others is often covert but the usual method is reliance on the orthodox, petitions, the tools of propaganda, agents and legates.

The reverse is the case when the enemy must be approached – the raw truth is still the core, the message often a dictat, and only during the end-game can a conventional diplomatic dialogue emerge – a prospect for which few movements prepare. Mostly the rebel sees the enemy as misguided – and so open to conversion – or in need of intimidation – and so open to threats – or beyond hope and so doomed and ignored. When the enemy becomes communicator once again the rebel finds contact a problem.

Communication is always a problem except when the act arises naturally without thought and without realization – the sit-in as communication, the graveyard oration as communication. Then, the returns of the faith display are so great as to disperse any technical problems. Otherwise communications are bad news, difficult, secret, narrow, aggravating.

At the core of the galaxy, operationally the secret army stays secret, keeps in touch, finds novel means or does without. Operational communications are thus secret, illicit, difficult but possible with care and cunning. There is always an enormous difficulty in maintaining such secure communications, especially the underground operational communications that permit command and control. The rebel tends to subsume any violent deed used as message into operational matters and all operational matters are weighted on the scale of assets and ease. There is little easy underground. Covert communications are always complex even with access to the latest technology. Illicit underground communications for whatever purpose by whatever means are a chore and so a challenge. No rebel wants challenges, only solutions. And so communication is considered as a problem by the rebel more often than a solution.

Still, communicating is not especially vital unless quite impossible and never a really strategic matter. The power of the center to hamper communication is the only real point of focus. With consensus, with initiative on the part of the gunmen and guerrillas, with the means to hand, the leadership can cope – everyone tends to know what to do even if the message to do it is lost along the way. The galaxy cannot long be maintained nor the armed struggle effectively pursued simply by recourse to the invisible force fields of consensus; the faithful and the gunmen must be pulsed, directed, deployed, commanded and controlled. The word must be sent as well as believed.

Romance would have every word, each message, transmitted by subterfuge, sent as a coded note in secret ink wrapped in butcher's paper and carried by a man in a trench coat. Those who can rely on the telephone or the mails, travel without watchers, move at ease, find the underground response to repression romantic rather than tiresome. The Italian and later the Irish public found that once the mails did not work alternative means were possible – but not as easy, not as happy, not at all romantic. Mostly undergrounds try to be conventional. Mostly they prefer paper and files and public meetings and all the forms of the orthodox.

Logic would indicate that recourse to the orthodox carries dangers to those underground, but the lure of the conventional is considerable. Still, there is little opportunity to build files and make copies. Except for those organizations with sanctuary and pretensions of grandeur, the result is that the record of communications for an underground, the paper, files, notes, agendas, the documents, is often scanty. Such paper can lead to years in prison. When there is haven, however, the paper can be as massive as that churned out by orthodox government agencies. The Israelis after the invasion of Lebanon and siege of Beirut in 1982 carried off paper by the truckload: books, records, academic journals, the paper trail of a generation. The hard-pressed underground, however, can hardly write anything down, can hardly afford the risk of personal memory – and, if efficient, destroy all traces that do exist as soon as possible. The documentation of the difficult years for the IRA – 1943 or 1950 – can be held in one hand; the historical remnants are usually hidden, often forgotten, scraps in code. There is little serious paper and a reluctance to accumulate data, even to remember too much. This is an irritant that if the struggle persists may become second-nature, and if not may result in considerable losses. In communications as in other matters, to mistake the returns of the conventional as desirable underground can be fatal.

As a rule there is more paper than there should be, more vulnerable communication in the field than wise, more risks taken in the name of expediency than the prudent would accept as needed. Simply because communication is an absolute necessity but a low strategic priority rebels are apt to be satisfied with what works today. Often with repression focused on the gunmen and not on their conversation or contact, if the order gets through then communication was adequate. And if the gunman gets through, no one remembers the difficulty of contact. It is certainly easier to use the telephone as a legal party does, like those organizing a protest do, like everyday people do.

And often this is how gunmen like to communicate, but such ease is seldom permitted for long, for surveillance is quickly prologue to repression. A state, once attacked, responds in such ways, often without intention, that even internal rebel communications become a serious matter. States seek to find enemies, seek to monitor the suspect, seek to break rebel cover. Sometimes the process begins long before the shooting, but always the state soon becomes involved in eroding cover. Soon the gunmen cannot telephone or meet in sight, nor can their leaders nor many of their advocates. The rebels must protect the cover of their conduits and nets. They soon may have to find different nets and conduits, close the open and open new, rarely as effective, alternative means.

Many, most, rebels have visible and legal assets, recognized parties and institutions, friends and neighbors, a legitimate constituency. These potential channels largely remain even after the armed struggle begins and the secret army and often much of the movement moves underground. These above ground, visible assets, may continue communicating normally, may provide simultaneously parallel channels for illicit communication, and must maintain underground contacts with covert communications. Underground communication is invariably covert on crucial matters but often must break the plane of secrecy to contact friends and enemies, the general public or some other target audience. And, as always, the means and the ends blend under the pressure of the struggle, but the conventional option is denied only to those deeply underground.

With the usual on-the-job training in matters of publicity and publication, propaganda and diplomacy, rebels can and usually do learn to manipulate the media and to deploy various means to channel the truth. They reach their own and also the others. While the message sent is filled with resonances for the faithful, it is often harsh and cold for the doubtful or the dissenters. Genial persuasion is rarely a rebel virtue: the truth is serious, pure, inviolate and best dispatched whole. And so the conventional is used to transmit the unconventional, the absolute.

Communications outside the core at times simply cannot be conventional because the cover is too thick or because the movement is too weak. The enemy may not listen. Then instead of a thrust to the orthodox, 'meaning' is piggy-backed onto operations: the details of the struggle, or on the armed struggle as the dream communicated, propaganda of the deed, terror tactics as strategy. In some cases an armed struggle must be structured as a form of communication rather than a means of coercion: propaganda of the deed or manipulative terror becomes a strategy.

Propaganda of the deed is not unique to the underground, although the conventional tend to use it as a tactical route to their enemies through military means – the Americans bombed Hanoi during the Vietnam war in part as message, just as symbolic air raids against Berlin or London carried more than the weight of bombs. The Doolittle raid on Tokyo in 1942 had military purpose to force Japan to allocate more resources to home-island defense. The raid was also targeted both on the Japanese, the establishment and the everyday citizen, and also on the Allied public starved for victory. The Allied war effort, however, was not dominated by armed messages but by the exercise of power. The rebel is not novel in making the medium one with the message except when such communications become strategic. And rebels take such a step reluctantly for they too recognize that such an option indicates weakness.

The entire armed struggle can at times be seen as a message writ violent: the weak attracting the attention of the strong, forcing a dialogue. Neither the rebel nor the state may recognize such a dialogue, consider matters only as a revolt or a matter of law and order. The British could not imagine that Africans had a message until the riots in the Gold Coast and the Mau Mau emergency in Kenya. Some despots often do not want to admit that anyone can send them unwanted messages. Even violent agitation is a dialogue of the deaf. The rebel is forced to act to be heard. EOKA began with bombs that Makarios if not Grivas thought would attract sufficient attention to allow a more political dialogue with the British authorities. The conventional propaganda of the deed anticipates that the message will transform the enemy, the galaxy, even the arena, while the bombs of Grivas were intended merely to open an orthodox political conversation.

The Italian radicals struck at the state in the person of Aldo Moro, who was stolen, interrogated, tried and murdered. The deed was operationally elegant but still neither the establishment nor the nation received as intended the rebel's message that history had doomed the system. The target did not change – in fact the target, the great conspiracy, gradually disappeared from underground perception and so transformed the rebel analysis. Those converted by the deed were in the end the rebels.

Assassination can more easily punish an individual, a symbol, a system than erode the power of the center. Such deeds – massacre, assassination, atrocity – are specific, operational messages of strategic rebel violence. If this is all the rebel can or will send, they may cause concern and turmoil but rarely lead to power. If they occur within campaigns, that, too, can be considered a form of communication. More specifically, more often, the rebel tends to speak through special deeds, often neither very spectacular nor especially violent, for special purposes: a unilateral truce, a shift in targets, a wave of wall painting. Mostly the meaning is clear enough.

The center, in fact, is often likely to assume more discipline and planning than the rebel invested. The center is *always* inclined to discount the inefficiency and murky nature of the underground, never more so than in assuming a greater coherence in operational matters than is possible. Still, a deed may force the recipient to respond in what the rebel feels is an appropriate response: fear or anger or despair. It is possible to carry out a dialogue with bombs or shots.

Rebels do not see an armed struggle as a means of communication even when all effort is focused on spectacular deeds. Rebels rarely see communication as more than a means, a means often denied by the state. Commanders are likely to focus on the details of operational matters, a nod to the gunman, a note to the column commander brought by hand. If the gunmen are frustrated, then the leadership may opt for a strategy of the spectacular in order to persist. Thus the rebel manages unconventional communications at two very diverse levels – first, the technical matter of operational orders and organizational function under cover and, second, a strategic means, often the only strategic means, to effect events. Much that is internal is involved in techniques, and much that is external is managed by recourse to the conventional. All, however, is adjusted by the reality of the faith.

For the rebel all communication is filtered through the faith. Inside the core of the galaxy, within the movement, among friends, this rarely gives great difficulty. Sending word outside the galaxy to the disinterested, the concerned or the enemy is more complex. The rebel prefers to send the truth alone. Since an armed struggle is necessary, the truth dispatched with explanations and rationalizations, serious, detailed, exacting, is necessary. Much of this activity can be orthodox: placards and statements to the press, position papers as the secret rebel sends conventional messages through the usual channels to particular targets. Many of these messages are hardly conventional in content or analysis, but then neither are the sermons of a fundamentalist or the explanations of the state. What the rebel lacks in such matters is restraint and subtlety. Friends may mount advertising campaigns or offer elegant rationalizations, but for the rebel the truth is too blinding to be displayed in pastel colors. Most overt messages thus display the analysis of the underground, the raw truth uneatable to many prospective consumers. There are thus few converted, few takers of the truth especially when it is coupled with recourse to violence. Such violence as a message-unit, a bomb on the corner or a politician's murder, is often treated as a quite proper means of communication by the rebel if not by the threatened. The rebel contention is that their gunmen are driven to such unpleasant means, though many outside the galaxy are not inclined to accept the pure truth whatever the form. Even the friendly often find the faith indigestible.

The rebel tends to ignore the poor returns on general communication just as the troubles of operational contact are minimized. The faith guarantees optimism. And it is not only the faith that imposes conditions on communications. As with all rebel dynamics, the degree of overt activity and the nature of the cultural arena set bounds and opportunities for communication. Some rebels are hampered by inherent cultural communication problems. All, Arabs or Germans or the Indians of Peru, have special problems, most unrecognized. Whether communication is covert or overt, regardless of the channel, the target or the origin, the process is substantially molded by cultural factors. Some languages are elliptical, some peoples reticent and others direct. The Irish messages are invariably late, the Italian elaborate, and the Arab too optimistic. Some assume their special language to be secret – who knows Hebrew or Basque? – and others communicate through understandings, consensus, gestures. No matter the detail, the armed struggle requires adequate contacts to any and all receivers.

Even when open communications exist so do traditional problems. The PLO, a huge, sprawling state-in-waiting, had to cope with various sanctuaries, with differing and shifting rules, with various constituencies, and with the international arena and with various levels of suspicion as well as communicate with the covert parts of the galaxy in Israel, the Occupied Territories, and operational sites. Each problem was different. Each message was sent to differing receivers and so required differing approaches. Each message in each arena required various degrees of cover. And all the messages were shaped by the existing Arab arena culture. The PLO is hardly unique in having to cope with such cultural complexities – in 1967 the Nasser messages out of Cairo were read by others not to Egyptian advantage. The same is true with the PLO: authorized publication in Arabic in obscure newspapers may contradict the official position in New York or Tunis. Authorized bombs often, almost always, disrupt authorized postures despite disclaimers; but a message to be read by the Arab population of Gaza may carry quite undesirable content to those receiving in Tel Aviv or Washington. All this was complex enough for the PLO with considerable resources, overt and covet, but often proves beyond even contemplation by those rebels with fewer assets and little conventional capacity.

Smaller organizations not only have these same problems in miniature – have smaller problems and often fewer prospects – but also suffer from the results more acutely. Small group dynamics, simply the constant abrasion of intimacy, may produce irritants that in time lead to schisms, betrayal, disaster as was the case with the Japanese Red Army. The pressures of necessity may lubricate some small groups. Seemingly the enormous advantage in miniature is that the secret army is a cell, all in contact with all by necessity. Such intimate communication is denied most armed struggles and is soon attenuated even with a band of assassins when operational requirements impose distance.

The PLO, increasingly dependent upon fax contact, could not be reached by this means immediately before the crucial meeting of the Palestine National Council in Algiers on 1 September 1991, because the bill had not been paid in Tunis. Unlike states with seemingly infinite credit, liberation movements, quasi-states, operating legally must operate efficiently, pay their bills even if with extorted or stolen currency. Communicating with the PLO leaders has never been easy from either the inside or the outside, a mix of Arab habit and revolutionary practice that the introduction of the fax ploy only alleviated but did not solve. At least conventional means exist to reach the PLO leadership, but the same is hardly the case with other groups.

Some groups cannot reach out nor can anyone reach them. Some groups do not want visitors, choose to communicate only through the operations of the armed struggle. Some deep underground, like *Sendero Luminoso* or the Khmer Rouge, are apt to kill the curious. For them the world is divided between the saved and the damned and contact is futile. Within the eco-system of the saved, in Peru and in Cambodia, communications were covered except in the liberated zones and so little different in cost than elsewhere.

Flawed communications, internal and external, make persistence difficult and escalation dubious. These flaws inflict direct costs in transmission and indirect cost in reception because of the limitations of the limited messages. And the involved are rarely aware of the implications of what is perceived as a technical problem.

First, then, to complicate every underground struggle even ideal communications would not penetrate the miasma of the faith that adjusts all incoming data to need. All the givens, the arena, the level of intensity, the culture of the involved, fade in significance to the effect of the faith. All messages are warped by the rebel dream before transmission and so before reception by the targets. The prism of faith affects all perceived data just as the medium of cover blunts any message. The rebel galaxy is a private world that bends reality to need and so skews messages even when the channel is clean and clear. And, second, messages must often be sent on matters beyond the technical or operational, sent to more than one target, sent to those outside the faith. Most rebels communicate in various ways with their own audience, often in such a way that the overt message is obviously at odds with the apparent reality. Never is great thought given to the problems of translation – the rebel shapes the message naturally or not at all. Mostly the message goes to his own and conforms to the dream.

The problem with rebel communications is that there is no solution. The underground that gives cover and assures persistence also makes intimate communications among the rebels difficult, in and out messages difficult, even everyday normal expression permitted by the center difficult. The most troublesome factor in every case is the need to pare the means and the message to permit access to the margins. Always, in all cases, the desired means to convey a message is personal contact. Instructions, operational details, solutions to problems and promises of comfort can all be sent in code or through elusion, dispatched by cable or openly on telephones, tied to a pigeon, carried on a stick, delivered by an innocent or a throw-away courier; but nothing replaces the actual contact. And such contact is difficult and dangerous.

Ideally every contact must reinforce the faith, not simply allow a practical exchange. The note on a forked stick is only part of a message – the needed contact is only partial, dry, unsatisfactory, even and especially after the letter is read. The medium is part of the message, the messenger often is the major message. With real contact, personal contact between the faithful, the formal message is enhanced through a rich mix of gesture and tone, redundancies and echoes, nods and winks, a warmth. There is a listener not just a letter. Facial expressions count and body language and the gestures matter. The courier is thus almost the message but the best message is the sender: how much more effective to communicate at touching distance. And this is rarely possible. Anything desirable is rarely possible in the underground.

The safest underground world is totally invisible, does not exist except in rebel minds, a cover that so far covers intention and implication, a nest of moles so far normal. Always, the best message for security purposes is no message at all. After that the degree of difficulty increases in direct proportion to the richness of the message – a pot in the window, a nod from the old lady, an advertisement in *The Times*, a cryptic note in the mail, the word from a stranger, all the way to what is truly wanted – a long, involved, and intimate conversation on the matters to hand.

Once there are deeds to hide, messages to send, the problems begin. Cover must be kept and so intimacy lost as well as assets redirected. Every effort is made to trade up to complexity by the rebel and to make this impossible by the center even when neither recognizes the duel. Both focus on operational matters not communications theory. In this dialogue all the power is with the conventional state center and the rebel must rely on ingenuity and craft, the consensus of the faithful and the independence of the commanders beyond control. These are never sufficient. There is no solution.

THE GALAXY AS FIELD

Since nearly all movements share a common faith that shapes the perceived world, this obviates the need for many explanations and much commentary. The faithful have a single agenda, similar priorities, and a predictable response to novelty or opportunity. Spread out through the galaxy of the faith is a force-field of common assumptions and unstated premises that goes far to allow communication at a distance. A singular event will automatically produce a similar response without the need for formal communication. Thus from the operational units who 'know' without being told that a target is appropriate to the mildly sympathetic who know the center is lying, communication comes through a medium. This, like a liquid, responds to disturbance in predictable ways. Thus there is far more communicating within the galaxy than is easily apparent. Even those outside can predict with some accuracy the impact of certain stones into the liquid: this will produce, somehow, some way, a rebel attack or a rebel denial.

While this field of consensus is enormously useful, it is inadequate to allow proper command and control. At the very least message units must be dispatched for operational matters and often simply to maintain the faith under pressure. And this can no longer be done as a matter of course, over open wires, in letters or public speeches, at the coffee house or over the back fence. The movement underground must camouflage the conduits and the contents of the messages for disclosure would give aid and comfort to the center, would prevent most operations, would close down the armed struggle. Cover for communication is as vital as cover for the volunteer. Cover requires time and effort, cover restricts. The whole ecosystem cannot be easily or adequately covered. The enemy is all about. Most of the rebels must exist in an alien atmosphere, always vulnerable to disruptions. Years may go by when any, every knock at the door could be dangerous. Yet during those years in theory the door opens only on a truly safe house, known to the very few, secure – but never, never absolutely secure. Thus the galaxy as field reduces some problems but the need for cover unveils so many unexpected obstacles that the rebel hardly notices the blessing.

OBSTACLES AND OPTIONS

The loss of the conventions of the normal, including conventional communications, is generally foreseen. With the leaders set increasingly on subversion, if not insurrection, the movement becomes increasingly covert. Minds close and meetings close and the underground begins to close around the pilgrims. If the movement is lucky, the ecosystem fades from sight starting at the core. If the movement is normal, wisps and shadows remain, points of suspicion: the galaxy is not a black hole, gives out light visible to the enemy.

There is rarely a sudden descent into secrecy so that the habits of caution, the need for cover, emerge as the start point as war nears. Once the fighting begins, most rebel communications are everywhere, and usually almost at once, restricted to those messages that can be hidden or coded. On Tuesday a telephone call can be made with some assurance of confidentiality but on Wednesday one can only speak with the assurance that not only are the authorities listening but also that the call may lead the police to those making and receiving the call. If the latter is not the case or not important, subsequent calls may be made but must be disguised, if not as normal then so as to hide the real message – even the call alone may be sufficient.

If there is no overt party newspaper, how is a constituency to be built? If everyone is in hiding, how can the enemy be contacted except through violence or random messages, notes in bottles tossed over the wall of the presidential palace? How can those abroad or those in authority at the United Nations be reached if conventional contact is denied? How does one cope in a closed world with cover hard to fashion, coding not easy to learn on the job, and command and control at stake? And this is not to mention the other and often unexpected requirements: morale must be maintained, rituals must be performed, and all sorts of *matériel* acquired. New weapons, for example, must be located as available, then acquired with the use of money and influence, packed and transported, hidden and distributed, and then at last deployed to operational advantage in a carefully monitored tactical operation that is orchestrated to strategic intention. It is a long and complex road from a gun shop in Texas or Pakistan to a dead soldier in Belfast or Beirut. And the road can not be traveled in silence.

All this activity must be hidden and so all messages from reports on progress to the acquisition of bank drafts or customs declarations must appear at worst impenetrable and at best normal. Everything suddenly becomes arduous, time consuming, enormously difficult. The covert world makes any everyday activity into drudgery. A 24-hour day is too short. All at once the secret world presents the first great bill and one if unpaid assures the bankruptcy of the dream. Normally a rebel movement first addresses the command and control problem that, unsolved, will prohibit effective operations. Some operations are usually on the books and others can be initiated locally by those comfortable with the reassurance of the galaxy consensus. Inevitably the police have either closed down the normal means or monitored them. So headquarters must find ways to maintain communications.

The rebel must make do. What is done almost automatically by most rebels is to move from hi-tech to low, from telephones to written or oral instructions taken by hand to the receiver. These may in time be regularized so that a man on a bike delivers the daily newspaper wrapped around the GHQ message. In an urban arena low-tech may at times prove more efficient than the conventional postal system if not the telephone. In rare instances when the resources exist within a covert society the pursued may go hi-tech. In another covert world the South American drug dealers who could draw on enormous funds could buy the fastest boat, commission a faster one, equip it with state-of-the-art electronic gear, load up on counter-deception trinkets at world-class prices and yet lose the whole lot without cutting the profit margin by enough to remember.

Rebels almost never can even contemplate such resources. They must manipulate the conventional or go down-scale. A few may for a time have access to haven state assistance, use a diplomatic bag or receive advanced electronics. Much of the time, most rebels must depend that an order will arrive eventually even if brought by bike. The *Brigate rosse* usually lacked money but not ingenuity and skill. They avoided the local Italian telephone system by recourse to the international system: when in Rome to talk to the Roman *Brigate rosse* one needed to call Toronto in Canada and so be connected back to Rome through a link that, being international, tended to work, unlike the local Italian system, and which was not monitored by Italian security forces who were seeking terrorists in Rome not Toronto. Still, the Irish low-tech bike delivery works, if not as well at least adequately.

Communications options are not simply a matter of resorting to existing technology for technology transfer involves far more than the purchase of machines or even their maintenance but an understanding of the nature of the skill. Nabil Maksumi, a major player in Ahmed Jibril's Popular Front for the Liberation of Palestine-General Command, was released by the Israelis in 1985 and immediately returned to active service. He moved to Cyprus and set up a telephone-relay system that allowed European agents to talk directly to Jibril through the link. This meant an agent in Germany could dial into Cyprus and the call would be transferred to a Damascus line – very elegant. The assumption was that the link would divert any interest that would surely arise if Syria was dialed direct. Instead of a deception ruse Maksumi had contrived to attract attention. His sophisticated transfer equipment was hardly novel. Any overseas telephone contact could be monitored. The reason that it had not been in Rome was a mix of official innocence, the assessed needs of the *Brigate rosse* – why would they need such a link? – and the choice of Canada, a turnaround node quite unrelated to Italian terror. Cyprus, on the other hand, had long been a key staging place for underground operations, was staffed by watchers and listeners concerned with all aspects of the Middle East. Maksumi could not operate freely on Cyprus nor could his friends in Germany. Calls in from Germany were as likely to be monitored – and were, of course – as calls directly into Damascus. And a great many Arabs in Germany were watched, their calls monitored because local German terrorists could be involved, not just transnational stringers. Any monitored PFLP-GC activity in German that involved telephone calls to Cyprus would raise security concerns immediately. And this happened. Sooner or later the computer would have clicked on the Germany–Cyprus calls even if the Germans had not monitored calls of the General Command agents. The revealed hi-tech option simply meant a serious operation was in hand and the Germans concentrated on the communications link.

Once the link was revealed, an inevitable step, such communication rated priority attention. Instead of providing cover, the link was an indicator of activity. Those involved on both the German and Syrian ends obviously had their doubts about their elegant, hi-tech cover. Simultaneously while using the link, they resorted to the standard down-market ploys for telephone communication by devising code words, often on the spot, thereby confusing the intended listener as well as any unwanted one. Surprisingly, these not very subtle codes – 'everything would soon be ready' and the 'medicine' was made 'stronger' – actually did seem to confuse the German listeners whose leaders felt that the course of events had become unclear. The Italians had missed the *Brigate rosse* ploy because they could not imagine it existing, and the Germans were confused by their intercept because they could not understand what was happening.

In any case, the flawed communications were not the prime reason that the General Command unit ran into difficulties but an indicator that low-tech responses have their place, especially when sophisticated alternatives are misapplied. Mostly rebels do move down-scale technically. The key Moro messages of the *Brigate rosse* were deposited in trash cans and the location called in – 'the basket nearest the front door of *Il Messaggero*'. When risk is involved, the rebels cut the message length, cut the number of messages, rely if possible on local initiative, suspect all usual means and so add ambiguity or codes to all communications sent over such routes. Thus some place advertisements in international newspapers, messages by references beyond the grasp of all but those with a shared background. All the nods and winks and asides inevitably lead to rebel confusion as well. In a thriller, after a coded telephone call, all the well-trained operatives show up on the dot across town three hours later on the next Tuesday. In the underground, the call is never made, the messenger instead loiters on the corner on the wrong Tuesday or the taxi is caught in traffic or the gunman forgets the appointment. In the underground the rituals of tradecraft are often badly served – and so at times make countermoves more difficult. And these countermoves are gradually factored into rebel calculations.

Increasingly, all serious rebel matters are never discussed by the involved if possible and then often in ways beyond all but the initiates. To overhear a meeting of the central command of some movements would gain few much insight: little said, obscure references, a muddle of names and asides, no neat agenda or show of hands, no briefing, no list of items. The meeting is often the message. The real decisions have been taken long ago.

The more ideological movements often have a constantly shifting language of analysis, ideo-babble that is difficult to penetrate and impossible for agents to reproduce as means of entry into a suspicious and inbred underground. In six weeks all the trendy terms have often been changed, sometimes the pace is faster than the monitors can translate: radical ideology requires a radical language. In effect, within the movement a private tongue is fashioned. Mostly the language is used in matters of the faith. Real operational conversations are limited to the involved, are short, technical, compartmentalized, and often integral to the deed. The destination of the carbomb is not decided until the ignition key is turned.

Quite unconventional means may evolve to maintain the faith field in the galaxy. The leaders of the Shining Path in Peru once – once was all that was needed – spoke to their own, the Indian peasants, taciturn, stoic, unresponsive, placid, difficult to organize, difficult to reach at all, to teach at all, to intimidate or to galvanize. The armed struggle of the Shining Path began not with atrocity, a convention for the Indians of the *altiplano*, but with dead dogs hanging from the lamp posts, more awesome, more mysterious, more effective than placards or proclamations or bombs in the police station. The rebel commanders were not interested in appealing to the masses or converting the enemy, often in fact they were not even interested in communicating with anyone but their own. The death of dogs was a sign for the faithful, not a threat, not a warning, simply a banner of defiance and determination. Such deeds appall and intimidate the representatives of the center and awe and intrigue those so wretched as to be beyond conventional messages.

The most effective messages, then, can readily be delivered, may be covered or revealed, and have a manifold and escalating effect. They may be strategic messages or simple propaganda, tactical or technical operations shaped as message. These operational units arise from the web of communications necessary to run the armed struggle. And such messages are subsumed in the general noise of that campaign, must be repeated, perhaps escalated to have the desired effect. And so, too, the rebel operational messages, always more vital and always more difficult to send. These are the real basic communications of the armed struggle.

Most such messages, however, are curt, stripped of elaboration, delivered slowly but surely, require no answer and permit action at a distance. Against all odds, against the grain of culture and the habit of history, despite the security forces and the limits of the rebels, even the most complex operations take place. The word can get through – usually does. Meetings do take place, even as planned. And meetings are always a risk.

Even when relatively safe, there is constant rebel concern about security so that contact is never simple. Arafat of the PLO often moved each night without warning. Famous and notorious gunmen are often displayed and available but seldom those who must run operations. And operations require but cannot received fine tuning, much adjustment, a great deal of preparation. Even the single gunman, the lone assassin, must be shrewdly commanded, constantly under control, deployed to shifting advantage – must be kept in touch and must be touched.

In the underground the problem of communications is considered a means, not an end. As in much else the closer the matter to command center, to the heart of the faithful, the more important. Those at the core must be in touch. There the armed struggle is commanded and there the purpose of the faith must be pursued and so communication must be a first priority. The habits and responses of the underground required to maintain the cover for communications are considered necessary and irritating but not of the order of acquiring gear or seeking informers. Keeping in touch is often a matter of avoiding being touched by the security forces. Only when communications must be dispatched as propaganda or weighted as diplomatic initiative, only when the message may be read differently by different targets does the center contemplate – and still as a lesser matter – communications as more than irritant.

THE SECRET ARMY

When they reduce the flow of communications and rely on internal conventions and argot, all movements further isolate the militants and activists from both reality and their own. The IRA gunmen of the 1940s often on the run moved from safe house to safe house seldom comfortable with the conventional. Safe houses are closed houses. And a very secret army is closed within the galaxy, isolated, sealed, sends few messages to the movement. The galaxy field alone is insufficient to feed the faith. The believers require sermons and services, contact with the center. The leaders cannot *just* pursue the armed struggle. Even then each soldier needs to be touched by the hierarchy. The note at the end of the forked stick, if not too late, brings not warmth and praise and bright spirits but only the operational word. The hard word alone is not enough, may run operations but does not satisfy the needs of the faithful. This does not – or not at first – concern the leaders of the secret army for they are focused on operations.

At least the hard word does allow the rebel to operate but not as normal. The secret army must deploy and operate more slowly than anticipated. Because Cyprus was small, an island, and so geographically limited the possible operations, a Grivas in a dugout coped – and he let others in the movement see to the faith. His hand-written orders not only would do, but also would tie in all the activists – he was dispatching tangible evidence of command. Others, however, have had not only a wider arena, could run more soldiers, escalate, but also more obligations, must see to the movement, reinforce the faith, deal with the needs of the galaxy.

If control is possible, most campaigns may escalate without trauma, most galaxies be served even if with difficulty; but if communications are too difficult, then the assets must be let loose to operate freely beyond regular control. Those on the margins can only be controlled by a detailed agenda without appeal. With troubled communications, a very common problem, the rebel center must choose between rigid control from the center or flexibility at the margins that assures lack of strategic direction. Halting communication prohibits fine tuning of operations except in special circumstances when the battle arena is small, when the rebel force is small, when a means has been discovered to direct details at a distance. In some degree all rebel organizations have this problem. Either there is too much control – slow, plodding communications that arrive too late, arrive and are irrelevant, or else the freedom to act and act often in ways that contradict the intentions of the center. Since communications never are fast enough for long, the rebel can never for long escape the dilemma. Blunted and blurred communication means no satisfactory 'solution' to the center–margin choice, a choice inherent in any case in all armies, secret or conventional. The general on the hill can see everything but cannot reach the men on the line while a general on the line can sense an immediate opportunity but misses the scope of the entire battle arena. Most generals opt for the hill, but rebels, often isolated under cover, often must defer to the margins whatever their preference. During much of the IRA–Free State conflict the 'irregulars' without benefit of a capital center were directed by a roving GHQ in military matters while the president of the republic de Valera drifted, largely unheeded.

However romantic secrecy may appear to the innocent and desirable to the orthodox, an enormous commitment of resources is necessary to cover each and every initiative. Secrecy is bought at high cost. Each operation is a bundle of difficulties intensified by the problem of maintaining cover. The involved must oversee the acquisition of identification documents, the opening of a bank account, forward the request from a unit for supplies, make the arrangements for two commanders to meet in a strange city. Each requires hours and hours, sometimes days of preparation for a slight gain, no gain at all. Just to persist is difficult. Even internal communication is limited. Less is always safe. Say nothing and so risk little. The price of the hard word, the short message, the wink will come later. Tomorrow for rebels has a low priority. The operation must work today or there will not even be a tomorrow. A wink will do, the hard word suffice.

PRISONERS

One novel challenge that inevitably emerges early in the armed struggle is the asset and liability of those captured by the enemy. The rebel commanders, no matter how skilled or how versed in command, find their focus unexpectedly broadened soon after the shooting begins. The rebel leaders find that the enemy in scooping up the suspect and the captured volunteer has not necessarily removed rebel assets from the board but rather broadened the game. The pieces, the faithful, have a different value in cages and cells but are a net asset still. While more useful outside, the prisoner is not without uses and not beyond communication. Within the prisons rebel losses are transformed into assets and assets must be managed.

The rebel prisoner focuses almost from the first on communication. Contact is made with other prisoners and with the outside as soon as possible. Contact, as long as there is an outside movement, is always possible. There is a pressing need to know, a need to remain within the active galaxy. So the rebel turns the technique of contact, an irritating technical obstacle outside, into a strategy of defiance. And this initiative, except for high priority escape operations planned on the outside, usually comes from within the cells. There is ample time and continuity to allow a rise in efficiency. And most of all the prisoner wants out – or at least to be in touch – far more than the commanders outside can imagine. And the commanders outside must continued to focus on the war not on the morale of those seemingly lost. The prisoners often force their way into the underground agenda. In time the prison option plays a greater role – the lost volunteer returns to active service, no longer simply a prison martyr, a name scrawled on a wall, but a veteran of a different campaign. Sooner rather than later, often long before any one returns to the underground from a cell, the leaders discover the power of the imprisoned and shift the old agenda.

For the innocent observer one of the more difficult obstacles would appear to be maintaining links with prisoners. This is rarely the case. The problems and solutions of operational units are both more obvious but also more daunting and dangerous than headquarters keeping in contact with those sealed away by the state in cells or camps. Prisoners pay fewer costs if their communications 'operations' fail. Already lost once, a second loss is less painful to the movement. And success, against such formal odds, seems even more a bonus, unexpected. The prisoners have infinite time, limited tasks, enormous patience.

Some political prisons are simply great and porous holding camps detaining the suspect and the subversive. With a steady traffic in and out, with new levees, with over-confidence on the part of the authorities communications are not a serious problem. Some camps are closed, isolated, islands almost beyond touch. Some gunmen and guerrillas end up in real prisons, sometimes purpose-built for convicted rebels. There isolation, long sentences, and craft create the basis for subverting the system.

The activist prisoners are engaged in waging unconventional war in one more unconventional area. Prisoners, too, serve their 24 hours a day and so often feel spiritually free. Some volunteers once captured do undergo a sea change, make adjustments to prison, adapt, wait out their sentence rather than persist in the struggle. They may retain the faith but not the necessary commitment once captured to continue to seek service. It is easier when the arena provides example and encouragement to a prison role; but always confinement has an effect, often unforeseen, on the faithful. Some are tempered, contribute most to the cause while in prison, and others drift away into isolation from the faith, into a private life of accommodation and patience.

The center has, thus, one more responsibility. The prisons cannot be forgotten or at least seen to be forgotten. The center must maintain contact, usually is eager to do so and thus disperses assets to aid their struggle. The cost is mostly in time and concern for even a major escape operation uses limited operational counters. The result is often encouraging to the center, for relatively little is spent for a visible, often immediate, return on the invest-ment. And communication, seemingly the prime problem, generally proves less difficult than imagined. Ingenuity, recourse to existing operational practice, and a willingness to deploy ruthless brutality largely solve even the most stringent restrictions of the prison system. Very, very few movements cannot turn a prison message around in 24 hours assuring a better service than the post if not the phone.

The easiest means to communicate is to intimidate guards whose services may be bought or extorted. Any physical in-and-out exchange that touches the prisoners permits messages: garbage taken out or visitors permitted in. There are all sorts of channels, from tiny radios to rags flying at a cell window. Food deliveries may be used, circulating library books or authorized mail or hospital visits. The prisoners have 24 hours each day to work on ends and means.

THE FAITHFUL

A galaxy of the faithful, pulsing and glowing, indicates the ultimate reach of the revealed truth. In theory the movement's constituency is all within the galaxy, where all should be faithful. The galaxy cannot depend solely on the field of consensus or even the news from the operations of the secret army to maintain morale and to renew the energy of the dream. The loyal and committed must be touched, encouraged, disciplined as well as used and exploited. The easiest means are found in the everyday world. And thus most movements make some effort to structure an acceptable face, an orthodox and legal means to communicate: a legitimate political party, a friendly newspaper, broadcasts from a sympathetic state. Many movements have visible organizations and not simply gunmen on call. Some do not.

As far as communications are concerned, most covert activities within the rebel organizations are treated operationally. However, interdiction of organizational communication is a continuing priority of the state. It is a natural security response of the threatened and, just as in the case of the rebel, always focuses on operational matters. The state has more assets to invest and so can at minimum make rebel command and control difficult. At times the entire spectrum of rebel communication to the organization, to the movement, out into the galaxy of the faith and beyond to the distant can be severely hampered. And the state always monitors what is known and above ground.

There are those who pay not dues, have no place on lists or rosters, but are touched by the faith, may sacrifice if asked, may be useful if touched. These, the believers, may not be a formal part of the organization – the solitary, the families and friends of militants, those fearful of the costs of the faith. Each and all identify fully with the dream and usually with the organizations of the movement as the vehicles for the truth. Some may contribute their life, more than the active service volunteer, and others offer nothing and are asked nothing. In communicating with the organization, command central touches much but not all of the movement. And beyond and around the movement lies the remainder of the often latent galaxy where belief often, sometimes, usually, lacks great intensity: dark matter waiting for the illumination of the deed, of victory, waiting on congenial messages from the center or the battlefield.

As far as the faithful are concerned, communication can come by varying means and intensities but always is best shaped by an individual, by personal contact. A crowd of the faithful, some carrying party cards, some in from the hills without contact for years, can be intimately touched by a single speech, by the hero moving through the crowd, by actuality. A meeting in a closed, upstairs hall or at a barn in the country can bring the war close. A gunman hot from the streets has the power and impact of ten thousand leaflets, a volume of programs. One whiff of cordite is worth a thousand words. The appearance of a commander or the maximum leader has vast effect over the next year – the messenger as message. This is true for the galaxy, for the movement, for the organization.

ENEMY

Those in arms against the dream are often seen as quite alien, occupiers, agents and pawns of evil. They fight history as well as the rebel. Some may be shown the error of their ways without need of ultimate conversion to the faith. Some universalist rebels, especially those with a general political ideology, hope that despite all evidence the enemy will accept the inevitable. Thus some enemies are misguided, some others may be converted, and some are quite beyond reach of the dream. The Irish always believed in the conversion of the Protestants once the British were gone, the Palestinians that Jews not Zionists could live in the twice promised land in harmony, but the volunteers of the Islamic *Jihad* see no future for a West dominated by the Great Satan. All enemies, however, are doomed by history.

The entire armed struggle sends this message. The rebel may explain atrocity to the victim, allot the blame to the enemy, threaten and cry vengeance without expectation of answer and often without concern about the impact. The center cannot hold. The rebel as history's agent, then, tends to communicate with the enemy in relation to the degree of success of the armed struggle, communicate about the power of the will and the certainty of ultimate victory. Such communication is usually garbed in grievances, the lessons of history, the fashions of the day but remains uncompromising in aim.

This communication may be done through conventional means – newspapers, press conferences, television documentaries, word of mouth, letters to the editor – or by resort to propaganda of the deed. When words have proven useless killing is chosen as means instead. Mostly, since an armed struggle requires killing, the rebel means are mixed, some propaganda and some bombs. All of this is what might be called general, strategic communication; for it involves the masses and history not details and items of an agenda. Rebel strategy is broad, vague, focused on invisible assets, the tides of history can be communicated adequately by slogans or with bombs.

The entire armed struggle then is a message, a means, to accelerate history that can be, should be read by the enemy at the center and by others. Rebels, like their enemies, tend to think of the campaign as a form of war, politics by other means, a protracted and violent means. Operations, even the most narrow and limited have multiple targets, the bomb maintains the gunmen's morale, encourages the faithful, terrifies the enemy, impresses the neutral, every bomb, every time has a multiple message – the rebel's missiles have multiple warheads for effect. These implications are not always foremost in rebel minds, mostly concentrated on persisting, on details, on the obstacles of the moment, but such merged targets, nevertheless, exist.

Violent message units, whether efforts at escalation or simply to maintain momentum, to persist, can for the underground prove as risky as every other underground maneuver. For over a century the Irish have bombed in England with various results, seldom foreseen. Elsewhere, too, rebels do not fine-tune the last act. The operation can collapse into a disaster not a foundation for explanation. The meaning may be lost or beyond the capacity of the rebel to articulate properly. The channel may warp the rebel message. More likely the targets will not respond as intended and the other watchers may be alienated.

The seizure and diversion to Uganda of an Air France Flight 139 on 27 July 1976, resulted in an enormous tactical victory for the Israelis with the raid on Entebbe. The terrorists had not planned on the shape of operational failure: death as martyrs was foreseen but not death as villains bested by a display of Zionist skill. At Munich, on the other hand, although the operation collapsed into chaos, murder, and a final gun battle, the basic fedayeen intention was achieved despite the apparent 'failure'. The West was appalled and wanted to know the rationale of the terrorists, the Israelis were outraged and punished, many of the Palestinians were encouraged by the visibility and ignored the killing, and the rebels felt that they had acted, persisted, helped history along. The risks both with spectacular and with the more complex manipulative terror are high – but so are the risks of the underground – especially so if the rebel has few other operational options.

Every violent deed sends the enemy, the specific target, some sort of message: the roads are not safe or traitors will be punished. At times the rebel center may organize special deeds to send specific messages amid the general din of a campaign. This is not really a strategy of propaganda of the deed but operations crafted to induce specific effects: prevent civilians from co-operating with the authorities or indicating that no quarter of the capital is immune to violence. At times such a meaning is tacked on by announcement to operations planned without reference to propaganda 'meanings'. And again the message may be misinterpreted, prove counter-productive or be ignored.

Reading the future of operational acts undertaken as message has had a mixed return. At times the rebel does not always craft the operation with delicacy or sophistication. A rebel spokesman may later explain the event to movement advantage when, in fact, the operation was haphazard, undertaken because it was feasible, unexpected, even undesired. The victim may be appropriate only in rebel eyes not in those of the target audience. The audience, a secondary target, may be lost unwittingly. Then, sometimes, the rebel may explain, again blame the victim, the nature of the war, others. Sometimes, rarely, the movement seeking to horrify or appall neglected to count on horrifying or appalling all instead of only the target with a hijacking or a no-warning bomb. The target audience may, therefore, respond in unexpected ways because the rebel has misread reality, sent an inappropriate message or one congenial or effective only to the faithful. The loyal may understand and approve but the yet uncommitted be alienated.

Sometimes, rarely, the message received is effective but unintended. Not always: strategically the activities of the Irgun in Palestine from 1944 to 1947 finally disgusted the British establishment. The unintended deaths when the Irgun bombed the King David Hotel in Jerusalem in 1946 were blamed in Britain on the Irgun and in Palestine by the Irgun on the British. The killings disgusted those responsible in London and so raised the crucial question: 'Why are we there amid the ungrateful and treacherous?' The British establishment was angered and disgusted at a general lack of sympathy for their policy, angered that Jews were the culprits and victims and disgusted with the entire Palestine affair. In 1947 London decided to turn the matter over to the United Nations. Soon Britain decided to withdraw, unappreciated, disgusted with everyone. The decision was not a strategic matter, not a legal or technical decision, certainly not a result of losses suffered or sacrifices that could not be made, but more than all else a desire to be rid of such disagreeable people, Jews more than Arabs, and an impossible responsibility that returned no advantage. Why must innocent civilians die in the King David Hotel for no good purpose? It is not worth staying. So the center did not hold. And the Irgun had not planned to kill with the King David bombs, had meant to send a message but not the one received.

Sometimes the message does work as intended: the United States withdrew from Lebanon after the carbomb attacks while denying any pressure. Later so too would the Israelis from much of Lebanon after constant irregular attacks while denying any need to do so. Governments seldom admit responding to coercion and are as likely to resist such messages. Few governments attacked at home can do other than resist. And often the rebel recourse to violent messages simply alienates the many. Mostly rebel explanations – that the civilians are a legitimate target, that a warning had been posted not to drive at night, that all who used the national airlines were enemies of the people – convince no one but the rebel, and not always them.

When the enemy must be sent communications directly and in relatively conventional ways, the prospects are either a continuation of covert means, especially if there is no truce or amnesty for such an exchange, or a move above ground to the normal with scheduled, safe meetings at the palace or in a public hotel room. The rebel tends to seek channels that can be trusted, message units that have worked in the past. Thus when there is need for negotiation the movement seeks not the conventions of diplomatic communication but agents, those who can be trusted and trusted to present the message properly, personally.

The problem is that communicating outside the necessary command-and-control within the rebel movement deals with the truth and the raw truth is diplomatically useful only if it can be imposed. Agents at least keep the dilution of the truth that diplomacy requires at one remove – the reality of others, the necessity of compromise, the need for concession can be denied or postponed or evaded at least for a time. The loss of purity can be a gradual matter: first distant contact, then the intervention of friends, the dispatch of agents, perhaps even, finally a real meeting. Each step overloads the channels of communication into the heart of the galaxy. And contact arranged in haste assures trauma within the organization, the movement, the galaxy no matter the outcome. In the midst of the outside world, the blinding light of the faith must dim, little by little, to let the messages be read, answered. In 1997, after years of contact, the IRA is still uneasy with the peace process – many are nostalgic for war. Those still unexposed to that world of negotiation are blind to the advantages if they come by any diminution in the dream.

Governments have often refused to talk with bandits, take tea with terrorists – at least in public view. Israel seeking to erode the very existence of a Palestinian entity has long refused to talk to 'terrorists' having nothing to say that would not be taken as concession. At the Madrid conference in November 1991, when Israel sat at the same table with a Palestinian delegation cleansed of the PLO, the 'terrorists' hovered just out of sight in their villa. The Israelis had, however, at least recognized that there *were* Palestinians. There were not yet direct participants in a dialogue, not fully into an end-game. The Israelis did not want to pay the price to include them, suspecting there would be no tangible return on the investment.

The rebel, too, must be willing to pay the cost required in open communications. Any change means costs, both imagined and unexpected. Any change in secure communications may be costly. The truth, absolute, pure, untainted must be communicated to pagans, must be shaped to reality, sub-divided into text and agenda and codicil. Reality, even victory, demands an adjustment of the faith. There are those who never will pay, who prefer a dream, a grail, the perpetual gunmen who always threatened the end-game. To deny these, to adjust the dream, to adapt to the real is a costly and painful process. The most faithful and uncompromising are often the first eliminated with the advent of peace, fill patriot graves dug by their old comrades. This is a cost seldom counted. Most attention is not on the cost but on the benefits. Most rebel diplomacy with the enemy is weighted by the leadership strategically. Have we won or won most? Have they decided to concede? Are matters in hand? Need the armed struggle continue? Is the sacrifice at an end? Has history moved?

THE ARENA AND BEYOND

Very rarely does the rebel have time to scan the general horizon, seek the good graces of the distant who should be attracted by the simple justice of the cause. No one considers that the messages sent to the faithful or to the foe may have an undesired impact on the disinterested. Effort declines proportionately with the distance from the core of the galaxy. A movement may, of course, have so many declared enemies and supposed allies that an effort must be shaped to the distant. Thus a Shi'ite villager up from South Lebanon must learn the techniques of a press conference in order to justify the hijacking of an airliner or the holding of a hostage. The provincial is thrust into the big picture and must cope. Inevitably the form is quickly grasped, the nature of pool coverage or the specific deadlines of various agencies and networks, and the guerrilla becomes a self-taught producer, over-confident, innocent, and at times effective. Usually the techniques of publicity come to dominate, at least for a time, the deed.

Certainly, for a far longer time the nature of the distant target remains elusive. There is little feedback about the real nature of the Great Satan, a mix of Hollywood and political cliches, or Mao, victor in the field and author of the Red Book. Rebels are parochial, take short views, accept the stereotype of the transmitted faith. Even the most sophisticated rebel still has the tunnel vision that the truth imposes. And there is quite often a struggle to fit the deeds, not always carefully crafted as strategic propaganda but undertaken because possible, into a coherent ideological message. No matter, the most important aspect of the message is its reality and transmission while the avowed purpose, the impact is less understood.

Only in time and only for some does the reality of the distant target take some form except as stereotypes. Those disinterested or simply away from the arena and as yet uninvolved are divided into potential recruits to the friends of the constituency – the United Nations or a Great Power or all Moslems – and those are beyond the pale of conflict or concern. There is always an exaggerated estimate of the armed struggle's importance, the appropriate nature of violent deeds, the skills in transmitting through conventional channels, and the impact of the message. Those rebels concerned are, like everyone underground, perpetual optimists – and in this case why not? The press conferences are crowded, the media is agog, the powerful away from the stage are, must be, interested. The underground is hidden away, closed, intense, self-validating; so that wishful thinking coupled with a lack of rebel sophistication in many armed struggles means that the commanders assume their own perception is general. The raw truth as perceived is dispatched to the concerned and interested with confidence that only the unrepentant will spurn such reality. Even the interested, however, are not always friendly or the friendly always constant – the communication may be counter-productive.

PROPAGANDA AND PUBLICITY

For the movement the rebels concerned with communication are often those assigned to the task of telling the authorized truth. They are specialists assigned to get the real story across. The involved insist and often believe that their target lies beyond the movement or the galaxy or even beyond their avowed constituency. In fact the message is really shaped for the faithful. The rebel cannot readily distinguish between faith and reality, the truth of the movement and the needs of the moment. What others call propaganda the rebel sees as information.

Really good propaganda and truly effective, conventional publicity is rare. There are few to buy rebel truth raw. The truth does not so much drive out error as destroy the subtlety that even commercial advertising demands. The armed struggle is always given a hard sell by the rebel. The rebel insists that the name be spelled correctly as well as used, that the text be transmitted as written, that the cause is ever righteous. Nothing less is really satisfactory. When subtlety appears it may, indeed, be a sign of rising conventionality, the institutionalization of the faith, the decay of zeal.

Again there are costs in such a hard sell as well as the benefits to the movement. The process makes the rebel into a fanatic. In a sense even to show the rebel as reasoned and human is a net loss for the regime at the center. The threatened are always inclined to hunt down 'terrorists' and 'mad dogs'. There are no revolutionaries, only fanatics and criminals. There is only a bandit problem or a few of the demented killing without good reason. The Indian authorities in 1991 faced with over 100 different guerrilla groups in Kashmir representing all manner of goals insist that all are simply proxy Pakistani gunmen: alien invaders in nationalist or separatist clothes. The Rhodesians fought communist terrorists not African nationalists. The Armenians or German radicals or the Japanese Red Army are mindless murderers. Only the mad Irish would bomb London. The Russians had tribal trouble in Afghanistan. All imperialists were troubled by outside agitators. Each rebellion is a matter of legitimacy – the right to rule – and so every center wants to deny the rebel recognition.

If the center is threatened by those not easily declared mad or simply criminal, then all can be 'terrorists'. The perception of the center does not always make for elegant propaganda – especially in an era where the rebel may be romantic. As long as the romantic rebel offers only the absolute truth, then the center benefits from the doubts or the disinterested.

Even with the death of the myth of the guerrilla, some rebels cannot simply be dismissed effectively as bandits or mindless murderers. The Irish have been bombing England for generations – for even if there is madness there must be a method to it. Rebel propaganda might relatively easily show balance, empathy for those outside the galaxy, some humor. Rebels rarely do so, not the Irish, nor the Arabs. The truth is serious business and the burden of the movement is to display the truth to the galaxy, and then to others. In this they are fanatical, gaining the continued loyalty of their own but not of the uncertain who hesitate at the edge of the galaxy. The distant and power-ful are, too, apt to be alienated by the absolutes of the idealists at the core.

The revolutionary posters out of Havana were most elegant but dis-patched only after Castro had won. The new Cuba used art and typography as an export item. Communism was best sold with arms and art. Then Castro's sponsorship of the Tricontinental (OSPAAAL) artists and illus-trators produced splendid designs advocating national liberation and world revolution. Costa Gavras directed the film *State of Siege* in 1973 on the Tupamaros – the rebels, more sophisticated than most, might have had the inclination but not the opportunity. In 1986, after the key events, Reinhard Hauff in Germany made *Stammheim – The Trial*, a sympathetic treatment of the RAF. These German rebels had concentrated on the ideological impli-cations of their armed struggle, not the artistic possibilities. A few of the more elegant terrorists have lived their lives as existential art work, but most leave art to the camp followers, who often follow some years later – paintings were still being made by Gerhart Richter with a RAF subject matter a decade after the key figures had died.

The real rebels seldom have any interest in elegant and esthetically demanding publicity. The Spanish communists did not like Picasso's dove nor did the Mexican rebels much understand the giant murals of Orozco, Rivera and Siqueiros – many painted after the revolution had failed in practice but triumphed in theory. Art is illustration and most effective when created outside the core of the galaxy by a Goya or Daumier. The Russian constructionists using the style of the day were too radical in vision for Stalin, the new Tsar, who once in power, like the everyday people, wanted recognizable workers and peasants, not white squares and radical ideas. During the armed struggle and often in newly in power, the rebels possess the truth, have no interest in beauty. In opposition the truth is all and in power the rebel wants reassurance not beauty, at least at first.

Sophistication comes with time, with talent, and often with the mellowing of the faith. Most true believers continue to dispatch the exact, pure text of faith – the truth – as the weapon that will most surely work. The truth does have a profound effect on the faithful, always the first target, but dissipates rapidly with the distance from the center of the galaxy. This is rarely apparent to the leadership who cannot afford subtlety and are blinded by the faith. Publicity is transmitting the exact truth. Some truth may be held back for operational purpose but even the spokesman speaks in the tongues of the cause. Propaganda is merely the elaboration of the truth. Others may focus on such matters but rarely those directing the secret army, resentful that the truth is not accepted but often too deeply engaged in maintaining the momentum of the campaign to fret long over secondary concerns.

The more sophisticated and extensive the underground the more elaborate and diverse the message. Here, a single, individual talent can elaborate on a small movement's assets. Such spokesmen, flexible, amusing, sincere, questioning, often are regarded with suspicion by some pilgrims. The faithful in declamation are seldom glib or charming. Still, each must sacrifice for the cause so the leadership will deploy the rare individual skilled in such communication. The most competent movements transform reality with the faith and channel the product to a general and special audience. Thus the reality of the Palestinian children in the occupied areas throwing rocks at Israeli soldiers was escalated and elaborated into a vast orchestrated international campaign. It was a campaign with messages for all: the core of the faithful, the galaxy, the sympathetic, the distant and important, the enemy in all forms, Israel, Zionist, Jewry, the West, were targets too. The stones were simply stones. The motives and feelings of the children and their parents were obvious, undeniable. Shaped as messages the stones were given specific meanings. These messages made use of all existing channels, often technologically sophisticated covert nets, as well as the deployment of the endless agents and legates of any Arab effort.

From time to time, such general efforts have been orchestrated by friends of the underground. These friends may be under control or may act independently. These allies may be members of the faith but cored elsewhere, pro-Zionists in New York, communists in Cuba, Shi'ites in Teheran, Arab nationalists in Cairo. These assume a rebel burden. This response is often institutionalized in universalist faiths so that the rebel knows that his big messages, his general messages, often even his strategic communication with the enemy can in part be left to professional hands. In the cold war most rebels counted on one patron or the other. In religious or ethnic struggles, in anti-colonial conflict, in wars of national liberation, there are usually automatic friends who will without prompting advocate the rebel dream, the rebel grievances, the evil of the enemy. Even the most parochial and isolated rebel can expect some distant sympathy – the advocates of a free Timor or support groups for the Corsican nationalists.

Mostly, however, such communication plays only a subsidiary, if highly visible, role in an armed struggle. Since such exercises require time, assets, and some sophistication as well in choice of channel and often destination, they pose difficulties for the rebel. Yet the movement never wants to cede control of anything, any asset, especially interpretations of the faith, not to anyone, not to those beyond the core, not to friends and not to the distant. And the leadership tends to assume that communication is not an art but a matter of channel. At the core where communication is largely a technical matter, obstacles to overcome, messages to the outside world are a lesser matter. Disseminating afar the truth, touching distant friends, touching the bases, all this is helpful in troubled times.

It is not, however, really a *vital* matter at all. Vital is close. Vital is tangible. The really vital matter is operational. And if matters there go well, external communication will deal with the dismayed enemy, with terms and details and concessions and timetables. Then, diplomacy will not even require tact and certainly not difficult and dangerous means or methods. Then, the distant can still be ignored or explanations left to friends since the near future is in hand. Only when the movement must emerge from cover, move conventionally, is an agonizing reappraisal begun on agenda and method and communications.

THE COST OF UNDERGROUND COMMUNICATION

No matter the methods of communication, each has a cost in visible assets and in general morale. Those messages that the rebel center feels less vital than the war effort subsumed under propaganda and publicity are the simplest to perform, often rely on overt forms and conventional means. Those less apparent – the rituals and the riots – more vital are only slightly more difficult. The more crucial the message to the armed struggle the more difficult is transmission and so the greater the cost. Always the underground requires that the faithful come first, even if others are alienated and so the general message ruined by particular needs. Only an increasingly conventional organization can speak with forked tongues if never with two minds, reach out effectively beyond the galaxy. Just as an armed struggle may move out of the underground toward unconventional war, so too is the case with dissemination of the truth. The closer to victory, the less need for the purity of the message and the easier transmission. During the hard times, all attention is focused on military matters, on the campaign. And every such message comes at a price.

Operational messages are inevitably short and rarely initiate a dialogue. In fact, personal contact is eroded along with the message length. This means that all the conventional richness of content and contention, from body language to the benefits of the dialectic, are lost. Even a taciturn society that moves on winks and nods receives them personally. To be isolated, surrounded by threat, living on nerves, and dependent upon sporadic and cursory communiques, may not hamper the actual operation but does erode the volunteer's skills and dedication.

Those at the margins who suffer from the benefits of such communication's democratic centralism even when the necessity is recognized – a war measure – in time become alienated. This is more true with the edges of the secret army, reached in matters of import only by covert communication, than the edges of the movement where overt contact is often possible. The center can radiate the faith generally but cannot communicate specifically with the active service volunteer except through narrow channels. In 1941 the IRA Northern Command became so alienated from GHQ in Dublin that the officers came to the conclusion that the Chief of Staff was a traitor, not simply inefficient or hard-pressed but an agent of the Irish Free State. Most rebels are unable to blame the movement center for functional difficulties, isolated and distant and doing the necessary, those at the margin often define dissent in ideological terms. Without capacity to discuss the direction of events, the alienated feel that the truth is being misapplied not that the commanders are ineffectual or unresponsive. They must seek a reason for their dissent – there must be a cause at the center for irritation at the edges. The first cause is the faith not its communication, and so the margins mistake the impact of the few and the faulty message struggling through the underground miasma and seek malice and betrayal on the part of the sender.

The gunman wants more or less, escalation or a pause, a new front or the closure of an old one, often something that hardly factors into the center's plans and programs, does not relate to the big picture – has not been discussed. There was no way to discuss the matter, any matter, no way to communicate and no seeming need. Suddenly there is an issue, disputation, schism. In a sense heretical dissent within the movement is an indication – a message unit – that more is needed than the existing communications. Such dissent means that command no longer means control because such commands as dispatched, as received, as translated, are uncongenial. The *Brigate rosse* command to avoid schism allowed Senzani in Rome to mount his own operations: better operational disaster than schism. Some movements tend to split easily. Some arenas, like Italy, generated many movements. All movements, arising from the explosion of a revealed truth, are open in time to disputes. These may be engendered by practical matters, by personal ambition, by too many defeats or the prospect of victory, by the costs of escalation or the boredom of persistence. Much disputation is very real: the Eritreans had to cope with the Christians and the Moslems, the Leninists and the nationalists, the choice of strategy – real issues. Real issues are often, even usually, transmuted into a reading of the truth. Disputes, whatever the cause, then are apt to be argued out on principles: who possesses the truth. The revealed truth always encourages organizations to fission.

IN SUM

The rebels must communicate within a specific cultural environment with varying degrees of overt means. Open or secret communications, never a high priority, work, sometimes quite well, if at a cost. The rebel ecosystem exacts a varying price in all matters of communication. Simply to persist operationally, to command and control, to run the war, to control the organization, and to marshal the movement, the necessary secrecy exacts a fearful toll in time and effort. Much communication is haphazard, the effective means often lost by the attrition of combat. Little consideration is ever given to communication priorities or implications. Always communication is focused on the faithful even at risk of alienating others or sending inappropriate messages elsewhere. Importance is measured out from the center of the galaxy: the secret army, the organization, the movement, the constituency – and then others, friends and even at some stages enemies. And communication of all sorts, channels of all sorts, are always considered a means – not a crucial concern.

Always the armed struggle demands the greatest effort. Even conventional communications with friends and enemies are troublesome. Then, even when channels have been found, messages shaped to risk, and the means of control institutionalized by necessity a second price must be paid. Because attenuated messages do not communicate fully, the normal aura that supplies secondary benefits – unity of purpose, enthusiasm, reassurance – is lost. Again, everything underground seems to hamper rebel dreams.

11

Deployment

FEW REBEL leaders invest any great interest in the functional dynamics of the armed struggle. All have a grasp of the strategic rationalizations, for this is the faith made manifest; and nearly all become concerned with deployment of the faithful. It is in the tactical options that are supposedly required by grand strategy that the leadership first recognizes the functional difficulties of the underground, the obstacles to control, the delays in communications. Once the beginning is made, the rebel headquarters is immersed in details: no one has time to move nominal columns and commands about a potential battlefield. Strategy analysis is for those with time and assets. The rebel has only a sense of urgency, a scattering of volunteers, and a need to act.

Deployment within the center of the secret army is more often a matter of the moment, a hasty scuffle to repeat yesterday, to use what can be found to assure a tomorrow. The real rebel problem with deployment is to find assets to deploy.

STRATEGY INTO TACTICS

All rebel leaders share a similar vision of reality; the contents of the vision varies enormously but not the mindset. Each reads history as text, perceives present reality as grievance and power in a dream few can accept. The means is the armed struggle. *All* such struggles require a vulnerable opponent, so the self-chosen, often self-educated rebel leadership know something others do not: the hidden vulnerability of the center to assets within rebel grasp. This is basically the strategy, a reliance on history and the validity of the truth.

Every rebel arena contains the vulnerable center and a rebellion powered by the truth. There is a conflict between the wretched present and the assured future. The authority that devolves from such an analysis legitimizes the rebel struggle, makes the war just, the ultimate victory inevitable. Authority is not, however, real power. The rebel believes it possible to tap and so to deploy invisible power – the nation, the people, the peasants. So the rebel deploys the existing visible and limited assets: a few gunmen, the tiny store of explosives, the snipers or the few in the *foco*; but the rebel commander also has recourse to the power of the will, an asset not as readily visible to observers.

The rebels have launched armed struggles when only two or three could be gathered together. A rebel strategy, propounded by Che, insisted that no preparation was needed. The lack of assets almost became a virtue: just a few guerrillas sited inside the battle arena would attract the many. The few would win in the end just like Castro. And far from Cuba or Bolivia in time and space, every rebel assumes that a lack of visible assets while distressing is not fatal to an armed struggle. Having no assets to deploy, one deployed a few and relied on history. Rebels have begun when a proclamation could be drawn up but no soldiers found. The vision makes up for all and the subsequent deployment is enhanced with hope if not fire power. For two centuries many rebels have opened an armed struggle without assets while others with long preparation and mature conditions begin with real if secret armies to deploy.

The rebel is optimistic about the end result but frets about the morrow, about the end of the week. At the beginning, when all rebels have to deploy for war, all share a similar strategic image. As soon as the shooting begins, that image becomes strategy and the rebels, no matter how complex and arcane their analysis, focus on tactical matters. Strategy is taken care of by the ideological text. Analysis tapers away except for the repetition of the faith. There is a move away from the nature of history to the needs of an ambush in the next valley. The less analysis, the weaker the universal myths and assumptions, the more likely the tactical options are practical.

Tactics is a search for the possible in order to persist. The avowed dream of the rebel is to find assets to change this persistence into escalation. Often the rebel in order to persist must shift deployment, open new fronts, take new risks, embark on tactics that engender problems and dissent. And even in practice, if escalation is possible this change too imposes undesired choices and sacrifices on the rebel command. Deployment is easiest, most congenial when yesterday can be repeated. Consequently the unconventional rebel is apt to be most conservative in playing with the limited assets available.

What can be done is done. And always if there is strategic optimism misted in pessimism of the moment. Enthusiasm is short and anxiety constant. And always, always, the effect of the deployment, the selection of operational tactics, the balance of intensity with risks arises in large part from the rebel vision of reality, a mix of hopeless optimism, cunning insight, strategic certainty, and daily desperation.

STRATEGY AS TACTICS

The few leaders must find a means to act, assets to deploy, when to the practical and complacent none exists. If there were assets, a swift coup, even a civil war would be possible. If there were nothing, not even hope and false optimism, then nothing would be possible. So there are always assets of a sort to deploy and if fortunate the secret army may even be a serious threat to the state. Something, often anything, can be found even if the leaders must deploy themselves. What is always to hand is a strategy that can be adjusted to perceive reality and so permit confidence in the deployment of the scattering of real assets. This strategy solves the need to act. Much else is tactics, the means of acting.

For most rebels their operations must be based on a grand vision – a strategy as icon. Before deployment even of the one man with a revolver or a straggle of volunteers, there *must* be a strategy. Not *any* strategy, but one that embodies the dream and, if there is to be a protracted conflict, related to objective reality.

Most rebels do not manage even this. Their strategy is grossly optimistic and their tactics dependent upon few assets hastily deployed. They are inevitably deployed within an unanalyzed arena either in pursuit of a grand theory or because little else can be done. There is always a grand theory, a revolutionary strategy, available, the one book to read, the map not the terrain.

OPERATIONAL COMMITMENTS

Since most strategic factors are consumed simply by the need to persist tactically, operational factors are determined by those tactics that offer prospects. And such tactics – operational options – are as diverse as the dream and so the strategy. These operations, the substance of most guerrilla guides, the focus of anti-insurgency in both theory and practice, and the daily routine of the underground, are the stuff of wars and thrillers.

Escalation in operations may offer simply more of the same or the same but elsewhere. Sometimes seeking to escalate the commanders will widen the target list or authorize more violent means. Each case is special, but each is determined by the perception of the rebel command about appropriate targets given the underground's capacity. Thus both assets and target determine deployment, what can be done and what should be done.

VOLUNTEERS AND CAPACITY

The great asset of the rebels can always be found in the faithful, many ready to act, all eager to help. The tradecraft and skills of those volunteers may, often do, leave much to be desired. Those who have military training often find much has to be unlearned and much technical has to be taught to the others on the run. Many rebels come to the underground with experience in a conspiracy, with years underground politically, but few with involvement in underground operations. Others have at least had military service. Many rebels, however, arrive without the skills of war. Mostly volunteers are young and untrained. A great many rebels learn on the job. Some have only fired shots in anger, never had target practice. Their targets have the capacity to return fire – which does not necessarily improve rebel marksmanship.

Most volunteers are badly trained but if they can survive, honed and seasoned by the real world of operations, danger and risk impose good survival habits. Experience under fire cannot in any case be learned well in camp. Battle conditions may allow the volunteer to survive long enough to deploy useful skills. Those who do survive may, in time be very effective, indeed, far more so than graduates of any formal course. Anti-insurgency may be a learned skill but the tradecraft of the rebel can only truly be learned by surviving the penalties of the conflict. The result is that the volunteers are often competent in one arena or with one weapon, can survive and persist but may be incapable of variety – the gunman hopeless in a corn field, the peasant dazed in the market – or coping with the complex. To bomb effectively more is needed than the capacity to tip a switch in a tote-bag as directed and leave the bundle on a door step. The entire spectrum of an operation from conception through intelligence and planning and the act followed by the inevitable explanation opens room for error.

Experience, hard bought, will often install care and cunning in operators. Those who too obviously loiter are arrested. Those who panic and flee are not sent back again. Those who blunder but persist may do better next time, if there is to be a next time, another ambush, another bomb.

The volunteer is the great asset to deploy even if the more often deployed the more often lost. If the survivors increase, then escalation is possible, even without foreign friends or new weapons or the state's despondency. If not escalation, then the rebels may persist for tomorrow and then the next day, persist for years.

MATÉRIEL

It only slowly dawns on the rebel command that an armed struggle is going to require more than arms and money and the odd publicity release. The volunteers – the great asset – must be housed and clothed, paid and protected, their families must be secure, there may have to be hospitals open and doctors on call, jobs found and cousins placated. There must be organizers to go forth on such errands. There must be means to control all of this – the care and feeding of the guerrilla who cannot live off bananas in the country or the gunman who cannot survive on coffee, nerves, and home cooking in the ghetto.

And this problem suddenly appears far more acute than the care and feeding of the operations of the armed struggle: there must be arms and money to go with the volunteers, but also intelligence, control and communication, repairs to this and replacements for that. Are cars to be bought or borrowed, stolen and returned? Who can move what? Are there trucks, ways across the border, safe houses, safe havens, means to keep in touch? What if there is a raid on a friend? What is the procedure for broken communications, lost gunmen, units out of contact? In the beginning there is a muddle of needs and requirements, no rules and regulation, no allocation of resources, no divisions in authority, no routine – that worst of all situations for command and control: no standard operating procedures. Transportation and communication can only for the shortest period be handled by borrowing a car and stopping by a public phone booth. The security forces almost at once force the rebel to take cover, seek low-tech solutions or covert options. So sooner rather than later the rebel commanders then realize that all sorts of material things are needed besides the chemicals that go into bombs or new barrels for P-38 revolvers. Usually the responsibility for the acquisition of the materials necessary to wage war – hospitals, trucks, safe houses, newsprint, radios – is allocated from the core. Usually those in charge hardly consider the process deployment – it is building a foundation under a going concern – the armed struggle.

Operational commanders may supply their own *matériel* – steal their own cars, find their own safe houses, feed their gunmen and contact a doctor. Thus, across the spectrum of armed struggles the nature of *matériel* acquisition varies, especially as a result of the degree of cover and also often the size of the secret army and the capacities of the galaxy.

LIABILITIES

The big battalions of the state, the real army, the police, the institutions of government, the opportunities to reward and punish, the legitimacy, all weight the scales for a surprise free future and so rebel defeat. Tangible assets tend to win and always appear to lend credence to the state's analysis of objective reality. A visit to Saigon in 1970 revealed the air filled with the clatter of helicopters, the streets jammed with military vehicles, and the seas dotted with naval vessels. Figures on poured concrete, building starts, sewers laid, communication wires stretched and barracks completed were all available on computer printouts. Any place the eye wandered, there were thousands and thousands of soldiers, special units, daily parades, heavy tanks, officers' clubs, parades and the offices of various bureaucracies, indigenous and imported. There was evidence everywhere of power and permanence, enormous commitment. And the rebels were but small men in dirty black pajamas, hiding in the jungle, crouched in hidden tunnels, depending on scientific socialism, the will of the people, and a generation of sacrifice. It appeared no contest. No contest in 1967. No contest after Tet and the ruin of the Viet Cong. Not even much of a contest after the American withdrawal of 1972. And at the end the rebels on their few tanks rode to power over the failure of the will in Saigon – just as Giap and Ho had promised. The will won: and the accumulation of orthodox assets. In the beginning the will seemingly was the only asset that the Vietnamese rebels had to deploy against the West and so it made everything possible.

OPPONENTS

The will does not win often. The powerful win; the big battalions win; logic wins. The flurry of rebel victories over imperialism in the years after 1945 that engendered the myth of the guerrilla was a special case. The big battalions were not deployed and the will – just as the rebels predicted – was not there. Empires were passé, colonies not wanted. Other means of rule, more contemporary and less costly, were available. And once the overt targets of imperialism disappeared, the will rarely won at all. The rebel challenged those who had more to lose than a distant colony – and won when the besieged nation turned out to be directed by a brutal and inefficient despot in Cuba and a limited family company in Nicaragua. The mullahs' victory in Iran, quite unconventional, was hardly an armed struggle at all but rather the withdrawal of national support from an arrogant and ignorant dictator. The armed struggle when it did come in Iran was from the mujahedeen of the radical left and was crushed by a regime, crushed without a regular army, without years of police files or much practice in repression but with absolute conviction and recourse to any necessary brutality in the name of the faith.

THE SYSTEM

The rebel must deploy against a system, mostly the modern state, although if the conflict is at the edge of power or with a provincial center little contemporary may be visible. What the state has to deploy is so overwhelming that the only effective means for the rebel to persist is to transform weakness into strength or the reverse. Protected by the ecosystem the rebel at least can pursue an armed struggle that may be focused on a perceived vulnerability of the state.

The famous rebel strategies mostly arise from the analysis of others. And no strategy can rely on ready concession All rebel deployment is seen as lethal. Who at the center wants to die in exile or at the end of a rope, appear at a show trial or eke out life as guest of a friendly despot? The British, the French, the Americans could go home again. The Russians withdrew from Afghanistan because it suited a Moscow edging toward chaos not because of rebel planning. Stalin would have stayed but Stalin was the past, dead in a different world. In Afghanistan the rebels had persisted, raised the cost, protracted the war beyond reason and so gave Moscow further reasons to withdraw. This is the hope of most rebels, to last long enough for the center to weary: surely the British do not think they are at home in Ulster?

PERSISTENCE AND ESCALATION

The rebel, incorrigibly optimistic, seldom foresees the extensive protraction of the conflict or the complexities that operating underground will entail – and rarely lingers over all the assets of the opponent. Few rebels really imagine that simply persisting will be so difficult – all foresee escalation and none the complication that it will entail. In fact few rebels have time to be operationally reflective, consider the implication of the deployment or the nature of escalation. Most simply are swamped by the daily crisis and most respond as always with the available dispatched to perform the usual.

If the rebels survive, the first operational factor that becomes crucial is that the center always raises the stakes, surprise is lost and simple communications and easy access to the entire galaxy and volunteers not easily replaced. The rebel must find new assets, new vulnerabilities, new methods, new friends – and then discover that victory is no nearer. At times and often for only a time, the rebel manages just that: the incident level increases, the perception of chaos and confusion increases, the numbers involved increase, the capacity of the secret army increases, recruits are at the door and the capital shudders with carbombs. Mostly, however, the rebel simply persists, deploys the available assets today as will be done tomorrow.

The rebel then always must try to deploy more when less is likely to be to hand. To make up for this the rebel – reluctantly – seeks new vulnerabilities and new means of approach always within the unstated bounds of the strategic analysis. The target may be broadened or novel means introduced or a new front opened. Rebels unless they are directing a real irregular war, seldom sit at a table and debate options, analyze prospects, draw on files or surveys. Change is forced and the menu read in a rush. What else can be done will be done.

Innovation is difficult underground. It is far easier to deploy even the most limited assets in comfortable routines. There is often little time to contemplate new options, little hard intelligence except on immediate needs, not enough talent and never enough effective volunteers. And worst of all when escalation looms so do the risks.

Most novelty, most big operations, most surprise moves by the gunmen or the guerrillas require risk and enormous risks. The state can lose a battle but the rebel often fears that the loss will be catastrophic. The rebel believes in inevitable victory but only the demented fails to recognize the obstacles – and risking too much is dangerous and not taking the risk is deadly.

So the assets are deployed with a careful hand and after a constant, if hectic, search for vulnerabilities that entail few risks, a search then for a means to maintain the pressure without endangering the underground unduly. Such means rarely exists. Still, the rebel wants, like everyone, to keep the cake that must be eaten to survive.

PROTRACTION

Surviving at all, surviving for years, a generation, is an aspect of many an armed struggle. The theorists and practitioners insist that the capacity to persist, to last out a protracted war, is a rebel asset. The movement is deployed to persist. Actually the rebel experiences various flows of time. There is the long, slow haul of history that will give ultimate victory, the fight for as long as it takes. There is the time of the gunman or the terrorists, a few spectacular operations on the dangerous edge where every moment is intense, enhanced by risk and power and meaning. No time is like that and no volunteer lives that way long – some do so only for a few moments each year and many have only a short span of active service as a gunman – a few months, a year or two. And few last the course even in retirement – the victims rarely forget the affront of horror. The rebel and the guerrilla may find security in exile or power but rarely the killer who enjoys his metier.

So no active gunmen can live on the high wire long. In between the moment of terror and the creep of history, most rebels live lives of hectic desperation often interrupted by the inevitable waiting. Deployment takes place in a mix of urgency and delay between the creep of history and the moment of terror. The rebel does not see protraction as a long, even flow but a matter of bursts and spasms, haste and delay, regular life in fact but played faster and for higher stakes. Persistence is hectic and no place more so than in deployment.

The rebel commanders deeply involved in the minutiae of the armed struggle that is dominated by the ramifications of the faith have little time to contemplate the implications of protraction or the special requirements imposed by deployment. The reasons of the underground, the requirements of the faith, if thought about at all, are assumed conventional, givens. *This* is the way we respond to challenge, to difficulty, to the needs of conflict for *this* is the appropriate way, the reasoned way, the way indicated by logic and the truth. Those commanders recognize the difficulties of deployment but, except in the manner of scarcity, seldom reflect on the reasons that so much is difficult, complicated, and dangerous. It is difficult enough to plan an ambush or pay the bills without fretting about first causes.

Those who control an armed struggle over time do so by deploying their assets in order to persist in various ways, for various strategic forces, selecting from the acceptable menu. Each armed struggle is operationally various; and as a result each deployment is limited and encouraged by certain special, underground factors. The formal chart of command, the size of the organization, the level of intensity may vary; but the essential obstacles are constants – as are the simple returns of the underground.

Choosing from an operational menu, a menu supplied by command perception, available assets, appropriate targets, the culture of the arena and the assumptions of the movement, is difficult, hampered by the rebel ecosystem. Each choice, any choice, every deployment will be hampered by the reality of the underground. The rebel can operate, deploy, from the security of cover but at severe cost – inefficiency, schism, incoherence, internal crisis, resentment at the edges, and adamancy when flexibility would pay, even the wastage of limited assets. All are assured, come as integral to the underground. And what is gained – besides the capacity to endure – is the willingness to endure with optimism. Even those with almost no assets to spend can survive, select from the top of the menu, deploy what exists in the name of what will be.

IN SUM

The requirements of deployment come, like much else, as a surprise to the rebel seldom aware of the complications of maintaining an armed struggle until the need arises. The choice of means, the techniques and tactics of deployment, are enormous, some cataloged in insurgency texts and some always novel; but every underground faces certain general obstacles – and few advantages – in using rebel assets. In the end, each deployment is special and the difficulties universal and the results unique.

12

Intelligence

IF DEPLOYMENT is always somehow managed it is in part because of the erratic but real flow of information concerning potential vulnerabilities that reaches the secret army. Communication may be difficult, the channels clogged and unsafe, the messages short and skewed, but information is moved into the movement. The information, data of all sorts, must then be filtered through the faith, analyzed, applied to matters of the moment and dispatched as instructions to chosen receivers. One way or another new data is transmitted, used for movement purpose, becomes transmuted into underground intelligence. And the rebel center needs data. What is happening above ground in the real world? Where are the state's vulnerabilities? Who can be sent on a mission and with what equipment? Where is the money promised, the demonstration planned, the messenger expected? How does the data fit the ideological vision and how can it be used technically for operational purpose? How best may the assets be deployed?

STRATEGIC INTELLIGENCE

Long before any crucial tactical question arises the rebel has presumed the actual nature of the real world that is real only through the adjustments of the faith. Everyone must tune the buzzing confusion of reality into sense, adjust up and down, view the day through experience and assumptions fulfilled. Much is not seen and some can be detailed that others pass over as invisible or irrelevant. The rebel is no different only more apt to have a special focus, fine-tuned to exaggerated proportions on details missed by the everyday. The rebel galaxy exists within this everyday reality but filters the actual in-coming light into the images expected and predicted by the dream. For the armed struggle this perception of the rebel matters enormously even in the most narrow, operational intelligence. Even to focus one's attention requires assumptions about the nature of reality, often unstated, often unrecognized. And the rebel has read history, found a reality not readily apparent to others – who at best are apt to accept rebel sincerity but still believe their own, the everyday vision is real and that underground illusion. The cynic cannot imagine love as anything but fantasy, a mystical experience as delusion. Real is real for the realist – but so too for the rebel.

Thus the faithful are scarcely aware that they wear special glasses. If everyone sees specially, the faithful sees more so than most. They have been transformed and thus are different. If history is as they predict, in time everyone will see as they do, transformed by Islam or the death of empire. And sometimes the vision does become reality – in fact such reality is mostly a matter of perspective and assumption, not some skewed totality: up is still up, the enemy powerful, the hungry unfed. It is the meaning of matters that matter, a case of interpretation, perspective.

This different perspective, easier to understand for the conventional as political conviction, maybe, then, closely related to the reality of both their opponents and of the disinterested but it is not the same. The nature of some movements, in fact, assures that not only is it different but also such rebel perception will grow more different. As times passes, as the sacrifices are made, as history unfolds without patent denial, the rebel becomes more not less assured even if victory becomes more distant. In fact as the coercion of the state on defense inevitably begins to restrict the activities and potential of the movement, the rebel is isolated, more distant from fresh data. The dynamics of the underground tend to restrict rebel intelligence from beyond the movement, certainly beyond the galaxy. Communication into the underground is difficult, always different. Trust is at risk. Operations absorb more time than planning. Consensus is difficult to build quickly or at all. Time runs simultaneously at varying paces – insufficient for daily living, adequate for the slow evolution of history, and like a warp in space suddenly transformed into an instant of terror and action. All these factors, from the perception of time to the cost of control at the fringe, often increase and always turn the rebel inward. Those involved in the minutiae of the armed struggle 24 hours a day lose balance and perspective over time, measure all against their immediate concerns. Reality – the reality of others – is hard to find and often unpleasant to contemplate, impossible to accept without editing.

As a movement contracts it does so not only in size but also in most cases away from the pressure of the state. Life underground becomes more intense. Even if the campaign escalates those involved are often driven closer to each other, their vision is compressed, intensified. Under state pressure, a given once an armed struggle has begun, rebels move deeper underground, further from the commonplace and so away from generally accepted reality. They associate only with the convinced, the dedicated, the volunteers. Too much reality destroys hope and initiative while too little destroys the rebel in futile and feckless adventures. Reality must be managed with care, word from outside is both necessary and potentially dangerous. Intelligence is not just the facts but also vindication.

Intelligence about the great scheme of things is thus muffled by desire, by analysis without recourse to verifiable results, by the reflections from the dream. The world may be seen as an expanding conspiracy, or may simply be discounted as not tactically relevant, as has been the case with the leaders of many rural insurrections focused only on immediate injustice and the neighborhood exploiter. The Irish have spent decades waiting for an opportunity to deploy, seeking within their constituency toleration and support, seldom focusing first on the avowed enemy. In 1969–70 what the IRA militants realized first was that an opportunity for an armed struggle existed because the nationalist community – the Catholics – in Northern Ireland needed a defense that only the volunteers could supply. The route from defense to provocation to attacks on the British army was obvious to the provisional Army Council – they, all republicans, knew the real enemy, the historic enemy; it was only the opportunity to strike that was often lacking and the loyalist attacks had opened the way.

TACTICAL INTELLIGENCE

It is easy to divide revolutionary intelligence into strategic and tactical. Strategic intelligence is data accumulated to give substance to the rebel vision and has, once the killing has begun, almost no further role to play except as exhortation. What is next needed is the most mundane operational details. Since most rebel operations are small, the tactical is often actually technical. Such technical intelligence arises from the operational needs of the battlefield, the turmoil and opportunities of the moment, and is transmitted upward and onward to control center. There for everyday operational purposes the data is used to wage the armed struggle. The filter seemingly does not matter greatly. An armed struggle introduces a very harsh reality to rebel assumptions. Strategic visions may encourage disaster and foolish daring but faulty tactical intelligence simply kills without returns of any sort unless the road to the future is to be paved solely with martyrs.

Tactical intelligence, however, is not simply technical. The entire movement is always shaped to the dream and thus any reality entering the ecosystem is fractured and reflected before interpreted. Even those distant from the center, the beggar on the corner or the clerk in the tax office, spies in a provincial capital, look where the faith requires, see what the faith suggests, report what the faith indicates. If they report fantasy, there will be operational disaster. They will, however, always and only report what they can see through the spectacles of the faith, some targets excluded, some reality ignored. The most mundane detail, the sentry's height or the train's schedule, is shaped by ideology. As those who report in grow fewer, the chance that gross reality will overwhelm interpretation declines. *Brigate rosse* went so far underground after 1979 after the Aldo Moro kidnapping-killing that not even friends could reach the activists nor could reality. The ideas of reality, honed and refined and elevated, reiterated in private increasingly warped what was already a skewed vision. Real life can no longer penetrate as the messengers disappear. Then only a little, filtered data arrives at the center of the rebel ecosystem. All that data is parsed for what is expected.

The center can often tolerate distressing intelligence that forces its way down into the underground by finding hints and indicators that all is actually as it ought to be. All rebels must be criminally optimistic or else there would be no armed struggle – and lack of contradictory data is crucial to that struggle.

Most tactical intelligence is so low key, focused on special directions and opportunities, seeking vulnerabilities or report on targets, that the data can hardly be called tactical. During an armed struggle there is always a mix of campaigns, both the directions of the military thrust and the agendas and activities of the other facets of the dream in action. Tactical intelligence can most properly be thought of as a vital, if often not delineated, often even not recognized, aspect of a campaign. The military needs are more obvious, target data, vulnerabilities, new arena information, weapons information, or enemy formations and so more traditional. The data needs of other campaigns, those of grievance or politics, secret diplomacy or commemorations and rituals, are as real but often are less covert, always less spectacular, and often go unrecognized – asking about to see how a candidate would do or talking with those who watched the parade or heard an oration to see what might be adjusted to advantage. Some tactical data is within the galaxy but mostly the movement actively seeks the details needed to pursue the various campaigns.

Mostly the intelligence focused on matters of relevance to the secret army coming into an underground will be analyzed to some degree as tactical and so to some degree prone to ideological adjustment; but the data is often hard and often so too the analysis. Tactical campaigns are pursued operationally and rarely organized specially, even specially recognized.

OPERATIONAL INTELLIGENCE

In the real world beyond the texts of the military academies, the distinctions between tactics and grand tactics, campaigns and regional strategies become blurred, certainly to the generals responsible. This is much less true in an armed struggle because, however complex the rebel ideological rationales, the rebel must wait, persist, and penalize the enemy so as to erode the will and let history proceed. All military operations are tactical, directed at this one end. Such operations may accumulate, be exaggerated, actually escalate, but this simply means more not different tactical counters. Intelligence used strategically will always encourage the rebels that they are winning or, if not, these being the times that try men's souls, that they must persist for victory is sure. There are even benefits in delay: the character of the people may be steeled, the nation may be forged in war or all else a disaster the armed struggle may act as witness, as blood sacrifice, as a necessary stage of history's drama. Only the perception that the faith has failed or the physical elimination of the rebels will impose strategic reassessment.

The focus is always on what to do next, what can be done not what should be done. For this the secret army concentrates on acquiring tactical, often technical, information. This real world intelligence need not be any more twisted by the faith than is the case for conventional states and orthodox intelligence agencies where organizational bias and convention play a similar role. While everything is filtered and transformed to proper writ, the cost of faith only rarely is simple fantasy.

Word does get through to the rebels, anyone's word when the newspapers are read or television viewed and someone's word when the tiny, coded communiqué arrives from a prison cell. The rebel is apt to be optimistic about tactical matters, optimistic often despite experience and the evidence of the immediate past. This is not novel. Successful generals are usually optimistic. Some may be cautious, delay battle or wait for reinforcements but in the short run most assume victory is possible. And for the rebel the long run is assured. The opponent of the rebel often is not, or not at first, a general but the orthodox state, denying the armed struggle is a war. Thus in the beginning the asymmetry poses a dreamer against a realist, the vision of the underground against the conventions of an orthodox government.

Nearly every rebel organization allots a considerable portion of intelligence assets to counter-intelligence, the search for conspiracy and spies, informers and heretics. No evidence becomes evidence of skilled penetration. The wilderness of mirrors that results is particularly deadly within inefficient and brutal secret organizations where the first resort is often to force.

It is not the disproportionate investment in counter-intelligence to find the informer or the heretic that is special about rebel data processing but the capacity of command central to find most news, any news, no news as good news. In-coming data, intelligence, tends to take on a heated glow of optimism as it moves towards the command center. Thus if conspiracy is everywhere and no one beyond suspicion, the countervailing result of all rebel perception is that all intelligence indicates matters are in hand. Thus the real world orbits about the galaxy, intermingled at times, but always aligned.

In low-intensity war the interpretation of the text of reality kills those who would too readily translate their heart's desire. It is one thing to send a man with a revolver against the empire but quite another, and obviously foolhardy, to send him down the middle of the street at high noon. There must be an operational adjustment. Without intention, unconsciously, rebel intelligence must adapt to reality, not risk the faith but not accept wishful thinking as reality. And this is easier than it might appear for the faith determines strategy while reality determines technical and tactical matters.

The rebel tactical estimates are often more accurate than those of the center. In order to defend the system's legitimacy, those under threat tend, certainly at first, to insist that the threat is minor, apolitical and alien. There is a continuing tendency to persist in focusing on rebel incompetence, all too real, on unsavory rebel motives, often true in a dirty war, and on flaws of the faith, again all too true. Thus the rebel benefits from the center's posture that tends to overlook the real virtues of the underground – that tends to stress, if at all, the romance of the secret and the lure of opportunism. The failures of the center's intelligence are compounded by the very evidence of reality, soldiers that can be counted, votes that can be counted, the numbers of prisoners and detainees and bombs defused, even the rising curve of kills. An armed struggle is not, however, a matter of numbers and quantitative triumphs but of the faith and will – and so the rebel persistence is ignored to rebel advantage.

Underground much of this is obvious. The rebel interpretation of reality and faith may be in orthodox Marxist-Leninist terms or the language of the mosque but always the commanders know what they need to know and what they want from intelligence is details. What is wanted is the bits and pieces useful to the gunman or the column commander. For this, most organizations fashion actual institutions, unlike communications, and place a positive not a negative value on assets so spent.

STRUCTURE AND INSTITUTIONS

Every member of the central military system, every member of the organized movement, each member of the galaxy and often their friends, neighbors, and contacts make up a huge intelligence net, a net in place of those conscious of movement priorities, those often alert, silent, working without trace – and, of course, often without result. The first asset then, is passive, arising from conviction. The armed struggle needs an input of information – targets and routines, habits and adjustments, vulnerabilities, secrets, and intentions. The galaxy, more particularly the movement, supplies this, often without refinement, often erratically, but always from proximity. From time to time, specifics may be requested from the center and the need filters out over the entire galaxy. The problems here are: first, the certain leakage of the nature of the need – perhaps to the enemy and certainly to the many; second, the lapse in time taken for the watchers to watch and report; and third, the difficulty of precision – there is no way to train the watchers but only to hope that the general returns will contain particulars of use.

The galaxy is the first asset in the search for all sorts of information, but the core of the operational intelligence is focused on the immediate needs of the organization. Nearly every organization, no matter the size, has the equivalent of an intelligence officer in constant contact with the core command. As the underground increases in size so may the complexity of the intelligence operation. Battle arenas or specific campaigns may have their own group, their own intelligence commander – and such commanders including those on special missions. These individuals may report directly to specific commanders. For all sorts of reasons there is a tendency in this the most secret of areas of the underground to maintain secret structures or special groups.

Most rebel, intelligence commanders, unlike their operational commanders and secret army leaders, do remember as much as they can; but they report only the necessary data and husband contacts and sources. They keep the secrets and when lost are in a real sense irreplaceable. One of the truly great losses for an underground, therefore, is the defection of an intelligence officer. First, as with any defection, this threatens the orthodox faithful, but unlike the loss of most volunteers the loss endangers the workings of the secret army but carries intact within him into heresy or the enemy camp much of the intelligence apparatus. A conventional defector carries only his own treason and what can be remembered, but the rebel intelligence defector takes with him as loss to the underground the surety of the faith and his memory – and his secret army often has only what he can remember. Only the most faithful, the most trusted and most cunning remain in rebel intelligence – and few can be tempted although some can be outwitted, manipulated, or if the state is fortunate found and eliminated. Thus, as in the real world, intelligence tends to be closed, compartmentalized, and crucial to the organization. Those involved keep the means to data isolated from all others.

The others at the center constantly feel the need for more and competing intelligence and so fashion other if very similar means. The system is cloned, a new net fashioned alongside the old. And always the responsible want to know more: what has happened and most of all what is about to happen? What is vulnerable? Who is faithful? Where can more arms be found? When will the police sweep begin? The usual questions. And quite often either the galaxy or the assigned volunteers produce viable results.

Again the movement does not have classes or texts or standard operating procedures to get results. Often the watchers are quite innocent and undiscriminating, lack imagination and rigor of observation but often are well placed and persistent. They do not so much learn by doing as act as conduit for raw data. For them there are no mid-career courses, no guides, often no real instructions, only an indication of GHQ interest. The underground applies their limited experience, seldom institutionalized, guile, enormous patience and long hours, and a great sense of urgency concerning the needs of the moment. The inherent inefficiency of the underground limits the result and as the subject rises from a technical matter to one of strategic analysis so do the strictures of the faith.

Quite often underground intelligence proves that necessity can triumph over lack of resources, formal skills and so confound the orthodox. In Belfast in the early part of 1979, the police undertook Operation Hawk, a major surveillance effort relying on highly sophisticated electronic equipment, covert operations, and existing files to track leading IRA suspects. In March an RUC checkpoint stopped a car to find they had scooped up the key IRA GHQ operational officer Brian Keenan – and, as a bonus, his coded address book. London informed the RUC that his notes suggested a raid on three houses. On 15 June, 300 police and another 100 soldiers swooped and discovered that the Provisional IRA had been running a highly sophisticated intelligence operation – running their own surveillance, keeping a watching brief on Hawk and many other supposedly covert security forces activities – and doing so unnoted, unsuspected for over six years. They were using military-style transmitters, specialized monitors, and position-fixing devices.

The Belfast IRA had set up telephone taps in the British Telecom network that included a tap on the private line on the Dunmurry residence of the general commanding the army garrison. Components had come from the Ulster Polytechnic and the Grundig and Strathearn Audio factories. And there were files, real files just as a real intelligence operation would generate: details of the houses, cars, lifestyles of civil servants and judges and security people. There were photographs, endless pages of transcripts of secret transmissions of the security forces. And they had used their skills and the electronic equipment from Grundig and Strathearn Audio to set up a modern factory producing elegant electronic and radio detonation devices for the IRA bombs: research and development underground as well as simple intelligence.

The IRA had cracked the codes for the RUC's Operation Hawk – and so watched the watchers, moving their own people around so that the authorities would track them using the police code word – one gunman was disgruntled to discover he had been code-named 'Chicken' and another 'Budgie'. The IRA had also followed much that the security force assumed was beyond reach of the lads off the Falls Road, the school leavers who somehow had friends who were telephone engineers and electronic specialists. And so the IRA had countered the intelligence of the security forces with assets unimagined by the conventional and shaped their own special intelligence – not one time but over the course of years.

In technical and tactical matters most undergrounds have been well served by their intelligence operations. Most armed struggles impose adjustments on the faithful that have spin-off intelligence benefits. The rebel perforce is easy with the requirements of secrecy for all the faithful are practiced subversives, and so draws on the rewards of sly cunning. Minds are concentrated and wary. The most wary are those in charge, fearful of conspiracy, fearful of the power of the state, dubious about internal security, and so secretive and elusive. They acquire habits never lost even after long years above ground in the everyday world. These rebel intelligence officers tend to have a longer operational life than gunmen or guerrillas and so over time accumulate trade experience. The great weakness of tactical intelligence is the lack of effective institutionalization of data and technique: no computer banks and no master classes. The compensation is that the craft can be relearned and even the networks and resources needed can be replaced. And because of the inclination toward multiple collectors even a major loss is not a total loss of underground intelligence capacity.

In the end all commanders want to know more, want to know the future, and want to know now. What is impressive is that for those, ill-trained or not, who are absolutely dedicated, completely focused on particular targets, that so much useful can be found. And what is useful is not really complex

– no details on computer circuitry but only how to bomb the electronics plant that makes the circuitry. Since it is easier to hide than to find, the more startling rebel successes tend to come when intelligence is sought and found about matters not thought relevant to the armed struggle, perhaps politicians' home addresses or the catering schedule in a government building. Whatever the operational matter, most rebel commanders never get what they want but generally get more than might be expected within an inherently inefficient underground. In many intelligence matters neither the faith nor the inevitable cost of persistence operate as usual, penalize as much. The very medium of the faith, the structure of the galaxy, is an asset; and the cost of secrecy, so dear to the orthodox, is no more painful for the intelligence function than any other aspect of the rebel ecosystem. What does penalize is the nature of rebel institutionalization. Strategic analysis, even much tactical analysis, found in governments and especially in the academies – the conferences, seminars, meetings and minutes, the situation reports, the files and monographs, the papers and articles and all the issues that rise and float on the paper simply do not exist. The few visible conferences, international gatherings, conventions and seminars focused on analysis are really exercises in internal propaganda, shadow plays to give legitimacy and depth to the make-do world of rebellion. If the analysis becomes truly important, if the seminars are real and the analysts paid, it is an indicator that the movement has become a counter-state, emerged from the underground as government-in-exile, runs to a different dynamic.

The rebel underground can effectively focus only on tactic data, fills in the strategic with a few broad strokes and concentrates on technical matters. This requires the establishment of intelligence officers and organizations that in turn are concerned with technical and tactical matters: bombing campaigns, assassination targets, infiltration by police informers, the acquisition of arms, the prospect of prison escape – and even at times the improvement of communications to get data into use. Sometimes assignments impose intelligence requirements – each operation – smuggling arms or shooting police agents in foreign capitals or robbing post offices – absorbs much time while data is accumulated. Even then, there are usually intelligence assignments given and perceived as a component of operations. There is very little concept of central intelligence and a great focus on what is needed now, for this operation or for that problem.

So just as all those in the galaxy are involved in data-gathering so too are all volunteers on active service. And the various institutions structured to acquire, order, and deploy this data are inevitably in place from early in the armed struggle. Intelligence is integral to operations – an expression of the faith – and to maintaining the purity of that faith. The other major facet of intelligence is to seek the schismatic, suspect the informer, counter penetration by the enemy or the apostate. Often separate from operations but arising from free floating suspicion, a conspiratorial atmosphere and actual evidence. This is the other rebel foci and central to underground concerns but divorced from operational matters. For the rebel the division between external and internal missions is so great that rivalry is rarely present as is the case in the conventional world. Operational matters are technical, tactical, detailed, day-to-day while penetration endangers the faith, a strategic matter that reverberates in every one of the saved. They are different, treated differently even as they merge and overlap. Still, just like the orthodox, every rebel army has in some form institutions for tactical intelligence and domestic counter-intelligence.

OPERATIONS

Since the underground always has less flexibility than imagined, unorthodox methods including the acquisition and use of intelligence arise from lack of formal assets not from skill or capacity. Thus rebel commanders rely mainly on the galaxy, the movement, on untrained observation, on luck, on sending the available for information on those few matters with sufficient priority to warrant early investment of assets. Mostly the investment comes after the initial indication from the galaxy focuses attention – on a means to escape, on the ease of access to a bank or military camp, on a vulnerability in security or office procedure or individual protection. There are various reasons that haphazard intelligence often produces such unexpectedly spectacular effects – the Dawson Field hijacking and hostage operation in September 1969 by the Palestinians, the assassination of Admiral Luis Carrero Blanco in Madrid by ETA on 20 December 1973, the kidnapping of Aldo Moro in Rome on 16 March 1978. The crucial fact is that the unexpected often works – first attempts or outrageously bold attempts are often effective. Then, too, the spectacular is exaggerated by the media. Everyone can watch and no one knows the last act. A little violence thus may go a long way, cause disproportionate impact on a well-ordered society. The World Trade Center in New York was bombed by a handful of emigrants. A violation of a convention, the breach of the assumed immunity of transnational airlines or the historic sanctity of diplomats gets results. And not every airliner or each embassy can be protected, and at times seemingly none can be sufficiently protected against the bold and determined. Worse for the authorities is a strike at those assumed quite untouchable, targets but safe: the British prime minister sitting in an office in Downing Street or the American Congress in session in the Capitol building. The audacious has more chance of success than might appear. This is especially the case for terror operations that factor in very low survival rates for their own. Most important, such targets can be attacked with quite limited intelligence.

The intelligence and planning, the assets needed to kidnap the Queen out of Buckingham Palace are far less than what is needed to spring someone from a British high-security prison. The authorities know all about prison escapes, have standard procedures, have hardened the targets, have not, as past experience indicates, made the prisons secure but certainly have lengthened the odds on escape even with outside help. As for the Queen, there has been much preparation but no experience. No one can imagine a vulnerability not covered but no one responsible can foresee all – and besides there has never been a visible attack. It is still the first time for Buckingham Palace.

Some targets, especially in open societies, remain vulnerable, particularly to those who take disproportionate risks with their own lives as well as everyone involved. Less intelligence is needed because audacity replaces assets. America is full of Federal office buildings – not just the one in Oklahoma City. Audacity in concept is crucial for this is often what makes the operation unconventional: the target is unexpected, the means of access unexpected, the result highly predictable but vitally important for the rebel eager to engender a maximum return on the investment. A fading urban guerrilla group seizing the Japanese embassy in Lima also seized world attention – at the cost of their own lives.

Data on potential targets is often not so much sought as discovered, arrives from the galaxy. And sometimes the galaxy is asked to watch, seek vulnerabilities, for most rebels have special targets, dream lists of victims – so many targets that no state is ever quite secure.

Target data

The unconventional approach, often difficult to distinguish from structured blunders, can pay enormous returns for those desperate to exaggerate operations. The four ETA volunteers dispatched to organize the assassination of Carrero Blanco spent a year seeking vulnerabilities in his routine. They became involved in all sorts of diversions that risked their freedom and so the operation. They were neither tidy nor skilled but, unsought, operated freely. The decision to dig a tunnel and place a bomb was not necessarily the most obvious and certainly not the best solution to their problem. The time and point in the admiral's routine, the moment on the way to church, was not the ideal, not even satisfactory. The whole undertaking, Operation Ogro, was unduly complex, yet nothing mattered but the result. All the unnecessary risks and their complicated methods still produced the desired result. And the explosion under the limousine had, as intended, a greater impact than a simple gunshot inside the church, the obvious, professional solution. In such operations innocence may pay and very little data do.

What is obvious about the intelligence gathering is that sufficient details were easily acquired. If the details of the target's routine had been really secret, the four innocent Basques without contacts or much experience would have failed. The details of the target's schedule were easily acquired and so allowed the four to plan the attack, complex, risky, but successful. The more notable aspect of the attack was that ETA had selected a type of target and then an individual. The intelligence did not drift in but had to be found. There was, then, a request from the center for specific operational intelligence rather than the arrival of news of a vulnerability. ETA chose the target, the first major strike away from the Basque country, in order to strike at post-Franco arrangements. The victim, Franco's chosen successor, would indicate that ETA would carry on the struggle – persist – and if need be escalate – operate in Madrid – no matter what the Spanish center did. The assassination was coherently planned by specific political purpose first and intelligence found later. Like most special rebel operations, the attack had many targets, delivered many messages but took only one victim. And like most special rebel operations audacity and novelty and a little hard data made success possible. The intelligence required was easily acquired if clumsily applied yet made possible ETA's greatest operation.

An easy means to reduce the demands on intelligence is to choose unprotected or novel targets. The more general the target, any judge and so all judges, means that access should be found even by the amateurs available. The more distant the target from the existing arena, the capital and not the colony, an ambassador abroad instead of a politician at home, the more complicated the intelligence problem but the greater the vulnerability and so the less information needed.

What rebel intelligence generally lacks is not adequacy but files. GHQ seldom has much of a corporate memory, cannot afford research or storage, and is tasked mainly for the next day not in general or for a distant contingency. It is not simply putting first things first but there are few second options for the rebel. Rebel intelligence rarely rises even to theater tactics – the central command may decide on escalation but this is often based on general perception rather than commissioned reports. More likely, operational data is acquired when needed, used and forgotten.

Internal data

Where intelligence is constantly wanted is on matters of internal security, the protection of the faith from the heretic or apostate and most of all the informer. This concern engenders a general anxiety, the more intense the closer to the core. Conspiratorial organizations fear conspiracy, fear effective cover, fear the corruption of the faith, fear in fact what is crucial to the eco-system. Knowing their own, they tend to fear their own may not be their own. Yet real counter-intelligence does not exist in the same way that operational intelligence does. There may be an inquisition, courts of inquiry, prosecutors and investigators; but most of these arise from suspicion confirmed. After a long campaign, internal security investigations may be institutionalized, as is the case with the IRA. Usually, someone is doubted and those, regardless of title or occupation, closest to the suspect are tasked with sifting the evidence.

In a sense, one of the forces that maintains the galaxy is free-floating anxiety, a weak force in contrast to the gravitational pull of the dream that generates a strong field but still a force, a factor. This universal anxiety intensifies both individual piety and public worship so as to deflect any unwarranted suspicion. The prospect of betrayal is thus the negative force for cohesion – and the reason that rebels seem more concerned about small schisms, a singular betrayal, than the intensity of the armed struggle. The armed struggle will in time be successful because the faith so assures the loyal but if the faith is spoiled all, including and especially the loyal, are lost. Thus the rebel is always alert for signs – even when no signs exists they are found by some. In the end much counter-intelligence rests on conspiracy theory where no evidence is the evidence.

With haste, anxiety, limited capacity to investigate, much counter-intelligence work is destructive, ineffectual, and vain since the anxiety arises from the nature of conviction not from actual betrayal. There are, of course, those who reinterpret the faith, cause a schism, lead an alternative movement. These may or may not be classified as enemies but are rarely welcomed. Rebels yearn for a single road to salvation, a single crusade, control of the truth and the faithful by the elect. Sometimes there are internecine conflicts over the faith, the movement, the organization or the secret army – a shooting war to solve ideological problems. These problems may arise from all sorts of reasons, personality clashes, communications problems, agenda differences or real theological problems but are always seen once the shooting begins as a struggle not between variables but over the control of the truth. Worse by far are those who jettison the truth entirely and betray the galaxy, betray their friends and fellow pilgrims. If this is done for money, so much the worse proving that the faith can be bought, if for fear of family or lack of nerve, so much the worse proving that the faith can not instill strength. Some at the center feel that even torture should not force betrayal. The faithful may not be able to move mountains but they should be able to withstand pain – for ever, for 24 hours, for three days, for the sake of the dream. Some betrayal takes places at the fringe, by friends and neighbors, some by those not under discipline but all informers within the avowed constituency are apt to suffer if discovered and the closer to the core the more certain the punishment.

Since the rebels have few options, some cases may be dealt with by maiming or compulsory exclusion – fleeing the country – but mostly the informer is shot, often in special ways, often after an underground trial. Always this procedure arises from the existence of intelligence. And such intelligence arrives in almost all cases spontaneously, unexpectedly, and rarely as the result of program or plan. Despite their enormous fears of betrayal, security checks are rare – the recruit is often known, has been known since born, has no secret life. When units are checked it is usually after not before information has been received or operations have aborted without good cause. Counter-intelligence operations are, then, not preventive but tied to prosecution. The original data is fortuitous, like so much rebel operational intelligence, and the subsequent information has been discovered as usual by a hasty, haphazard if sincere search for the guilty.

It is crucial to realize that with very few exceptions the amount of time and concern invested in protecting the faith, seeking potential apostates or operating against informers is enormous – and often is not considered a matter of intelligence at all. Yet all touched by the dream acquire as one role that of counter-intelligence officer, guardian of the ideal. The faith is everything for an underground, the source of the crucial energy and although eternal and valid somehow also vulnerable. Thus each volunteer, every member of the galaxy, believes the faith beyond reproach, the other believers just and saved; but yet, somehow, great care and constant caution must be exercised, not just against those who would betray the armed struggle out of greed or fear or failure of nerve but especially against those who would renounce the faith, deny the truth. Each galaxy is in part held in place not just by the magnetic power of belief but by the force of doubt – and to ease this doubt data is needed and so intelligence is sought by all even if not institutionalized. And often the underground does, indeed, have those structured for no other purpose, to seek, discover, try, and punish the unfaithful and every underground has as priority the hunt for the spy, the mole, the informer.

Special cases

Two other areas that involve intelligence in a classical sense are usually assigned by rebels to special units and not considered as 'intelligence' at all. The first is the problem and potential of prisoners. Inside the prison units may have an intelligence officer and are apt – having much time – to have more intelligence planning and review than those active outside. Those outside concerned with prisoners tend to subsume the various problems under special prison operations – vulnerabilities of guards, means of communication, strategies of resistance and prospects of escape. Each is handled in turn and if intelligence is needed acquired without recourse to central assets or even to the use of the word. The second area is the acquisition of arms and at times funds through illicit means. Again those units involved acquire their own intelligence and even more than those involved in prison operations, compartmentalize their systems, nets and contacts for security purposes – thus assuring that the loss of a key volunteer means the loss of the files kept in his head. In any case, most of such operations merge diplomacy, commerce, covert tradecraft, and special operations with each phase generating its own needs and own means to acquire the appropriate information.

Intelligence, then, is very closely tied to operations like most aspects of the dynamics of the armed struggle except, again as expected, when dealing with the faith. And when dealing with the faith the details are operational although the results are crucial. Most intelligence is not very crucial and not very difficult to acquire and almost never kept for contingency planning. Individuals may become resources, may even be isolated away from the center for years and return with still valid assets in their head. Some individuals may prove apt at intelligence tasks, but this is a matter of luck. Some individuals may find conspiracy and betrayal everywhere and this is unfortunate if predictable.

Fortunately for the rebel operational needs are relatively easy to fulfill and the sanctity of the faith can never be fully protected. In the first case, the unconventional coupled to the acquired data can produce formidable and spectacular results. In the second case, the inevitable anxiety and allotment of resources does return not so much purity as deeper and certainly more visible commitment. Somehow the movement manages to acquire what is needed, what is needed to operate, what is needed to purify the system, what will allow the secret army to persist and at times to escalate the campaign.

IN SUM

In rebel operational matters a little has always gone a long way. As in all else strategy falls to the text of the faith, seldom intrudes except as exhortation in rebel considerations. Tactical intelligence is closely tied to specific operations on one hand and to a general fear of penetration and betrayal on the other with very little central control. Intelligence is assigned to individuals, those with skill and brutality who are sound of faith. They possess procedures, contacts, the data but have no files. They are one of the underground's greatest and most vulnerable assets. And these, the best and the brightest, may be lost and so the data, the contacts, the control. Much is not done or not done properly in matters of intelligence – a facet of operations not a special discipline. And much, therefore, is handled elsewhere or not at all, left to the gunman or the purchasing agents or the publicity office, left to the galaxy. And, at the end, Moro is dead and Carrero Blanco; the airliners smashed on Dawson Field; Downing Street mortared; and the World Trade Center bombed. Not much data was needed, just enough was enough: could the mortars reach, was there parking inside the Trade Center? In a sense the real world is unduly penalized by the secrecy surrounding the acquisition and analysis of intelligence data, a cost not paid for most orthodox actions, while the rebel always under cover, at risk and without skills, copes by necessity and without surprise or recriminations unlike the conventional who assumes secrecy a blessing. The rebel is penalized as always by the nature of the ecosystem but needs little to persist, less to cause trouble. The world can be moved if there is but a tiny spot to place a fulcrum and in the campaigns of the armed struggle even the innocent and ignorant have found appropriate sites. A little intelligence can go a long way – and does.

13

The Campaign

FOR NEARLY everyone, most certainly the involved, the campaign, the killing and risks, the spectaculars and prisons, is the core, the armed struggle, the faith as deed. The gunmen sponsor the thrillers and history books, the academic studies of this movement or that, the television cameramen show up at bomb sites and the journalists write of strategy and tactics, hearts and minds. The campaign is seen, again by the involved as well, as a war, a special war, unconventional but still a war, not a form of social mobilization, not the outward and visible sign of a revealed faith. The campaign is mostly all above ground, visible in result if not in operation. This is the tangible face of the armed struggle, the aspect, defined and shaped as central by the conventional theorists – and by the threatened state. And justly so, for the rebel campaign, whatever else, is violent, a matter of killing, often spectacular killing, the essential dynamic of any armed struggle. The factors that make it possible, the support and toleration, the means that extend, expand and exaggerate the effect through other kinds of action may in the end, may in all cases, be more important; but the war is the core, the matrix, the means to transform a dream into power.

To divide up the war, the campaigns as military or conspiratorial, protracted popular war or urban terror is to mingle intensity and means, time and opportunity. All these bleed and blend in real life and only the rare campaign, like Che's in Bolivia, fits neatly into a pigeon hole. The more serious the armed struggle the more complex, the more simultaneous fronts and so the more categories involved. The divisions between country and city are real but always blurred. The necessity of protraction appears in all sorts of circumstances. Still, certain armed struggles fit conventional expectations: the focus is the rural peasant slow to organize, slow to escalate, deterred with items from the anti-insurgency text or recourse to state terror. The *Brigate rosse* were classic urban terrorists, and generated a classic campaign, a text. The arena shifts as the rebel seeks vulnerabilities, finds cover, exploits whatever limited assets exist. It bounds the attitudes, agenda and assumptions of all involved, is a stage but not central to the drama any more than the details of the dream or the predilections of individuals. The campaign is, in effect, where the rebel focuses physical force, opens fronts of all sorts, enters into the asymmetrical lethal dialogue with the state.

NATURE OF THE STRUGGLE

What becomes difficult for the analysts is that the armed campaign, the visible and violent struggle between the state and the rebel, is not amenable to conventional approach as *merely* a campaign. Real wars, even irregular wars, are won and lost, have tangible results, body counts count, high ground matters, a retreat changes the arena. This is war. The orthodox army would so like to treat insurrection, both in description and in reality, deploy tangible assets following the conventions of the unconventional and roll up the guerrillas. Sometimes the state does so – lets the military loose on the gunmen or bandits, admits there is a campaign if not quite a war. Sometimes the state prefers to declare peace and pursue the rebel covertly by military means disguised as peace-keeping or police action.

It is then the campaign requires, as sooner or later all armed struggles do, rationalization to explain the special nature of what the state insists is not a war but not quite peace. A campaign arising from an armed struggle is neither war nor peace, not just the gun in politics, not a covert but parallel world opposed to the center. All these are true and adequate and add very little to the description of the campaign but are crucial factors in describing the dynamics that produce the campaign. These dynamics operate for the underground and so for others as a result of perceptions of reality: what is taken on faith matters, not body counts or the high ground.

Later the generals will write books easily read as military history, the analysts' works to be filed under politics or sociology, and the rebel, if fortunate to survive, political memoirs. Grivas, a professional colonel promoted general at the end of the EOKA struggle, wrote both: a guerrilla manual and a substantial memoir. Mao, a political general, wrote about revolutionary war not military history. Begin – as always – wrote as if his pages would be pasted up on walls. They all covered in detail the most visible and most exciting part of an armed struggle, the campaign, the killing, the prison breaks and ambushes and heroism and cruelty. Grivas, being a regular, gave his campaign regularity; and Che, being a revolutionary theorist, made his fit theory. These rebel campaigns are, justifiably and understandably, material for films and novels. And so real and compelling that the generals and analysts and even the rebels are inclined to think it the main story, often the only story even while they insert references to political context or the hearts and minds of the people, the will of the state – the intangibles that seemingly played so little part in the real killing.

The intangibles, those assets and liabilities, those historical imperatives and moral boundaries, that do not show up easily on the battlefield, in the bush or down a back lane, shape the killing, insert meaning into murder, even in large part determine the winner. The armed struggle and the visible facet, the killing campaign, is in great part a matter of perception, unarticulated assumptions, organizations and movements controlled by unstated consensus, matters that unlike the classical account of a cavalry charge or a naval battle cannot be exactly described. The evolution of battle tactics, the construction of cruisers, the class structure of the combatants, all may play a role – no less in fact than the weather or the terrain – but the battle is the key. And the winners and losers, the course of the day, the toll of the dead, the ruined ships are not a matter of dispute, not a matter of perception. This is far less so with an insurrectionary campaign – then it is often difficult to determine if there is a war at all much less who is winning for there are often few casualties to count and the battles are not over at the end of the day or the month. The involved must assume much.

THE ANALYSIS OF THE CAMPAIGNS

Those who describe or analyze the armed struggle beyond the spectacular events tend to focus on a particular aspect of the campaign – see events ordered by perception. First, most concentrate on the armed aspect of the campaign, the killing, but then the means of entry onto the stage indicates the special interest. Generally analysts organize around the arena, the ideologies, the intensity of the war, the length of the struggle or the tactics involved. Thus books can be found focused on a compelling aspect of the armed struggle: the urban guerrilla or rural insurgency, the arena; on communist subversion and national liberation movements, the ideals; on the terror network or revolution, intensity; or on protracted conflict or the year of the guerrilla, the time; or on low-intensity warfare or the war of the flea, the tactics. The most satisfactory means of approach has been traditional narrative history that imposes, as do the involved, a beginning and an end, includes aspects of the real and cultural arena and may expose social facets – psychological or economic – of the campaign as well as the more military events. Almost certainly the concerns of social science and policy analysts will not be as well served, but in turn such methodologies often are concerned more with general facets of behavior than with a specific campaign except as a case study.

In all cases the approach indicates not simply the interests and favored methodology of the investigator but also assumptions about the nature of reality and often a special agenda. To explain the nature of the Irish problem is to assure the nature of a cherished solution – a religious war requires a different accommodation from a national liberation struggle. In general many are dedicated to order or to change, focus on the means to power or the protection of the center. Some write, then, of special operations, anti-insurgency tactics, internal war when they treat the campaign. Others are apt to seek romantic heroes, crusades for justice, or the inevitability of history. The scholar may see war as politics or politics as war and have recourse to the means of social science. Those who seek only the truth, whether with charts and graphs or narrative history, who hope to be value free, still focus on an amenable aspect of the campaign and somehow no such focus is ever quite sufficient, can enclose all the variables, all the factors, find a consensus on the meaning of the killing. At least all focus on what can be seen, the tangible campaign undertaken by rebels against the center.

The campaign in an armed struggle is, then, the visible aspect of an asymmetrical conflict between those with a compelling vision of a promised future and those, conventional in most matters, who possess legitimacy, usually the state, and always the center with tangible assets. It is the rebel ideal, the dream, that imposes the responsibility to revolt on the faithful. And the dream also imposes form on the faithful, assures a galaxy of believers that contains a movement – not a party or a secret army or not alone, not a spectrum of organizations but those who see reality in a special way and so feel impelled to act in certain ways. They must so act even when their acts are feeble or few, when the devout are not mobilized or when the avowed constituency denies them. They feel a clearly defined responsibility. And once engaged in seeking to change history the rebels must respond to the inevitable opposition of a powerful center. The movement must react both to the imperatives of the ideal and the reality of the opposition.

The movement does in fact contain organizations and for the armed struggle a secret army. All are united in the faith, held in varying degrees of intensity, and all accept as well the strategic readings that arise from the texts of that faith. Regardless of the text or the message, the imperatives of class or the gods, the secret army operates as a means that will allow individuals to pursue the responsibilities of the truth. To exist the rebel must fashion, often unconsciously, a protective ecosystem that allows persistence if at cost, that assures a campaign that will be countered by the center. The center's inevitable response follows a pattern that then shapes rebel capacity and structure.

Even the nature of what consists of a campaign within the general struggle is elusive. Small rebel organizations can organize only a single campaign, persisting in hopes of escalation or deploying at least as witness for those deprived or those to come. The Stern Group – LEHI – was tiny but with assassination could threaten the equanimity of the British empire. Within the Palestinian fedayeen movement, there was after 1970 until about 1974 a general terror campaign but only as a single facet of the whole armed struggle and that struggle one component of the entire movement seeking to establish a nation. Within the terror campaign certain organizations would focus only on tactical terror. Their campaign was their armed struggle, terrible, spectacular and not without effect. Some movements, smaller and less competent than the Palestinians, can pursue but one campaign until defeat or escalation: EOKA or the Mau Mau, different in all else but the narrow limits on possibilities. Grivas managed to open a second rural front in the mountains more as symbol than reality, but the Mau Mau after the early days could only seek to evade the security forces. The Irgun's revolt was in fact a campaign run parallel to that of LEHI and briefly in alliance with Haganah. All other campaigns and fronts were beyond control if directed toward a similar end. At times a movement may engage in serial campaigns, try this approach, attack next that vulnerability, failing which look elsewhere with other means. This has generally been the case with the Irish.

Over two centuries the Irish have never managed to intensify their struggle for long at a stage of irregular war where cover is not needed. The early French-backed forays failed and are far in the past. Since then the republican leadership opting for physical force selected a course that makes use of perceived English vulnerabilities, Irish assets and the toleration of the nationalist constituency. Thus each campaign varied in scope, mix of techniques, point of focus. There were distant attacks by the Fenians, bombs in English cities and invasions of Canada, conspiracies and insurrections, guerrillas in the country and gunmen in the cities. The Anglo-Irish War of 1918–21 saw many fronts and so in a sense many campaigns – mostly a rebellion on the island under cover, in tandem with the establishment of an alternative government to represent the risen nation. Later the IRA focused on the Free State as enemy or the reality of the British presence in Northern Ireland or the English mainland – only after 1971 could the secret army deploy against more than one target in more than one arena. And after 1974–75 with the beginning of the long war, the IRA actively sought other fronts and varied targets to maintain the campaign, a campaign that could not escalate but could not be closed down. The IRA could neither win nor lose but persist – a congenial if costly posture. Generally, however, an Irish campaign had a beginning and an end, always relied on physical force and usually focused on one approach, one front, one vulnerability. In the campaign's end, however, was the beginning of the next one.

The Irish republicans, like other rebel movements, represented with their campaign one aspect of the battle against the present. Many non-military fronts were controlled by other and different nationalists, usually more moderate and often more flexible: for them the dream was real but more pragmatic. Thus Grivas had to depend on Cypriot Greek nationalist organizations that he could not control, and so too Begin – who presented Ben-Gurion with a physical force capacity he could not command – or control. Mostly a military campaign in theory makes use of all the other fronts just as is the case in orthodox war, but as in orthodox war force dominates the dynamics.

In Ireland over two centuries, nationalists have sought power and control within the island by recourse to conventional parliamentary politics, by means of boycott, monster meetings, demonstrations and strike, by use of threats and through alliances with Britain's allies and enemies. The political leadership has sought concession, reform, advantage, made use of the militant republicans and denied them. Thus in a broad sense all IRB-IRA campaigns are but a facet of grand strategy, often a grand strategy with central command, single direction, or certain end. Within the secret army, the republican conspiracy, a campaign is seen as time-linked – this genera-tion's effort – and arena focused – this time in England or in Northern Ireland. In 1994 after a generation of struggle, the IRA leadership sought through a ceasefire and negotiations a means to avoid both the persistence of the struggle and the necessity for physical force but did so with a move-ment that distrusted politics as well as the British enemy and the establish-ment in Dublin. Few were sure whether the ceasefire was a beginning or an end, a stage, a concession or an indication of strength: what was clear was that the immediate future held no recourse to an armed struggle even if the struggle was to continue. After 17 months the campaign began again, lasted 17 months and ended with a ceasefire in July 1997 for the same reasons.

A campaign may when thwarted in one arena seep into another, same campaign but different focus, formerly guerrilla raids but now international terror but without abandoning the guerrilla. Rarely has the rebel center considered two simultaneous campaigns, defining new fronts not as new directions but a form of escalation, and almost never the existing campaign as an aspect of a more general historical event – Fenian bombs as part of the nationalist drive for British concession on national and social issues – Home Rule or fixed land tenure. Almost always the IRA has seen the campaign as the contemporary deployment of physical force to coerce the British into submission not concession. A campaign for the Irish rebel is war – maybe as in 1921 war supported by politics or later with Sinn Féin but war first with a lesser political front. A campaign in Ireland has been war but unconventional war, rarely even irregular war, war always with a cover, covert, illicit, and based on long experience. The IRA volunteer is thus apt to take a conventional view of the unconventional: after all, each recruit came to an army, became a volunteer in a secret army, sought to fight as a soldier not as a revolutionary gunman or an ideological terrorist.

Those at the center are comforted that the IRA volunteer can be categorized as underground soldier. The conventional tend in print as well as reality to miss the enormous power of the revelation on the perception of the involved. The rebel sees reality differently and so is different. The IRA volunteer realizes the difference but not the reality of that difference within the underground. The IRA volunteer persists in thinking as soldier but must exist as rebel, under cover without uniform or recognition, relying on legitimacy not from the titles awarded by a secret army but by the perception of republican galaxy and at times the declared constituency. The volunteer is different, legitimate as rebel but not a real soldier at all.

This difference is often noted by appropriating other names for the gunman: guerrilla, defender, freedom fighter, fedayeen, partisan. The campaign, however, is waged mostly by the unorthodox deploying irregular means. And a major difference is the compelling, transcendental aspiration of those underground that fuels the campaign. The Irgun and the British were neither ignorant nor innocent of the real in their conflict; but the authorities could not imagine the impact of either the holocaust or two thousand years of Jewish history – or, of course, their own conduct – on the rebels. The rebel with so little else is driven by the intangibles that quite often the center denies exist or at least are relevant – the British response to Zionist ambitions in Palestine had very real psychological roots as well as pragmatic considerations. The British had given up over hegemony in Ireland in 1921 because they no longer wanted to maintain domination over Irish nationalists, largely Catholic, by recourse to state terror – and because it was too costly in tangibles. They did not, however, then or later discard their intangible attitudes on the nature of the Irish, Anglo-Irish history, and English – British – nationalism that were never measured out in policy choices. The center has dreams too; but the faith has faded, the pragmatic counts too, and reality cannot be entirely denied.

For the rebel the faith will provide, not only history as promised but salvation for all. What is good for the faith is good for the individual. The faith can use but does not require explainers. The truth to the believer is obvious and subsequent actions adjusted to it. Thus everyone who believes serves if by no other means than as witness to the power of the dream. Reality in expectations and understanding is not tangible. All the glitter and power of those in place, Louis XVI or Nicholas II, the Shah, Farouk, was revealed to be patina over obsolescence.

Rebels never appear winners. Lenin was thought a fool and Hitler a crank. Every movement's office is seemingly interchangeable, small, seedy, on the wrong side of town, filled with old banners and posters, unread pamphlets and dirty cups. These rooms are merely way-stops to the future for the faithful. When the faithful step into the underground, they are seldom in step with the orthodox, still appear hopeless, limited in assets and warped in analysis. This move underground is perceived by those involved as in cadence with history, empowered by considerations beyond quantification: the truth will set them free and the truth is underground. And so the campaign is based on the faith and shaped by the perceptions of the faithful: national liberation or Islam redeemed.

If the vision can be maintained, if the armed struggle can continue, if the campaign persists then truth will in time prevail. The world is by no means turned upside down, for the dead are still dead, the horrified no friends of the rebel, the military in control of the country, the gunman hunted and the suspect in prison; but what all this means is read differently underground. The asymmetry in the struggle and so the campaign is not simply a matter of assets, big battalions there and bandits out there, but a matter of interpretation. For the terrorists the massacre by the Japanese Red Army at Lod was a splendid success. For Giap the destruction of the Viet Cong during Tet turned into a splendid victory. For the Irgun the presence of ninety thousand British troops was a sign of progress. For the *Brigate rosse*, however, the Moro operation that riveted the nation for two months – the Fifty-five Days, a seeming operational and symbolic triumph, was the beginning of the end for the faithful had misread history. In the underground excess optimism may be necessary but a determined reliance on a vision at the expense of everyday reality can lead to disaster: all those *focos* in Latin America, comforting in theory but lethal in practice, arose from a misreading of reality. The faith mattered more than the facts, it always does, but facts matter – even to the faithful who shape the campaign.

Many lose this faith in the inevitable and necessary triumph of the revolution. Their dream evaporated even if they would not deny their service, past commitment. In Italy, for example, there was no longer purpose in pursuing a campaign but the dwindling dedicated core continued as long as there were a few with guns. For these the dream was still real, still mattered, the campaign still valid. What matters is what is seen to matter. So there is, indeed, real killing, a real campaign with battles and casualties, raids and sorties and all the rest but the result cannot easily be counted up in numbers, charts and graphs.

CAMPAIGN CASE STUDIES

If there is any analytical consensus at all concerning those conflicts that can be grouped under the rubric of armed struggles, it is that the case study method is useful, if not the most useful means then always a use to those even with other interests and different foci. The social scientists often leave such chronological studies to historians or shape their own cases in language that hides the fact they are contemporary history, if too often from secondary sources. There is an inclination by analysts not trained as historians to assume that narrative case studies are more rigorous than they are – that 'history' is fact rather than an artful presentation limited as well as shaped by data. Still, whether done as history, disguised as social science, or undertaken by those involved, journalists, policy analysts and bureaucrats, whether published as books, as part of anti-insurgency training manuals or as memorial to the slain, the results tend to a pattern: campaign studies. There is an introduction at times offering promises that the text must keep, then the arena as prologue, sometimes this is merely a cursory beginning and at others a deep cultural history. What follows is the core, the political-military developments over time, that culminates in a result, winning or losing, and a final summary with at times reference to lessons learned or theories proven. Rebel campaigns must perforce follow the form – there must be a beginning and an end, a series of events and usually be lessons learned. Mostly the campaign is seen from the outside and the dynamics described if at all from analogy and the evidence of those once involved.

The visible and even agreed events of the campaign – the King David Hotel was bombed in Jerusalem, Tet occurred, Che is dead – are the tangibles of the rebel dream at work. The important factors of shifting perception, the intangibles of will and optimism, can be inferred, more often than not inferred with considerable accuracy – certainly after the events. The center can usually be treated as real, the evidence traditional, the motives as displayed, the operations as indicated from the documents – perhaps enhanced by some insights on the assumptions and misperceptions of the involved. The rebels are more difficult since there is less traditional data and the key factors are often the assumptions and intangibles later adjusted by the involved to account for victory or defeat. Still, a great many observers have fruitful insights into the covert, are not unmindful of the weight of perception and the impact of the ideal.

The result is that there is a most useful literature of case studies, even when those studies, as is often if not usually the case, written to forward a specific agenda – counter terror or buttress the national cause. There are as well a series of case studies strung together as example or displayed as basis for more general concerns: transnational terrorism or anti-communist guerrilla organizations. Many are political–military history that indicate an innocence of the nature of the underground or are based on an assumption that an exposure to the covert is ample to understand a secret army: that secrecy provides an affinity, that the faith of the gunmen is no more than an underground patriotism. Hence the case studies display an asymmetrical conflict where the key difference is not perception but capacity.

In a sense what most case studies lack is the understanding to transfer the result of the cultural shock involved in entry into the underground to the reader. The gunman is not a soldier in a raincoat but an individual driven by a dream that transforms reality. Novel reality is hard to grasp and hard to describe. It is one matter to read of starvation another to see it. An exposure over time to the alien often produces trauma, must, indeed, produce psychic trauma, if there is to be learning. The boat person or the Eskimo seldom writes of the impact of the complex on the simple, but the cases of the complex in the Peace Corps or the military being stunned by the different are legion: cultural shock. And what makes the armed struggle different – traumatic for analysts – is that the underground is alien. Surely the volunteer who drives to certain death in a carbomb is not a simple soldier any more than the Japanese volunteer who slaughtered those in reach in the Lod massacre. What makes them explicable is the impact of a dream that few analysts can experience or apparently imagine. So unconventional campaigns are often described by the conventions of the orthodox, often for conventional purpose. And this often is satisfactory for most uses and many analysts.

The rebel ecosystem cannot easily be grasped by projection or analogy any more than can romantic love or a religious conversion where description is apt to advance by negatives or similes – not this but like that. Thus even the best of the case studies face the obstacle of explaining what is largely inexplicable – the mind of the convert and the world this shapes, a reality sharp, vital, compelling and beyond the reach of the conventional. Explaining from the known, the orthodox, usually indignant and outraged at the pretensions and brutality of the rebel, ever inclined to seeking base motives, seldom credit the ideal as quite real. A mystical experience is thus explained as a delusion, real to the saint but not to others. The rebel reality is thus discounted because it is rebel not real and so the reality of the underground remains misunderstood.

The conventional at home in book-lined studies or in large offices, in front of computers with references to hand, area experts on call, tend to be orthodox in approach. Those who have participated in anti-insurgency campaigns are no better for they assume an experience in the black world that they have in fact not had – they did not see as rebels but saw rebels as real. Few of those deployed by the state, by the system have ever been driven by a rebel dream and so explain to each other. Such history must, because that is the nature of history, have a beginning and an end, must touch the crucial events and the spectacular operations, must cover the data. And many works do so with care, cunning, and with serious efforts to explain the rebel. Where the rebel has become a familiar as in Ireland, the astute recognize the power if not the legitimacy of the dream. Elsewhere the orthodox focus on the tangible, assets, deployment, campaigns, things that can be counted.

Campaigns tend to be described from the perspective of the state-center, particularly by rebels in from the cold. Rebels have risked all to be at the center, to control events from the center not from a vision, to be taken as legitimate and conventional. And so the rebel is often less forthcoming on the underground than the disinterested scholar or the observant journalist. Bob Fisk, reporting for the London *Times* and then *The Independent*, describing how stories are gotten in Lebanon during the chaos gives greater insight into the atmosphere of the underground than in his more formal books – Lebanon for nearly everyone in the country became an underground driven by nightmares, tribal fantasies, broken dreams.

Those who write fiction and films even as they compress events into a novel or a feature, still give indication of that strange atmosphere. And most of that atmosphere is found in perception not in visuals; spy novels do better than spy films for very little visible takes place in the secret world. A secret army is secret not because of the camouflage alone but because the ideal cannot be shared with the conventional. No one, however, can manage to infuse a case study with the reality of the dream, only conversion can do that, not insight or proximity or talent. Most case studies subsume the dream under ideology or motivation and make the years of the campaign explicable in orthodox terms.

Most studies are apt to reveal the singular of the particular event examined. The Huks might have been communists, rural guerrillas, might have exploited traditional grievances, deployed in traditional ways their traditional assets but were special, were not like the rural communists of Malaya or the African Marxist-Leninists of Eritrea or Angola any more than one African nationalist movement is the image of another. Case studies tend to indicate that one rural campaign is much like the next but that each is special. There have been classical struggles, long, complex, spectacular and intense – Vietnam, Algeria, Palestine, Ireland – that contain models for the general. In fact such campaigns did provide models for many other rebels who read reality through faith-tinted glass, then adjusted the distant campaign to the local conditions, and so produced material for case studies of their own.

Begin in 1944 felt there were only two relevant case studies, India and Ireland. The first was alien – and offered means unsatisfactory to the needs of his own at that particular moment – but Ireland seemed more promising. In 1971–72, the Chief of Staff of the Provisional IRA Seán MacStiofáin was reading about South Arabia: How many British soldiers had the NLF-FLOSSY killed before London lost the will to remain? The tendency of Begin, MacStiofáin and the others is to read the case study, note the results, borrow the tactics and techniques for their own dream supplies the strategic imperative as well as the necessary energy. All case studies are useful to the gunman even if in reality only one book is read. There is always an enormous amount of energy invested in speculation and disputation at most beginnings, but this is rarely focused on military–political strategy but rather the dream so disguised. It is an exercise in faith, a catechism not an operational plan whatever may be published later.

The Ireland that Begin took as case study was largely the classical period of revolt between 1918 and 1921 after the Easter Rising of 1916 and before the irreconcilables of the IRA went underground. In some form, often quite truncated, this Black and Tan war or the Troubles that include the entire 1916–25 decade of violence has been case study and primer for an enormous number of diverse and often very distant rebels. The Irish appeared first on the scene although the IRA felt ancient in experience and expectations, weighted with history as well as opportunity. Some Irish history is real enough – 1798 to 1918 was rich in events, options, campaigns. It is the Tan War, the glory days of the IRA, that others found most useful.

The charm of Ireland is that the rebels without many assets took on the British empire and won some if not all of the dream – the distant rebels are particularly attracted to both Irish tactical means and also the errors in culmination to avoid, the good lessons and the bad examples. The Irish have always had trouble with selecting the appropriate from their rich history – any posture has precedents – and so MacStiofáin looked elsewhere as well but not to great advantage. The reality of the South Arabian experience meant little for London when engaged, yet again, in Irish Troubles within the United Kingdom. Ireland was special for London as well as for the Irish.

While the more extended treatments of the Irish Troubles always stress the special, more often the Irish special than the British special, distant rebels look to the general: the creation of a secret army, escalation not only through tactical ingenuity coupled with a ruthless determination but also by means of parallel institution – an underground government, by recourse to diplomacy, the mobilization of the Diaspora, propaganda, subversion. These were, correctly, assumed factors for export. The long Anglo-Irish historical dialogue, the history of radical Irish republicanism that shaped rebel assumptions, the divisions in island society, particularly the religious divide, the nature of British society, the attitudes and assets of the British establishment, and the atmosphere of the world arena in general in 1918, all were particular and vital and largely ignored.

The rebels in Africa or Latin America wanted to know what to do and what not to do and focused directly on the campaign with a singleness of purpose. And those charged with defending the center so focused for they needed to know what to expect and to respond. For these purposes the Irish case study was attenuated to lessons learned – and what has interested the rebels and their opponents not at all has been Irish history, Gaelic particularism. Beyond the fact that there has always been an Irish rebel in the rebel pantheon, a gunman in trench coat then and now, who has generated goodwill for the Celt in revolutionary circles, the active guerrilla wants evidence and operational instruction not history.

The Irish Troubles, a failed provincial rising planned with German aid, collapsed Easter Week in 1916 into a blood sacrifice. Instead of future generations being inspired, the Irish nation, mostly Catholic, mostly content until 1916, was immediately inspired to support or to tolerate three years of escalating rebellion that tactically included classic actions in the country, although no full-time guerrilla columns wandering the green hills, and terror in the cities. The core of the secret army broadened by political leaders also escalated the struggle through the entire spectrum of new fronts and new initiatives ranging from rural courts dispensing justice to assassins sent into London. In 1921 the British, unwilling to rule solely through coercion, a costly process fiscally, militarily and morally, switched to a path that led to a diplomatic accommodation. This maneuver, made visible in the Anglo-Irish Treaty, engendered a civil war and a long-lived secret and subversive IRA on the island but for 50 years removed Ireland as a political issue from British politics. As a case study Ireland did more for the observers than they did for the Irish who learned little that did not fit the desires and devices of their own hearts.

Then in 1969–70 the Irish republicans were presented with what had long been sought – an opportunity to apply lessons as then learned. These lessons described reality more accurately in 1970 than any other model presented and meant that a campaign was possible. What came next had not been considered at such length because since 1921 beginning had always been the great obstacle. Once the campaign began, the IRA simply sought to escalate and then to persist by seeking new options and new targets. What previous campaigns in and out of Ireland indicated no longer mattered in that British resistance and Irish persistence established a special and lethal dialogue that regularly saw novelty but no real change in the correlation of forces.

CAMPAIGN MODELS

To make it real the rebel as well as the professional soldier must shape the campaign to tangibles, the environment of war and the presence of assets that cannot be vaporized by dreams. The rebel sees much the same as does the general or the paratrooper, takes cover, shoots with a clean weapon, worries about fire lines and back-up, is not maddened crusader immune to all but silver bullets – although Africa has produced a few of these more primitive, less perceptive rebels. The tactical purpose of the rebel is to persist, to spread turmoil, to cause more trouble – and so erode the will of the center. All the means to do, to wage the campaign, are relatively orthodox, guns and bombs and threats; but because these means are limited they are deployed in unconventional ways, covertly, unexpectedly, audaciously, often ruthlessly against those assumed safe, innocent, or protected. In effect, a rebel campaign is unconventional because the rebel has to make do with limited means in the service of maximum ends.

The campaign can be protracted because of this time differential, intense action on the operational front, endless moments of terror, and little of event on the strategic level as history dawdles. To the orthodox this rebel persistence often seems unreasonable, supported by neither the evidence of the conflict nor the support of the supposed constituency. And in order to rectify this the rebel seeks campaign means to hurry history, inspire the galaxy, inflame the constituency and so prove the faith. Although some campaigns have been very protracted – Vietnam, Eritrea, Ireland – this is hardly the general case. And some long campaigns, the campaigns of Malaya and Colombia, the final years are truly futile. The rebels cannot go home again, cannot imagine winning, cannot really hold to the dream but are trapped in the reality of the wilds – career rebels without valid cause.

Any campaign is often an array of novelties, classified unconventional, that generally fit into patterns. Rural insurgency moves on the toleration of the environment – the cover of the bush, the resources of the countryside, the support of the people are either won or not. Few of the deprived love a despot, support a system that exploits their pride and denies their potential. A few, often many, have been co-opted by concession or mobilized for the center by the threat of a mutual enemy and the rest can be – have been – intimidated unless the dream offers both an ideal and a possibility. If the rebels have a reasonable chance, are engaged so in a just war, fair and with potential, then protraction is possible. What is protracted and perhaps escalated is a classical campaign that spreads out from the wilds, cuts communications, fashions liberated zones, spreads disorder and violence into the villages and cities, appears at least in the capital with middle-class support. The most classical examples have been in Latin America but the African anti-imperialist struggles followed much the same course. Always in such a rural struggle, the will goes, the door to the capital opens, the old ruler rushes by limousine to the waiting airplane, and the will wins.

The other side of the guerrilla is – in theory – the terrorist found within the city, often in the heart of the post-industrial West. Many have millenarian dreams rather than nationalist ones but in essence their campaigns are little different but in the matter of cover. The rural guerrilla can hide in a bush but the gunman appears as delivery boy or investment banker, often lives above ground. The purely urban guerrilla may as well have rural allies, as is the case in Ireland and Spain, but not so with the middle-class post-Mao radicals in Italy and Germany. In many countries rural simply means the gunman lives in a small town, works on a farm, has a daily life, does not live on the run in beret and combat jacket. One can hide in an orange grove or apple orchard but not for long. Mostly unconventional campaigns must depend on constant cover, not the countryside as camouflage.

The classical guerrilla is, with the decline of the wilds, endangered. The famous guerrilla column with Zapata, crossed bandoleers and ten-gallon hat, is a historical artifact. Still, in Chad in December 1991, a column of rebels crossed the border and marched unsuccessfully toward the capital, an African anachronism. In 1997 there was an echo of the column on the move in Zaire – a long march, more hike than campaign, to power. On the other hand, the classical gunman, the Irish model with trench coat and slouch fedora, has evolved only in style and ruthlessness not essential, purpose or daily cover. Today, the tourist in the line at the airport, the mailman, the student on the way to class may be a gunman, a terrorist for one cause or another. There are presently all sorts of gunmen and guerrillas, all sorts of campaigns. Most rebel campaigns are a mix, moderately intense, not unduly protracted, occur on a variegated stage, and employ what is available in ways congenial and not alien to others in the same trade.

Some few campaigns are classics. The rebel campaign for a variety of reasons evolves along special lines: the cult terrorism of the Japanese Red Army, the irregular, increasingly protracted bush war in the South Sudan, the late national liberation struggle in El Salvador, or the defenders of Croatia evolving into militia-army. Some campaigns are more various, that of the Provisional IRA, the world of the fedayeen, the new tactical directions of the fundamentalist Shi'ite Hezbollah or the primitive rural wars of Africa – the Congo or Somalia where the dream is too parochial to inspire more than clan vengeance and pillage as goal.

In the more traditional campaigns, the guiding rebel principles are always the same: to survive, to persist and so maintain the dream and a high level of turmoil, to escalate by intensifying the struggle, employing novel means, and spreading the conflict – and so to erode the will of the center. The course of the campaign is always determined by rebel perception, by the lack of assets, the need to act, the competence of the center, and at times the contingent and unforeseen. The key points from within the undergrounds relate to changes in intensity – the inability to persist or the need to escalate that always require crisis management. And the rebel seldom has the assets to manage easily. Every campaign includes effort to extend the battle, involve diplomacy or the law, acquire new weapons or new friends, open up a new front or establish a political presence. Each effort must further the dream, further the armed struggle, change history. Rebels while engaged are all apt to find the past unbearable, the moment difficult but the future comforting.

Those at the center are apt to find today not unlike yesterday and assume that tomorrow will be the same. The campaign may not even unduly trouble those in power except at key moments. The orthodox at the center tend, like historians, to see the shooting campaign begin, spread and either win or fail and contract. The armed struggle is organic, a child of challenge and response rather than a rising curve of expectation that the rebel pictures. Mostly until the very end and the bandits are at the gate the world looks normal, is perceived as normal, and so there is always room for confidence, optimism that has tangible basis – look out the palace window at our tanks.

Reality may impose the pattern whatever the perception of the involved. Assets may erode either underground or at the center. A rebel may waste legitimacy by recourse to atrocity or acquire it because of the repression of the government. The context, the stage of the struggle may be changed far from those involved in the campaign – who will still dream when their gods are dead or be able to struggle when their vital supplies cease? Those who believe in patterns imposed by dreams or that tomorrow will always be like yesterday tend to shape the meaning of campaigns in ways quite different from those of distant observers. These, equipped with their methodologies, agendas, prejudices and special sources, nevertheless are most concerned with what has really happened. And each campaign is the same and different and at the end means what the winner perceives, what the observers imply, for by then someone has truly lost or won.

IN SUM

The campaigns of an armed struggle are the visible and violent component of a rebel process to transform an ideal into reality. Such a struggle is asymmetrical and so unconventional, arises from a covert underground, and, being in large part a matter of perception, difficult to describe and to counter solely with tangible assets. Reality, tangible assets, the big battalions do matter, may even win alone but often do not play a dominant role. Thus the kinds of campaign, the stages or intensity, are less relevant than the perception of the involved – the campaign concerns will and persistence and ideals. The American intangible assets were quite different before and after Tet, just as their opponents' tangible assets had been severely eroded – but in return for an advantageous change in the perceptions of the Americans.

In the end, force may and often does win – the bandits march into the palace or the rebels hang from lampposts – but often perception, even in such winning, is vital: nerve goes or the ideal, *Brigate rosse* give up the dream and terror, and the regime implodes in Saigon. Each campaign is different but the basic dynamics tend to be similar – if not divisible by stages or explicable because of length or location or operational directions.

14

The Enemy

FOR THE rebel there are always two enemies. The first is that defined by the dream and by history, the state, the bourgeoisie, the infidels, and the other is the soldier at the road block. The first is doomed by history and the latter dangerous. It is crucial for the underground to distinguish between the two. The grand enemy is usually shaped as stereotype but the soldier with the gun must be treated not as the text requires but as caution dictates.

Once the dream is transcribed for use during the armed struggle, the rebel generally has little time to explore the strategic enemy. All is known that need be known. Slogans will do for the gunmen and for the publicists and while any attached intellectuals may detail the ideological nature of the opponent usually those who do the killing are content to focus on the specific. In highly ideological movements the specific may be surrounded by a cloud of analysis that would appear to determine detail – which make of car to steal, which rank of policeman to shoot; but the distance between the great system and the constable with the Uzi remains. Later, if there is need to treat with that enemy, the reality in power instead of the stereotype of the text causes difficulties. This is especially true when the truth has been detailed by intellectuals, where the ideology has answers to everything instead of to all. In a sense the nationalist or ethnic stereotypes are easier to set aside than the intricate formulations of contemporary ideologies: for the IRA, the British are the historic monster and the soldiers at the end of the lane: in any end-game there will be a need only to change the monster mask not discard an elaborate analysis. And even this is not easy, for the monster has most readily shown its true face when engaged in negotiations – a dirty war is merely a dirty war, but British duplicity is special.

In the midst of most campaigns, the rebel does not really plan to treat with the enemy, only to replace the system, to scatter or to kill those responsible for holding back history, the capitalists, the Tsar, the imperialists. In the meantime the enemy, the Great Satan, the Empire, a Multinational

Conspiracy, must be opposed in arms by those opposed with real and tangible opponents.

Some of these opponents may be irredeemable. This is often the case when the clash is over the universe of the faithful or a great struggle between the saved and the damned, Islam and the rest, the workers or the peasants and the doomed classes. Lenin saw the aristocrats as candidates for history's boneyard and most anti-imperial rebels against the empires imagined a future with no colonial role for anyone. Sometimes the enemy is simply misguided, tools sent to do a monster's job. Most and most times all of these men with guns, the police and army, their allies the clerks and administrators are perceived as pawns in the great game. The truth has been denied them, the logic of history is hidden. If exposed to the revelation of the dialectic or the justice of the people, these pawns would, if not change sides, certainly no longer collaborate with institutionalized injustice. Even those engaged in the great apocalyptic struggles may see hope for some of the enemy: converts from the middle class led the workers and peasants, Paris was worth a mass, and priests could be found as guerrillas. National liberators did not want to occupy France or Britain but rather seek a fair future where there would be no empires – the world would change but most especially their arena, their submerged nation would be changed.

For the rebel the core of opposition – the system and its defenders and explainers – need hardly be reexamined. They are not suspected enemies but real ones. The enemy has guns, is lethal as well as evil. The enemy is vile, a dreadful if passing survivor in a world the rebel did not make but is busy reconstructing. Those who innocently do the bidding of the center, make up the death squads, fly ground support, may not be innocent but can often be redeemed. A few of those too enthusiastic, too brutal, may incur the people's justice. The rebel is not always pure of heart, ideologically sound in matters of personal vengeance: those who torture or delight in oppression may not only be beyond redemption but favored targets – as symbols, of course, but as individuals as well.

Still, for most underground, the soldiers and the citizens of the center are not to blame. History is to blame and the enemy. That this is so means that once exposed to the truth these innocents and those at a distance will understand the historical necessity of the struggle and so appear on no enemy's list. That list at the most extensive may include whole classes or peoples but often is limited to the despot and his circle. Anti-colonial struggles simply wanted the imperialists out, not necessarily destroyed, while the millenarians of the Euroterrorists wanted a different world where there would be no roles for oppressors. No matter the scope, the enemy is either defined by history or met in the wild with ambush.

The enemy who heeds other voices, lives in history's other rooms, may bear only marginal resemblance to the portrait in the rebel text or may, indeed, fit the mold. Often the rebel ideology presents if not an accurate picture or the only one of the center then one that does really reveal: Lenin's description of Tsarist Russia, or Castro's of Batista's Cuba, the separatists' view of Addis Ababa or Madrid is not without reality. The enemy, however, sees matters differently, of course. Above ground vision is not as skewed by the faith, by the filtering and warping inevitable in the underground, by the desperate needs of the rebel. History for the state is in part disinterested, inherited from scholars as well as found in polemics. The ideals of the state may be artificial, scavenged symbols, flags and titles and constitutions; but they have a patina of legitimacy denied the rebel. The state may confuse self-interest, continuity of power, stability and the good of the nation, but must operate in full view and so is subject to the real. What is difficult for the orthodox to grasp is that in such matters reality may be a matter of perception, that even tangible assets may not play any real part in a revolution: an army may be, as well as seem to be, merely a crowd in donated uniforms not a real force at all. Certainly the regime in Saigon found this to be the case in 1975 just as the Americans had accepted that tangible assets – the long rows of airplanes, the huge supply dumps, the Marines and the carriers – could not in the end counter the intangible and persistent dream loose in the countryside.

The rebel always seeks to stress a reality unseen but at times such a reality is less than convincing. Many rebel targets are not greedy and vicious elites, mad-dog cannibal kings, despots or lackeys of an international conspiracy. Many are legitimate by most standards but those of the rebel. Many are elected and admired. The great Irish republican enemy, the British, really the English, have established as example for the world the rule of law, a genial and tolerant society, detailed the rights of man and propounded democratic principles. The lapses, if real, are considered by most aberration, if considered at all. The majority of the population of Northern Ireland feels British, claims not to be Irish. And the other island Irish, Catholics, nationalists, largely oppose the armed struggle. Yet for the republicans the British establishment is not only anti-Irish in attitudes and assumptions but also long involved in policies and programs that from the smaller island seem despotic and dreadful. And so the British are illegitimately present on the island, an imposed presence that is the source of all Ireland's ills. The British, their allies and associates, most of the Irish, much of general opinion finds such analysis eccentric, twisted, the logic of the gunman.

Gunmen engaged in an armed struggle always find their opponent spurious, always are apt to find their truth denied. Yet for them the target is illegitimate but for few others. Many states, most states, are counted legitimate by all but a tiny radical sect – the Japanese Red Army speaks for class history not for the Japanese. LEHI had a tiny Zionist galaxy of support for personal terror: a few dozen gunmen and a few hundred friends. The PFLP-General Command represents no one but Ahmed Jibril. And until 1989 those who spoke for the submerged nations of Armenia or Latvia or Serbia were thought relics of a distant past or romantics unable to recognize the reality of the present. Those who do recognize the gunmen are often damned as equally illicit – according to Ronald Reagan the whole contemporary lot were 'outlaw states, misfits, Looney tunes and squalid criminals'.

Most target states, target regimes are acceptable to the world community, have seats in the United Nations, have faults but are real. Many states, if not perfect, have been long accepted by their citizens, by their neighbors, by the international community as adequate, necessary, perhaps irreplaceable. The Union of Soviet Socialist Republics was a fact, maintained in part by terror but in large part because the system operated out of Moscow was accepted as legitimate heir to the Tsars. Ethiopia under Haile Selassie benefited from past history, contemporary friends, the dangers of tribal schism in Africa and the weight of habit. France was ready to assure continuity in Francophone Africa by flying in troops to support any threatened regime – the regime was the state and even if the state was no nation the elite spoke French. Those targets without a respectable history, without many friends, those with similar problems benefit from the rewards of habit. The state-center is in power and so legitimate, often representative of more than the dictator's family or the dominant or lucky tribe. Always power, however grudgingly given, assures international acceptance in many places and on many levels, acceptance even for the pariah states. Zaire has a lake named Idi Amin Dada and a main boulevard Emperor Bokassa. With Mobutu gone, they may have new names offered by a new democratic despot. Those who can run up the flag, move into the palace, can anticipate some returns. And even if unrepresentative the new government is still responsible for the system, for a vote at the United Nations, for issuing postage stamps and collecting taxes. The center as system is always legitimate to some degree until someone else sits at the United Nations and someone else pays the clerks.

During the era after 1945 when the Western powers dismantled at varying speeds their overseas empires, those in London or Lisbon were always surprised at the natives' anger and ambition, lack of patience, misreading of history. The difficulty by the involved in gauging the speed and scope of the winds of change, let loose by the diffusion of power and the ebbing of Western will, engendered a generation of armed struggles. This was a time of national liberation, a series of successful if costly armed struggles that surpassed most previous records for rebel success. There had been other grand eras, the collapse of the Spanish Latin American empire, the 1848 nationalist rebellions, the rise of revolutionary class action – especially revolutionary anarchism – and the two great earlier examples of Ireland in 1916–23 and of Indian non-violence that had by 1935 and the India Act assured a British withdrawal sooner rather than later. The anti-imperialist struggles, however, were classic and often highly successful, sometimes combining the previous ideological strains and tactics with local usage but indicating for all that the rebel could win. That there were rebels at all was unwelcome to the imperial powers. And all rebels begin as illicit criminals if not Looney Tunes.

The French were outraged with the Algerian nationalists, indignant that a few unrepresentative agents of alien interests, the FLN, would dare to kill for so bizarre a 'cause'. Algeria was French. And a generation later the military successors to the French were outraged that Islamic fundamentalists would oppose their government with an armed struggle. The authorities are always outraged and indignant, and often everyone else is too but the rebels. The anti-colonial struggles drove imperial governments to concession cloaked in magnanimity. More general struggles force more general concessions – what can the Algerian generals, the Egyptian bureaucrats offer the faithful?

The next generations of rebels did not have the advantage of an overt occupier. They might, like Castro in Cuba, attack imperialism at one remove – America as center of a capitalist-imperialist system, a congenial interpretation to Latin American radicals and a posture assuring outrage in Washington. Others simply relied on the new truth, Islam revived or the Fourth Sword of Marx. For the West, most revolts were aspects of a global conflict or from time to time, but only rarely minor matters dominated by parochial concerns, Eritrean separatism or Italian neo-fascism. For those outside the classical bounds of the West, the First World, rebellion was in some cases a permanent condition, the peasants of the outback always uneasy, or indication of dangerous ideas inflaming the innocent, Che as traveling salesman of trouble or the mullahs preaching *Jihad*.

In any case each generation of armed struggles provoked indignation, outrage. And this was true as times changed and the guerrillas and the gunmen suddenly appeared not at the frontiers of the West but in the heartlands. The enemy of the armed struggle whether ancient of lineage or recently in power tended to respond as one: surprise, outrage, righteous indignation and, of course, recourse to force.

Some states lack only the capacity to slaughter the rebels not the will at the center nor need to consider ethics or the law but only survival. Many regimes are barely legitimate. Others duly elected or generally accepted govern uneasily with limited means over truculent citizens. Often large districts are beyond control, beyond the law, breeding grounds of parochial dissent. Some governments habitually repress the potential for revolt, sweeping away symbolic targets; this village, these organizers, those peasants, relying on the reality of specific coercion to intimidate. Some states have both the means and the determination to respond to provocation with ruthless and efficient brutality: kill the asp just out of the egg. In Syria in February 1982, Hafez al-Assad, head of a Ba'athist, secular government dominated by dissident, Alawi Moslems, ordered the utter destruction of a revolt led by Moslem fundamentalists. The city of Hama was besieged by the army, shelled, destroyed with a death toll estimated at ten thousand. No fundamentalist would soon imagine that an armed struggle was a viable option to accelerate the inevitable end of the sect in power in Damascus.

In fact, if harsh and thorough repression by an effective security force seems likely, then few rebels will rise. There must be *some* hope and many, most, rebels are incurably hopeful. But few rose against Stalin or for that matter in the United States, for the capacity to adjust to legitimate grievance, to accommodate all but the mad and the few millenarians is a great strength of successful democratic states – that coupled with prosperity is a defense that means recourse to force, except in matters of nationalism, is not needed. Mostly the rebellious seek enemies that can be perceived as tyrannical but vulnerable. Some rebels, many rebels, misjudge the state.

Some in Latin America realizing the immense power of those in authority sought a strategy of leverage. In Uruguay and Argentina the radicals for varying purposes challenged the system in order to produce an excessive reaction. They wanted to provoke the military into seizing power and so polarizing the country. Then assets would flood into the rebel camps. The alienated would rush to the barricades. Instead the military provoked, destroyed the rebels while their constituency – the people – watched. The rebels were hunted down and killed. The suspected were seized and disappeared. Democracy was suspended and the most parochial generals institutionalized repression. The rebels had misread history.

At rare times the rebel may feel there is no choice but to bear witness in arms to the intolerable – but as example not as coda – as was the case with the Irish Easter Rising in 1916 that had originally been planned to succeed, or the Warsaw Ghetto Rising by the Jews who in part hoped to inspire resistance to Nazi extermination but certainly evidence of militancy even without practical hope. Blood sacrifices, more often found in poems than on the barricades, have few takers. The delirium of the brave may lead a man to die for his children's future but seldom when there are to be no children, no future. So rebels have enemies perceived to be at least slightly vulnerable. And for many of the desperate such perceived vulnerability is enough to begin. Sometimes it has been enough for the rebel to win.

Since World War Two there have been the several generations of rebels who perceived a vulnerable opponent. The enemy nearly every time was portrayed as strategically obsolete. A few rebellions are narrowly tribal, a matter of other times, other arenas, and a few do arise and persist through personal ambition thwarted but mostly the killing rests on an underground vision of history. And history is always change and opportunity, new vulnerabilities and dreams, new dreams and old but always adequate for the guerrilla. In 1969–70, the IRA read history as opportunity, seized the chance to defend the threatened Catholic nationalists in Northern Ireland so as to provoke the British into creating conditions that would allow a campaign; and unlike the guerrillas in Uruguay and Argentina the gunmen in Belfast and Armagh provoked not bloody repression but a graduated reaction that shaped a generation of violence producing neither victory nor defeat but a classical armed struggle different from past experience, different, as is each armed struggle, from all others.

In an era of terror and violence, those governments that escaped serious threat were either the brutal and efficient or the democratic without a nationality problem. The former could crush the rebels and the latter co-opt them. There were still a great many targets with the capacity to resist a swift coup or permit an unopposed seizure of power. All of these target regimes – enemies – when faced with revolt, revolt in a colony, revolt by ideological millenarians, revolt by anyone, reacted with repression related to the values and capacities of the center. Some, like the British, deployed other options as well as the army. Others had no such options to hand and relied on force. The values limited the deployment of the capacities and these assets in turn, especially when limited, were not always sufficient to prevent a protracted conflict. Mostly a center with reasonable resources and no restraint could ward off the rebel. The Euroterrorists had limited galaxies that violence and the state eroded. The separatists, unlike the Eritreans, mainly failed. The *focos* failed. The Asian communists failed. The collapse of the Soviet empire opened the way for new nations, new irregular conflicts but rarely armed struggles. There were always new dreamers and so new attempts. India was arena for all sorts of gunmen, but huge, various and stable, the country could absorb disorder. At the other end of the spectrum, the failure at the center in Somalia and Rwanda produced not classical armed struggles but anarchy and slaughter. The enemy was the gunman for there was no longer a center.

The difficulty for the state occurs when there is a paucity of resources or a lack of capacity or an erosion of will. The refusal to rule by resort to terror that would destroy the purpose of governance, however admirable to theorists, is a decay of will – and is so seen by potential rebels. Restraint, recourse to institutionalized justice and accommodation is a luxury of the rich and strong: America or Britain or France need not resort to terror to manage local gunmen, even as dangerous as the IRA or as spectacular as those of the faithful who come to the center of the Evil Empire at the World Trade Center to display grievance. This is not the case when the rebel is domestic, threatens the system not simply valuable assets. Many states, especially in the Third World, cannot quite stamp out armed subversion because there are not enough assets. The government, the state, is both too strong to topple and too weak to impose order by coercion. And if there are not enough assets, state command and control may be lacking or the army may be corrupt or in some way the center inefficient. Those in power, however, want to remain in power.

When the rebel persists, the state must find a balance between repression and normality: a place between internal war without limit and peace with full freedom. Democratic states have different problems, different priorities, different assets from despots or authoritarian governments; but all have a problem of allocation of resources, the need to maintain the conventions, and the dangers of losing legitimacy by over-reacting. Every government, even the most personal and despotic, is in some ways legitimate beyond merely the right to collect taxes or appoint ambassadors. Those who have institutionalized terror, cleared the board early, given no indication that moderation is an option, often display a will too great for those with grievance to counter.

A general response from the state that falls between recourse to absolute repression and a rush by the elite to flee, fueled by outrage and indignation, is to define the threat. The enemy tends to determine the shape of the armed struggle. The rebels are demonstrably illegitimate. The individual rebels are mad, wicked evil men, criminals or alien. They are in rebellion for personal gain. They have no real cause but greed. They are mad, certainly criminal. These categories may be contradictory but are run up as banners of state defiance not only at the beginning of the armed struggle but at every opportunity during the years of internal war. How intense that war is depends on the state's allocation of force and accommodation and the rebel's skill and attractions. Both the center and the rebel prefer a monster as enemy, one both dreadful and inept, brutal and unreasoning and cunning. The rebel hunted and marginalized can most easily imagine the enemy as without merit or moderation. The rebel finds evil incarnate but encased in everyday people. The visible enemy is a single soldier or the civilians who inform. They are real enough people but the great enemy is seldom seen: the enemy of truth, the system that imposes injustice.

At times the rebel outrages are too distant or too traditional to have serious or at least lasting impact. Even to achieve outrage the rebel may have to escalate, move closer to the center, resort to terror, make more noise. In a sense the rebel must listen for outrage to be certain that the campaign continues – the enemy has many roles and one is to act chorus to insurrectionary violence. If rebel escalation is impossible, the level of violence and so noise low or the battles distant, the regime, the state, the people may simply tolerate the rebel turmoil.

It is not only in Ulster that the rebel can be forgotten by the enemy. This has been especially true with large, largely rural states or those tolerant arenas long used by rebels. War can be waged in the Sudan or Angola or the far islands of the Philippines without unduly troubling the government. Law and order in Western terms hardly exists in many areas beyond the presidential palace. Thus internal war can be tolerated by those, even the sophisticated, regularly exposed or without need for order. The governments of Chad or Burma can accept lack of control in the far parts as long as the convenient assets can be exploited – and the last asset is always the existence of the regime.

The rebels' enemies by nature have enormous powers of resistance and recuperation. Even advanced, delicate, hi-tech societies littered with exposed nodes of control can tolerate an armed struggle. The World Trade Center is reopened or the City of London more closely guarded. A few bombs are spectacle not lethal threat. In Oklahoma there will be new Federal offices. Post-industrial society may be complex and vulnerable to systemic attack but such societies are also huge with enormous redundancies beyond the reach of most gunmen and bombers. This has been the case with the Palestinians or Holy *Jihad* operating in Europe and was the case with the Euroterrorists in Italy and Germany. Killers can snatch television coverage and bombers slow commuter traffic but the system is hardly at threat.

Terrorists may bring down airliners with bombs. Pan Am's Flight 103 was destroyed over Lockerbie in Scotland in 1988 with a loss of 270 lives and the next year the French UTA 772 was brought down over the Niger with a loss of 171 lives, but international air travel continues. No rebel, no state claimed responsibility, the threat may still exist; but no flights are canceled, and in time reluctant passengers are back in the air. In Germany the authorities and the people were enormously concerned about the forays of the radical terrorists, tiny bands of urban guerrillas without real support of any sort, because random disorder was alien, because a government is supposed to fashion a tidy society. The British had suffered with the Irish for over a century so that indignation and, of course, inconvenience seldom lasted long. The Italians did not expect order, even competence, and so withstood a very high level of violence, perceived and actual, without vast adjustment.

The enemies of the armed struggle, then, may respond strategically across a spectrum of toleration and outrage; but all governments that must cope with the problem must defend the center in similar ways. Some governments cannot resort effectively to counter-terror, cannot co-opt or accommodate the rebel, cannot avoid a campaign of repression. Then, essentially, the state seeks to kill the rebel with the security forces and simultaneously erode the rebel appeal with the display of the conventional rewards of power. The state has recourse to legitimate force, the attractions of order, a menu of rewards. Generally these assets can be deployed effectively, allow a variety of tactical initiatives on varying fronts: political or economic, diplomatic or social. And at times the state can have recourse to special operations, play the terror game, murder the murderers, but always this will be at the risk of legitimacy – often not a serious consideration with governments determined on retaliation or unresponsive to the goodwill of the distant. And besides with the power of the state covert operations can be denied and retaliation declared legitimate, the rebels kidnapped as an act of state, the suspects bombed as right. The rebel often finds the state quite wily, apt and brutal in pursuit of its own interests, hardly a brittle and fragile opponent as first imagined.

There are all sorts of ways for the state to proceed but unlike the rebel the center tends to persist, even escalate, without trauma. The rebellion may be largely ignored, contained, in time repressed or in the worst case scenario require sufficient center resources to shift priorities. A rebellion then can be a most minor matter or the major, sometimes almost the only, priority of the state. Mostly the latter case is rare. Mostly the state can rely on the security forces alone and if not on the assets of legitimacy, the inertia of stability, the aid of friends.

The protracted conflict means that the center has gradually to adjust to provocation and violence. Some regimes have done so more easily than others, some used revolt to advantage and some skewed traditional priorities not always to advantage; but all acted within the imperatives of the arena. Just as the campaigns of the rebel follow no general rules beyond the focus on persistence and escalation so too the target response is various. With time the response is more efficient, more effective, often more extensive – or at least as persistent. The longer the campaign usually the more astute the repression and by necessity the rebel. In a sense center competence imposed rebel capacity – the arrival of the Russians and Cubans in the service of Ethiopia meant that the Eritreans had to move from the congenial irregular war of the shifta into a more formal conflict involving armor and artillery and large units. It often seemed that the halting Portuguese response to the nationalists in Mozambique and Angola in part accounted for the difficulties of the rebels – they had trouble learning on the job without an effective enemy to impose discipline. Still, over time, learning takes place if the rebel can protract the struggle – and most cannot. If the underground proves exceptional then in time most states face more efficient revolts that they have in part tutored even as repression has kept the conflict from escalating. The IRA in 1994 or even 1996 was far more effective in skill and capacity than in 1972 but the intensity level of the armed struggle was far lower: the British authorities had been even more successful in learning their trade.

The key for states without pressing is largely the deployment of assets. How serious is the rebel threat? How should repressive assets be allotted? Will delay in such decisions – always a ready choice – be advantageous or necessary? Should external aid be sought? Often the decision can be weighted and factored into later calculation – this worked and this did not. Should something else be tried? Is anything new really necessary? All these questions are addressed, except in the most primitive centers, with care, often with good advice, and always with hope. There may be from time to time a crisis, a need for decision without adequate information, but in contrast to rebel dynamics the state's response is ordered, amenable to analysis, and closely focused on tangibles and repercussions. Time and contemplation are different even in the most chaotic moments and the results usually can be judged success or failure.

The most complex response and the most difficult for those charged with responsibility has been found in democratic states that in theory should have no armed dissent. History should have produced consensus, democratic institutions endowed the center with legitimacy. There are many who insist that elections assure legitimacy, the courts are fair and just, the system works. It has not worked well enough for Irish republicans or Italian fascists or has worked in such ways that an armed struggle has been encouraged. The most intriguing problem for democratic states is, then, to find an appropriate balance between full internal war and conventional peace. Internal war destroys the society it is meant to protect and persistence in normality does so as well by allowing the rebel free play. Pragmatically the best strategy is to do as little as possible, to maintain normality, to ignore – like the regimes who allow the rebel to run loose in the bush – the provocation. This is rarely possible. The people – and their leaders – are outraged, indignant, want action.

The security forces by wont and practice seek an active role, a mission, an end to disorder. Something must be done even when nothing should be. Some armies want to do everything or nothing, crush the rebels even if hidden with tanks or let the police cope. Other armies find destroying subversives congenial but rarely so in democratic states. There soldiers generally want real wars and only the eccentric seek a career in special operations. Internal 'war' – subversion, an armed struggle – has too many political components and too little opportunity for orthodox tactics. The armed struggle falls between peace and war, law and order. It presents difficult problems. And the real problem for the democratic state – unlike most of the other decisions of the threatened – is that there is no solution. Peace cannot exist in the midst of war nor war be waged with the restraints of peace. If the Basque is a Spaniard, he must be so treated or there is no Spain. If the Basque is the enemy, then war is waged over the future of the arena not the integrity of the nation. If Northern Ireland is a legitimate part of the United Kingdom, with the unionists voting repeatedly so, then the IRA gunman is a citizen, albeit a criminal, like any other and must not be shot on sight.

Many far newer nations tend to be defended by an elite determined to maintain their power and the existing bounds of the arena even at the expense of consensus – the threatened will wage war since peace can only thus be promised for the future. Many states in Latin America are dominated by an unrepresentative establishment where the military has often traditionally been a defender against subversion thus protecting the nation's honor. The rebel is seen as monster and the military, attuned to deploy the harshest means to erase any threat, often deploy force over long periods of time as a monitoring measure even when overt rebellion is hardly visible.

Each arena has its own imperatives that shape repression of an armed struggle. Only and almost always, the democratic governments are the ones that find any response uncongenial, all viable reactions lumbered with penalties. Democracies do not want to have recourse to state terror, to gross expediency, to corruption of the law, to detention and torture and all the readily available policies of repression. The people, the government, like the generals, would prefer war, traditional, conventional, not an armed struggle that imposes problems without solutions.

All of this appears, again and again, in the tactics of the campaign of repression, most notably when the democratic center erodes peace in the name of war. The soldiers who shoot to kill violate the accepted norms, impose enormous political damage on the government, often outrage the rebel constituency that assumes an armed struggle can be waged within the peacetime rules of the state, and rarely repays long-term tactical benefits. The Irish Free State after 1922 had to defend itself from gunmen who advocated the ideals of the government, who had the toleration and at times support of many in the country, who would and did kill their countryman for the cause. And as the years passed the problem remained: the secret army sought to hijack the national issue as well as maintain the right to use the gun in pursuit of unity. Such gunmen must be shot, detained, treated as guerrillas even in prison or the state will collapse. The Irish state was rarely in danger of collapse and so could often tolerate a secret army if the gunmen were not too blatant. During the present generation of turmoil, both London and Dublin sought to impose their own definitions, deny that the IRA was waging a war of national liberation. Any threatened state must wage at least a limited war while proclaiming that all is normal, peace prevails – or mostly prevails.

For the rebel the difficulties involved for the state are largely exploited without reflection or discussion. In opposing a tyranny the rebel hopes to exploit the enemy's lack of support, inclination to repression. In an open society the rebel seeks the benefits of peace while waging war, seeks to use toleration or concession or good will to advantage. The rebel almost until the end sees the enemy, the regime in particular and the system in general, as relic. At times ideology makes all the enemy, all Zionists, all Croatians in Serbia, all the English, instead of a small ruling clique. At times the ruling clique represents a general ideological enemy, the bourgeois or the convinced communists, the Alawi of Syria or the pagans of the South Sudan. The enemy, however defined, exclusively or inclusively large or small, always illegitimate, tends to remain the same over the course of the struggle.

To the rebel the state appears to have the capacity to shift at will, change gears and fronts and postures with ease – a capacity those in power cannot even imagine. In turn those in power at the center can scarcely credit the desperate efforts of a rebel leadership to adjust to shifting state repression, to a changing agenda of response, to the imposition of a real world. Both imagine an efficient opponent and not a hurried and harried one. And the rebel most often imagines an enemy as focused on the armed struggle as is the underground leadership, neglecting the reality of governance that must open the schools, deliver the mail and see that the trains run on time as well as kill the gunman on the corner. In the asymmetrical campaign what both share as enemies is a lack of empathy and so a failure to understand the reality of government or the dynamics of the underground.

For the rebel this may be just as well for too much reality could be fatally disheartening; and for the 'enemy', the state, the regime, the democratic government, a grasp of underground dynamics might not alter priorities at all, might at best give operational advantage and at worst induce despair: how could an enemy so brutal and cunning arise from such a perverse reality? Neither know their enemy and for the rebel this may be useful. The rebel in any case concentrates by necessity on operations and rather less on the impact these may have on the enemy – however defined.

Mostly, however, the rebel sees the enemy as implacable and grand but vulnerable. Those with guns are deployed as counters not as personal enemies. The real enemies are elsewhere and always prove more persistent and more artful than anticipated. Mostly, the rebel does not spend a great deal of time on analyzing the enemy, that is for the prologue, for the intellectuals, for the editorials in the party paper and always in ideological terms. Mostly the rebel focuses on operational matters, the soldier at the crossroads, the tangible enemy and the one amenable to physical force. The other, more distant and strategically more important enemies, will be thus reached.

IN SUM

What the rebel believes exists so that the enemy – the monolithic, obsolete, evil enemy – becomes real. Such an opponent is the end product of a history shaped to patriot need, and such an opponent is rarely a factor in the actual events of the armed struggle. There, amid the turmoil and confusion of killing, the rebel treats with the other enemy, quite real, not a matter of perception but of experience and the tangible, not the Queen but the SAS. That enemy is often known quite well so that tactics and techniques are adjusted to battle arena conditions, so that reality of engagement if not ultimate purpose is maintained and exploited. Thus an armed struggle always opposes two enemies, that necessary to the dream and that dangerous to the individual dreamers. The first is doomed and the second if deadly is often misguided – led astray by an elite doomed to ultimate defeat.

15

The End-game

ALTHOUGH MOST armed struggles begin with the certainty that history will vindicate the conflict as the dream is transformed into reality, few give great thought to the details of the end; not Marx, not Che, not the IRA nor the *Brigate rosse*. Mostly the end comes almost immediately, unexpected, incredible, in violation of theory and the revealed truth. The struggle fails. Often the struggle fails almost at once, fails even before the movement can get underground or under cover or off the beach. The faithful have organized not a crusade with operations and deeds and movement but a massacre or worse – a humiliating series of arrests without a shot being fired. Some armed struggles have not only no arms but also no time to struggle. Such failures produce not triumph but the scorn and even the amusement of those in power, even of the people. The dream is denied and the gunmen ridiculed and the armed struggle becomes no more than a blip for analytical analysts.

When the end-game comes almost before there is a game, as was the case with most of the efforts to emulate Castro, the armed struggle is apt to be mistaken for a failed coup, a riot, random vandalism, a frustrated conspiracy – not an armed struggle at all. Many analysts assume that one of the more salient aspects of low-intensity war is protracted conflict – not the end at the beginning, not the blip that indicates the death of a dream often long incubating. For a significant and so salient end-game, for analytical purposes, the armed struggle must be a struggle at least somewhat protracted and not simply an initial disaster. Whether the disaster is initial or not may prove crucial to those in power: just what is crushed in the egg matters. Some dreams survive the death of most of the dreamers. In Ireland generations of volunteers have been recruited to replace those who compromised, retired, despaired, accepted imposed reality or simply private life. The Irish dream, however, and so the militant republican movement, was not so easily crushed and dismayed.

It is the perception of the faithful that is vital, more so than the ruin of their initial hopes. Those who would seize power through an armed struggle always assume that there *will* be a struggle, even another struggle, an unconventional but ultimately successful struggle as the will defeats the oppressor. Others, more confident of their assets, assume instead that force can win at once or at least soon, that by recourse to conventional means, a coup or a civil war, power will be grasped. Castro tried this route at Moncada Barracks in Santiago, Cuba, in 1953 and the Irish volunteers in the Easter Rising in 1916. Neither foresaw a protracted underground struggle – or, of course, defeat. And for some even such force is not needed but rather the marshaling of votes or even recourse to riotous assembly, threats, monster demonstrations, coercion without guns. Agitation should be adequate, perhaps at most armed agitation but not an underground, not war but politics.

Those who lack such capacities fail because of their poverty of both conventional and unconventional means, because of bad luck or skilled opponents. The times are wrong and the people cold. The army shoots first or the police cannot be intimidated. The center holds. And so they find their prologue is transformed into epilogue. Some few manage protraction and if not escalation then a triumph when the center does not hold. All this means that end-games are far rarer than beginnings, than dreams deferred or destroyed.

As has always been the case, the underground faces massive difficulties at the end as well as at the beginning and, again as always, largely unanticipated difficulties. The key to the end-game has to do with the salvage of the dream. If there is to be victory, how much of the dream can be made real? For some, perfection is not really possible, the struggle is all; but as the underground emerges, swiftly at the palace door or slowly as negotiations drag on, the dynamics of the underground have to be replaced with an orthodox agenda. And so who has really won and what has been won? And the men with guns and those who want office and those who come later all tend to quarrel over the process that sought to make the dream real.

The key moment in an end-game that moves toward violence is when the primary oppressor is redefined. The Irish idealists in 1922 saw those who evolved into the leaders of the new Irish Free State as the immediate enemy not their British backer. The NLF had seen FLOSY as too conservative, too close to Egypt, ideologically incorrect and so more dangerous than the British. The purists, the old gunmen who have found a career in revolution, often find their more compromising colleagues intend to put them down in the name of order if not expediency.

In the Palestine Mandate in 1947–48, the emergence of Begin's Irgun can be traced in detail as the realization spread underground that the British were actually evacuating and that the local Arabs were determined to replace them with the aid of their friends in the Arab League. The Irgun had always focused on the major enemy, the great power, the alien occupier. It was with reluctance, even more pronounced in the Stern Group, that the old British enemy was discarded, that cover was largely discarded, that the techniques and tactics, faulty in regular war, were discarded.

Mostly end-games take place beyond the armed struggle, indicate in fact that the protracted war against the center has produced power to contest. Ben-Gurion ordered an attack on the Irgun arms ship *Altalena* to assure that the state would be unchallenged, just as the Free State attacked the irregulars to assure that the future was no longer in dispute: the orthodox had power and the right. At the far end of any armed struggle one finds the conventional. Mao or Giap or Castro ruled by right and with power – their visible struggles over real or anticipated power had culminated and so ended the dynamics of the underground, long eroded in Asia and discarded on the wild ride to the palace in Havana.

Back in the past, at the other end of the armed struggle, there is often little more than a dream, a dream that is apt to lead to an aborted beginning. Some few protracted struggles last long enough to become institutionalized, beyond suppression but are denied foreseeable victory. There must be sight of victory or fear of the unthinkable – not defeat but endless denial – before an end-game becomes reality in the center of the galaxy. The guerrillas in Colombia are local barons, rebel war lords of the backlands, living on a black economy, an available but unlikely option if the ruling elite were to collapse. Their struggle has entered a long last act, the game has ups and downs but no viable end, no one seems likely to win or lose. Others still have hopes of escalation that will finally after decades take the faithful into power like the Eritreans and Tigreans. They won on the ground as the new empire of Mengistu collapsed in Addis Ababa and so found themselves in the unusual position for a separatist organization: dominating the whole. Thus the end-game could be played out to independence by those acting orthodox roles above ground. A few separatists, like the Ibo in Nigeria, manage an orthodoxy, a schismatic state, a rebel army, an irregular war and then fall to the power of the center without hope of persisting underground. Some, like ETA in Spain, simply persist, never with prospect of any advance unless Madrid decides to compromise the integrity of the state instead of regularly co-opting those Basque willing to settle for less than liberty. Many end-games are no more than the tactics of the center deployed to corrupt the pure, reduce the intensity of the struggle, compromise the idealists. The

Irish republicans have for generations suspected *any* political prospect as the corruption: end-games in Ireland have always ended before the dream could be made real. And after the ceasefire of 1994, there were many in Ireland with little faith that an unarmed strategy could succeed, that the gun had brought the movement deep enough into the end-game with power intact as to be no longer needed. And so they began again and replayed the second end-game act as futile and, still reluctant, moved on again – another ceasefire. What the hard men want is victory not concession.

It is when the prospect of serious discussion about transforming the ideal into reality looms that an end-game becomes in fact a matter of moves and ploys, sacrifices and gambits all bound by rules that indicate an agreed culmination, a draw of some sort. The rebel may assume the dream will convert without resort to the gun or that the dream need not be achieved pure and at once. The Irish republicans believe that the Protestant Irish now loyal to the Crown will be transformed when British sovereignty is withdrawn, and will accept an Irish future.

Everywhere the dream, however, must be adjusted, perceived differently if there is to be any negotiation. The zero-sum game must be replaced with an end-game. This might be done because the reality of power imposes itself on rebel consciousness, concentrates minds: the necessary patron of the underground disappears, the rebel constituency denies the struggle, reality imposes itself on perception no longer blinded by the faith, or the faith proves for some reason faulty. Armed struggles in the South Sudan, in Yemen, in El Salvador, here and there, often at the margins, but yet real enough, have evolved into end-games with negotiated settlements – even if such settlements led to renewed fighting in the Sudan, dissonance and disorder and war again in Yemen, and uneasy turmoil in Salvador, the end-game was real and different from an armed struggle. In Colombia the center is concerned with co-opting the rebels on the margins and in Northern Ireland the British with finding a way out of the maze with honor intact. Both are serious and both need the underground to respond in orthodox ways to real offers.

Those underground may assume that the end-game is simply a new battle front – a variant of political pressure or accumulating international support; but the crucial difference is that for an end-game to be more than a propaganda exercise the rebels must perceive the nature and responsibilities of the dream differently. The dream, never denied, need not be achieved whole, at once, soon, without discussion – achieved at the point of a gun. The dream itself may have evolved – undergone a sea change underground; but most important is the perception of the rebels. Some, like many of the Irish in 1921, feel that with major concessions the armed struggle has achieved sufficient gains so that the dream can eventually be achieved without recourse to the gun. Some in Ireland in 1998 believed so again – more of the underground this time but not all – there are those who hold to the purity of the dream.

There are too few cases of end-games to make easy generalizations but there are indicators. First, the dream must be amenable to adjustment. What was it that *Brigate rosse* wanted? How can the Great Satan be destroyed? Second, the dreamers' perceptions must shift in ways congenial to negotiation. The IRA accepted that they could not win nor could they lose, so if there were to be movement rather than persistence a new means must be found to go forward, a new front: and so the concept that with negotiations underway the gun was no longer useful but actually counter-productive. Third, those who would destroy the armed struggle must, of course, find advantage in co-opting it: and those in power rarely cede power without coercion so that perception there, too, must shift.

If an armed struggle is protracted, especially if escalation is denied or halting, the prospect of negotiation is logically always present. The dream tends to deny any reality to proposals to adjust – those who would negotiate, conciliate, accommodate, modify behavior, offer good offices, find another road seldom can find a meeting between the imperatives of the dream and the reality of power at the center. In an armed struggle the emphasis must shift for there to be an effective end-game. Most often this occurs as a desire to win by other means than killing: offer something but give up nothing. This means the dreamer still dreams and the powerful still hold power and there is no middle ground to exploit.

Such adjustment, such change, is the rarest of all outcomes for armed struggles. Most fail. Those that persist tend to push against open doors if they are to win – and during the anti-imperialist years although the will at the center failed from the first it did so at various paces across the colonial spectrum. Most armed struggles, then, win in one rebel generation, under ten years led by those who first went underground and who become the government. The Irish armed struggle that evolved from the failed coup of 1916 was typical: began small in 1918, escalated in all ways until 1921, forced an end-game that led to partition, the Irish Free State – and the persistence of the republican galaxy. The ceasefires in 1994 and 1997 have hardly dispersed that galaxy, if anything increased the size, and failure is not apt to destroy the core who will hold to the dream – form the genesis of still another struggle when conditions permit.

Some few armed struggles simply persist on and on without culmination nor prospect; any escalation seldom troubles the center sufficiently to force an end-game until the arena is transformed: Angola and Mozambique won for the rebels when a coup succeeded in Lisbon but order collapsed from multiple factors into a generation of war still not over in Angola. Some armed struggles, like those in the Huks in the Philippines or the communists in Malaya, gradually decelerate until they flicker out without need of an end-game. The more protracted the more likely that someone will seek to define the present as the last act and initiate an end-game.

Rebels justly fear the necessity of an end-game. A great many rebels learned from the Irish Tan War that the conventional power can be perfidious, that formulas may in the long run fail to disguise the realities of power, that a flag flying free does not necessarily make a free nation. For the British at the end of empire beginning with the Irgun's revolt in 1944, the situation was reversed in that the colonies – Begin and the Irgun excluded – accepted the Commonwealth formula that gave London the impression that concession of independence had been out of magnanimity not because of weakness. In a real sense Nasser's seizure of the Suez Canal and the subsequent collapse of the Anglo-French recourse to force in 1956 was so traumatic for the British because at last their limitations were realized – and, London felt, somehow unfairly revealed by an Egyptian demagogue. Nasser in some curious way used words and emotions – will – to counter justice, legitimacy and power. And it was dreadful to discover that justice meant what Nasser said, British legitimacy was denied even by allies. And then came the realization as well that British power was lacking. The Egyptian will – as all armed struggles insist – had won for a flawed cause, won for the dictator Nasser, won for the disreputable, won over tangible assets – and worse – won in plain view and, unlike Ireland in 1921, without need for an end-game formula that left British pride intact. Leaving Algeria was no less traumatic for the French who on departure took their own with them in sullen resentment uncertain as to fault, to responsibility; those who blamed de Gaulle were blamed by de Gaulle.

Most armed struggles seek victory at the end and no games. Most armed struggles, however, arise within a galaxy where currents and assumptions exist that permit initiatives taken as a means of either escalation or persistence that might permit movement toward an end without need of unconditional victory. Even the most uncompromising crusaders may reveal flexibility when the prospect of partial power beckons. And yet many protracted struggles simply continue: dwindle away into the jungle as in Malaya or continue on in the countryside of Eritrea until the center collapses in Addis Ababa. And in a few cases, like Cambodia, the rebel arrives at

Year Zero without compromise or concession with the dream intact, the banners unfurled, and at last the power to make history comply with theory.

As for the few successful terminations of armed struggles through agreement, there are obvious parallels with any negotiated process and these parallels are more conventional, since the secret army in an end-game is not secret, not an underground army, and often not a factor as spokesmen and legates take over the direction of events. In Cyprus, the game was taken out of the EOKA rebels' hands by the Greek government. Grivas and Makarios were given a package which could not be more Greek than the Greeks and signed for an independence neither wanted. In Yemen after the civil war 1962–70, those involved – republicans and royalists – found that an accommodation could be reached to share rather than contend for power because the urgency of their patrons, Egypt and Saudi Arabia, had eroded as costs had increased.

Each case was special but all included at least two factors: the perception of the underground particularly and the conventional shifted over time and then the reality of the arena changed dramatically to the advantage of accommodation. In the Irish case in 1921–22, those within the nationalist galaxy perceived the advantages of some power immediately and the risk of seeking all power while their British opponents recognized that major concession was necessary if swift and terrible war were not to be the only option remaining. After that, Irish republicans repeatedly entered politics as a means, only to find that the prospect of the republic, the ideal, continued to recede. In 1994 the IRA–Sinn Féin ceasefire was based not on the premise that the gun would get the dream no closer as much as that an unarmed strategy was a way forward. Putting aside the gun allowed the end-game to accelerate toward what the republicans saw as a desirable direction that might shape a means into the future – in other words the peace process was a continuation of an end-game that had begun with contacts with the British and had no final time-line. When 'progress' was not apparent, the gun was reintroduced, foiled, and everyone – minds sharpened – tried again in 1997. The assumption was not, as with the moderate republicans in 1922, that the freedom to be free had been won but that a means to proceed had been chosen, the major front of the campaign had shifted, not the process.

What had changed in the arena in 1921–22 was the recognition of the cost of the armed struggle in lives, influence and self-respect and the risks inherent in continuing, risk for the empire, for the Irish, for the nationalist cause and British private and political interests. Unlike Cyprus or Yemen outside factors were not crucial, important but not crucial; rather it was the perception of the involved that shifted – and did not shift as far as might have been imagined when the conflict was assumed to be a zero-sum game. Some of the Irish could see the Anglo-Irish Treaty ushering in the real end-game after 800 years and others only the betrayal of the dream – and so, as is often the case in revealed religions the pure confronted the pragmatic and in Ireland in 1922 lost and went underground to wait until the Irish people would tolerate the next act in the long march. And so the Irish in their time of troubles rather than being *sui generis* and very special indicate all the factors at work during an end-game. In 1993–94 the republicans were very conscious of the risks for the movement, for the IRA in continuing the end-game. Yet merely to continue the armed struggle into another generation offered continuity, secondary benefits, and sacrifices – willingly made – but to no practical purpose. Certainly, Britain, too, had changed in public on Irish matters: claimed no reason to stay on the island except as a matter of honor and responsibility and practicality. Honor might be difficult to negotiate just as was the republican dream but what the optimists hoped was an end to the zero-sum Ulster game. The unionist and the more militant loyalist had not changed at all except in that the fear of betrayal was even greater – they believed in the zero-sum game, could imagine no benefit equal to the continuation of the British connection. Only if everyone could find sufficient advantage in an accommodation could the gun be taken out of Irish politics – and yet in 1994 the hard men, loyalists and republicans, as well as the intransigent in London still saw little prospect of breaking the unionist insistence on British sovereignty that assured an IRA armed struggle. No matter that similar hard views in South Africa and Palestine had seemingly been changed overnight, the Irish had, if nothing more, persisted with the integrity of their quarrels, which moved on through violence, another ceasefire and intense negotiation.

The galaxy must have those who prove flexible as well as faithful, the movement must permit sufficient data to penetrate the galaxy so that the faithful can recognize shifts in objective reality. The conventional must be able to imagine concession short of collapse. And once the process is recognized the secret army, no longer secret, no longer merely an army, will discover that emerging into the everyday is merely the last and most difficult of the obstacles in an armed struggle. The enemy must tease away the covert, involve the entire galaxy, and attract the core commanders within the bounds of potential compromise. None of this is easy in the midst of a dirty war, during an asymmetrical conflict often defined in absolutes, amid a clash of destinies where talent may be limited on either side. The simple lack of tact, diplomatic talent, the capacity of empathy may abort an end-game. Thus the imposition of a greater reality – the wishes of the Greek government in the Cyprus case or the shift in Nasser's priorities in Yemen – can be of enormous assistance to those who seek accommodation. And even then it is more likely that there will be no end-game but merely persistence to victory or more likely to the end of the struggle when the faithful falter or the tanks destroy the safe haven over the border or the *foco* is found.

IN SUM

End-games that lead to accommodation, then, are special. They are, however, always an opportunity for the pragmatists on both sides of the asymmetrical conflict. Both must adjust perception and assumption, and so reality. And so any end-game is always a risk for the faithful who cannot stand too much reality – and not all the faithful are found within the armed struggle, for once the conventional had a dream and some still do, while all those under challenge at least have interests.

16

The Dynamics of the Dream

A T THE very beginning the rebel moves, often reluctantly, grudgingly, accepting the inevitability of force. A few are eager to revolt, begin shooting from a foundation long in place or in reaction to provocation or escalating oppression. Always there is the assumption better now than never. Defense cannot wait or the dream cannot be abandoned because conditions are not ripe. Some, like Che, can always find a reason to begin – just as the pragmatic can find reasons to delay, seek other roads into the future. At times events force the rebel into the underground, there organized as a national resistance, as an illicit militia, as the remnant of a lost civil war or a coup, as those who would witness injustice in arms or seek slow redress of sudden grievance. At times, but not often, the rebel rushes to revolt, eager to catch the tide of history, deploy the fashion of the moment, volunteer in a long tradition. In 1970 the Provisional IRA saw the prospects of a campaign emerging as the volunteers were first defenders and then provoked the British security forces. The Official IRA, on the other hand, committed to more conventional politics, tended to see the turmoil in Northern Ireland not as opportunity but as distraction even as their own volunteers began shooting. Nearly everyone else, including the British security forces, imagined that amelioration of grievances, justice with order, would be the prime focus arising from the civil disturbances. The Provisional IRA's analysis proved more accurate and the Army Council got their campaign, but a long war not an escalation to triumph.

Mostly rebels must balance the options and the prospects with the enormous need to act imposed by acceptance of the dream. Those without a dream, without a text or a commanding vision, engage in endemic insurgency, random violence, play a violent role in anarchy, take advantage of chaos. Columns of peasant killers, lone assassins driven by private demons, tribes without banners but gross appetites, killers hired with a slogan, all often highly visible, add to the din. These may play a role in real revolt but are not engaged in an armed struggle. That struggle arises from a special perception and a particular analysis, a rebel reality available often only to the committed, the saved; such a crusade into the future requires more than those eager to use a gun or live on the dangerous edge.

Analysis had led the rebel leaders to a belief that history can conclude appropriately only if arms are used. The ideal encumbered with contemporary grievances, then, can only be achieved through an armed struggle. The ideal is as various as the rebels, often is bedded in the most local aspirations, often is expressed in the fashionable language of the moment, the dialectic turned to tribal grievance, vengeance dressed in national colors. The language of the Left was apt to capture many rebel dialogues even when the cause was parochial, for Marx saw struggle as a means forward and Mao had won. The Right was more apt to aspire to a defense of order or what order should be and so often seek not so much the future as a replay of the past. In all cases the dream imparts a certain urgency to personal lives, quiet desperation. Tranquillity is not compatible with the revelation of the nature of history. Action is required and yet frustrated. Prospects are always real but poor.

The risks of revolt are at times ignored, must at times be ignored and always minimized; but the rebel is rarely a fool although often foolish. Rarely is there a rush to the barricades by those concerned with self-interest, with getting and spending, with general injustice. The classical rebel is an idealist no matter that the ideal be flawed or that the volunteer is focused on the parochial and the perceived grievances. And all dreamers are not pure in heart or cunning in analysis. Some volunteers simply find the revolt congenial, are not self-absorbed or even self-interested, follow the special riptide of rebel history.

An armed struggle for the reasoned and logical, those not saved, is often difficult to grasp because so much is a matter of perception. The reality that all must accept can be transmuted by the rebel faith so that time stands still, power evaporates if only by definition, and defeat is transmuted into victory. If the rebel thinks that an event is a triumph, then it is a triumph for the underground. Pointing to the body bags, the numbers in prison, the hopelessness of resistance simply offers a reality the rebel chooses not to accept. Then, too, an armed struggle is not only, not at all in fact, a simple low-intensity conflict, a war over power, an event to be categorized, but a means to shape a dream to effect. Conventional military victories may play only a small part in the ultimate outcome, a glorious failure, a mix of martyrs and the murdered, hunger strikers dead and leaders hanged; a long litany of apparent losses may, in rebel perception, be all to the good.

As Giap pointed out, his cause did not in the end need military victories.

So, too, with many armed struggles – as long as those involved can survive to shape reality to the dream. Then, if the struggle falters, is insufficient, the dream must die or the rebels reconsider. Most campaigns do fail, many dreams fade, the intensity lost in exile or as time moves on.

THE REBEL GALAXY DISPLAYED

The orthodox accept the tangible as real and the definitions and assumptions of most rebels as imaginary, useful to the desperate but not adequate to determine a real world outcome. The loss of the Mandate of Heaven is difficult to observe. The disappearance of the Soviet Union was easy to watch but the erosion of legitimacy took place beyond easy view. And who was to blame, who is to blame became a matter of perception, history examined in sullen disappointment. The meaning of events, what truly matters, is always a matter of focus and perception.

The conventional may, as an act of analysis as a means of understanding, accept that the rebel world is real to the rebel. Children believe they see the Virgin, Christ bleeds and hermits claim to visions. The ideologue sees a risen people not a hired mob and the gunman dies for Ireland, for the Republic. Truth is a function of need or time, is not quite everyday and not easy to factor into orthodox analysis.

The habits of a lifetime, the assumptions of the conventional world are not easily discarded, not even as exercise, a willful act of empathy. And without marginal empathy there is no realization of the role of the dream – a dream few of the orthodox can credit. It is the dream that supplies the energy, shapes the perimeters of the struggle, imposes the dynamics of the underground.

If the role of the dream is ignored, the nature of the armed struggle is only partially understood: the apple falls to the ground because ripe or the wind, for special reasons in every case unless Newton is read. In an armed struggle, in any armed struggle, the dream and the consequent energy shape all the subsequent dynamics, inspire the galaxy, assure the campaign. For the innocent, these campaigns are apt to be not mandatory but special cases: the Irish clumsy in an Irish way or the Arabs in theirs, not because the dream underground imposes penalties in return for the capacity to persist. It is the dream that gives and the dream that limits; but without the dream there is only banditry, tribal conflict, killing on the margins, crime and murder done. And many of the orthodox are apt to believe that this is the case: who else would say no to convention, kill for the intangible, go in harm's way for such improbable gain?

Mostly the conventional assume the rebel is deluded, dangerous but deluded. Some may be sane, many surely are self-interested, but all are criminal if not foolish. Their reality is wishful thinking, their analysis rationalization, their assumptions outrageous. Rebel reality is not real at all. The state intends to impose reality, deploy the tangible, ignore the dream. And mostly analysts are conventional, if not part of the state almost certainly beyond the power of dream, often beyond accepting the implications of the dream.

TRUTH

Truth does not ordinarily arrive in a flash of enlightenment, a single moment of revelation – the prophet accepted, love at first sight. Few are blinded by a single moment of revelation. Love at first sight exists but is rare. The truth may, rather like most romantic love, appear in an ascending commitment, a rising arc of certainty and hard-to-suppress excitement. The truth may, indeed, be perceived after enlistment by osmosis or by example, by the heightened awareness of the power of the idea made manifest in the movement. Converts often come from within the movement just as they do within the Church, with a growing maturity of both spirit and body, an acceptance that imposes urgency and returns order and purpose. Recruits take instruction and so become initiates, sooner rather than later, but rarely all at once.

The Truth, the faith that fuels the reactor of revolt, everywhere has certain structural similarities: amenable to elaboration and rich with resonances and ambiguities the dream can still be wrought as slogan, emblazoned on flags or shouted through a bull horn. It is thus open to those who would probe reality with the new insight and those unlettered, filled with unarticulated grievances and ruined hopes. The dream of nation or God does for all, can be tool to fine minds and brutal. The dream in contemporary politics often shaped as radical ideology, even if an extension of a more traditional religious faith or tribal base, offers to all an explanation of what has gone wrong with reality, what is to be done, and thus what will transpire.

The answers to these questions, whatever the level of elegance and scholastic refinement, may, often are, crude but effective – slogans that recruit and kill: Peace, Land and Bread; Free Ireland; Let God Rule; Liberty, Equality, and Fraternity. Unlike everyone else, the government, the analysis, the complex and sophisticated, the converted, stumbling over the words of the wall poster or scrawling graffiti, know The Truth. The workers will unite and win. The nation will emerge. God's law will prevail. All is made clear. Nothing more is needed but audacity and arms. And the clarity can be elaborated. The militant nationalist create a glorious, golden past, contrast the long denial to others' ultimate success, offer a glorious and preordained future, available to those who will take up arms against history as written by the center, the alien oppressor, the enemy to justice.

HISTORY

For those who have found the truth and so changed the run of time, the end of History is Justice. History is not only a chronicle of justice denied but also of the stage for the long conflict that will assure the triumph of the truth. All the battles and dynasties, all the relevant events entered in the chronicles, all the useful pass as witness to the great current that leads on to the realization of the dream: the Mega-Greece, the Fourth Rome or the Second Temple, the Basque Republic or the Dictatorship of the Proletariat. None of the faithful wants exposure to the complexities of historians, varying interpretations or explanations. Those with certificates and degrees are apt to elaborate on the ideas rather than the ideals, on the design of the truth; but slogans will do for most, for the gunmen, the new crusaders.

History is weapon fashioned from front to back, from now to then, a tale of justice denied, opportunities lost, a matter of bright flashes of martyrs and golden eras long gone and the black eras of oppression and denial. A Serb or a Tamil, however simple, knows the litany of misery inflicted, the stations of humiliation, the bitter beads of long defeat by arrogant power. History is witness to present grievance, example to be avoided, buttress to a protracted conflict. Most armed struggles are led by those and supported by others who unable to transform the past – a thousand years of Arab defeats or the failure of a new Black Africa – would rewrite the future in order to adjust history. In a small way the armed struggle reflects this larger effort: a protracted struggle between the just and oppressive where the will triumphs over power because the truth has set the faithful free.

Beginning in 1958, the Eritreans, joined by others on the margins of Ethiopia, struggled on in their obscure corner of the Horn of Africa, ignored, denied, forgotten, until the center collapsed in Addis Ababa in 1991 and their guerrillas, allies from Tigre, appeared at the Hilton bar. The center had not held but had not fallen for a third of a century. Eritrea, long denied, ruled by no one, and then the Italians and then the British, then an annexed part of Ethiopia, had thus after a generation emerged from history. It was a history rewritten by the nationalists from scraps and myths but perceived by them as valid. So in May 1991, rebel reality became manifest as fact. The nationalists took Asmara and their allies from Tigre marched into Addis. History rewritten as justice demanded.

To grasp the rebel dynamics, the structure of history, the definition of justice is as vital as a sense of the truth, the power of the dream, to determine action. Humiliation, pain, repeated defeats, the cost of attrition can, if at all, only slowly erode the Truth, impose history as written by others, deny the hope of justice. The Kurds may have no friends but after centuries of oppression still have hope, different hopes, hope for a haven in northern Iraq for some, hope for a victory over the Turks for others, hope for better times for all. The center may hope that pain will adjust perception but there is little evidence to this effect; even time rarely works, or at least not swiftly, to the center's advantage. So history for the rebel remains as adjuster and justice as defined and the struggle protracted. Victory will thus come with persistence not because of the lesser kinds of power deployed by the state.

POWER

There is, then, a principle of Futility of Quantity in every rebel perception. Power arises from history's verdict, from an undeniably just cause, from the will of the people, the inevitable triumph of the proletariat or the working of God's will. All the tanks and planes and flags, the empire displayed, are illusory. Like the Eritreans or Vietnamese or the Cubans, each rebel knows that in time someone will arrive at the palace on a tank or order a drink in the Hilton, sees the beginning of history's last act because of the impact of the faith, the capacity of history to shape events with rebel aid despite the surface reality, despite the seeming power at the center. Numbers do not matter any more than clock time or the orthodox verities or history as written by others.

What matters is persistence in justice's cause, the validation of history. At the end the imperialists or the alien occupiers, the heretics or those others, generals and statesmen, will have to accept that will has power beyond weight and measure. In the meantime, will fuels the struggle, feeds on the ideal, persists beyond reach of the palpable assets of the state.

It is enormously difficult for alien observers or the orthodox opponent not to believe in numbers, not to discount the power of will or the invisible people. The Americans in Vietnam back in the imperial sanctuary have remained immune to this lesson of rebel reality, still often believe that 'more' would have triumphed – more fire power, more support at home, more tactical freedom over the arena, more. All the generals, the media, the visitors and most of the troops could see the vast array of equipment, the flights of helicopters, the ranks of vehicles and artillery, the infrastructure of airfields and computer banks, the officers' clubs and government offices, the miles of poured concrete, stretched cables, the new roads, the whole enormous visible American presence. And all this was opposed by a few bands of terrorists in black pajamas. Enormous weight of metal could and was concentrated, whole districts devastated, free fire zones turned into killing fields and the outback into a cratered wilderness. The weak, punished by power, would in time concede to the visible reality.

What Washington never could possess nor ever understood was the power given by the Vietnamese dream. The dream explained the past, promised the future, and required persistence in the meantime. The 'meantime', tried men's souls, cost the faithful lives and treasure and their future but was worth the cost. Time was on the side of the underground, the irregulars, those with a dream. This strategic scorpion Time assured a combat so protracted that the visible assets of the Americans would erode, this decade or next, because the will in Washington, in the country, in Vietnam was vulnerable, was not for the long haul. And so the dream won and only then proved fallible: after a generation that cost the inchoate Vietnamese nation millions and led not to the ideal but a failed Marxist–Leninist state ruled by old discredited men. Ho and Giap and the rest had been quite right about the armed struggle and their hidden assets, if not as perceptive about the next stage of history. So they did achieve the power they sought if not the future.

Power arises for the rebel only from history, from justice, from the will of the people or the axioms of the faith, never from numbers or armadas or the consensus of the conventional. The power of the center in theory and often in practice can only be effective if sufficiently awesome to kill all, all the dreamers, all the converts, all those resident in the nebula of the faith. And sometimes, mostly, the center can so do, for the big battalions usually win; but sometimes not. Other means may work, corruption, co-option, compromise – all gunmen fear the end-game that may change time into an enemy and the dream into tawdry. So some persist until the center falters: the imperialist counts again the colonial costs or the life-president opts for the Riviera. Then, in time real, countervailing rebel power will arise, often in conventional form. At last the center fails to hold and the victorious ride into the capital on tanks or at least without opposition.

For the disinterested observer, for an analyst outside the conflict loop, much rebel analysis is often taken as propaganda, largely preaching to the faithful or, more cunningly, to the innocent at a distance. To grasp the nature of the rebel ecosystem empathy is required – a willingness to accept the perception as valid. Few of the orthodox can so do. Rebel dreams are flawed, self-serving, rationales for terror or imported as cover by the greedy and ruthless. Few of the orthodox believe rebel dreams matter when faced with the big battalions. And mostly the orthodox are right: the dreamers can usually be killed and so the dream. This is not quite always so for sometimes if very little is left that residue is the dream, a conviction that may lie fallow waiting for a new generation of faithful.

In any case, for centuries, generals and statesmen had been urged to understand the foe and for centuries many have felt no urgency to do so. The Romans knew little of the Gauls and less of the Germans. The Christian crusaders knew only that the infidels were cunning. Such enemies were seen as absolutely alien and enormously dangerous. The fedayeen driving a carbomb to glory for Islam never met a Zionist and those gunmen who know their own – landlords or officers or communists – need no details. A dream may offer details, may define the enemy at length, but, like those in power, the opponent is more easily shaped as monster.

Most armed struggles, however, pit a dream fashioned from the old ideals at the center into a powerful new ideal. The center sees not the alien but the corruption of the old faith by new men. These are violent, self-serving, ruthless and ultimately deluded by false prophets. Those in power recognize facets of rebel pretensions and perceptions but usually fail to understand the nature of the rebel challenge – see war or politics or subversion as the category, power and profit as the solution. Empathy with fanatics, even those not too alien, is no easy matter when the dreamers claim the rights and legitimacies of the establishment as history's reward.

To understand too much, to know too much, makes the defense of the conventional more complex. Do the Zionists need to read Palestinian history to understand fedayeen who target women and children? Do decent men in the Quirinale Palace in Rome need to grasp the slogans twisted from Marx or Mao by rabid terrorists who gun down professors and journalists? Why bother? Why should the British care about Wolfe Tone's ancient dictum or even the latest word from the Sinn Féin offices on the Falls Road? And so few bother but rather depend upon numbers and tradition and inertia. And if there is to be peace, if Sinn Féin comes to talk without a gun or the *Brigate rosse* is repentant then that is a different game, different people who speak not of vision but details.

Those who do analyze the rebel do so with orthodox tools: number of gunmen, foreign aliens, arena cover, sanctuary and arms. They focus on the variety of motives or the location and intensity of the campaign. The perceptions the dream, any dream, imposes are missed or ignored, if not irrelevant, less compelling. Those analysts concerned with dreams tend to focus on the specifics of the text or the typologies of belief, not the general rebel perception that shapes the dynamics of the underground. This is, after all, what makes the conventional conventional: the conventions of the irregular are so regularly defined, edited, and published in traditional form for traditional purpose.

THE PERSISTENCE OF THE DREAM

Once the killing begins, the movement increasingly becomes focused on the requirements of the unconventional campaign, those investments most closely related to the military deemed most appropriate. Facing rising competence at the center, greater repression, the penalties of the under- ground, the rebel is hard-put merely to persist. The campaign gobbles assets. Propaganda may come by the deed, may come only by deeds, or prison may be chosen as an arena but only because of necessity or overwhelming opportunity. The *real* thrust is toward war. And when, as is almost inevitable, this thrust is blunted, the rebel may seek other targets, other theaters and fronts but always as a means to further the armed struggle – the outward manifestation of the dream at work. A rebel campaign is shaped operation- ally by the nature of targets, access, vulnerability, appropriate form, and often the haphazard factored in but not discussed. Inevitably the key to the armed struggle by all the involved is assumed to be the deployment of rebel violence in a campaign usually treated as war rather than as a dream in action, or a nation in arms or a class rising or even a form of politics. The move underground means that the actual manifestation of the dream is the armed struggle, an ideal transmuted into an act that will determine the direction of history. The rebels kill, choose targets, seek power and so the future, with a gun.

Targets

The movement's tactical operations are usually determined in the balance between chosen and desirable targets and what can be reached. The rebel may want to attack the army but will settle for the police until difficulties force a switch to the militia or to civilian friends of the regime. Most rebels want to be in power, assume at least the titles and tactics of power, act if possible even if counter-productive as would the state, the regime, the center. Often this is not possible and is never convincing to the orthodox so that the rebel is left with titles and rationalization – this young man in a boiler suit carrying a lunch-box bomb is a commandant and that explosion in a public square was the justified act of an urban guerrilla.

In response to violence and provocation the defenders of the center, attacked by the unknown without warning or remorse, seek an appropriate response that will neither damage legitimacy nor prove ineffectual. Some worry little about legitimacy and use all the force available, others ignore the provocation if possible, but violence within democratic states is always complex, hedged, and unsatisfactory. Any response to the rebel assault will inevitably begin as defensive and bleed out into offensive operations that are, in fact, mostly active defense from a more advanced cordon.

The protection of targets comes quickly, often first. Who or what will be attacked? If the military is at risk, will this include off-duty navy recruiters, cooks and bakers – who? Which of the categories, which point within the category will be attacked? Which cook is endangered? When will an attack be likely to come and how and by whom? Why will such an attack come? What is the rebel dynamic? The latter is often thought too academic by those at the point where the shooting occurs. They are, of course, questions of great interest to the analysts and academics who, more often than not, assume rebel priorities are the same as their own and the skills of the conventional easy to transport underground. And few, whatever their past service, have the same sense of urgency as those deployed in the killing game. There, underground, answers, properly so, like their questions, are often academic.

A lack of empathy usually results in an error by the defense, an error in commitment of resources. Right question. Wrong answer. Often these questions are not asked directly, often some answers are known or assumed – or read off rebel placards. The more precise the answer and the more general then the more carefully calibrated the response – a cost-effective move that will not beggar the center.

Defense

The ideal is to protect all potential targets, if it be the military then defend all soldiers, their families and retainers, their friends and neighbors. This, hardening targets, often is difficult, expensive, but not by any means impossible. In imperial situation the army and its train can be isolated in defended camps. In an everyday world uniformed military can be deployed only on active service when armed and ready and then hidden away the rest of the time in mufti or even camps. When out of sight, isolated and protected, neither they nor the barber, the girl friend nor tea boy will be in the firing line. All targets can be hardened. There will be concentric rings of defense, static and mobile. The secret service would like to protect the president by sealing off central Washington and the British have devised 'rings of steel' about Belfast and London City – not to great effect but in general view.

Simultaneously the routes to such targets can be monitored: the way in and the way out covered by observation posts, air surveys, undercover patrol cars, informers, sensors, whatever will work. Thus an attack flowing through the only access road may be blocked or thwarted at site or if successful hit on the way back. It is crucial that the defenders hone a swift and effective operational response: hard targets give time for a quick on-site response, time to close the doors, and if necessary first cut off havens and then check the suspected. Even then a swift investigation through intelligence assets may reveal operational details even before the smoke clears.

It is even more effective if the targets, hard or soft, can be made invulnerable by dissuading rebel commanders. There can also be deterrents that may make hard defenses unnecessary. These may range from psychological moves that make certain targets ideologically unattractive: the rebel will find them so or his constituents or the general public.

Too often the defender assumes that rebel priorities are similar to those of the state, criticizes this target or that as inappropriate – feral murder or the slaughter of innocents – while the guerrilla, assuming no one is innocent, finds the victim ideologically congenial. The IRA could never understand why their little bombs in London so outraged the English given the Royal Air Force bombing campaigns against the Axis. Convinced that 'no one was innocent' the Palestinian fedayeen simply ignored the global outrage that attacks on civilians engendered. Rebel grievance is often assumed ample provocation: no justice for us, no peace for anyone.

The rebel movement, the galaxy certainly, even perhaps the avowed constituency, finds unsavory targets acceptable. Croatian irregulars, the gunmen of the IRA, the Holy *Jihad*, realize they are misunderstood by observers, but the rationale of necessity convinces their own, their galaxy. Each tangible target, the army camp or the airliners, has as well other targets, the galaxy and the distant, the United Nations or the heretics at home. These must be taught by the deed. In Algeria the crusade slaughters whole villages, old men, women, children, to prove the government futile and foul. And indignation and outrage from the threatened, editorials and media condemnation, sermons from the establishment will not have a deterrent effect – perhaps the reverse.

The threatened may discard the rationales but seldom ignore the danger. There can be the simple deterrent of highly visible protection, highly visible deployment or assets that will intimidate or dissuade. Filtering at the airport rarely catches a terrorist but may well deflect some, certainly the incompetent or hasty. Simply building the fences higher or adding attack dogs may work. No chance to attack *there*. Psyops can exaggerate capacity – or even stress real capacity – in effectiveness of response, skill of units, intelligence to hand, technology in place, and operations to come. The leak of disinformation about sources may not only cause havoc with rebel security but also inhibit operations that require large numbers of people. Obviously it helps if the center's assets are real and seen to be deployed as well as paraded by spokesmen. The center must *appear* to respond to provocation: rings of steel about the City that do not dissuade the IRA or inspection at the airport that does not deter the hijacker. The state must not only have assets but display them.

Rebel reactions

The authorities can scarcely select effective items from a menu of response without the rebel changing the price or the list – and at times the very restaurant. The rebel at great cost must shift assets to persist, change the deployment under pressure in order to continue the campaign. Hard targets mean an immediate search for soft targets. First, almost at once, the target categories are increased: soldiers in and out of uniform and, if they prove elusive, then their suppliers – barbers and bakers. If all the military withdraws behind effective walls, then there will be other enemies on the list: the clerks and typists of oppression, capitalist contractors; all those who give aid and comfort to the oppressor are as one with the oppressor. The ultimate list can be made so extensive that hard defense becomes very difficult: everyone who flies to Israel, any manager at Fiat, all Sikhs, any white face or brown. And such a lengthening list may not be shortened by deterrent, by propaganda and by persuasion – all slow processes – but require greater if ineffectual defenses.

Ultimately, some of the Palestinian fedayeen felt any Israeli would do as target, any friend of Israel, most Westerners. The target list changed and so the method and even the arena because of operational necessity. The lethal dialogue resulted in a situation where access to any prime target grew harder: killing Israeli soldiers was very difficult, killing Israelis nearly so, killing Zionists abroad presented novel problems, even killing people in El Al or Pan Am boarding lines in Europe and escaping was not a simple matter. The fedayeen found that the resort to terror engendered all sorts of problems that hampered persistence in a seemingly invulnerable tactic. And the easier the operation, a time-set bomb in an airliner, the more distant from the legitimate, the less military, the more likely to alienate certainly the distant and even the constituency.

In fact the fedayeen, like most rebels, found no solution to their problems, no costless means to escalate and grave difficulty in persisting. What did not change was the obligations of the dream. When the dream was in part co-opted by the faithful of Hamas, they too begin to seek the vulnerable: those in the Occupied Territories, those riding a bus down Dizengoff Street. And their success assured that once again the Israelis would close off the vulnerable – and, as had been the case for the fedayeen, for the faithful in Lebanon, more than likely send the gunmen and bombers further afield.

The rebel, like the Palestinians, in order to persist – or if lucky – to escalate, may take the war elsewhere, another arena where the targets are not as hard. The Stern Group in 1944 went to Cairo to stage a spectacular in the murder of Lord Moyne, and the Palestine–Israel war was often fought out between agents in foreign capitals with diplomats and legatees as targets and the streets as battlefield. The Gaza–Jericho accommodation and the rise of Hamas as an aspect of the revival of fundamental Islam only means that the context of the struggle will change: terror will be as valid in New York's World Trade Center as in Dizengoff Street. If the parochial IRA could dispatch volunteers to Germany and Gibraltar, in an interdependent world where a credit card and a passport gives accesses to all sorts of undefended targets, any underground can target the ends of the earth. Airliners filled with innocents targeted because of the logo are destroyed a world away from the primary arena. Turkish diplomats can be shot in California and the struggle against Zionism brought to Uganda or pursued in Argentina.

The spread of international, even transnational, terror is an example of broader target selection on a global scale. The Armenians simply struck where Turkish officials could be found – any place, any capital, any arena but historical Armenia. Mostly the arena is more modestly extended: ETA comes into Madrid in 1973 from the Basque country to assassinate Admiral Luis Carrero Blanco or the Official IRA detonates a bomb in 1972 in paratroop headquarters at Aldershot in England. In turn, the Spanish authorities arrange with the French to search for the Basques across the border and the Protestant paramilitaries bomb – if not often – in Dublin. Always the first choice is what is to hand as much as what will be most effective. Some symbolic targets, like the World Trade Center in New York, are easy, unguarded, vulnerable even to the clumsy and untrained – ideal.

If there is nothing to be done about the target or its location, then the rebel may improve and elaborate those techniques under threat from the defense: find new ways in and new ways out, new ways to construct an operation. The harder the target, the more difficult access and withdrawal, the more ingenuity or skill required. A proxy bomb can be devised that will force an innocent driver to pass by security for fear of retaliation. Another route is hi-tech, bombs that can be detonated from a distance months after siting; the introduction of a new weapon – a heavy machine-gun or a novel explosive device or a special mortar. Newly acquired electronic radio channels scanners or night-sights can open up not only targets but also entry and exit. And there is a case for low tech: poison in the soup or a bomb in a letter are hardly novel but come as a surprise the first time. Even operational innocence disarms a too highly sophisticated opponent. Who would have anticipated the IRA moving arms into Ireland in small boats, a replay of previous failures, using Malta filled with British citizens as a transhipment point, going back once again to Libya? Both the old and new may work. Michael Collins on his bike may ride by the British patrol but so may a wanted man with his own face and a borrowed passport slip by border controls on the alert for disguises and elegant documentation. Often reduced to the simple and obvious for lack of talent, lack of assets, lack of experience, the gunmen triumph over the elegant defenders prepared for hi-tech assaults by their peers. The rebel, sound and available, seeks any means to act, responds to any vulnerability.

The lethal dialogue

Each of these rebel responses engenders a counter, other targets hardened, other operational areas protected, entry and access to the vulnerable defended more closely, assets adjusted or redeployed, more machines and more cunning applied. And in return the rebel responds. Since there is no match between two players but an unconventional war, much of the lethal dialogue occurs without proper planning, without much thought, ad hoc. One shot sailor on leave in a foreign port concentrates all minds. One proxy bomb means new instructions for the guard at the gate not necessarily seminars at the military academy. It is easy in the long view, from a distance, to parse the expansion of the battlefield, less academic when the evidence is sprawled dead and bloody opposite, at a café table far from home.

The tendency of the threatened or simply horrified when war erupts across the table, amid civilians, in the front lobby of the Carlton Club bombed by the IRA or the line at Rome airport when Palestinians gun down the passengers, is to assume that the rebel has free play. The gunman can kill where he wants, when he wants, who he wants, makes the running, selects with cunning and care the atrocity of the moment. The actual rebel, of course, is hedged around with both cultural restrictions and often more effectively by the enormous difficulties of operating underground in secrecy with all those penalties and very few assets. Mostly the limitations are what the rebel notes, the difficulties, the cost of persistence and the elusive nature of escalation. The IRA would prefer to deploy as an army not as messenger boys leaving bombs at the front door just as the fedayeen would prefer to drive tanks against the Zionists rather than dispatch those who kill passengers in the wrong airport line. Mostly the gunman is left with second best, the target that can be defined as valid and is within reach.

It is no small matter to exist while wanted, to acquire a weapon, to find a soldier isolated and vulnerable, to shoot, perhaps to kill, and to escape, hide the weapon, find haven, evade the hue and cry until the next time. It does not to the gunman seem an easy matter. At least some rebels try to escalate through resort to unconventional means, novel targets or new fronts but most find simply to continue, to keep the dream real, ample challenge.

THE ARMED STRUGGLE ANALYZED AS CONFLICT

Analysis has focused on the nature of the armed struggle as war, as rebellion or revolution, as unconventional conflict with the arena, the ideology, the tactics, for example, as the primary definition: a rural nationalist insurgency or a war of national liberation. A persistent and understandable motif in many studies is the discernible stages of these low-intensity conflicts. Obviously events in history move through time and once a focus is decided, a subject chosen, then there is a beginning, the middle, and often an end. There is the expectation of the idealists that the stages will be distinct, the direction of events progressive and at last a final act, an end result. There is a feeling that revolutionary war, like Mao's theory, should start small and end big and conventional outside the palace. It did, in time, for Ho and Giap and even for the Ethiopian rebels.

Real life is not always so congenial. The communist insurgency in

Malaya was underway before the British noticed, peaked quickly and tapered off bit by bit for years and years in the jungle, rather inside out, back to front, for successful campaigns. Some 'campaigns' arise from endemic insurgencies when new banners are raised and maintained for decades as in Burma or Cambodia or the Philippines or even Eritrea where the center at Addis Ababa could no longer cope and the rebels could move on and up to irregular war. In the Philippines, Cambodia and Burma there are tides and eddies but as yet no end. In Ireland even with the IRA second ceasefire of July 1997, no one, least of all the Army Council, was sure that the end-game would pay sufficient dividends, that the campaign was on hold or over.

Only a few campaigns evolve into overt negotiations. The American rebels signing the treaty of Paris at the end of their revolutionary war was not harbinger. The center seldom deals but like the rebel wins or loses. Only on occasion does the dialogue emerge into convention – as it did in Ireland in 1921–22 with a treaty that removed the Irish problem from British politics for 50 years – but assured its reappearance and so another troubled generation. Gaza–Jericho appears even less promising, transforming the context of the conflict but not the intensity of the persistent dream.

The analysts concentrate on motivation – what ideology or loyalty inspires the rebel, on the arena and structure of the campaign – whether the rebel is an irregular soldier or a rural guerrilla, on phases and stages, theoretical and real. In the latter case the observer has the nature of time as ally, for revolts must begin, must persist, and sooner or later succeed or fail. Thus there is an effort to find stages as did Mao, after the fact, as do most rebels who must start small and want to grow grand.

Those responsible for order focus on orderly stages that relate to shifting capacity not to the intensity of perception that drives the real rebel. The British General Frank Kitson, theorist of low-intensity operations, suggested three stages: the Preparatory Period, the Non-Violent Phase, and Open Insurgency. The difficulty with the Preparatory Period for a government is that a factor in most revolts is the surprise of the center at the audacity of the rebels, heretofore ignored. No government can quite imagine that the rebel is preparing to contest the state. This is true even when the state is founded on such assumptions, directed by those always fearful of their vulnerability, and exposed to visible evidence. Revolts still surprise and preparatory periods go unnoticed. Surprise may be tempered by previous and parallel experiences and, as Kitson urges, by civil–military preparations, a step opposed by the habits of lethargy, the invisibility of the threat, and the varying institutional agendas.

The British in the Irish case, in fact the Irish government as well, are always aware of the potential of the IRA, but in that special case everyone has institutionalized Irish republican persistence. The fact that the armed struggle was put on hold in July 1997 hardly guarantees that the Irish underground will not opt for a renewed campaign if the dream is denied, if the existing leadership fails to deliver – and most of all if the conditions for such a campaign reemerge. And after generations both London and Dublin are aware that the republican dream has had a very long half-life. Generally the state is inclined, no matter how fearful, to miss the rebel preparations. In Ireland in 1970 the Provisional IRA had needed no preparations until the arena proved ripe – and this the state always misses for to accept intolerable grievance would be to admit a failure of governance.

The non-violent phase can be very short indeed for the rebel often feels that the preparatory analysis has gone on so long that once the time of decision comes the shooting should begin. Some revolts move into war still debating the options. Some rebels are always violent, some even suspect any option but force. And as for the Open Insurgency, this is the stage that most theorists seek to parse and divide, build general models so that an appropriate response can be structured by the threatened.

Most states cannot be concerned with each foolish dream, with the newest perception of the discontent, with the grievances beyond remedy or the gunmen who threatened only a few. A few states, like Germany, feel absolute order is necessary, an order the Italians neither miss nor admire and an order far beyond the dreams of the most secure, legitimate and successful Third World government. No matter the degree of turmoil, the mere presence of rebel dreams is seldom a source of great alarm. The police are wary but have other priorities. The exiles often have no real prospects for a campaign: who really imagined a Croatia reborn or a Spanish Bourbon restored?

Governments have other priorities and only respond to provocation – and exiles and old rebels often regroup and provoke further reaction. The Iranian mujahedeen prepared to rebel against the Shah, contributed their assets to his downfall only to be destroyed and driven into exile by the mullahs. With sanctuary in Iraq, they proved a constant but minor irritant and eventually in April 1992 in a public display Teheran bombed their Ashraf camp near Khalis 40 miles north of Baghdad. In a carefully coordinated and previously planned response, the mujahedeen seized and sacked ten Iranian missions and offices in Europe as well as the United Nations Mission in New York. This end-game falls outside most of the conventional stages theory just as the set of acts occurred beyond the primary arena. Still, most revolts do tend to have beginnings, action, and a final act even if the epilogue may drag on. Most intended revolts, of course, never for one reason or another reach much beyond the prologue, and often the action is brief and final when rebel theory, rebel perception, gunmen pretension meets tangible reality.

In any case, neither the theories of the rebel strategists, often as academic as their opponents, nor the maxims of counter-insurgency, often common sense as field tactics, are as dominant in the field as they are in the academies. Much of the technical and even many tactical responses are readily codified. The ground rules of war are still valid. There are effective ways to pursue guerrilla columns in the outback or safeguard cities from gunmen. People's wars have generated conventional and often effective government responses. Often the theories of the state, the ideas of the academics, the models of social scientists are irrelevant, do not help or hamper the soldiers and the police until the rebel persists and the model imposes untested on the campaign. Even then a state can make errors, readjust theory and practice. A state has assets to waste, however painful the loss. The rebel does not.

17

Epilogue

T HE TRIUMPH of the dream is the universal aspiration of those
embarked on an armed struggle and one of the rarest of all political
phenomena. Those great struggles that produce major revolutions in
governance, attitudes, institutions and the balance of power are justly
detailed in history: the American Revolution or the French, Lenin in Russia
or Mao in China. Even the lesser triumphs of Castro or Ho and Giap are
saga, great historical moments albeit with less potency. There are vintage
eras for revolution like the wave of emulation spreading out from France
and America in the eighteenth century that in the next century found Latin
America transformed, and there was 1848 that left behind tricolors and
causes not yet realized. The rise of class revolution was more apt to leave
socialist parties and martyrs in the nineteenth century – and new soviet
regimes in the twentieth. The great contemporary event was the global
anti-imperial campaign after 1945 just as the last classical revolution in
China climaxed; each anti-colonial armed struggle was special, some only
symbolic, but all ran to a pattern and many were successful.

For many small countries the moment of liberation defined all that went
before and made all history since less pedestrian or corrupt: the glory days
were spent underground in the Palestine Mandate or the suq of Algiers.
Because the era of decolonization generated such a wide spectrum of
violence – liberation by riot, by non-violent demonstrations, by assassination
or association – the imperialists often crushed one rising only to concede
to others. The British could not imagine the Mau Mau or the Malayan
communists in power but welcomed more presentable candidates to the
Commonwealth table. Vietnam concentrated Parisian minds on Algeria.
In fact the cost exacted by the FLN in an armed struggle that was frustrated
militarily in Algeria but triumphed politically in Paris concentrated many
minds. French African 'concessions' were transformed into a new invisible
African empire. Each colonial struggle, the will against the center, seemed
certain to triumph in the end. Opposed to corruption and despotism in

Lisbon, the Portuguese rebels conceded in Africa to their colonial rebels and thus encouraged the African National Congress to persist against the seemingly immovable indigenous Afrikaners.

Thus a generation of success clouded rebel minds to the previous failures, to what became a special case. The Huks did not win in the Philippines, nor did their successors. In Latin America, before Castro generations of despotism and exploitation had produced revolving military coups and only one revolution in Mexico soon corrupted by power. And after Castro there was no victory until the Sandinistas in Nicaragua when the regime imploded. Then the new revolutionary elite proved not so corrupt as incompetent. And there were armed struggles against old revolutionaries in Afghanistan or new ones in Africa. Yet, despite the plethora of despots and selfish elites brought to power with the gun, the cannibal kings and life-presidents, most armed struggles were snuffed out by the police. Those despots knew too well the routes to power in the palace. The democracies could adjust to radical demands. And the efficient dictators were seemingly beyond challenge.

Mostly it was a case of a few men in an upstairs room swept up and forgotten. Many failed in the field, on the beach, when the riot petered out and the survivors were put before walls or into prison. The dream dies at least for a generation of the bold. Even most of the colonial rebels struck a blow and died, found a place in future history texts but no route to power. And after the overt empires were gone vulnerable targets appeared scarce if rebel ambitions no less intense. Fueled by ethnic aspirations, religious sureties, national purpose or the ideology of the moment, every year revealed new armed struggles in the service of one dream or another. The world changed, the Soviet empire collapsed and often democracy not the gun had takers as well as advocates. Always there seemed a role for the rebel with a cause, however flawed the cause, however faint the prospects.

Only a few at any time survive underground competition, the attrition of the years, the heresy and informers and the simple trap ambush around the corner, survive the reality of those tangible assets and win through to the palace and power. And some, like the NLF in Aden, triumphed over Arab rivals. In South Arabia the NLF ultimately imploded, killed off the triumphant generation and opened the way first to unity with the Yemen to the north and then for a time to civil war. At the same time, most Arab revolutionaries were swept up, shot, and forgotten. A few, Arabs or Asians or others, do reach power relatively quickly, a matter of years on the run, time in a hide, in the back of a closet or a stranger's house, time intense with responsibility and danger, each day desperate but then an end and, unlike South Arabia, no new gunfights in the streets and murder in the cabinet room.

The Arab Revolt in Palestine lasted three years – from 1936 to 1939 – and the Irgun and Stern Group were active only from 1944 to 1948. Most *focos* failed quickly and in fact the great model in Oriente in Cuba was not the site of a protracted conflict but one that in a few years escalated from a hunted handful to control of Cuba. A few, such as Mao and Giap, like the Eritreans, persist in a single long campaign protracted beyond reason, slipping through stages, often more readily seen in retrospect than at the time to those engaged, until the center collapses and/or their own power predominates. And the irreconcilables in Ireland in the IRA kept the faith, tried repeatedly to inspire general dissent and at last succeeded in 1970–71 in establishing a military IRA campaign that might not be able to win but after a generation could not be defeated. The Irish example of protracted conflict was in a sense novel: in Ireland sacrifice paid in dividends, secondary benefits, if not in conventional power.

All such struggles, short or long, at the beginning assume that the center will fail to hold, is fatally flawed and so fragile, damned by history. Thus the center may collapse in time if the rebels merely persist, but most in the grip of a dream do not want to wait, are engaged in an armed struggle to accelerate the course of history. They have assumed for one reason or another that justice cannot wait on time and an armed struggle is, therefore, necessary. Once the struggle begins, however, the great decision taken, the dream moved underground, the rebels intend to win if they cannot escalate by simply persisting. The Irish republicans have persisted for two centuries – a ceasefire does not mean the gun no longer has validity on the island. Mao took decades and fashioned a real army, a counter-state, another China, that in 1949 simply subsumed the old, scattered the disheartened fragments of opposition.

Ho and Giap haltingly repeated the schedule in a long Vietnamese war during an era when other national liberation movements came swiftly to power as the empire accepted the rebels as respectable or too expensive or too unimportant to quell. If the center, sensitive only to its own agenda, sought to persist as well, as did the Portuguese, the rebel generally had to rely on persistence rather than accumulated power. Mao might have acquired more power than his opponents, but elsewhere the rebels were right: the assets at the center were too strong until the will broke. In Havana there was a rush to the Miami flight. In Vietnam the French and the Americans conceded on the installment plan, leaving their local allies behind to keep up payments without funds. In Ethiopia the center, cruel, corrupt, incompetent, dazed by memorized magic formulas from abroad, brutal without efficiency, collapsed and left all the country to the Eritrean and Tigrean separatists. The margins had won a victory beyond expectations, possessed the whole country, not simply their just homeland.

Victory, rare but real, is almost always the case of accumulated assets suddenly being sufficient if the center fails: the Cuban army did not want to fight nor the Ethiopian, and those few in Saigon who did had insufficient assets to repulse a conventional invasion. Mostly, however, it is the will that goes and lets the rebel emerge into power, heir to history. If the British decide Ireland is not worth the effort, that secondary rewards are secondary, their departure will be precipitous if disguised as a magnanimous gesture; and if they stay, as in some form has always been the case, it will only be as duty, as responsibility, as symbol of a will still virile. Many nations and most regimes rest on the will to rule. If Moscow no longer feels an empire crucial, control vital, all may go, did go – great Russia became little for no one had the will to send out the tanks. The center tends to hold until the price is right: then Baby Doc or Mobutu withdraws and the liberated nation falls into other hands, then the Shah accepts the inevitable and the ayatollahs their promised land. At times there is no choice and the center holds until the very end with the gunmen at the gate, but mostly the will goes and so the center fails and the rebel wins.

Winning, however, is not everything, for little attention has been paid to the reality of power. Often the text, especially those imported, have details and plans and charts, but real life requires real rules. The gunman must become a general, put on a uniform, go daily to an office, activate the phone and the fax, call meetings and administer, authorize, deny. A different set of dynamics rules when the underground emerges. It is not always a simple matter for a counter-state to become a state overnight, go from cabinet meetings in attics and agricultural courts held in palm groves to the flourishes and rituals of the capital. Those movements, however, that have shaped themselves not as secret armies or vanguard parties but as states denied, governments in internal exile, have a shorter road to travel toward legitimacy.

The Irish founded a Free State and the Zionists Israel, not overnight but in the underground and often above ground in sight of the opponent. Those counter-states sited abroad with exile governments and often a tenuous understanding of their cherished homeland liberated by guerrillas and gunmen not always ready for the easy life or amenable to directives and formal agendas have other problems. The successors to Tito or Stalin follow no set underground pattern, are irregulars seeking legitimacy, ethnic conspirators in power, the powerful appearing under new banners, players deploying factions and gunmen and faced with all sorts of novel problems not easily defined, much less addressed.

There are two struggles for legitimacy. The first by the galaxy to become recognized in whole or in part as the vessel of the future: not just a secret army but the army of the republic, not criminals, not gunmen alone but soldiers in a just crusade. This thrust is found on all fronts: the army has titles and uniforms in the top of the closet; the leaders are presidents of liberation movements, make treaties, are accepted at international conferences, appear on television panels and before the committees of friendly governments; the faithful see themselves as the real citizens, the truly loyal, heirs to the future, proper people patriots not criminals or traitors. At one end of the spectrum, Arafat speaks to the United Nations in paramilitary gear with an empty holster, or Gerry Adams of Provisional Sinn Féin becomes the media flavor of the year in 1994 during the ceasefire events; and at the other end a frantic young man in a ski mask, holding a revolver to a pilot's head, speaks for a liberation movement without substance, for a cause no one understands that requires hostages and victims to become valid. The masked gunmen of Hamas move down the road abandoned by Arafat in a miasma of grievance and violence – and none are sure that such a road may not arise again in Ireland, and if so few will need a map.

At times there is almost no movement toward legitimization – the struggle is too far underground, too far out in the wilds. What could Che do – toss proclamations into the jungle? Even the elegant terrorists of Italy were reduced to communiques left in waste bins. Still, in the case of the Euroterrorists, friends above ground, outside the secret armies, out of touch with the underground, could and did endow them with legitimacy, rationalizations and explanations. Ideological friends, sometimes in state offices, offered aid and comfort because the professed ideas of the underground were deemed ideologically correct. Some struggles are so protracted that the guerrillas involved accept that the dream is mirage but still fruitful, that the struggle appears the end but is not without rewards. The guerrilla in the process of the struggle grows, matures, is empowered if not in power. At times, hope of conventional power must be discarded but not the life underground. Persistence means the underground is viable, a factor in any equation: insurrection institutionalized. Then a guerrilla commander has a legitimate role in the Colombia *altiplano*, has power, prestige, position, operates underground and is recognized on the ground, never perhaps to be able to impose the dream but beyond reach of suppression, not a bandit, not a liberator. And who knows what the future holds for the rebel-in-perpetual waiting. The Irish have from time to time bombed their way to the peace table only to be thwarted. There were hundreds of cease-fires in Lebanon and in Angola and Mozambique that proved prologue to war.

Despite the uncertainties on the ground, those engaged in any armed struggle recognize the need to be engaged in more than murder from a ditch. An army without banners must still have cause and credentials. There is a legitimacy to the Irish armed struggle many elsewhere recognize and seek to emulate. And no ceasefire yet has fully denied or denied for long the desperate and frustrated who seek the republic. And those without tradition, without authorization from God or a great party, with only their own, still claim history as vindicator.

Even the most parochial clansman or bandit from the outback if at all exposed to the fashions of the times, the rubrics learned on television, seeks some vestige of legitimacy, represents the people not greed, is a commander not a killer. Some armed bands come with titles and ideological manuals borrowed for the occasion. No warlord is without uniform or aides or airs and graces but many have no dream, no prospect of recognition as more than dangerous. The mountains of Bosnia had local commanders and commandants self-appointed, dressed in the fashion of the times, representing power imposed.

Most European capitals are home to the faithful few denied visibility and prospects but insisting on the legitimacy of their special dream. Exile is almost as traditional for the faithful as the military campaign. Exile in any case is apt to last longer, impose alienation as a career but may lead home again. Who cared about Lenin or Garibaldi or Ho Chi Minh in exile? The effort to be someone, to be respectable, to be not killer but crusader is everywhere found, found in the miserable offices and bedsitters, found in the hills beyond the media. Few of the bandit chiefs or clan killers really aspire to proper power and all its prerogatives but rather to prominence and a modicum of respectability. On the other hand, every gunman with a dream assumes legitimacy, assumes that the denial of this legitimacy by the center is a tactic not a reading of reality. The sniper in the ditch or the car bomber has not only been empowered by the dream but made legitimate if not respectable.

There are those involved in real armed struggles who seek not simply the costume of legitimacy but also to shape actual institutions and so achieve recognition. During a brief truce in 1975 in Ireland, Provisional Sinn Féin set up authorized Incident Centers, visible if minor evidence of the movement's legitimacy – hardly enough for the hard men who wanted the

Republic not small concessions. These seedy offices of the Sinn Féin public presence, a telephone, a deal table and mismatched chairs piled with old newspapers, tea cups and activists, were far from the realities of real revolutionary power. The Rwandan army in exile in the Zaire camps, brutal men late engaged in pogroms and ethnic cleansing, were still armed, still lethal, and still claimants to military status and the right to impose order on *their* Rwanda. These pretensions are far from the complex financial net of the Palestinian Liberation Organization or the Tamil control of the Jaffna peninsular in Sri Lanka, but are one with the thrust to be recognized.

At times all such efforts merge to produce the counter-state, one with the power to make history real in Mao's case or that of the Zionists in Palestine. There may be pretensions of grandeur in the case of the Palestine Liberation Organization when the Gaza–Jericho compact was signed or a fragile reality in the successor states in the Soviet empire. The yearning for recognition has at times been sated by recourse to strategies that thus entailed great risks. Governments-in-exile are often in danger of isolation and irrelevance, cut off from the battle arena and the secret army, custodian of secondary assets and a dream less blinding. Other counter-states are never proclaimed but can emerge into power as often was the case with the anti-imperial rebel. A liberation movement in Africa could shift from the armed struggle to ruling the nation swiftly if not easily, many in fact were already recognized as real governments by African friends. And some 'real' governments are recognized by almost no one: the Turkish Republic of Cyprus, Somaliland, or the regime of the moment in Liberia or Sierra Leone.

The keys to legitimization in every case as far as the armed struggle is concerned are the aid in escalation and the reflection of actual power. Legitimacy aids the galaxy's perception of the validity of the dream, aids the movement in its public image, and so aids the escalation of the armed struggle. At best the claims are validated by perceptible evidence: the Tamils control Jaffna, the IRA had no-go zones until 1974, no one travels in the combat zone without authorization issued by the movement. Movement through the roadblocks of Beirut left a paper trail through obstacles and checkpoints where the wrong document could have fatal consequences. Yet in the midst of murder, documentation mattered. At times legitimation is a matter of titles and banners and rituals, bits of paper, parades on back streets and the color of a beret bought on the corner; but more important at times such postures and pretensions are real, indicate that there is power as well as facade in those rituals and titles. Some underground reality is real, some pretensions legitimate. Mao's Red Route Armies *were* real armies and on route to power.

In power the movement must legitimize control of the center and in this there is no lasting and often no major role for the underground. When the Dáil voted for the treaty with Britain that created the Irish Free State, the old IRA became at once the new Irish Free State Army hurriedly togged out in uniforms and deployed against the armed dissent of those anti-Treaty forces still organized as the Irish Republican Army. The rebels were not rebels, but, loyal to the Republic of 1916, were *the* Irish Republican Army, the only legitimate Irish army but only to their own. To the new government in Dublin they were the 'irregulars'. The real Irish Army, that of the Free State, tended to respond as a real army should, even borrowing artillery from the British, and the IRA responded in turn irregularly, unable to fight effectively even in an irregular war. And so the IRA lost and went underground, a revolutionary conspiracy organized as a secret army. The Free State Army was shaped by the state and the IRA by the dynamics of the underground.

It is not always easy to get rid of old gunmen, who are loath to give up the purity of the dream. It is in fact not easy for the new state to deploy those gunmen as they emerge from the underground. The dynamics of the galaxy shape a particular capacity where persistence pays and victory can be postponed, where ideological loyalty rather than competence is most important, where operational details are hampered by the nature of the environment and so have engendered certain precautions and responses not needed in conventional war. Thus when the Irgun and the Stern Group came partially above ground in the face of the Palestinian Arab attacks before the state could be established their operations were notably unsuccessful, less so than those of the Haganah which had little combat experience, a less intense exposure to the dynamics of the underground but was organized as an army-in-waiting and so could be deployed more conventionally.

Successful rebels in irregular wars are often those who possess nearly regular armies, forces that can be structured in liberated zones or safe havens, away from the mold of the underground. Thus the dynamics of the armed struggle are poor military preparation for conventional war if vital for an underground struggle. These dynamics made real by recourse to myths and rituals seek as purpose power but when that power is grasped all is utterly changed – if not overnight then over time.

The new institutions may have problems adapting or none to the dynamics of the orthodox. For the individuals the everyday, even if the movement is victorious, is a strange matter. All the intensity of the underground, the life of conspiracy, the risks around the corner is simply gone, replaced for some with positions and power and for others with a lack of purpose. Some old gunmen are killed for good cause, some are broken and discarded, and the others, those who sacrificed and succeeded or failed, lasted the course, must find their way in a conventional world driven by other priorities.

The great dream that energizes the armed struggle can never emerge into practicalities and power whole, untouched, still incandescent, nor can those once in the underground ever quite leave all those days of anguish and glory behind. Some will seek to do so by embracing all that is conventional, slaughter those still addicted to dreams, especially the purity of their own dream, while others simply lead orthodox lives but still sit in corners, cross open places cautiously, take care on the telephone, never quite give up the habits of survival and often never despair for the dream. The habits of survival once learned are not easily forgotten nor the addiction to the ideal.

Few who have lived on the dangerous edge without assets or prospects, who have been too committed, who have survived sudden death around the corner and the risk of betrayal, are ever again quite the same. Some never forget, never live lives as fulfilling. Some forget almost everything, find normal careers and new lives. Mostly those who emerge remember the intensity of the experience and even in victory the power of the dream unredeemed. Mostly their epilogue is written to a different beat with a different perspective. Their ending is the beginning of peace and quiet for some, the prerogatives of the state for others, and a different perspective on the real for all. The faithful must live in the everyday, with goals pursued with different means for other purposes. There are other voices in other rooms, another dynamic and so the compelling logic of the underground is forgotten.

For those who have survived the present has charms and the future is not without real promise; so the past is adjusted to present need and then neglected, left to historians and at times a few still caught up in their own dreams still unredeemed. The rituals of persistence, the rites of the incorrigible and uncompromising are apt to wither, fewer subscriptions, fewer commemorations. Those who did not die on the beach or in the hills, did not take a position offered by the successful, did not give up the dream, die a little each day.

Some few are never content, never satisfied unless the dream is incandescent, pure beyond reach. Some gunmen find in the underground a vocation not a process. Some few find in persistence a way of life. The others, the living and the dead, were shaped by the dynamics of the armed struggle while underground. Those who survived the campaign, campaigns with a visible end, win or lose, rarely can imagine a replay, another act, a new season underground. Those who can, who live in hope or in exile, who appear as ghosts passed at commemorations or the exile office are special. They still believe that their day will come.

There are always those who believe that the future can be made to match aspiration by recourse to the gun. Like a cunning virus they exist on the flaws of reality – and reality, reason and governance are never ideal, only at times brutally efficient or capable of adaptation. The dream seldom can adapt and so those so emboldened shift with the times, are immune to extermination, beyond reward or threat. Like a virus they can penetrate each new defense, shift with perceived reality, retain the capacity to do harm, often for generations. For the faithful the area is a great medium for expansion. And if most expire seeking to exploit that medium, some do not and all so engaged are apt to be deeply shaped by the struggle. A few never grow old, never accept history, prefer fruitless exile or barren conspiracy. Many so touched are never the same but no longer aspire to the gun. A few find other faiths, but most survive in the everyday, keep in their own way the faith, become in most matters orthodox and like their faith are no longer shaped to an armed struggle. Their day has come and it is not incandescent with hope and sacrifice, but they may be reconciled to reality as found, gain recorded, the future as lived. And not unmindful of past service, past sacrifice, time spent in harm's way on the dangerous edge, a time shaped to the dream by the dynamics of the armed struggle, they have found their way out of the underground.

The others, still aspiring to change the world, to change history, and all those soon to do so, soon to appear seemingly spontaneously driven by a new dream or an old faith, all these believe their day will come. Before then, they too will be shaped by the inevitable dynamics of the armed struggle, each will be special and all will be alike.

Sources

THE SOURCES for the text are no more conventional than the subject, in that the analysis rests on conversations and interviews, thousands of hours of questions-and-answers, tens of thousands of hours of political conversations, years and years talking with the involved. Some of those involved have become friends, some are long retired, some are in for life. Some have been met once at a café or a party office, during a convention or at a seminar. Some have become regular stops on my terrorist tours and some I see all the time. At various times I have passed through an arena but once, but briefly, seen everyone I could and moved on. But mostly I tried to go back, if not every year at least often – or until Asmara or Amman or Berlin no longer seemed worth the trip. Some places I go regularly and in the case of Ireland, my ground-zero of the revolutionary world, I have spent seemingly much of my life amid subversives of one sort or another.

These conversations, shaped to my own agenda or random, have formed the basis for a variety of studies, mostly published: works on one movement or one arena, especially again Ireland where the past is long, the present intense, and the sources available. In time with age and rising prudence, I first restricted my travels to the line running from Belfast through Rome to Tel Aviv and Cairo and then gave up active gunmen altogether. The gunmen have not, however, always given up on me, finding few outside their galaxy who can talk about their business without rushing to print. Sometimes, of course, it is not wise to rush to print ever, to become a stop on someone else's terrorist tour; but generally as time has passed I have become not only *passé* but also no longer attracted by the smell of cordite. In any case, late and soon, at home or in strange places, the active have supplied the data for the text.

Conversations often without notes, never with a tape recorder, have been collected and remembered but are not the rigorous source scholars prefer. How does one file the remarks about the difficulty in moving Semtex into Europe? How can a long dissertation on the malice of the press by one who bombs newspaper offices be noted? Either may give special insights into the nature of command and control or the world view through spectacles of the faith but exist only in recollection. And some recollections about who did what or who was to blame supplied data not wanted. To know everything has also meant knowing things best left mysterious – a gunman's and a political scientist's idea of hard data vary considerably. Too much precision can be fatal.

If often general rigor was not advisable, often – certainly for a long while – I did not know exactly what I wanted to know in any case. To want to know *everything* is often to end knowing very little, often the wrong things, and alas knowing things better forgotten as soon as possible. So much of the field research – not in fields but hotel rooms and parlors, party offices and back rooms – took place with scant immediate reward. And rewarding or not, it is difficult to slot into a neat bibliographical section. A list of names, those I remember and those I knew, would be impressive: all those Palestinians later prominent and often dead; those in Africa who would have become presidents and prime ministers if they had stayed the course; gunmen who would appear on the front page of the newspaper in an identikit likeness. The contacts look significant: the Huk leader, the kidnap victims in Italy or Brazil, the Chinese general who had been on the Long March, secret policemen in Jordan and Britain, survivors from Bolivia, ministers from Sri Lanka, most of the IRA Army Council members over the years, the Welsh and the Kurds and the Moslem Brothers, all sorts of Zionists. The residue of their discussions would be something less impressive: a few notes, sections of books published, scraps and quotes scribbled down and my recollections. The real source, then, is recollections, which over the years sharpened and focused on the actual workings of revolutionary organizations.

These movements at first seemed so special and peculiar, so Arab or Irish, so shaped by special times and particular arenas – the reaction of a historian trained to suspect the general. The similarities were apparent – a gunman's life is similar whether in Cairo or Paris. What in time also became apparent were the general aspects of all armed struggles, imperatives that determined the nature of the gunman as well as the daily life of the volunteer. Then over the very years I began to give up my wanderings I had questions that could be directed to special points – how decisions were actually made or what recruits believed was on offer by the underground. Once there were categories I could look elsewhere, back to other interviews and even at times toward the conventional sources, those available to anyone, those anyone could check.

Very few subjects have generated as much concern or as many books as low-intensity conflict: terrorism, revolution, insurrection and irregular war, the conflict of the bush, subversion, oppression and radical politics. The Irish Troubles have generated over 8,000 titles, mostly different. The Palestinians' own library in Beirut seized by the Israelis filled a truck convoy. There are biographies and bibliographies, chronologies, databases, computer files, endless shelves of paper. Nearly every movement has engendered as many commentators as gunmen. And the gunmen if they survive are apt to write memoirs, histories, manuals and studies. LEHI and the Irgun produced not only politicians and everyday people but a remarkable number of PhD dissertations by participants. The threatened, the orthodox, the scholars and journalists produce the printed word on the gunmen, the arenas, the small wars and spectacular violence of our times.

These, the secondary sources, often by primary people or those who were present at the time, have all the virtues and vices of any such genre. What they lack is recourse to hard primary data. Despite the enormous amount of paper the underground generates, there is no really satisfactory documentation, nothing to equal the files of the state or even the minutes of the Elks or General Motors. Data are the province of the center, for mostly the rebel focuses on grievance and goal, publishes exhortation and the party line, keeps the details, the underground reality away from paper. In fact, those underground are rarely interested in the process, in the dynamics of the struggle. Beyond operations – how to acquire arms and money, how to escalate or persist – even the most articulate of the involved devote their time to the beginning and the end, not the housekeeping, the process, the mechanics of the struggle. Thus the vast library of case studies, examples and experiences, is apt to supply works focused on underground dynamics. The United States Defense Department, long ago, funded clip-and-paste studies that focused on matters such as rebel communication, or for that matter the use of mules. No general reader wants to leaf through hundreds of books, seeking odd examples: how Begin made decisions for the Irgun, how Grivas communicated, how Arafat formed a consensus. It is a comfort for that general reader to know that such examples do exist – once a point of focus is found. Often, however, the involved and the observant are not interested in such a process or choose not to examine some aspect of the struggle – the implications of charisma on Arab ideologically shaped movements. No matter there are so many studies, so much published, that most of the conclusions of the text can be tested against reality but not by recourse to a few good works.

There *are* a few good works on the armed struggle: in fact there is a small library of rich analysis and useful recollection. This text simply shapes underground reality in a certain way. Other ways exist, other perspectives, other voices. For the bibliography section of my much earlier *The Myth of the Guerrilla, Revolutionary Theory and Malpractice*, which described the inefficiencies inherent in the underground, the gap between theory and practice, there was a short survey, a dozen pages, of sound, interesting, and representative work. There were the theorists of insurgency, the practitioners, the analysts and those focusing on my special case studies. This was almost a necessary addendum to give weight to a work that largely rested on those elusive, unrecorded interviews: too short for the scholar and irrelevant to a general reader who is not concerned with reading General Grivas or the conclusions of Ted Gurr. It was an exercise not worth repeating: a library on terror that would terrify even the intrepid, shelves on assassination, on the attempts on de Gaulle in French, on the death of Moro in Italian, on the theory and the practice by Americans shattered by the Kennedys and King and the others, books on tradecraft and the Viet Cong, on this facet or that of the unconventional.

What is wanted for the general reader is a list of a few books that give a feel for life underground, for the process of the armed struggle, and perhaps a coherent overview. Mostly these do not exist or not in a form readily available. Begin's *The Revolt*, like most memoirs, like those of Che or Mao or Grivas, tells it not like it was but like it ought to have been, a struggle with heroes and villains and sacrifice, no brutality, betrayal and blunder, no gross errors and corruption, no despair. Those on the other side of the hill are good with details, chronologies, events but rarely have empathy with those underground, rarely can catch the feel of life outside the law, life made real only by aspiration and kept through luck and cunning. For that, fiction does better, imagined gunmen engaged in imaginary wars. And since the gunman and the terrorist have become great stereotypes of our times, most often monsters, fiction is apt to credit them with unreal capacities, improbable insight, skills found only in films and thrillers. Still, films and thrillers do better than social science where blood is compressed into numbers, charts, and graphs – and if not amenable to quantification ignored. The problem is not without solution but certainly with no easy solution – no short list of good books, good thrillers or good social science.

So the general reader is left with a few suggestions – the works focused on one struggle by those intimate with the scene even if not concerned with analysis, for example: Paul Henissart, *Wolves in the City: The Death of French Algeria* (New York, Simon & Schuster, 1970); Alistair Horne, *A Savage War of Peace: Algeria 1954–1962* (New York, Viking, 1978); Patrick Bishop and

Eamonn Mallie, *The Provisional IRA* (London, Heinemann, 1987); Jack Holland and Henry McDonald, *INLA Deadly Divisions* (Dublin, Torc, 1994); Kevin Toolis, *Rebel Hearts: Journeys Within the IRA's Soul* (London, Picador, 1995); William Finnegan, *A Complicated War: The Harrowing of Mozambique* (Berkeley and Los Angeles, University of California Press, 1992); Jonathan C. Randal, *Going All the Way: Christian Warlords, Israeli Adventurers, and the War in Lebanon* (New York, Vintage, 1984); Robert Fisk, *Pity the Nation: The Abduction of Lebanon* (New York, Atheneum, 1990); and anything that Ryszard Kapuscinski writes, especially on Africa, for no one manages as well to introduce the eerie world of the irregular, not quite the same as the armed struggle but a parallel reality as divorced from the everyday of the West as imaginable. For those who want purely imaginative entry into the underground most thrillers add capacity where none exists, drama when there is actually little, and coherence that all commanders seek and few find. In this one case fiction is not stranger than reality but rather far more coherent. Still, for those with access, one film – *The Battle of Algiers* – indicates nearly all that can readily be displayed about an armed struggle.

Index

Titles of Related Interest

Western Responses to Terrorism

Alex P Schmid, *Leiden University* and Ronald D Crelinsten, *University of Ottowa* (Eds)

This volume combines case studies of national responses to terrorism with analyses of conceptual, political, economic and data-collection problems surrounding the control of terrorism in democratic societies over the last 25 years.

374 pages   1993, repr. 1998
0 7146 4521 4 cloth   0 7146 4090 5 paper
A special issue of the journal Terrorism and Political Violence

Action Directe
Ultra Left Terrorism in France, 1979–1987

Michael Y Dartnell, *Concordia University*

'Dr Michael Dartnell has written an excellent ideological and operational profile of the French terrorist group Action Directe. To my knowledge it is the only book written in English on this group.'

Dennis Pluchinsky,
US Department of State, Terrorism
& Military Intelligence

In defining Action Directe's mixture of millenarianism, workerism and nihilism, the study explains why the group turned to a strategy of murderous strikes and how a revolutionary political faction emerged in a stable western society.

224 pages   1995   0 7146 4566 4 cloth   0 7146 4212 6 paper

Inside Terrorist Organizations

David C Rapoport, *University of California, Los Angeles* (Ed)

Original essays by prominent authorities describe the internal life of terrorist organizations. They contend that no descriptions of terrorist behaviour is adequate without a grasp of the deep tensions which often characterise the groups and without appreciating how firmly implanted in our culture terrorist traditions have become, since the middle of the nineteenth century.

268 pages   1988   0 7146 3332 1 cloth

Political Parties and Terrorist Groups

Leonard Weinberg, *University of Nevada* (Ed)

'Along with abundant information on the political party-terrorist group nexus, there are many useful insights to be found within the pages of this book.'

Shannon Lindsey Blanton,
University of South Carolina

This collection offers examples of the relationship between political parties and terrorist groups in different parts of the world, including Northern Ireland, Latin America and Italy. The contributors also investigate how changes in the party politics of these and other nations in the 1960s and 1970s were associated with the emergence of political terrorism.

152 pages 9 tables   1992   0 7146 3491 3 cloth
A special issue of the journal Terrorism and Political Violence

Europe's Red Terrorists

The Fighting Communist Organizations

Yonah Alexander, *George Washington University*
and Dennis Pluchinsky, *US State Department's Bureau of
Diplomatic Security*

This unique volume explores Europe's most dangerous communist
terrorist organizations and reveals how they use violence as a
means of political communication and persuasion. It outlines seven
terrorist groups from Germany, Greece, Spain, France, Belgium,
Italy and Turkey and gives their modus operandi, rationale and
political messages in translated communiqués never before
available in English.

272 pages   1992   0 7146 3488 3 cloth   0 7146 4088 3 paper

Technology and Terrorism

Paul Wilkinson, *University of St Andrews*

This volume will be of interest to all students of terrorism,
policymakers and security practitioners involved in combating
terrorism from government officials, law enforcement, military and
intelligence agencies to specialists in industrial security including
the aviation and nuclear power sectors.

162 pages   1993   0 7146 4552 4 cloth
A special issue of the journal Terrorism and Political Violence

Violence and the Sacred in the Modern World

Mark Juergensmeyer, *University of Hawaii* (Ed)

This book explores the relationship between symbolic violence and real acts of religious violence with reference to some of the most volatile religious and political conflicts in today's world. These involve the Hizbollah movement in Lebanon, the Sikhs in India, militant Jewish groups in Israel and Muslim movements from the Middle East to Indonesia. The contributors also respond to theoretical issues articulated by René Girard in his well-known book, *Violence and the Sacred*.

168 pages   1992   0 7146 3456 5 cloth
A special issue of the journal Terrorism and Political Violence